380A7

£~~2:00~~
£7.95

Finch

THE GROWTH AND STRUCTURE OF THE CHILEAN ECONOMY

A Publication of the Economic Growth Center, Yale University

THE GROWTH AND STRUCTURE OF THE CHILEAN ECONOMY: FROM INDEPENDENCE TO ALLENDE

MARKOS J. MAMALAKIS

New Haven and London, Yale University Press, 1976

Designed by Sally Sullivan
and set in Times Roman type.
Printed in the United States of America by
The Alpine Press, Inc., South Braintree, MASS.

Published in Great Britain, Europe, and Africa by
Yale University Press, Ltd., London.
Distributed in Latin America by Kaiman & Polon,
Inc., New York City; in Australasia by Book &
Film Services, Artarmon, N.S.W., Australia;
in Japan by John Weatherhill, Inc., Tokyo.

To Angelica and
Anna, Katja, Marina,
John, Andreas, Philip,
Irene, Peter, Joanna,
Alexandra, Emmanuel.

Contents

Tables

xi

Figures

Foreword

This volume is one in a series of studies supported by the Economic Growth Center, an activity of the Yale Department of Economics since 1961. The Center is a research organization with worldwide activities and interests. Its research interests are defined in terms of both method of approach and subject matter. In terms of method, the Center sponsors studies which are designed to test significant general hypotheses concerning the problem of economic growth and which draw on quantitative information from national economic accounts and other sources. In terms of subject matter, the Center's research interests include theoretical analysis of economic structure and growth, quantitative analysis of a national economy as an integral whole, comparative cross-sectional studies using data from a number of countries, and efforts to improve the techniques of national economic measurement. The research program includes field investigation of recent economic growth in twenty-five developing countries of Asia, Africa, and Latin America.

The Center administers, jointly with the Department of Economics, the Yale training program in International and Foreign Economic Administration. It presents a regular series of seminar and workshop meetings and includes among its publications both book-length studies and journal reprints by staff members, the latter circulated as Center Papers.

Lloyd G. Reynolds, Director

Preface

The significant though uneven economic climb of Chile between independence in 1818 and the military junta of 1973 was associated with pioneer social and political progress—and retrogression. With its $800 per capita income, it has been in the vanguard of the moderately developed nations. As the rays of Chile's proud and independent star came to be a source of universal light, its experience became the object of intense international interest and curiosity.

To explain the record and meet the challenge of unveiling the country's economic morphology, this study concentrates on identifying the features of production, distribution, and capital formation and the interactions among them. Development is considered part of, and the consequence of, underlying changes in production, distribution, and capital formation. This approach is, I believe, unique. Treatment of production, distribution, and capital formation for the 1840–1930 and 1930–73 periods divides the survey into two parts, but the time distinction has necessarily been blurred in the chapters on sectoral production.

During my tenure at Yale between 1963 and 1967 and ever since, I have received the unstinting support of Yale's Economic Growth Center, the sponsor of this monograph and of the "Historical Statistics of Chile, 1840–1965" (4 vols., available in mimeographed form; to be published by Greenwood Press in 1977). A collective credit is due to the center's members, whose widely varied interests, orientations, and skills provided a greatly stimulating environment.

During my visit from 1964 to 1966 the Instituto de Economia of the University of Chile provided a unique setting to undertake research, to develop and exchange ideas, to teach, and to make lifelong friends. In the course of my visits between 1964 and 1972 countless private and government officials, from Antofagasta to Punta Arenas, assisted and guided me and answered my questions. Special thanks go to the members of the National Planning Office of the Presidency of the Republic (ODEPLAN) for their statistical help and to the Chilean Development Corporation (CORFO) and its affiliates for providing essential information and facilitating my work throughout the country.

The research on services was partially carried out with assistance from the Social Science Research Council and the Graduate School of the University of Wisconsin at Milwaukee. Valuable support has also been provided by the UWM Center for Latin American Studies.

I received useful comments from Carlos Díaz-Alejandro, Howard S. Ellis, Arnold Harberger, Simon Kuznets, Gustav Ranis, and Lloyd G. Reynolds, who read the entire manuscript, and from Albert Berry, Juan Crocco, Herta Castro, Luis Federici, Eduardo Garcia, Keith Griffin, Bruce Herrick, Shane Hunt, Teresa Jeanneret, Harry G. Johnson, Rolf Lüders, Raymond Mikesell, Oscar Muñoz, Andrés Passicot, and Gert Wagner, who read parts of it. The responsibility for the framework of analysis and content of the study is, however, exclusively mine.

I am also indebted to Harold Blakemore, Carlos Hurtado, Ricardo Lagos, Roberto Maldonado, Carlos Massad, Anisur Rahman, and John Strasma for provocative comments and discussions. Samuel Mardones and Arturo Malbrán of the Instituto de Economía greatly facilitated my basic research in Chile.

Peggy Limbacher gracefully and cheerfully performed for five years the indispensable functions of typing and putting together the "Historical Statistics" and this study.

Angelica, my wife, and our children are directly responsible for the completion of this study. They created and were part of the ambience that made it possible to look at the research as a unique challenge rather than as a maddening and seemingly endless exercise.

PART 1   EARLY GROWTH: 1840–1930

1

Progress in Production

Chile was an isolated, colonial, noncapitalistic economy in 1840; in a bucolic frontier environment the mixed-blood descendants of the conquistadores and Indians were still at war with Araucanian Indians of the South (fig. 7.1 depicts the regions of Chile). The country's progress since then has been generally continuous and massive, if not spectacular, but it has neither satisfied the rising internal basic needs nor matched the progress of the United States and Europe. Nevertheless, by 1930 the economy had evolved into a relatively advanced, partially modern production entity that enjoyed a high degree of specialization and, through manifold linkages and interaction mechanisms, was deeply woven into the fabric of the international economy. This progress encompassed not only the per capita output of goods and services but also such variables as life expectancy, educational opportunities, employment alternatives, and the economy's ability to adjust to and promote change.[1]

1. Some monographs stand out in terms of the broad contours of Chilean development they describe and the deep insights into the speed and problems of change they provide. I give below the few that I believe comprise the minimum amount of literature to which an economic historian interested in Chile should first be exposed. Although the approach of the present chapter is almost totally distinct from that followed by these monographs, it is considered a complementary extension of their work and can be best understood within the historical context set and so illustriously described by them. The monographs are Daniel Martner, *Historia de Chile, Historia Económica* (Santiago, Chile: Balcells and Co., 1929), vol. 1 (hereafter cited as *Historia de Chile*); Santiago Macchiavello Varas, *Política Económica Nacional, Antecedentes y Directivas* (Santiago: Establecimientos Gráficos "Balcells and Co.," 1931), vol. 1; vol. 2; Luis Galdámes, *Geografía Económica de Chile* (Santiago, Chile: Imprenta Universitaria, 1911); a useful bibliography for the pre-1900 period is the one by P. Lee Phillips, *A List of Books, Magazines, Articles and Maps Relating to Chile* (Washington, D.C.: U.S. Government Printing Office, 1903); Francisco A. Encina, *Resumen de la Historia de Chile*, 4th ed., prepared by Leopoldo Castedo, vol. 1, 1535–1821, vol. 2, 1822–1879, vol. 3, 1879–1891 (Santiago, Chile: Editorial Zig-Zag, 1961). This summary and the original version contain major sections on

INCOME AND POPULATION GROWTH

Using perhaps the best available measure of economic performance, Ballesteros and Davis estimate that Chilean per capita income, starting in 1855 at $100 in 1957 prices, rose at a rate of 1 percent each year between 1855 and 1957.[2] Their estimate was based on production indices that covered only the 1908–57 period and excluded commerce, health, education, and personal services.[3] However, many factors suggest that it was above that level. First of all, per capita income excluding services increased at an average annual rate of 1.45 percent between 1908 and 1927 and at a rate of 2.7 percent if 1927 is replaced by 1929 as the terminal year. Second, the Ballesteros–Davis argument that shifting the weights of sectoral indices could eliminate the difference between the 1.0 percent historical rate and the 1.45 rate of growth between 1908 and 1927 is not convincing. Any effect of shifting weights between the commodity indices could be more than offset by a correction in the income of the service sectors that Ballesteros and Davis ignore. These services accounted for almost 50 percent of domestic income.[4] Third, the 1927–29 years were not as exceptional in terms of capital inflows and government expenditures as Ballesteros and Davis believe. Net capital inflows mean little in Chile unless they are compared to net factor payments abroad. If capital inflows and factor payments for 1927–29 are compared to earlier ones, the Ballesteros–Davis argument receives negative support.[5] Also, government expenditures on public works peaked far before 1927–29.

Ballesteros and Davis used their estimate to reject the hypothesis of long waves, according to which the performance of the economy was much better before than after 1930. I believe that the annual growth rate between 1855 and 1930 was closer to 2.0 percent than to 1.0

Chile's economic history during 1840–90; see also Francisco A. Encina's classic *Nuestra Inferioridad Económica* (Santiago, Chile: Editorial Universitaria, 1953). Encina lucidly describes in this monograph how the forces that transformed Chile's economy from 1830 to 1900 led to its *Economic Inferiority* (the book's title) at the turn of the century.

2. Marto A. Ballesteros and Tom E. Davis, "The Growth of Output and Employment in Basic Sectors of the Chilean Economy, 1908–1957," *Economic Development and Cultural Change* 11, no. 2 (Jan. 1963): 152.

3. *Ibid.*, pp. 152–54.

4. In 1950 the non basic S-sectors excluded from the Ballesteros–Davis income estimates contributed 45–50 percent of GDP. Their extraordinary importance in the labor force during 1907–30 suggests that they were almost equally important then and that their omission could grossly distort the overall pattern of growth.

5. See chap. 3 on the intercountry distribution of resources.

percent. Because a growth rate of 2 percent doubles income every thirty-five years, per capita income would have risen to $200 in 1890 and $400 in 1925 or 1930. Such a figure is far from inconceivable for 1930, and stagnation or even decline between that year and 1957 may have pulled the overall rate down to 1 percent for the entire 1855–1957 period.[6] Significantly, because income of services was hit the hardest by the Great Depression, its inclusion in the 1850–1957 estimates could intensify the difference in growth performance before and after 1930 and could strengthen the long-waves hypothesis.[7] Although such an interpretation would turn the pre-1930 period into a golden one, at least if compared with the 1930–57 performance, it cannot be totally dismissed.

Moreover, per capita income may have been much greater than $100 in 1855 and underestimated ever since. If Rengifo's estimate of agricultural production in 1841 at 40 million pesos is correct, the income in that sector alone would be approximately $30 in 1855 prices, or at least $100 in 1957 prices.[8] Also favoring the hypothesis that the pre-1930 performance was better than the one that followed are the high growth rate of the commodity sectors between 1907 and 1930 and the reliability of data on which it is based, whereas the performance during 1930–37 and 1952–56 was poor and the data for the 1930s are not reliable.

The major dimensions of the Chilean economy's transformation are reflected in the growth rates of aggregate income, population, and per capita income between 1915 and 1972, all of which are given in table 1.1. Existing estimates of per capita and aggregate growth have been based exclusively on commodity production indices and are not therefore strictly comparable with the more complete post-1940 data for those items. In order to correct this deficiency, I have suggested for the pre-1930 period alternative estimates of the growth rates for domestic aggregate and per capita income including the service sectors; they are presented in parentheses in table 1.1.

Aggregate domestic income has grown at a relatively steady rate throughout the subperiods between 1915 and 1964. Only in the first

6. After 1957 the growth rate spurted upward.
7. However, if only the commodity sectors were analyzed, the Ballesteros–Davis thesis would receive stronger support but still would not account sufficiently for the uneven performance of the Chilean economy before and after 1930.
8. Rengifo's estimate is cited in Martner, *Historia de Chile*, vol. 1, p. 175. Chile's population in 1843 was 1,084,000, as shown in the introduction to the demographic section of the Statistical Appendix.

Table 1.1. Average Cumulative Annual Growth Rates of Total Domestic
and Per Capita Product and Population, Chile, 1915–72
(In percentages)

Period	Domestic product	Population	Per capita income
(1)	(2)	(3)	(4)
1835–65		2.0	
1865–75		1.3	
1875–85		1.8	
1885–90		1.2	
1890–1900		1.1	
1900–10		1.2	
1910–20		1.2	
1915–24	4.3	1.6	2.7
1924–37	3.4	1.4	2.0
1937–45	3.5	1.7	1.8
1945–52	3.9	1.8	2.1
1952–57	3.0	2.5	0.5
1959–64	3.7	3.0	0.7
1915–64	3.6	1.9	1.6
1960–70	5.0	2.4	2.6
1971 (official Allende)	4.7	1.8	2.9
1971 (official junta)	4.3	1.8	2.5
1971 (author's)	(4.4)	(2.0)	2.4
1972 (official junta)	−0.8	1.7	−2.5
1915–1930 (author's)	(6.0)	1.5	(4.5)

Sources: The above figures are based on data from the following documents. The sources for the domestic product data are as follows. For 1915–24, M. Ballesteros and T. Davis, "The Growth of Output and Employment in Basic Sectors of the Chilean Economy, 1908–1957," *Economic Development and Cultural Change* 11 (Jan. 1963): table 1, pp. 160–61. For 1927–40, the source is Economic Commission for Latin America, *Economic Survey of Latin America, 1949,* Spanish ed. (New York: United Nations, 1951), p. 300. For 1940–64 the source is Markos Mamalakis, "Historical Statistics of Chile, 1840–1965" mimeo, pt. 1, "National Accounts," table IF3, pp. A-155–A-158. The figures for cols. 2 (domestic product), 3 (population), and 4 (per capita income) for the 1960–70 period as well as for 1971 referred to as "official Allende" were obtained from ODEPLAN, *Cuentas Nacionales de Chile, 1960–1971* (Santiago: ODEPLAN, 1973), table 16, p. 54. The data for 1971 and 1972 referred to as "official junta" were obtained from ODEPLAN, *Cuentas Nacionales de Chile, 1965–1972* (Santiago: ODEPLAN, 1974), table 16, p. 37. The figures in parentheses are estimates by the author. The source for the population data for the years 1835–1960 is Mamalakis, ibid., pt. 2, "Demography," table IIA1a1, p. A-61. As already mentioned, the sources for the 1960–72 data on population are the aforementioned ODEPLAN publications.

(1915–24), which includes the prosperous years of World War I, did it reach 4.3 percent per year, a figure almost 20 percent higher than the long-term average. If services are included for the period before 1930, the growth rate of domestic income rises to 6.0 percent—and this I believe is on the conservative side—per capita income rises by 4.5 percent annually, and the rates for 1930–40 and 1930–64 are reduced to negative and negligible levels. Although the overall level of growth after 1930 is suggested here, specific figures are not given, because the wide fluctuations of income during 1930 and 1940 cast doubt on the use of trends that began in the 1930s.[9]

The most pervasive transformation of the Chilean economy concerns population growth. Before 1930 population grew at less than 1.6 percent per year. A mild upward trend set in between 1930 and 1952. The real population explosion started in 1952 as annual population growth climbed to 2.5 percent until 1957 and rose to 3.0 percent during 1959–64, an increase of almost 100 percent in thirty years.

The shifts in the birth rate, death rate, and natural rate of population increase are shown in figure 1.1.[10] The death rate rose between 1870–74 and 1885, after which it began a downward trend that was uninterrupted after 1920. The birth rate experienced a substantial decline during the decade of the 1930s but did not enter a downward trend so pronounced as that incurred by the death rate. The corrected statistics on the crude birth rate, standardized birth rate, crude death rate, and natural increase rate prepared by Collver[11] show similar general trends but less significant variations than the statistics in this monograph.

Since the growth of aggregate income has remained stable, the increase in population has inevitably had a depressing effect on the

9. If as a consequence of including S-sector income, domestic income for 1914 were raised, it could mean a reduction in the 1914–64 growth rate.

10. An extensive discussion of demographic trends and statistics is found in the "Demography" section of the "Historical Statistics of Chile, 1840–1965" by Markos Mamalakis (Economic Growth Center, Yale University, 1967), mimeo. See also Juan Crocco Ferrari, "Ensayos sobre la Población Chilena," Memoria en Economía (Santiago, Chile: Universidad de Chile, 1947); Octavio Cabello, "The Demography of Chile," *Population Studies* 9 (March 1956): 237–50; Miguel Cruchaga, *Estudios sobre la Organización Económica y la Hacienda Pública de Chile* (Madrid, Spain: Editorial Reus, 1929), vol. 1, pp. 459–540; O. Andrew Collver, *Birth Rates in Latin America: New Estimates of Historical Trends and Fluctuations* (Berkeley: Institute of International Studies, University of California, Berkeley, 1965), pp. 76–85. See also Vital and Health Statistics, *Recent Mortality Trends in Chile*, ser. 3, no. 2 (Washington, D.C.: U.S. Department of Health, Education and Welfare, Apr. 1964), pp. 1–34.

11. Collver, *Birth Rates in Latin America*, pp. 76–85.

Fig. 1.1. Live births, deaths, and rates of natural increase per 1,000 population,
Chile: five-year averages, 1870–74 to 1895–99, and selected years, 1905–69.

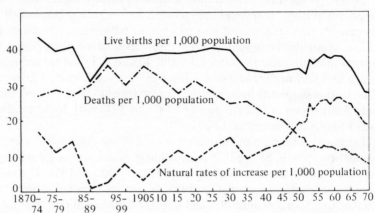

Source: For birth rates see "Demography," in Mamalakis, "Historical Statistics,"
table 11A1c1, pp. A-65–A-70; for death rates and rates of natural increase, see
ibid., table 11A1c2, pp. A-71–A-73. The data for the years 1950–69 were obtained
from República de Chile, Instituto Nacional de Estadísticas, *Demografía, Año 1969*
(Santiago: Instituto Nacional de Estadísticas, 1972), table 2.2.2., p. 6.

growth of per capita income. If the income estimate including services
is used and only the 1914–30 and 1930–64 periods are considered,
domestic income during the earlier period rises at a rate far above that
of the latter.[12] But whichever estimate is used, the crucial fact remains
that population growth has been catching up with or even exceeding
income growth. Insofar as welfare is defined in terms of life expectancy,
these figures suggest that the post-1930 Chilean policies have met with
spectacular success. But the adoption of the health standards of the
developed nations was not matched by an equally effective injection of
their technical, educational, and organizational capabilities. As a
consequence, the income gap between Chile and these nations grew
larger.

Information is unfortunately very incomplete on the factors that
determine the increase of output per capita: the growth of labor and
capital and technical progress. We know that during 1915–30, when
the population grew between 1.2 and 1.6 percent per year, labor force

12. These differences in per capita income growth rates are likely to be smaller, but
still persist, if national income is used as the denominator. Although national income
always fell short of domestic income, the available evidence suggests that the difference
between the two increased between 1880 and 1930 and has declined secularly ever since.

participation, which had reached 38.6 percent in 1907, declined to 36.2 in 1920 and 34.1 percent in 1930.[13] This suggests that the labor force was growing at a rate of approximately 1 percent per year. Since output grew by at least 4.0 percent annually during this period, labor productivity must have risen by at least 3.0 percent. With the government's developmental (investment) expenditures rising at an annual rate of 4.0 percent,[14] the capital stock may have grown even faster,[15] depending on other types of investment and given the massive rise of investment between 1905 and 1920. Keeping in mind that the pre-1930 Ballesteros–Davis estimate does not include services—some of which, as will be seen in chapter 4, experienced their most rapid rise from 1880 to 1920—and therefore is likely to have underestimated both the level of income and its growth rate, we can say that productivity rose by as much as 3.0 percent because of the increase in capital stock. Production throughout the economy may have increased at a substantially faster rate as a consequence of extensive investments and improvements in human, social, and institutional capital.

This discussion has not yet dealt with one of the most important changes in Chile. While the gap between its per capita income and that of the developing countries was widening, the internal income differences were apparently increasing at an even greater pace. In 1850 all Chileans may have been living at a similar level of tolerable poverty, but since that time inequalities between the income levels in urban and rural areas, in various economic sectors, and in different social classes have tended to rise. These inequalities and the underlying unequal degrees of sectoral transformation resulted primarily from the efforts of some, largely the most advanced, segments of the Chilean economy to keep constant or even to narrow the gap between their and the developed nations' income.

In spite of a healthy growth between 1900 and 1930, the unemployment problem had not been resolved by the end of the period. According to the 1930 census, unemployment had reached the level of 123,000 out of a labor force of 1,364,000. Of those openly unemployed, 23,000 were in agriculture, 3,000 in mining, 23,000 in industry, 13,000 in trade, 5,000 in transportation, 4,000 in construction, and 52,000 in various

13. Ballesteros and Davis, "The Growth of Output and Employment," p. 176.
14. Calculated from information found in Carlos Humud, "El Sector Público Chileno entre 1830 y 1930" (Santiago: Universidad de Chile, Memoria de Prueba, 1969), table A-6. Hereafter cited as "Sector Público."
15. See chap. 4 on accumulation of capital before 1930.

other categories. These figures give the rather astonishing unemployment rate of 10 percent of the labor force.[16] Even if adjustment is made for a potentially larger underestimate of the labor force than of the unemployed, the rate of unemployment must have been at least as high as 8 percent. The rate for males between 15 and 19 years old was 15 percent.[17]

Although the forces responsible for the open unemployment and general slack are complicated, a few stand out. The rather rapid rise in industrial output was achieved in the manufacturing segment by means of increased efficiency and productivity rather than by larger labor inputs. The nitrate sector was well past its apogee. Railroads and government tended to emphasize labor-saving devices, and the spectacular copper boom was achieved with technologies that were capital saving as well. The extensive use of the nitrate resource surplus for consumption rather than investment and for the expansion of wages and salaries in the service sectors rather than for investment in the commodity sectors also reduced the demand for labor.

THE PATTERN OF SECTORAL TRANSFORMATION

The sectoral distribution of income and of the labor force serves as an indicator of an economy's level of development, the demand and supply forces shaping its sectoral and aggregate production and growth, and the unique and basic characteristics of its capital accumulation process. The reliable information on sectoral distribution in Chile, which is available only since 1907 and with respect to the labor force, is summarized in table 1.2 and figure 1.2. The findings of a tentative attempt to estimate the relative sectoral income and productivities during the 1907–30 period are presented in table 1.3.

Between 1840 and 1907 the primary transformation was the relative reduction of agriculture in terms of both income and employment. Having functioned efficiently as a producer of food and raw materials even before 1840, agriculture experienced a long cycle, with a spectacular boom until 1880 followed by slow stagnation. By 1907 agricultural labor already accounted for only 38 percent of the overall labor force,

16. Chile, Dirección General de Estadística, *X Censo de la Población, 27 de Noviembre de 1930*, vol. 3, *Ocupaciones* (Santiago, Chile: Imprenta Universo, 1935), pp. VIII, 1–18. Hereafter cited as *1930 Census.*
17. Ibid., p. 18.

Table 1.2. Estimated Relative Employment by
Sectors, Chile, Selected Years, 1907–70
(In percentages)

	All services	*Services excluding transport, storage, and communications*	*Agriculture*	*Industry and construction*	*Mining and quarrying*
	S_{L1}	S_{L2}	A_L	$I_L + C_L$	M_L
1907	41.9	38.5	37.7	17.6	2.8
1920	44.5	39.7	36.2	15.2	4.1
1930	41.9	38.1	34.7	18.3	5.1
1940	35.5	31.0	37.3	20.9	5.7
1950	37.9	33.3	32.2	24.0	5.0
1960	41.4	36.2	30.7	23.4	4.0
1970	46.7	40.5	23.2	26.2	3.5

Sources: The data for 1907, 1920, and 1930 are found in Marto A. Ballesteros and Tom E. Davis, "The Growth of Output and Employment in Basic Sectors of the Chilean Economy, 1908–1957," *Economic Development and Cultural Change* 11, no. 2 (Jan. 1963): 176; the data for 1940 and 1950 are found in "Demography," in Mamalakis, "Historical Statistics," table IIA2a6, pp. A-160–A-165; and, finally, the data for 1960 and 1970 are found in ODEPLAN, *Población Ocupada por Sectores Económicos, 1960–1970* (Santiago: ODEPLAN, 1971), table 1.
Note: It is not known to what sector Ballesteros and Davis have added the gas, water, and electricity employment figures before (inclusive) 1930. For the 1940–1970 period those employment figures, which are not included in the table, were as follows: 1940, 0.6; 1950, 0.9; 1960, 0.5; and 1970, 0.4.

but it declined to 35 percent in 1930 before surging upward during the 1930s.[18] As can be seen in figure 1.2, a distinct downward trend in relative agricultural employment was not apparent until 1940, but because the rural population was substantially higher than that attributed to agriculture, it is possible that both the absolute and relative figures for agricultural employment were underestimated throughout the period.[19] However, even if upward adjustments are made, no more than 45 percent of the labor force could have been employed in agriculture in 1930, and the economy could not therefore be termed either exclusively rural or agricultural. As table 1.3 indicates, agriculture was

18. All the labor force information is presented in table 1.2 and fig. 1.2.
19. The rural population was 1.830 million, (or 56.8 percent of the total) in 1907, 1.991 million (or 53.6 percent) in 1920, and 2.168 million (or 50.6 percent) in 1930. The participation rates suggested by the census data are extraordinarily low. See "Historical Statistics," table IIA1f2, p. A-89.

Fig. 1.2 Estimated relative employment by sectors, Chile, selected years, 1907–70.

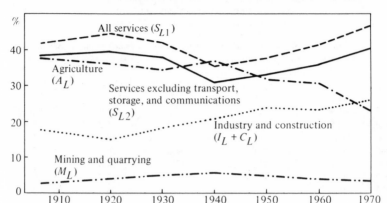

Source: See table 1.2.

also the poorest sector, with a low relative productivity and a contribution to domestic income of less than half the share that its portion of the labor force would indicate. Although in absolute terms per capita agricultural income probably did not decline but increased during 1840–1930, the income gap between it and the richer mining and service sectors increased. Relative productivity declined from a possible high of 0.8 in 1840 to 0.4 during 1907–30. Physical agricultural output, as measured by the production index presented in figure 1.3, increased sharply between 1925 and 1930, but only mildly from 1908 to 1925 and during the depression decade of the 1930s. In the development toward a pluralistic instead of a dualistic economic society, agriculture occupied the lowest level, and the welfare of workers in that sector was below that suggested by its relative productivity.

The second-lowest place on the income scale was occupied by industry, with a relative productivity of 0.9. Industrial employment (including construction) rose steadily until 1907, when it reached a level of 17.6 percent of the total labor force. Between 1840 and 1930 industry was also transformed from a minor to a major source of income, demand, stability, technical progress, and resource surplus—and to a lesser and uneven degree, of capital goods, both primary and secondary. Industry performed increasingly and generally efficiently the functions of supplying to the consumer processed agricultural goods and other consumer goods and of producing those goods (as well as capital ones) necessary not only to maintain but also to improve the quality of life and the quality of Chile's human, physical, institutional, social, and political wealth. Its early growth was due largely to the general prosperity and the special stimuli provided under Presidents Manuel Bulnes (1840–50) and Manuel Montt (1850–60). The progress in both consumer and capital goods production before 1900 was remarkable, and by the turn of the century the sector was already highly advanced in terms of the variety of goods produced, the size of its labor force, and the income generated by it.[20] But it did not succeed in establishing a permanent capacity to create those few activities and products capable of meeting international competition. Thus neither its export potential nor its capacity to produce capital goods needed by other sectors was developed.

Industrial employment accounted for 17.7 percent of the labor force in 1907,[21] declined to 15.2 percent in 1920 (when, according to the census, it employed 326,000 persons), and has risen mildly but steadily ever since.[22] The Great Depression of the 1930s seems to have had no impact on this trend, though it received a minor setback after 1950. Because of its relative stability during the last two decades, industrial employment—including construction—surpassed agricultural only in 1970.

Before 1930 the major segment of industrial employment was in agriculture- and mining-based activities. Autonomous industrial subsectors became increasingly important as the sector became more substantial and was transformed from self-sufficiency to dependence

20. CORFO (Corporación de Fomento de la Producción, or the Chilean Development Corporation), "Industria Manufacturera," in *Geografía Económica de Chile* (Santiago, Chile: CORFO, 1962), vol. 3, chap. 3, pp. 145–224, 152–53. See also Marcello Carmagnani, *Sviluppo Industriale e Sottosviluppo Economico. Il caso cileno (1860–1930)* (Torino: Fondazione Luigi Einaudi, 1971), and *Les Mécanismes de la Vie Économique dans une Société Coloniale: Le Chili (1680–1930)* (Paris: École Pratique des Hautes Études, 1973).

21. The advanced state of industrialization in Chile in 1909 is described by Luis Galdámes, "La Industria," in *Jeografía Económica de Chile* (Santiago: Imprenta Universitaria, 1911), chap. 5, pp. 180–211. Hereafter cited as *Jeografía, 1911.*

22. See Dirección General de Estadística, *Censo de Población de la República de Chile,* Levantado el 15 de Diciembre de 1920 (Santiago: Litografía Universo, 1925), p. 406. Even if definitional corrections are made and the 15.2 percent share figure prepared by Davis and Ballesteros is used, industrial employment accounted for at least .25 million persons.

on capital goods imports, from exclusively artisan work to manufacturing processes, and from selectivity to diversification.[23] The sector
remained a dynamic, leading, and strategic element in the economy.
Nevertheless, it did not become a source of technical progress and only
partially improved the quality of inputs and outputs. Although Chile
was a major producer of capital goods, tools, and instruments before
1900, it largely lost this function when industry failed to acquire the
internal capacity to modernize or transform production to the degree
necessary for self-sustained growth, in either its own or other sectors.
As a source of modernization and transformation it was neither
dynamic nor leading.

Whereas a complete explanation of industry's partial success would
require further research, some tentative hypotheses provide useful
insights.[24] Consumer- rather than producer-oriented throughout this
period, the industrial sector's primary function remained the transformation of agricultural, forest, fish, and mineral products for the
urban population. Within this framework the educational or technological foundations were too limited to encourage or stimulate widespread
production of sophisticated consumer goods, machinery, and equipment. Despite the relatively small 1930 market, a few highly efficient,
technologically advanced industries could have competed in international markets. Instead, the economy opted for more diversified
production. Thus, although by 1930 industry was modern in that it
utilized capital and energy to augment labor productivity, it was not
developmental and modernizing enough to increase and transform the
overall economy's productive capacity sufficiently to meet the ever-
rising and -changing needs of the population.

The evidence for this interpretation relates to the underindustriali-
zation hypothesis advanced by, among others, Hernán Ramírez

23. According to the partial figures of the industrial survey, which Luis Galdámes
has used, more than half the industrial employment in 1910 was in agriculture-based
industries, and food industries dominated the scene as late as 1923. By 1910 there were
14,750 workers in the livestock agriculture-based industries and 29,350 in the nonlivestock agriculture-based industries. The mining-based industries employed approximately one-sixth of the reported industrial labor force and autonomous industries the
remaining 23 percent. See Galdámes, *Jeografía, 1911*, p. 206.

24. For a partial analysis of the causes of Chilean overall and industrial under-
development see Osvaldo Sunkel, "El Marco Histórico del Proceso de Desarrollo y de
Sub-desarrollo," *Cuadernos del Instituto Latino-americano de Planificación Económica y
Social*, ser. 2, Anticipos de Investigación, no. 1, pp. 1–64.

Table 1.3. Estimated Average Relative Income and Employment
of Sectors in Chile, 1907–30

	Sectors / Income groups and employment	Services	Agriculture	Mining	Industry	Total	
1	Relative employment (R_1)	43%	36%	4%	17%	100%	Total employment
2	Relative income (R_y) of	50%	14%	20%	16%	100%	Total income
2t	Government	50% Distribution not known	2%	8%	2%		Taxes
2π	Capitalists or landowners	}	6%	8%	7%		Profits
2w	Labor		6%	4%	7%	100%	Wages
$\frac{(2)}{(1)}$	Relative productivity $\frac{R_y}{R_1}$	1.2	.4	5	.9		

Sources: The statistics on relative sectoral employment were obtained from table 1.2. The income estimates were made on the basis of information found in the various official documents on sectors cited throughout the present chapter.

Necochea[25] and Claudio Véliz.[26] Ramírez Necochea argued that after
a free trade policy had been adopted from 1820 to 1879 because
it satisfied the three essential poles in the national economic configuration—merchant–banker capitalism, feudalism, and mining
capitalism, primarily English—the coincidence of their free trade
interests prevented the flourishing of industries other than those
complementary to mining and agriculture.[27] According to the more
recent version elaborated by Véliz, the lack of industrialization in Chile
both before and after 1930 resulted from an ignominious coalition
uniting the mining exporters of the North, the agricultural exporters
of the South, and the great importing firms established in the central
provinces of Santiago and Valparaíso. These three pressure groups,
which allegedly ruled the country during the nineteenth and part of
the twentieth centuries had vested interests in perpetuating a policy of
absolute free trade and supposedly hindered the industrialization and
development of Chile by preventing the tariff protection required by
the infant industries.

This rather naïve thesis hardly provides an explanation for Chile's
moderate growth performance. It ignores the very substantial overall
progress and industrialization, as measured by industry's share of
employment and income, that took place before 1930. Also, industrial
output, as measured by the production index presented in figure 1.3,
rose continuously and occasionally even sharply between 1908 and
1924. Furthermore, the slower process of industrialization after 1930,
when protection was complete to the point of excess, is overlooked.
Lacking a wide and technically sophisticated base of higher and vocational education, Chile may in fact have committed the error of over-
industrialization by developing, behind high protective walls, many
inefficient industries rather than a small number of highly productive
ones.

The most spectacular increase in both relative and absolute employment that emerged from the production transformation between 1840
and 1930 was in services. The employment share of that sector—broadly
defined to include trade, banking, government, personal services,

25. See Hernán Ramírez Necochea, *Historia del Movimiento Obrero en Chile, Antecedentes, Siglo XIX* (Santiago: Talleres Gráficos Lautaro, 1956), pp. 58–59. Hereafter
cited as *Movimiento Obrero*.
26. Claudio Véliz, "La Mesa de Tres Patas," *Desarrollo Económico*, 3, no. 1–2 (Apr.–
Sept., 1963): 1–15.
27. Ramírez, *Movimiento Obrero*, pp. 58–59.

Fig. 1.3. Aggregate and sectoral production indices, Chile, 1908– 40 (1929=100).

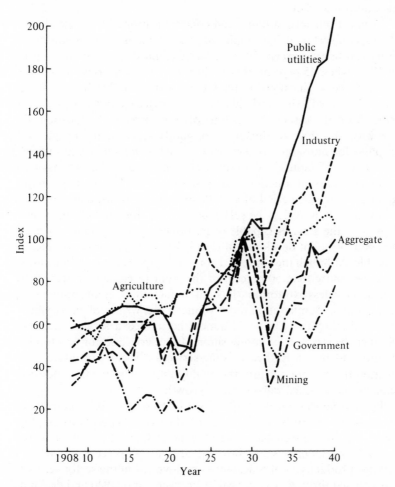

Source: Marto A. Ballesteros and Tom E. Davis, "The Growth of Output and Employment in Basic Sectors of the Chilean Economy, 1908-1957," *Economic Development and Cultural Change* 11, no. 2 part 1 (Jan. 1963): table 1, p. 160.

transportation, and electricity—rose secularly to 41.9 percent in 1910 and 44.5 percent in 1920. It has accounted for at least one-third of the labor force in all census years since 1907 and has generated 50 percent of the relative income. With a relative productivity of 1.2, it has been dominated by relatively well paid white-collar workers, but even the large group of household servants fared better than the many destitute agricultural workers.

Even if transport, storage, and communications are excluded from the service sector, it has employed more persons than agriculture in every census year except 1940. Relative employment reached its peak in 1920, when 45 percent of the labor force was absorbed in services, but declined so sharply after the Great Depression that by 1972 it had not yet returned to its pre-1930 level. The service sector was called upon to perform the essential functions of transforming the location, the quantity, and the time dimension of goods, services, and people. The demand for autonomous services required to maintain and improve the quality of inputs and outputs also increased. The expansion of complementary production and autonomous services was apparently greater during the period of growth strongly propelled and supported by exports than during the subsequent era of domestic orientation.[28] However, the services capable of improving quality, though in rising demand, were not developed internally but were imported as much as possible. Although the combined commodity-producing sectors always absorbed more than 50 percent of the labor force, the services' share was nevertheless extraordinarily high. In fact, the conglomerate service sector was so dominant, in terms of income as well as of employment, that Chile before 1930 could almost be termed a service economy. Neither the size nor the composition of the service sector was too low or too inadequate. Rather, existing services efficiently facilitated production but did not perform the quality-improving function indispensable for accelerated self-sustained growth.

The mining sector was set apart by itself from the other sectors in the economy by its exceptionally high productivity. Whereas its employment share may rarely have exceeded the high of 5.1 percent achieved in 1930, its income share hovered around 20 percent, giving it a relative productivity of 5. Relative employment in the sector seems to have passed through a sixty-year cycle, rising until 1940 and declining ever since. But the employment figures, which ranged from 2.8 to 5.7 percent, are an inadequate index of mining's role in Chile's growth. Although the label "export-mining economy" gives a one-sided view of Chile's complex production system, the mining sector was certainly in a strategic position. It generated almost all quasi-rents, earned most of the country's gold and foreign exchange, was the principal contri-

28. The service sectors are analyzed in detail in chap. 9.

butor to government coffers, and ultimately determined the fortunes of both industry and services. As its hard currency revenues were converted into capital goods, agricultural products, or vital service imports, the mining export sector acted as a quasi-capital goods, quasi-agricultural, quasi-service, or quasi-industrial sector. Thus, at one time or another it performed all the functions of other sectors from the basic transformation of location and quantity to the sophisticated improvement of quality. This tremendous versatility was as much a God-given gift as an anathema in disguise. It permitted Chile's growing and diversified needs to be satisfied promptly through imports, but it also concealed the unstable fortunes of the export sector and the imperative need for a concerted internal effort to overcome the excessive dependence of the economy's future on it.

An identifiable increase in the absolute and relative magnitude of capital-goods production also continued until 1910, followed by stagnation and decline. The system was quasi-complete throughout the 1840–1930 period, with needs satisfied through domestic production and imports directly or indirectly financed through exports. There was no import bottleneck.

GOVERNMENT REVENUES

As a consequence of changes in sectors and rising inequalities in sectoral productivities, the size, composition, and stability of the revenues of the Chilean government underwent transformations that warrant specific attention. During the 1830–80 period total revenues rose at an annual rate of 6.4 percent, whereas from 1880 to 1930 they grew at a rate of 4.3 percent.[29] The first transformation affected the relative importance of ordinary and extraordinary revenues. In terms

29. These and most of the calculations that follow have been based on the information found in Humud, "Sector Público," and Mamalakis, "Historical Statistics of Chile," pp. A-684–A-728. For a complete series on revenues and expenditures see table IIG1a1, p. A-684. Both Humud's and my work on the public sector for the pre-1899 period owe a major debt to the masterpiece by Evaristo Molina A., *Bosquejo de la Hacienda Pública de Chile desde la Independencia hasta la Fecha* (Santiago, Chile: Imprenta Nacional, 1898). Hereafter cited as *Hacienda Pública*. Molina presents a detailed discussion of all items of the public sector and those relating to it with extensive methodological notes that have never been matched. Also very important is the document by Spottiswoode and Co., *Resumen de la Hacienda Pública de Chile, Desde 1833 Hasta 1914, Summary of the Finances of Chile from 1833 to 1914* (London, England: Spottiswoode and Co., 1915), pp. 1–95. This is a summary presentation of all basic time series on the public sector in Spanish and English.

of composition, extraordinary revenues—which included internal and external borrowing, the issuing of paper money, and sales of gold—contributed an average of only 5 percent of the total between 1840 and 1860, but during the period 1860 to 1930 they contributed 30 percent.[30] They first rose to that level when they were relied upon to meet the contingencies of the wars against Spain (1865–66) and against Peru and Bolivia (1879–1881) and to finance railroad construction. Extraordinary revenues declined between 1879 and 1900 but rose again, to an average of 40 percent of the total, during 1900–13, when they were once more used for railroad construction.[31]

The second transformation occurred among ordinary revenues, and the relative importance of customs duties changed over time. They contributed at least 50 percent between 1830 and 1860, reached a maximum of 78.8 percent in 1895 as a result of the nitrate boom, declined slowly to 48 percent in 1925, and fell to 41.3 percent in 1930.[32] The introduction of income taxes in 1924 explains this change, but the actual composition of customs revenues also changed—giving rise to the third transformation.[33] The nitrate sector generated enormous resource surpluses, and the Chilean government absorbed more than half of them through customs duties. Whereas before 1880 these duties consisted almost entirely of those imposed on imports, the advent of the nitrate bonanza brought about a rise in the share of export duties from 3.1 percent in 1875 to 60.1 percent in 1890 and to a high of 70.9 percent in 1920. With the gradual eclipse of nitrate, however, export duties declined to 58.0 percent in 1925, and import duties regained their importance, climbing to 67.7 percent of the total in 1930.[34]

Changes in the stability of government revenues brought on the fourth transformation. The long-term fluctuations in the growth rate of total revenues reflect a transformation in the structure of the public sector that not only relates to the transformations already mentioned but also does much to explain the performance of the Chilean economy during this period. Between 1830 and 1860 revenues rose at the relatively high average rate of 6.2 percent per year. This growth resulted almost

30. Molina, *Hacienda Pública*, pp. 58–73 and Humud, "Sector Público", pp. 109–10.

31. Humud, ibid., p. 93.

32. Ibid., p. 111.

33. With the advent of political stability and the boom in trade, the contribution of customs duties to government revenues had risen from 13.4 percent in 1817 to 59.1 percent in 1829 (see Humud, "Sector Público", p. 84).

34. Ibid., pp. 130–31.

entirely from the 7.2 percent increase in trade during 1844–60.[35] This falls within the era of the presidential system (1833–71), when the strong executive power of Prieto (1833–40), Bulnes (1841–51), Montt (1851–61), and Pérez (1861–71) was characterized by concerted efforts to open the economy to the international trading system. The growth rate of total government revenues declined to 4.8 percent per year during the 1860–79 period, when trade rose by only 1.0 percent annually, and then to 4.6 percent during 1870–1900 (or 2.8 percent if 1880 is used to begin the period).[36] However, ordinary revenues rose 6.4 percent each year between 1879 and 1900 (3.5 percent if the 1880–1900 period is considered).[37]

Government revenues could have risen more had Congress and the people not chosen to abolish the agricultural land tax, the excise tax, and dues on sales of real property. The tax structure, which even in 1840 was heavily dependent on revenues from foreign trade, was transformed still further after 1880; as the share of the non-export sectors was reduced, the taxes derived from nitrate exports coincided with a rising outflow of resources and hence an export gap. Among the other long-term fluctuations that can be seen, the growth rate of total revenues rose to 5.3 percent during 1900–13 and fell to 2.2 percent in the 1914–24 period. Trade growth, after falling to 1.8 percent per year while extraordinary revenues were also shrinking considerably, finally bounced back and experienced an uninterrupted growth rate of 10.2 percent annually between 1924 and 1930.[38] Taxes on Central Chile and the non-mining sector were not only minuscule throughout the 1840–1924 period but declined after 1880, when the economy's capacity to pay them was at a maximum and the need for governmental resources to enrich the educational and institutional stock of capital was most evident.

The 1880–1924 era offered the most opportunities for development, and extensive transformation did in fact take place. But Chile unfortunately lost its best opportunity to accelerate its growth and transform itself at a rate unprecedented in most of Latin America. At first glance this failure seems to have resulted from the changes in government revenues that brought about such a high degree of instability that

35. Ibid., pp. 83, 85.
36. Ibid., p. 88.
37. Ibid., pp. 90–91.
38. See ibid., p. 94. Foreign trade rose at a 0.9 annual rate between 1924 and 1929 but at 8.6 percent between 1924 and 1930.

objective, longterm thinking, planning, and action became impossible. Certainly the size of some short-term fluctuations in total revenues was staggering: before 1866 they were relatively stable, but they declined by 30 percent or more in at least six years between that date and 1930 and experienced constant but lesser upward and downward fluctuations throughout most of the period.[39] The magnitude and frequency of such movements in ordinary and extraordinary revenues were even greater and continued over a good number of years in the same direction. This instability was a direct function of the low and declining degree of diversity of the tax base, the preponderance of trade-related taxes, and the continual and violent fluctuations in trade. Even when the composition of government revenues was altered after 1860 by raising extraordinary ones in an effort to offset the short-term movements, neither internal nor external economic, money, and capital market conditions permitted a successful pursuit of a stabilization policy. Not only was Chile dependent on a few taxes, which were in turn dependent on favorable market conditions abroad for one or a few products, but also the extraordinary revenues could not in most instances be obtained or serviced without the export-generated revenues.

Throughout the 1840–1924 period the revenue pattern of the central government was out of harmony with the economy's actual production pattern. The tax base was in closer correspondence with the spectrum of productivities but, with the exception of nitrate, failed to recognize, reflect, or utilize the ability to pay of either economic sectors or social classes. The large landowners, industry, and most of the service sectors (all of which could afford to pay) escaped except for the minor burden of indirect taxes. The reduction of government income resulting from the increased reliance on nitrate taxes and extraordinary revenues decreased the investable resources in the government's hands and thus increased the instability of its revenues to the point where overall growth suffered.

ECONOMIC INSTABILITY

Another major transformation was the increased instability in prices, money, and foreign exchange as well as in government finances. During the War with Spain in 1865 and 1866, when customs revenues fell and new tax sources could not easily be found, a brief experience with

39. Ibid., table 8–11, p. 100.

inconvertible paper money had no negative impact on the total money supply or on prices.[40] A marked and prolonged era of instability, primarily in the foreign exchange markets, occurred between 1875 and 1894, when the value of the Chilean peso fell from 43d. to 12d. before rebounding upward until 1907. Clear and strong cycles developed within a downward trend, with steep declines in foreign exchange occurring during 1877–80, 1883–86, and 1889–94.[41] Government deficits were small in 1871, 1872, and 1873 but assumed formidable proportions in 1878, forcing the government to turn to the already overextended banks.[42] According to Fetter, the suspension of specie payments in June 1878 was the consequence of "unhealthy relations between the government and the banks, coupled with unsound banking."[43] The nascent structuralists of the 1890–1930 period, however, found the ultimate cause of the poor financial conditions, payments suspension, and instability in Chile's unfavorable trade balance.[44] According to the theory of sectoral coalitions and clashes, instability was a symptom as well as a consequence of a narrowly based coalition involving mainly government and the export sector, but also to a lesser extent agriculture and services. The War of the Pacific, the Civil War, and especially World War I caused increased fluctuations in export revenues, prices, the money supply, and the foreign exchange rate.

Both the causes and effects of economic instability are complicated and interdependent, but it is clear that this instability acted as a major deterrent to Chile's growth. By preoccupying leading scholars, policymakers, Congress, and the president, it shifted attention away from and overshadowed the more fundamental issues of the welfare of workers, the level and rate of real savings, investment opportunities, and capital accumulation. It also added to the massive sacrifices of mining and agricultural workers without any significant long-term social benefits. By maintaining and even strengthening the unequal distribution of income, it led to a social crisis of slowly but unmistak-

---

40. Frank Whitson Fetter, *Monetary Inflation in Chile* (Princeton: Princeton University Press, 1931), pp. 9–16. Hereafter cited as *Monetary Inflation*.

41. Ibid., pp. 13–14. To a large extent the steep declines in the foreign exchange rate coincide with the contraction phase of the wheat cycles. See the discussion of the wheat export cycles elsewhere in this chapter and also Sergio Sepúlveda G., *El Trigo Chileno en el Mercado Mundial, Ensayo de Geografía Histórica* (Santiago: Editorial Universitaria, S.A. [Sociedad Anónima], 1959), p. 59.

42. Fetter, *Monetary Inflation*, pp. 26–27.

43. Ibid., p. 30.

44. Ibid., pp. 30–31.

ably rising proportions. And, finally, it was largely responsible for the outflow of resources from Chile, which between 1889 and 1909 was equal to two-thirds of the capital inflows to Canada during 1900–07.[45] Thus it reflected and shaped the fabric of the Chilean economy, which was relied upon to harness internal economic forces and to minimize outside shocks.

That fabric was also heavily determined by the diffusion of the tax burden, which fell increasingly on the export sectors. Any fluctuation in the direct or indirect resource surpluses generated by the exports reverberated through the government's economic program. The treatment of transitory mining surpluses exclusively as ordinary government revenues appears to have been the major structural factor behind this continuous instability. But since in the short run the government's policy favored all classes and most sectors and was advocated by almost all Chileans, it is difficult to assign responsibility for the problem to any one group, though the landowners may have been more responsible for its introduction and perpetuation than others.[46]

URBANIZATION

Finally, the changes in the urban–rural composition of the Chilean population provide further insights into the pattern of transformation. By 1930, as can be seen from figure 1.4, 50 percent of Chile's population was urban, up from 35 percent in 1865. This growth was determined by the geographic contours of the country as well as by its institutions. With its extremely high length/depth ratio (4,300 kilometers by 180 wide) Chile is shaped like an elongate, narrowing comb. Separated by its solid backbone, the Cordillera of the Andes, from Argentina and Bolivia to the east and Peru to the north, the comb has a series of river valleys as its teeth. In each of them a city was built during the colonial period. Only in the center of the country is there a concentration of cities: Valparaíso, Viña del Mar, and Santiago.

---

45. See Agustín Ross, *Chile, 1851–1910, Sesenta Años de Cuestiones Monetarias y Financieras y de Problemas Bancarios* (Santiago, Chile: Imprenta Barcelona, 1911), pp. 253, 256. Hereafter cited as *Cuestiones Monetarias*. At a time when Canada was enjoying an influx of resources through an import surplus, Chilean national saving exceeded domestic investment by a large margin and gave rise to an export surplus.

46. According to Fetter, paper money, instability, and devaluation were favored by the ruling landed aristocracy, which had accumulated heavy mortgage debts, not always for productive purposes "but for the purchase of luxuries, the financing of European travel, and the construction of manorial houses" (Fetter, p. 87).

As the inhabitants of each city established control of the surrounding area and its people, the increasingly limited availability of agricultural land slowed migration from the Spanish cities to the Indian-held hinterland and lessened the capacity of the rural areas to absorb a share of the total population growth. Hence, by the time of independence the proportion of the population living in cities was rising again. Within this general development, one city, Santiago, experienced a growth rate far greater than that for the rest of the country.[47] The proportion of urban population in its province rose from 40 percent in 1865 to 80 percent in 1930. The concentration of economic activities in Greater Santiago, Valparaíso, and Viña del Mar, the lack of open agricultural land after 1880, the absence of any major subdivision of *latifundios* (large estates), the lower mortality rates in the cities, and the push of surplus labor out of the latifundio-held land were among the key factors that made Chile more than 50 percent urban by 1930 and Santiago its leading city.

A third trend in urbanization was relatively temporary. As can be seen from figure 1.4, the urban population in the North rose from 47 percent in 1865 to 77 percent in 1895 but subsequently declined to less than 50 percent during 1905–30. Although the spead of the *oficinas salitreras,* or nitrate mines, between 1880 and 1900 had slowed the urbanization process, the nitrate collapse of 1930 gave further impetus to urbanization in the North.

Throughout this period the riches directly and indirectly created by nitrate and other export commodities not only permitted urban expansion but furthered a lopsided concentration of investment in the cities and in the Santiago–Valparaíso region. While the limited needs and wants in rural areas stayed within the limits of, or possibly below, the productive capacity of their inhabitants, the urban population's needs and demands for health, education, transportation, water, and electricity multiplied—a result of the density factor as well as of the revolution in the awareness of potential living standards—and rose far above the cities' productive capacity. Primitive skills were an important factor here, but even if the workers acquired education, the necessary capital for appropriate investment was not available in adequate quantities.

Thus although rural agriculture had an income that exceeded its wants, needs, and demands, the urban productive capacity fell short

47. Bruce H. Herrick, *Urban Migration and Economic Development in Chile* (Cambridge, Mass.: MIT Press, 1965).

Fig. 1.4. Percentage of urban population in Chile and in the provinces of Santiago, Magallanes, and the North (Tarapacá, Antofagasta, and Atacama), census years, 1865–1930.

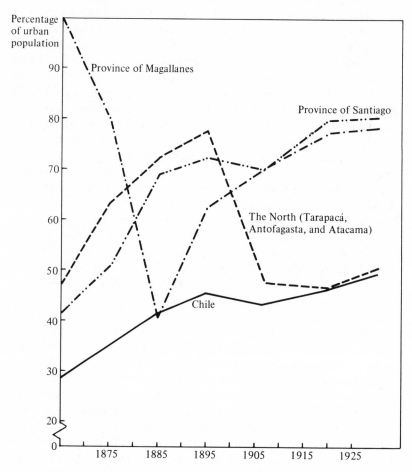

Source: Calculations made from data found in "Demography," in Mamalakis, "Historical Statistics," table IIA1fl, pp. A-84–A-88.

of its population's demands. By covering the urban expenditure–production deficit, the nitrate resource surplus made the cities increasingly more attractive than the rural areas. A rational investment decision would have favored the rural areas, where better health, education, transportation, and other services could be provided to a population with already low income but receiving small or no transfers. However, the traditional control of the nitrate surplus by the urban interest groups, political institutions, and intermediaries promoted investment in facilities that served the subsistence needs in cities: roads, vehicles, water, gas, and electricity plants, and public administration buildings. Since few of these facilities were oriented toward producer rather than consumer goods, the increments in productive infrastructure that might have had a lasting impact on the economy's capacity to modernize and transform itself remained small.

2

The Export Sector and Production

From the end of the colonial period (1817) to 1930 the expansion of
Chile's export sector was phenomenal. Although growth was restricted
by the limitations imposed by the colonial government, a move toward
freer trade had started even before independence. "Freedom of commerce between Spain and Chile was not decreed, however, until 1778,
when the Spanish Government issued the Royal Ordinance for the
Free Commerce of Spain and the Indies."[1] Trade liberalization became
a motto of the revolutionary government, which in one of its first
decrees stated "that the inhabitants of the country, will be able to
engage in free commerce in all the parts of the world belonging to allied
or neutral powers."[2] The right to trade directly with foreign countries
"represented the economic emancipation of Chile from the restrictive
commercial policy of Spain" and "was not intended to expose the
country's agriculture and industry to the rigors of competition, but to
provide a market for their output, ... was not a direct product of the
economic liberalism" of nineteenth-century Europe but "represented,
rather, a reaction against the excessive prohibitions and regulations
which had restricted the colonies to trading with Spain."[3]

The phenomena that critically shaped the ever-changing mechanisms
of interaction between exports and internal growth were:

1. The size, composition, and stability of export demand
2. The country's ability to attract and assimilate foreign private
and public physical, monetary, and human capital

---

1. See Robert Milton Will, "Some Aspects of the Development of Economic Thought
in Chile (ca. 1778–1878)" (Ph. D. thesis, Duke University, 1957), p. 11.
2. Boletín de las leyes y decretos del Gobierno (1810–1814), Santiago, 1898, p. 27,
cited by Will, ibid., p. 81.
3. Will, ibid., p. 82.

3. The country's capacity to retain export revenues, income, and resource surpluses

4. The size, pattern, and stability of import demand

5. Chilean government's desire and ability to invest the export-generated resource surplus.

Only factors relating to export and import demand are examined in this chapter. The country's capacity to retain export earnings and to attract and assimilate foreign capital is treated in the chapter on distribution, and the government's tendency to invest export-generated resource surpluses is examined in the chapter on capital accumulation.

By 1930 an unprecedented growth in export-import trade had developed. But there was also widespread skepticism, if not disillusionment, concerning the beneficial effects of this expansion to Chile. Exports were determined by the demand of developed nations for mineral and agricultural products and by Chile's ability to supply these products with the assistance of domestic and foreign human, physical, and technological capital. Both the demand and supply aspects were favorable for all or part of the 1840–1930 period for nitrate, copper,

Table 2.1. Growth Rates of Exports and Imports
of Chile during 1850–1930

	Growth rate of exports	Growth rate of imports
1850–1900	5.3	4.8
1870–1920	6.9	5.7
1880–1930	4.4	5.6
1900–30	3.3	4.4
1850–60	7.2	6.2
1860–70	0.6	2.4
1870–80	6.7	0.4
1880–90	2.8	8.6
1890–1900	9.3	6.6
1900–10	7.0	8.7
1910–20	9.0	4.3
1920–30	− 5.8	0.2
1920–25	− 4.4	− 2.2
1925–28	1.7	− 0.4
1928–29	16.0	34.0
1929–30	− 42.0	− 14.0

Source: Calculated from statistics found in Mamalakis, "Historical Statistics," pp. A-562–A-563 for exports and p. 567 for imports.

wheat, silver, and other products. Although the growth of exports was
phenomenal by Chilean standards, it was not continuous but subject to
long- and short-term cycles, as can be seen from table 2.1. The dominant
though not exclusive force behind export fluctuations was the nitrate
sector. Exports rose drastically after 1880, as can be seen from table 2.1
and figure 2.1, as a consequence of the incorporation of the Great North
into the Chilean economy, heavy foreign investments in the extractive
industries (particularly copper), rapid technical progress, the reduction
in transportation costs, and the boom in nitrate and copper demand.

Furthermore, it appeared to many that the economic independence

Fig. 2.1. Exports and imports, Chile, 1850–1930 (in millions of dollars).

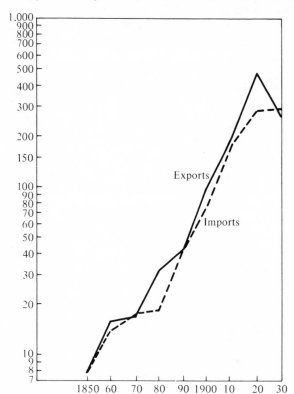

Source: Mamalakis, "Historical Statistics of Chile, 1840–1965" (mimeo), pp. A-562
–A-563 for exports, and p. A-567 for imports.

that Chile had gained by severing its ties with Spain was partially offset —in addition to rising foreign ownership and reliance on two or three export products—by the concentration of export and import flows to one or two countries, first Great Britain and then the United States. In 1850 each country bought 32 percent of Chilean exports. The Chile–California export trade declined with the opening of the Panama Canal and revived only in 1910 as American capital started moving into both copper and nitrate. Between 1860 and 1900 Great Britain purchased an average of two-thirds of Chile's exports—in 1880 as much as 78 percent. As can be seen from table 2.2, Chile's export fortunes depended not only on a few products but also on England's economic growth.

The concentration of imports was also substantial but never as high as that of exports. Between 1850 and 1910 the lion's share of imports originated from England. After World War I the Chilean–British trade relationships began a seemingly irreversible downward trend as the United States slowly displaced England as a source of capital and export markets.[4] At the same time Chile established increasingly strong links, especially on the import side, with Germany, France, Peru, and Argentina.[5]

Dependence on one export product and on one country dominated Chilean export trade between 1880 and 1910. Before 1880 Chile's exports included silver, copper, and wheat. After 1880 they were almost totally dominated by nitrate mining until 1910, and then by copper as well. A two-product two-country dependency pattern developed between 1910 and 1928. Only at the end of the 1920s had Chile acquired a diversified trade pattern in both exports and imports.

The links, interactions, and effects of export growth, as witnessed by the nitrate sector, were manifold. Mining assumed a singular place in the Chilean economic scene because it created massive riches and enjoyed an economic superiority that had broad foundations. The export sector was more modern and had a higher capacity to accelerate progress in response to market forces than the other sectors. Its superior managerial, financial, educational, and technological abilities were the by-product of a web of links and contacts with Europe and the United States. In addition, the export sector generated economic

4. See table 2.2.
5. The regional and country distribution of Chilean exports and imports can be found in Markos Mamalakis, "Historical Statistics of Chile, 1840–1965" (Economic Growth Center, Yale University, 1967), mimeo, vol. 3, part 3, tables E1e1 and E1e2, pp. A-562–A-568. Hereafter cited as "Historical Statistics."

Table 2.2. Regional and Country Distribution of Exports and Imports, Selected Years, 1850–1930
(In millions of dollars)

	1850	1860	1870	1880	1890	1900	1910	1920	1925	1928	1929	1930
Exports												
Total	7.8	15.7	16.7	31.9	42.3	103.6	203.2	481.3	386.8	404.6	472.5	273.6
United States	2.5	1.8	0.2	1.5	5.3	3.9	41.8	212.9	151.1	137.3	120.0	69.6
Great Britain	2.5	9.0	10.1	24.8	28.4	76.1	81.3	101.3	133.2	139.0	63.1	40.2
U.S./Great Britain	100.0	20.0	1.9	6.0	18.6	5.1	51.4	210.1	113.4	98.7	190.1	173.1
U.S. % in total	32.0	11.4	1.1	4.7	12.5	3.7	20.5	44.2	39.0	33.9	25.3	25.4
Great Britain % in total	32.0	57.3	60.4	77.7	67.1	73.4	40.0	21.0	34.4	34.3	13.3	14.6
Imports												
Total	7.5	13.7	17.5	18.3	42.0	79.4	183.8	281.2	251.9	247.3	333.2	288.0
United States	0.6	1.3	1.2	1.0	3.2	7.5	22.6	86.7	69.9	76.0	107.3	96.5
Great Britain	2.6	4.6	7.9	8.3	18.2	26.3	58.1	11.8	52.8	43.8	58.9	44.0
U.S./Great Britain	23.0	28.2	15.1	12.0	17.5	28.5	38.8	734.7	132.3	173.5	182.1	219.3
U.S. % in total	8.0	9.4	6.8	5.4	7.6	9.4	12.2	30.8	27.7	30.7	32.2	33.5
Great Britain % in total	34.6	33.5	45.1	45.3	43.3	33.1	31.6	4.1	20.9	17.7	17.6	15.2

Source: Mamalakis, "Historical Statistics," vol. 3, part IIE, table IIE1e1, pp. A-562–A-566 for exports, and table IIE1e2, pp. A-567–A-568 for imports.

wealth and an investable surplus of resources that had no parallel in another sector or era in Chile. A major part of export-generated income went to the government, which, always afraid it might kill the goose that laid the golden egg, reciprocated by granting privileges.

To some extent the export sector's superior economic power, which arose from its exceptional capacity to modernize, to generate a resource surplus, and to provide government revenues, was intentionally used to improve its own welfare. The export sector and government formed a mutually beneficial coalition. The export sector was privileged in that it was free of government intervention and control (except for taxes), ownership was open to nationals of any country, it retained a major share of its quasi-rents, and movement of factors of production and payments to it were uninhibited.

Both the foreign capitalists, who repatriated massive riches, and the Chilean capitalists, who enjoyed above-normal profits, were immediate beneficiaries of this coalition. Furthermore, as Robert Dix has pointed out, "if government policy favored the export sector, it was at least in part because such policies benefited Chileans who were not associated with the export sector,"[6] such as those paying lower taxes or receiving nitrate quasi-rents in agriculture, services, and industry. However, it should be added that this was a simplistic quid pro quo (taxes for freedom). The government made few attempts to transform the export sector by developing more products, by attempting to diversify it, or by reinvesting part of the mining-generated resources into research and development. If true laissez-faire ever came close to existence in Chile, it was in nitrate and copper mining.

AGGREGATE DEMAND CHANGES

The interactions between exports and aggregate demand dominated the links between the export sector and the rest of the economy throughout the 1840–1930 period. A gradual transformation in the external versus internal composition of aggregate demand occurred in three stages. During the first stage a boom in the demand for the agricultural staples and mineral products of Central Chile presented a challenge that was met through national efforts to augment the nationally owned production apparatus. As exports grew at an annual rate of 7.2 percent

---

6. "Comments on 'Sectoral Coalitions and Clashes in Chile: 1880–1930' by Markos Mamalakis" AAAS meeting, Boston, Dec. 1969, p. 1.

during 1850–60, aggregate income increased rapidly and imports rose at an annual rate of 6.2 percent. But exports, imports, and income stagnated during 1860–70 as the international market for agricultural products deteriorated and the economy also suffered from the War with Spain. It was during the 1850–80 period that Chile felt the impact of a rise in aggregate demand through the incorporation of an extremely unstable export component. The rate of export growth fell from 7.2 percent during 1850–60 to only 0.6 percent during 1860–70, and drastic annual and cyclical fluctuations in exports became an integral part of the economy.[7]

The second major change in the composition of aggregate demand occurred during the War of the Pacific. After 1880 nitrate became not only the dominant export product but also one of previously unparalleled magnitude. This challenge was met through joint foreign and national efforts, and the system developed its first major leakages: heavy amortization, intermediate product, and factor payments overseas.

A third and more subtle change came with the revival of the copper sector between 1910 and 1930. This was significant in that foreign demand was met exclusively by an output increase through foreign ownership and in that a true enclave sector with maximum links to the metropolis was established for the first time. This new copper sector replaced nitrate in the export scene after 1930.

The transformation in the external versus internal composition of aggregate demand had a critical multiplier impact on the rest of the economy, especially on investment opportunities in other sectors. There were derived changes in the income and purchasing power of several sectors. Agriculture catered to two markets, its own and the one in the mining North and the cities, and the value and volume of its sales were most intimately joined to export demand. A second wave of induced changes in aggregate demand resulted from the repercussions of variations in real agricultural and mineral income upon the industrial, construction, and service sectors. The derived expansion of the nonexport sectors tended to reduce but not eliminate the economic significance and power of the export sector.

Wheat, nitrate, and copper are of special significance in understanding the relationship between Chile's exports and its internal growth. Each will be examined separately after a brief discussion of the growth and pattern of imports.

7. For all these statistics see table 2.1.

IMPORTS

A mere inspection of the rates of growth and level of exports does not provide an accurate picture of the growth rate of foreign exchange resources available to the Chilean economy for payments of imports and servicing of foreign capital. It is necessary to estimate the payments to the foreign factors of production employed both in the export sector and elsewhere in the economy as well as the portion of export earnings accruing to Chilean factors of production and government in order to determine the country's capacity to retain its export revenues.

The ability or capacity to import was determined by the value of exports minus gross payments to foreign factors of production plus total foreign capital inflows. Capital inflows were dependent on the economy's ability to attract short- and long-term foreign capital. Although foreign capital inflows have been treated in development theory as synonymous with foreign financing of internal investment, their functions have been substantially more complicated in the Chilean economy. These inflows partly offset the leakages that arose from the repatriation of profits and interest payments on existing foreign investments and the capital flight by Chileans. The level of imports has occasionally come close to the level of exports only as a consequence of these capital inflows.

The interactions among exports, the capacity to retain export revenues, and the ability to attract foreign capital determined in turn Chile's capacity to satisfy its own import needs. As can be seen from table 2.1, imports grew at the healthy rate of 4.8 percent per year between 1850 and 1900 and at the even higher rate of 5.6 percent per year during 1880–1930. The growth rate of imports was generally below that of exports. Imports did not grow so rapidly as exports when exports boomed and did not decline so rapidly as exports when exports stagnated or declined. Imports grew much faster than exports from 1880 to 1890 because of the pent-up demand after the War of the Pacific and remained stable during 1920–30 despite of the precipitous decline in the growth rate of exports.[8] Only after 1920, when the fortunes of the export sector deteriorated irreversibly, did imports as well as exports suffer, as can be seen from table 2.1.[9]

8. See table 2.1.
9. A number of forces may distort the real value of exports and imports. Before 1930 there do not exist official statistics concerning payments by Chile for services abroad. Although we do not know their magnitude, ample indirect statistical evidence makes it safe to speculate that payments by Chile for imports of services were a multiple of pay-

THE GREAT WHEAT TRADE

During the onset of Chile's incorporation into the international production and trade systems, agriculture played an important role
through wheat exports.[10] Peru, which was the original and thus the
oldest and most traditional market for Chilean wheat, remained the
most regular one.[11] The opening up of California and Australia
supplied an enormous if transitory impetus. Wheat exports to these
areas, which in 1848 amounted jointly to only 6,000 qq.m., reached a
peak of 276,664 qq.m. for California in 1850 and of 323,607 qq.m. for
Australia in 1855.[12] The decline was as precipitous as the rise, and by
1855 exports to California had collapsed to 15,004 qq.m., and those to
Australia had also fallen by 1861 to only 10,536 qq.m.[13]

The years between 1865 and 1926 have been referred to as the era of
the Great Wheat Trade.[14] The boom began in 1865–67. Along with
the War with Spain, the customs ordinance of 1864, which opened all
passenger and cargo traffic to foreign vessels, destroyed the national
merchant marine but greatly facilitated wheat exports by reducing
transport costs.[15] The boom was supported by increased internal production and the introduction of steamships. The great expansion of
exports was characterized by complete predominance of Europe beginning in 1867, rising importance of England as a consumer, a production
level during 1867–1900 that was at least double that of the peak of the
1850s and never fell below 800,000 qq.m., and complete dominance of
exports by wide cyclical fluctuations. The cycles lasted from seven to
eleven years with major booms during 1852–55, 1867–73, 1880–83,
1893–94, 1903–05, 1908–09, 1916–18, 1922–24 and contractions

---

ments to Chile for exports of services. As a consequence not all of the export–import gap
reflected a "net resource transfer abroad." Moreover, there exists a tendency to underestimate imports whenever they are subject to import duties and to contraband as they
were in Chile. These forces also tend to inflate the size of the export–import gap. Finally,
the gap reflects partially a flight of Chilean capital abroad induced by monetary and
foreign exchange instability rather than any real weakness of the economy.

10. Sergio Sepúlveda G., *El Trigo Chileno en el Mercado Mundial, Ensayo de Geografía
Histórica* (Santiago: Editorial Universitaria, S.A. 1959). Hereafter cited as *Trigo Chileno*.

11. Ibid., p. 33.

12. Ibid., pp. 44, 48.

13. Ibid., pp. 44, 48.

14. Ibid., p. 56.

15. The number of ships under Chilean flag declined from 276 in 1860 to 27 in 1868
and 75 in 1875 (ibid., p. 72).

during 1856–61, 1874–79, 1884–86, 1900–02, 1910–11, 1914–15, 1919–21, and 1929–33.[16]

Wheat exports imparted to the system some of the great instability that characterized it between 1850 and 1930. In 1878 wheat exports fell to less than 25 percent of the 1874 level, and the decline in 1890, if compared to the cyclical peak of 1885, was even worse.[17] Most contractions were violent. The booms were as extraordinary in magnitude as the sudden declines were in intensity.

The turning point for Chile's wheat exports came during the export collapse of 1900–01, which was caused as much by bad harvests as by the rise of Australia and California as producers. From 1900 onward a declining trend set in, and even the recovery of the Pacific market that began in 1914 could not alter it. From 1865 to 1900, years of low exports were the exception. In contrast, the exceptions during 1900–25 were the years of high exports.[18]

The long-term outlook after 1900 was shaped by a demographic expansion that exceeded the rate of growth of internal production and by rising international competition, in which large producers squeezed out such marginal ones as Chile. Negative government pricing policies after 1930 only added to this deterioration.[19] The very forces that operated in Chile's favor before 1900 or 1930, such as demographic growth and technical progress, worked against it later.

The case of wheat shows that Chile was capable of exploiting investment opportunities to the maximum whenever circumstances in the international markets were favorable. Before 1900 it produced a major exportable surplus of wheat. This surplus shrank gradually after 1900 as the growth rates of new land cultivation and of agricultural labor productivity failed to match the internal demand generated by the demographic increase and also failed to meet the external competition that resulted from efforts toward self-sufficiency throughout the world and from the emergence of large producers.

Chile's experience of agricultural success before 1900 turned into failure after 1930. Agriculture has been unable to provide enough food for the population, and Chile has experienced rising food deficits and net food imports since the 1940s. The golden opportunities inherent in

16. Ibid., pp. 72–74, 56–57, 59.
17. Ibid., p. 55.
18. Ibid., pp. 55–56.
19. Ibid., pp. 122–23.

specialization in fruit and vegetable production for exports to Europe
and the United States during their winters have remained unexploited.

THE NITRATE BONANZA

The nitrate boom began after the 1880–82 War of the Pacific and the
conquest of the provinces of Tarapacá and Antofagasta from Peru and
Bolivia. Its collapse after 1930 was a far greater landmark in Chile's
history than the rise and decline of wheat. Chilean ownership of the
world's single source of natural sodium nitrate revolutionized the
structure of the economy, the society, and the political system. Thus the
boom is almost as significant as the achievement of independence.

The nitrate sector became the most important source of foreign
exchange and government revenues. From 1900 to 1930 more than 50
percent of total government revenues or expenditures was financed out
of nitrate and iodine export taxes.[20] The nitrate sector's resource surpluses averaged 14 percent of gross domestic product (GDP) between
1882 and 1930.[21] A major employer, its labor force rose from 4,500 in
1886 to 60,800 in 1925 and never fell below 43,000 during 1910–20.[22]

Both before and after 1880, a new frontier in the nitrate-rich North
created heroes, adventurers, and capitalists—Ossa, Puelma, and
others. Above all, it acted as a vital source of modernization and transformation of the whole economy.[23] Forced into the mainstream of
modern capitalism and direct contact with Europe and the United
States through nitrate, Chile acquired not only the benefits but also the
hazards of defending, and the responsibility of using properly, this
flow of riches.

The bonanza began with the technological revolution following
Alfred Nobel's discovery of nitrate's value as an explosive. But the
sector entered its golden age after Justus Von Liebig had established the
fertilizer value of nitrogen by turning it into the principal input of food

20. See Markos Mamalakis, "The Role of Government in the Resource Transfer and
Resource Allocation Processes: The Chilean Nitrate Sector, 1880–1930," in *Government
and Economic Development*, ed. Gustav Ranis, (New Haven: Yale University Press,
1971), p. 195. This document, which also reviews the literature on nitrate, will hereafter
be cited as "Nitrate."

21. See Mamalakis, "Nitrate," p. 195.

22. Ibid., p. 185.

23. Some implications of nitrate growth are discussed in Carlos Keller, *Un País al
Garete* (Santiago, Chile: Editorial Nascimiento, 1932).

supplies. The fall of nitrate was as swift as its rise, and technical progress was again responsible for this change. Cheap synthetic nitrate, which the Western powers (particularly Germany) were inspired to invent from fear of starvation or defeat in war, signaled the end of Chile's monopoly power and precipitated the doom of nitrate in the 1930s.

The nitrate experience molded what might be called, in contrast to the staples theory, a minerals theory of economic growth. Such an approach must consider three special aspects of this case: the product, an exhaustible export mineral with limited or no internal demand; the technology of production, which led to almost total obsolescence of the natural product by creating a near-perfect substitute and provided very limited, short-term expansion potential; and finally, the interaction mechanisms—taxation, induced capital inflows, backward and forward linkages, resource transfers, and technological diffusion—that were as massive as they were ephemeral. To varying degrees, the minerals theory shares with the staples theory such critical determinants as foreign ownership, heavy resource leakages abroad, and highly volatile demand. To a lesser extent it involves deplorable working conditions—the nitrate desert was described as Chile's Siberia.[24]

Carlos Keller has pointed out "the social tremors and earthquakes ... of ... public life" and the "constant seismic vibration" caused by the wild fluctuations of nitrate fortunes.[25] All these disturbances reflected the government's excessive dependence on nitrate[26] and the tax immunity of agriculture, industry, and services. Moreover, the nitrate riches were used not only for education and overhead investment but also for wasteful imports—French wine exceeded machinery imports—and for government employee wage and salary increases. The neglected use of nitrate revenues to stimulate productivity was inevitable once they were completely classified as ordinary and as a consequence other revenues were reduced over the objections of Don Pedro Lucio Cuadra, President Domingo Santa María's treasury minister

24. Jorge Vidal, *Veinte años después la tragedia del salitre* (Santiago, Chile: Imprenta Universo, 1933) pp. 7, 9.

25. *Un País al Garete*, p. 7.

26. Between 1880 and 1909 the total value of nitrate exports was $217 million and the amount of taxes paid $81 million. Thus, 37.3 percent of the export value went to government. See Alejandro Bertrand, *La Crisis Salitrera* (1910) (Paris: Louis-Michand, Editor, 1910), fig. 1, p. 12. Employment increased from 2,500 in 1880 to 39,653 in 1907, 40,835 in 1908, and 37,792 in 1909 (ibid., p. 14).

from 1882 to 1884.[27] According to the minerals theory, boom is accompanied by sudden, spectacular, massive riches and quasi-rents; stagnation follows the demise, misuse, or withdrawal of these determinants.

COPPER STAGNATION AND REVIVAL

The 1840–1930 period witnessed a gradual shift of copper production from rudimentary extraction and use of rich natural resources to one requiring a sophisticated, elaborate, modern production apparatus. Though this trend was obvious in all sectors, copper underwent a uniquely radical transformation within a short time. Furthermore, it achieved this through complete integration into the international production system.

Until 1880 Chile was the world's largest copper producer, but it experienced a rapid decline as the high-content deposits were exhausted. Its share in world copper production fell precipitously from 43.6 percent in 1878 to 25.3 percent in 1880, 9.7 percent in 1890, and 4.3 percent in 1910. And in 1918, when Chile's share had risen to 7.54 percent of world production, Chileans were responsible for only 4.5 percent of the Chilean production, whereas 86.72 percent was produced by North Americans and the rest reflected a contribution by other foreigners.[28] The relative loss to Chile as a copper producer was more than matched by the almost complete loss of ownership in domestic copper production through a rapid process of denationalization.

The era of easy, unsophisticated copper exploitation was over by 1880. Chile had been able to respond to the initial shock of an increased external demand for its export deposits only for as long as it could use crude, simple, even noncapitalistic methods of production. The capacity of the copper sector to modernize by itself and the capacity of the rest of the Chilean economy to assist it in this effort were limited, if not nonexistent.

The outcome was clear but in some respects avoidable. With Chilean nationals unable to shift from small- and medium-scale copper production based on rich deposits to large-scale production based on

27. See Martner, *Historia de Chile*, 1: 392, 409. Carlos Keller refers to these well-paid government employees as parasites contributing nothing (*Un País al Garete*, p. 7).

28. See Santiago Marín Vicuña, "La Industria del Cobre i el Mineral de Potrerillos," *Boletín Minero de la Sociedad Nacional de Minería* 32, no. 24 (Jan. 1920): 15, 21, 23.

poorer deposits, output stagnated. From a peak production of 52,000 tons in 1869 and a relatively stable production up to 1884, a declining secular trend set in. Although the trough occurred in 1897, stagnation lasted until 1906, when output had fallen to 26,000 tons.[29] But this year marked the beginning of a new era.

During the presidency of Germán Riesco the change and progress were spectacular, a "miracle introduced by foreigners."[30] In 1906 Marcos Chiapponi and William Braden, both pioneer engineers from developed nations, opened the El Teniente mine and created the Braden Copper Company. By 1910, however, the lack of expansion capital that had forced its Chilean owner Enrique Concha y Toro to sell and Chiapponi to enter into partnership with Braden and Nash had forced the withdrawal of Braden and Chiapponi and had led to a transfer of Braden Company's ownership to the Guggenheim financial colossus.[31] William Braden moved on to develop the mines in Potrerillos, Chuquicamata, La Africana, Lo Aguirre, and elsewhere.[32]

The transformation was massive. To paraphrase Churchill, never before had so few men transformed a sector so rapidly, so permanently. Never before had so few created so much wealth. The Chilean copper sector became an integral part of the international production system. Output growth enjoyed a more than tenfold increase between 1906 and 1929.[33] The new Gran Minería (large-scale mining) of copper, operating on a mammoth scale, required huge financial resources, and by 1915 Braden Company had changed foreign ownership three times in less than ten years.

Pervasive, powerful, quickly responding, and changing interaction mechanisms in the financial, engineering, and institutional fields were established between the copper sector and the United States. The financial and institutional superiority of Europe and the United States led to widespread introduction of foreign entrepreneurs, financiers, managers, technicians, and, last but not least, capital. The revival of copper was a contribution of foreign resources.[34]

---

29. See for this and other almost complete information on copper production, Mamalakis, "Historical Statistics," vol. 4, table IID1a6, p. A-486.

30. Luis Hiriart, *Braden, Historia de una mina* (Santiago, Chile: Editorial Andes, 1964), p. 65.

31. Ibid., pp. 29, 30–34, 112–16.

32. Ibid., pp. 310, 114.

33. Mamalakis, "Historical Statistics," table IID1a6, p. A-486.

34. The best study of the copper sector before 1930 is Santiago Macchiavello's *El Problema de la Industria del Cobre en Chile y sus proyecciones Económicas y Sociales*

The interaction mechanisms between large-scale copper production and the rest of Chile were limited and slow to develop. Unlike the nitrate boom, during which export taxes had been established, the largest part of the copper-generated wealth and resource surplus before 1930 left Chile. The process of nitrate extraction was accompanied by an industrial process of lixiviation and purification,[35] but because copper production was confined almost exclusively to extraction, labor costs and participation were minimal. Operations were guided and controlled from New York. Almost all capital goods and the majority of intermediate goods were bought abroad and imported to Chile. The Chilean share in ownership of large-scale copper mining was nil, its share in profits negligible. Chile played a minimal role in supplying capital goods, bought virtually no copper, and provided none of the managerial elite. The participation of Chileans in the labor force was extensive, in lower skills total. Chilean participation in copper wealth rose gradually between 1920 and 1930, especially indirectly through contributions to medical, savings, and retirement funds and the like. Even so, in only one out of seven years before 1930 did the share of copper revenues returned to Chile exceed the resources that went abroad.[36]

More than in nitrate, the copper case showed that foreign penetration was easy as well as feasible. Chile had neither the capacity nor perhaps even the interest to establish the linkage and interaction mechanisms that would provide maximum benefits to the economy. If a Chilean welfare function existed, it was unknown. Again more in copper than in nitrate, the de facto freedom and laissez-faire that were established by default and ignorance won the maximum degree of dominance for the export sector. Lack of capital,[37] the declining quality of mineral

(Santiago: Imprenta Fiscal de la Penitenciaría, 1923). Hereafter cited as *Cobre*. In 1920 only 11 percent of copper was produced by Chileans, an increase over the 4.5 percent produced in 1918. Only in the production of borax was the contribution of Chileans less than that in copper. The share of nitrate output produced by Chileans in 1920 was 56 percent, while the share of Chileans was highest in coal, to which they contributed 91 percent of output in 1920 (see ibid., p. 108).

35. See the excellent study by Santiago Macchiavello Varas, *Política Económica Nacional* (Santiago: Establecimientos Gráficos Balcells and Co., 1930), 1: 253. Hereafter cited as *Política Nacional*, vols. 1 and 2.

36. See C. Reynolds, Statistical Appendix, in M. Mamalakis and C. Reynolds, *Essays on the Chilean Economy* (Homewood, Ill.: Richard D. Irwin, 1965), p. 379.

37. The argument that the scarcity of capital and low saving have handicapped the expansion of copper by Chilean nationals has been questioned and attacked by Macchiavello, *Cobre*, p. 109. See also chaps. 4 and 11 of the present monograph.

deposits, shortage of technicians capable of solving these problems, falling copper prices because of the increased supply by the United States and Australia, a shortage of labor during the nitrate boom,[38] underdeveloped capital markets, and lack of Chilean entrepreneurship —all these factors that contributed to the stagnation of small-scale copper mining also created this partially de facto, partially de jure coalition pattern between the Chilean government and the foreign-owned copper sector. This large-scale, modern, capitalistic sector was flourishing by 1920.[39] However, the foreign complex of capital, labor, and entrepreneurship provided a temporary, not a long-term solution. Modernization and response to changes in external demand restored the copper sector's internal capacity but changed in little or no respect the internal capacity of the Chilean economic system to assist this or other sectors in similar problems in the future. Chile seemed to abrogate its responsibility of providing the capacity to modernize in this area. The copper sector thus became an integral part of the advanced capitalistic societies that controlled it, and its relationship to Central Chile was confined to a payment of tribute to the Chilean government, payments to local labor, and a few other operating expenditures. A critical problem was solved by giving the copper sector up, but its sacrifice to the developed West in return for a modest share of the income it generated could hardly be called a solution, and it has haunted Chile until now.

THE IMPACT OF FOREIGN DOMINATION

The penetration of foreign financial, administrative, and engineering capacity and structure into the heart of Chile's economy represented a shock as pervasive and lasting as the Great Depression that was to follow in 1930. This shock was subtle and inconspicuous but incredibly strong. Awakening Chile to the complexities, speed, and vagaries of modern capitalistic development, it cemented the labor movement in key sectors before 1930 and partially set the background for the government's entry into the economic sphere in the 1940s, the joint ownership in mining in the 1960s, and nationalization in 1971. The lag in response,

38. See Macchiavello, *Cobre*, p. 176.
39. This new segment of the copper sector was capital intensive with respect to the capital/labor ratio but almost always operated with a relatively low capital/output ratio of a value close to 1.

a tribute to the Chilean system of democracy and incremental change, is proof that Chile preferred slow economic progress to radical economic and political change.

Foreign penetration was acting as a catalyst of an old order as it forged national forces required to turn Chile into a modern system. Its most visible impact before 1930 was ideological. Encina, Macchiavello Varas, and others argued that economic development could not be successful unless Chile and the Chileans participated in all decisions. This nationalistic stance was pro-Chilean labor, pro-Chilean capital, pro-Chilean government. During that epoch, use of the terms *nationalization* and *Chileanization*, emphasized participation by Chilean production agents, not necessarily by government. The anti-foreign and anti-imperialist overtones in this ideology were secondary. The need for Chileanization as an instrument to change and retransform the structure of the economy toward greater national participation was eloquently advocated by Santiago Macchiavello Varas. In order to achieve "economic independence," he advocated the establishment of rules requiring partial Chilean ownership, maximum involvement of Chilean labor at all levels, and heavy taxation of profits.[40]

The characteristics of export demand fostered a special relationship between the export sector and government. Since the demand for copper, nitrate, and other mineral products was external, it could not be directly controlled by either government or producers. Nitrate demand was also created by technology and was unstable in the short run and secularly declining with respect to Chile. As a consequence the export sector was in a constant state of flux. Within a general climate of uncertainty and instability, it underwent crises and cycles and was exposed to continual shocks. The export sector's capacity to generate a resource surplus for government fluctuated drastically and strongly affected the Chilean-owned nitrate *oficinas* (mines), which were the less efficient ones. The demands of national and foreign nitrate oficina owners for favors and better treatment made the government constantly aware of the instability. The inefficiency of the national nitrate operators and the reliance on export rather than income taxes set limits on the magnitude of export taxes that could be imposed. Increases that would presumably have hit primarily the less efficient Chilean enterprises were politically unacceptable. Although the need for reform in

40. See Macchiavello, *Política Nacional*, pp. 184–85. See also the later discussion in the section on the distribution of income.

all aspects of the export sector was persistent, the instability of demand tended to delay its fulfillment. During boom periods solutions were postponed; during crises institutional reforms in production, marketing, and the like were instituted, but policies for a changed taxation system were bitterly resisted.

A de facto coalition developed as government acted defensively rather than aggressively. Although it could have appropriated all nitrate-generated resource surplus through taxation, nationalization, or other measures, its action underscored the fact that it was receiving massive resources for only one basic reason: the presence of massive quasi-rents resulting from a natural monopoly within its territory. Had government been able to provide protection from foreign competition and fluctuating demand, either through relative income stability or technological advances and a capacity to modernize, it could have acted from a superior or equal position of strength. Since it did not, the terms of the coalition were dictated by the export sector in conformity with circumstances. Massive intervention or a takeover could have been justified by ideological reasons, but no ruling party between 1880 and 1930 provided them.

3

Resource Distribution

The transformation of the resource, income, and surplus distribution process that occurred between 1840 and 1930 affected the sectoral, regional, class, international, and urban–rural dimensions of the Chilean economy. Although sectoral divisions had been important ever since 1840, they gained an unchallenged preeminence in shaping a sector-based and -oriented distribution process when the nitrate sector emerged as the dominant source of large quasi-rents, resource surpluses, sectoral income inequalities, and resource transfers to industry, services, and agriculture. The primary forces in the development process were the attempts of each sector to receive a maximum share of the aggregate resource surplus. After nitrate was incorporated into the Chilean production system during 1880–83, each sector, except nitrate mining, succeeded in retaining its own resource surplus. The struggle narrowed down to the distribution of the nitrate-generated surplus.

Because the nitrate sector was located in the North and the resource-recipient sectors were in Central Chile, the pattern of sectoral dependence was matched by a parallel pattern of regional interdependence. The cities of Central Chile became dependent upon the unilateral resource transfer from the arid pampas of the North. Furthermore, as foreign ownership in mining increased after 1880 and a major share of nitrate and copper resources, income, and surpluses was appropriated by the developed nations, the international dimension of the struggle over the distribution of these elements, though derived from sectoral forces, entered the limelight and assumed lasting significance. An inter- and intra-class struggle over income and surpluses also developed, especially in nitrate, but remained derived in nature and of secondary importance. The massive transfers of nitrate riches by government to agriculture and urban services may have created the impression that the surplus was controlled by the landed aristocracy and the emerging urban middle classes. In reality, however, nitrate quasi-rents were distributed according to a compromise brought about by the pressures of incipient sectoral pluralism.

THE INCOME SHARE OF CAPITALISTS

The distribution of income among classes had its sectoral idiosyncracies. At the aggregate level it can be argued that the labor share fluctuated between 40 and 50 percent of the gross national product. Profits, rents, interest, and so forth accounted for between 50 and 60 percent. However, the aggregate income distribution between labor and capital concealed significant peculiarities. The major income recipients among the employer or capitalist class were the landowners, the urban commercial, banking, and industrial capitalists, and the miners of nitrate and copper, in particular the English and American. At least a third of profits accrued to foreigners and immigrants. In agriculture, 50 to 60 percent of value added was appropriated by the landowners, a class accused not only of backwardness but also of exploitation of labor.

According to some influential authors, the extremely unequal distribution of income that dominated agriculture hindered its growth severely. It has also been argued that greedy landowners, unable to satisfy their luxurious habits and appetites with the limited agricultural resources available to them, relied on heavy mortgage borrowing to augment their expenditures and supported proinflationary policies to reduce their debt burden.[1] This widespread thesis has had such a profound influence on the government's post-1930 agricultural policies that it deserves a more thorough examination.

The distribution of agricultural income must have been unequal, especially after 1900, when demand for labor appears to have tapered off in most key sectors. It is also true that the educational, health, and welfare conditions of labor on the farms were among the worst in the country, bordering on the primitive in some areas. Both the landowners and the latifundio land-tenure system were in part responsible for this. In addition, landowners and the agricultural sector as a whole were

---

1. For this view see Frank Whitson Fetter, *Monetary Inflation*, p. 87; Hernán Ramírez Necochea, *Historia del movimiento obrero en Chile, Antecedentes, Siglo XIX* (Santiago: Talleres Gráficos Lautaro, 1956), pp. 45–54. Hereafter cited as *Movimiento Obrero*.

beneficiaries of the nitrate boom, which permitted them to carry a lower tax burden than would have otherwise been necessary.

But although landowners must share responsibility for the inadequate performance of the economy, they were by no means the dominant force in development. In particular, the "debtor–inflation" thesis that blames the landed aristocracy for Chile's pre-1930 upward price movements seems to be founded more on imagination than on either reason or facts. This popular argument, which is especially relevant to the issue of income distribution and spending habits of the rich, insists that heavy mortgage indebtedness among Chile's landowners created a vested interest in inflation, instability, and an induced redistribution of income to the landed aristocracy. The assumptions behind this hypothesis are doubtful, to say the least. Although statistical evidence to refute the theory has been found only for the 1920–27 period, there is no reason to believe that the trends would be significantly different during the rest of the 1880–1930 period.

First of all, the lion's share—between 25 and 50 percent—of real estate credit during the 1920–27 period was incurred in the industrial–commercial Santiago and Valparaíso provinces for nonagricultural business purposes.[2] Second, a substantial part—generally about 10 percent but running as high as 50 percent in 1925—of mortgage credit was extended in the mining provinces of Antofagasta and Tarapacá and reflected indebtedness of the mining sector and the use of credit for mining business.[3] Third, an average of 40 percent of mortgage credit was given in primarily agricultural provinces, presumably to farmers for agricultural purposes. These credits were extended by mortgage institutions, commercial banks, and private capitalists. Fourth, a major part—about 50 percent—of real estate credit was extended by one group of capitalists to another, that is, by farmers to farmers, by miners to industrialists, or by merchants to miners and vice versa.[4] Since each group of capitalists was not only a major debtor but also a major creditor, it would be inaccurate and misleading to argue that landowners or any other single capitalist group could benefit from inflation. Fifth, most of the mortgage credit (more than 50 percent

2. See República de Chile, Dirección General de Estadística, *Sinopsis estadística de la república de Chile, 1926–27* (Santiago: Litografía Universo, 1929), p. 87. This serial publication will hereafter be cited as *Sinopsis.*

3. *Sinopsis, 1926–27,* p. 87; *Sinopsis, 1925,* p. 127.

4. See *Sinopsis 1921,* p. 128; *Sinopsis, 1922,* p. 128; *Sinopsis, 1923,* p. 126; *Sinopsis, 1926–1927,* p. 87.

of the total in 1924) was short- rather than long-term, making potential benefits from price changes uncertain, generally minuscule, and possibly even negative. Furthermore, three-fourths of short-term credit was extended by private individuals, who would be least likely to become willing victims of inflation.[5] Finally, short-term exceeded long-term mortgage credit in agricultural provinces, suggesting the absence of a deliberate policy by landowners either toward heavy long-term indebtedness or toward promotion of inflation that would reduce the debt's real value.

This evidence suggests that no capitalist group was persistently either a net debtor or creditor and, more particularly, that landowners were neither net debtors nor heavy long-term debtors. Therefore, a consciousness of net indebtedness could not have been formed by a capitalist group even though it was possible for individuals. As a consequence, it would have been irrational, if not impossible, for any given capitalist group to either pursue or support an inflationary policy. If an inflation-induced redistribution of income did occur, it must have involved a random redistribution from one capitalist group to another or from one individual to another, rather than from workers to capitalists or from workers to landowners. Therefore, the theory that attributed the pre-1930 Chilean inflation to the high propensity of the landlords to go into debt and to their attempts to redistribute income in their favor through price manipulation seems to be without foundation.

The income share of the capitalist class in the urban industrial, construction, trade, and banking sectors must have also been in the neighborhood of 45–50 percent. After 1840 an elite group of professionals, government functionaries, and high-level white-collar workers developed slowly but uninterruptedly in the urban centers. The income levels of this group were far above those of the working class and occasionally matched those of many capitalists. Unfortunately, the statistical information in this area has not yet been elaborated systematically.

THE SHARE OF FOREIGNERS AND IMMIGRANTS

Both the internal and international distributions of income were apparently affected by the presence of foreign and immigrant monetary

5. See *Sinopsis, 1925*, p. 127.

and human capital in various sectors. The inclusion of foreigners and immigrants in the labor force led to the establishment of an efficient, well-paid, and well-educated group. Foreign capital thrust into the foreground the issue of national versus foreign ownership. This distinction assumed special significance because foreign enterprises tended to be more efficient than national ones. The differential made possible the superiority of foreign-owned sectors or subsectors in resource surpluses, survival capacity, and economic power. Furthermore, institutional, technological, and political linkages, as well as flows of payments for intermediate products and factors of production, were different in the foreign-owned and nationally owned sectors. The extensive association of the foreign-owned sectors with the developed West formed and made these sectors an integral part of the international production mechanism. National enterprises were operated primarily in the internal economy. Both, however, determined and were part of the domestic economic fabric.

The ownership transformation that started almost immediately after independence involved an increased share of factors of production contributed by foreigners and included a wide range of patterns. This trend was accelerated after 1880, and its magnitude, speed, and nature differed among sectors. The factors that determined it included the sectoral needs for immigrant human and physical capital, the need for advanced foreign technology to maintain or increase international competitiveness, the barriers to entry, the capacity of Chileans to meet foreign competition, and, finally, the government's degree of willingness to permit foreigners to operate on their own rather than on the terms most advantageous to Chile.

Maritime movement through Chilean ports increased more than tenfold between 1890 and 1900, but the tonnage carried by Chilean vessels fell by 20 percent.[6] Chilean ownership and income declined in absolute terms as such foreign-owned international companies as the Pacific Steam Navigation Company, Grace and Company, Roland Line, Veloce, and Trans-atlántica Italiana handled an increasing share of export–import trade.[7] The enormous increase in traffic that followed the nitrate bonanza and that was facilitated by the opening of the Panama Canal forced the government to undertake massive public

6. See Claudio Véliz, *Historia de la Marina Mercante de Chile* (Santiago: Universidad de Chile, 1961). For the data cited in the text, see pp. 375–76, 384.
7. Chile, *Geografía Económica* (Santiago: Imprenta Cervantes, 1923), p. 172.

works in almost all ports, but the majority of external maritime traffic[8] was handled by ships of British, American, Norwegian, and other foreign flags. Whereas the Japanese merchant marine almost quadrupled between 1890 and 1900, the Chilean merchant marine failed to grasp the opportunity inherent in massive trade expansion. The response to the challenge of increased demand was withdrawal and retreat rather than expansion and aggression.

Although many other sectors relied also on immigrant managers, entrepreneurs, technicians, and other highly skilled personnel, Chile was not without distinguished national entrepreneurs, pioneers, and explorers. José Tomás Urmeneta, a miner and industrialist, contributed to major mineral discoveries in Coquimbo and strongly promoted the incipient national industry. Matias Cousiño first exploited the Chilean coal mines. One of the most celebrated pioneers was José Santos Ossa, whose continued mountain and desert exploring led to the discovery of nitrate. The pioneer and statesman Vicente Pérez greatly assisted in the colonization of the provinces of Valdivia and Llanquihue. Pedro Nolasco Mena pioneered agricultural systems of land utilization and establishment of workers' unions. Maximiliano Errazuriz Valdiviesco won fame by being among the first to develop the coal mines, by financing public works (including the railroad between Santiago and Valparaíso), and by fulfilling the roles of industrialist, agriculturist, and public benefactor. Finally, special mention must be made of Arturo Villaroel, who along with Ossa, discovered massive nitrate deposits.[9]

Nevertheless, Chilean entrepreneurs and managers were still in short supply, and foreign talent was invited to exploit the numerous investment opportunities, especially in industry and commerce. In 1915 one-third of the manufacturing establishments responding to the questionnaires of the statistical office reported that their capital was foreign. The actual figure may have been higher since the record does not include foreign capital invested in anonymous corporations.[10] Moreover, in both 1925 and 1926, one-third of the owners of commer-

8. Approximately 20 percent of the ships entering Chilean ports flew the Chilean flag (ibid., p. 172).

9. See Jorge Vega, *Cartilla de la Chilenidad* (Opúsculo patriótico) (Santiago, Chile: La Nación, n.d.). A complete biographical list of the members of the Sociedad de Fomento Fabril is found in Pedro Luís González and Miguel Soto Nuñez, *Album Gráfico e Histórico de la Sociedad de Fomento Fabril y de la Industria Nacional* (Santiago: Imprenta Cervantes, 1926), pp. 124–228.

10. *Oficina Central de Estadistica, Sinopsis estadistica de la república de Chile, Año 1916*, p. 102. Hereafter this serial publication will be cited as *Sinopsis*.

cial establishments responding to the questionnaires were foreigners, with the Spanish, Italian and Ottoman nationals leading the group.[11] The mere presence of foreigners and foreign capital was a major factor in Chile's growth and transformation and permitted the establishment of the conditions that led to a process of internally controlled modernization and considerable subsequent economic independence. This contribution is admitted even by the Marxists.[12] The degree of absorption, reduced importance, and assimilation of foreigners and immigrants in the industrial and trade sectors was high, measured by their relative importance in newly established enterprises.[13]

The first and larger group of foreign nationals in Chile before 1930 was composed of Argentines, Bolivians, and Peruvians. They were extremely volatile, heavily migratory, and primarily of the labor class. In 1920 this group accounted for 50 percent of all foreigners. A second group consisted mostly of Europeans who were employers in trade, industry, mining, and agriculture and were predominantly permanent residents of Chile.[14] Although foreigners accounted for only 3.2 percent of the population in 1920, their share in Tarapacá was 15.3 percent and in Magallanes 21.5 percent. Foreign nationals had accounted for as much as 51.6 percent of Tarapacá's population in 1885.[15] By 1930 the number of foreign nationals had fallen to 105,000, with 63,000 belonging to the labor force, 32,000 of whom were employers. Among the employers, 12,000 were in trade.[16]

Chile has not been a country of mass immigration. The influx has always been thin in volume and often interrupted. But though the

11. *Sinopsis, Años 1926–27*, p. 78.

12. See Ramírez, *Movimiento Obrero*, pp. 32, 58–59.

13. Chileans including children of immigrants accounted for 73 percent of new incorporations before 1932 and 77 percent from 1933 to 1937. The pattern of Chileanization was even more evident in trade. In incorporations of trade establishments Chileans outnumbered foreigners by a factor of 2 before 1923, by a factor of 3 during 1923–27, by a factor of 3.1 during 1928–32, and by a factor of 5 during 1933–36. See República de Chile, Dirección General de Estadística, *Censo Industrial y Comercial, Año 1937* (Santiago: Dirección General de Estadística, 1939), pp. xxxii–xxxiii. Hereafter cited as *Censo Industrial 1937*.

14. See República de Chile, Dirección General de Estadística, *Censo de Población de la República de Chile*, Levantado el 15 de diciembre de 1920 (Santiago: Litografía Universo, 1925), p. 276.

15. Ibid., p. 277.

16. See República de Chile, Dirección General de Estadística, *X Censo de la Población*, Efectuado el 27 de noviembre de 1930, vol. 3 *Ocupaciones* (Santiago: Imprenta Universo, 1935), p. 18.

immigrants have always represented only a small proportion of the total population (2.16 percent in 1950) their cultural and economic significance has been of the greatest importance.[17] The landmarks of economic progress are linked with the names of immigrants. The beginnings of the textile industry are due to Heytz, who was Swiss; those of the paper industry to Rudloff, a German. Chilean metallurgy was created and prospered as the result of the efforts of Englishmen, Germans, and Spaniards such as Orchard, Morrison, Klein, Kupfer, and Victoria. The German Anwandter initiated the brewing of beer.

The history of mining, navigation, and railroading is also marked by the names of immigrants. The definite contribution made by German, Spanish, French, Italian, and Swiss immigrants to the colonization of the southern regions is a cause célèbre in Chile's development history.[18] A Spanish immigrant, José Menéndez, and a Russian, Maurice Braun, started the breeding of livestock. In addition to the immigrants, the initiative of foreigners is responsible for the development of clothing, printing, books, chemical and pharmaceutical products, glassware, window glass, ceramics, foodstuffs, furniture, utensils, and building industries.[19] Thus, in the economic development of Chile, immigration has played a role vastly superior to that suggested by its modest proportions.

The greater part of the immigration has been free and spontaneous. Planned immigrations were few in number and small in volume but were successful both in the economic sphere and in their cultural, social, and political aspects. Qualitatively, Chile has possessed a remarkable gift for welcoming foreigners and an outstanding ability to absorb and assimilate inflows from Europe and parts of Asia that

17. During the century of 1850–1950, 212,000 presumed immigrants settled in the country, implying an average annual rate of 2,120, or 0.5 per 1,000 of the average population during that century. However, immigration from 1906 onward has been definitely lower than this figure. See UNESCO, "Immigration in Chile" (Santiago, Chile: E/CN.12/169/Add 2), mimeo; plus tables, appendixes I, II. This excellent study which provides the foundations of the present section, has unfortunately never been published. For the aforementioned information see ibid., p. 56.

18. The literature on German colonization of the South is extensive. See Emilio Held, *Documentos sobre la Colonización del Sur de Chile de la Colección Histórica de Emilio Held* (Santiago: Talleres Claus von Plate, 1970). This has a detailed description of German immigration during 1840–75 and a short bibliography. See also the excellent essay by Jean Pierre Blancpain, *La Tradición Campesina Alemana en Chile* (Santiago: Camilo Henríquez, 1970). This essay was originally published in *Boletín de la Academia Chilena de la Historia*, no. 81.

19. Ibid., pp. 65–67.

occasionally displayed profound differences in language, culture, and ways of life.[20]

The ownership transformation in maritime trade (where an increasing share of value added was turned over to foreign countries), and in industry, banking, and other services (where foreign became immigrant ownership with maximum local ties, absorption, and assimilation) was accompanied by similar changes in mining. These changes had a transcendental influence on resource distribution and on the country's long-term growth and economic policy. In the case of nitrate the transformation involved, on the one hand, the satisfaction of a rising share of world demand by externally produced, foreign synthetic nitrates and, on the other hand, a simultaneous increase in control of domestic production by foreigners. Another variety of ownership transformation occurred in copper. As we have already seen, the Chilean share of world copper output dwindled as national ownership remained associated with small-scale exploitation of the rapidly disappearing high-grade-ore deposits. Eventually, foreigners entered the sector and revived domestic production through large-scale operations and almost exclusive foreign ownership. These Schumpeterian innovators exploited new markets, raised capital, introduced new techniques, and continued where discoverers and pioneers had left off. This displacement of nationals by foreigners has been described as the process of denationalization. The relative significance of Chilean and foreign production in various mining subsectors is shown in table 3.1.

Both Chilean Marxists and various nationalists have cited nitrate mining as the prime example of either imperialist exploitation or structural dependence. The exploitation theory argued that the latifundio aristocracy exploited farm labor, the commercial-banking community exploited urban workers, and the foreign, particularly British, capitalists exploited the nitrate proletariat.[21] International exploitation was accomplished first through an alleged penetration of

20. There exists very little evidence that in Chile "immigration policy was as irrational and shortsighted as in Argentina." This statement is from the study by Carl Solberg, *Immigration and Nationalism, Argentina and Chile, 1890–1914* (Austin: University of Texas Press, 1970), p. 171. Solberg does not distinguish clearly between immigrants and foreigners and the internal reaction to these groups. Without an analysis of this distinction and its problems and implications, it is impossible to impart the correct historical perspective to the relationship between immigration and nationalism.

21. Hernán Ramírez Necochea, *Balmaceda y la Contrarevolución de 1891* (Santiago: Editorial Universitaria, S.A., 1958). Hereafter cited as *Balmaceda*.

Table 3.1. Chilean Share in Mineral Production, 1920

Principal products	Production in millions of Chilean pesos of 18 pence		Chilean percentage
	Total	Chilean	
Nitrate	473.0	264.7	55.96
Copper	107.5	12.0	11.21
Coal	71.2	65.1	91.35
Iodine	8.1	3.8	47.27
Silver	8.1	3.1	38.14
Sulfur	1.7	0.9	56.96
Gold	1.8	0.6	35.13
Borax	4.1	0.016	0.39

Source: Santiago Macchiavello Varas, *El Problema de la Industria del Cobre en Chile y sus Proyecciónes Económicas y Sociales* (Santiago: Imprenta Fiscal de la Penitenciaria, 1923), vol. 2, p. 108.

British imperialism into the Chilean nitrate sector. The English share of the nitrate industry gradually rose from less than 18 percent in 1875 to approximately 34 percent in 1882. Spearheaded by the Englishmen John Thomas North, Robert Harvey, Maurice Jewel, and others, English entrepreneurs and capitalists established or controlled the Liverpool, Colorado, Primitiva, London, San Pablo, San Jorge, San Donato, and San Sebastián Nitrate Companies Limited, the Bank of Tarapacá and London, the Nitrate Railways Company Limited, the Tarapacá Water Works Company Limited, the Nitrate and General Investments Trust Company Limited, the Nitrate Provision Supply Company Limited, and the Tarapacá Nitrate Company Limited.[22]

Ramírez Necochea does not point out that the nitrate fields were conquered by Chile in an act of imperialism and that the Chileans who controlled less than 20 percent of the nitrate industry in 1875 had also increased their share to 36 percent by 1882.[23] According to the figures of Ramírez Necochea, the nitrate resources were distributed between Chile and the rest of the world in a proportion of 60 and 40 percent. The 40 percent that left the country reflected payments of interest and dividends, amortization of capital, and imports of machinery. Two-thirds of the Chilean share—that is, 40 percent of nitrate resources—

22. Ibid., pp. 18, 30; 32–33.
23. Ibid., pp. 18, 30.

reflected export taxes. The share of workers was only .50 pesos per
nitrate quintal out of a total price per quintal of 2.85 pesos. The labor
share in nitrate resources was a maximum of 18 percent, or, in terms of
value added, probably not much more than 25 percent.[24] In reality the
share of nitrate income that accrued to England and other European
nations was far below 40 percent of nitrate resources because imports
of machinery and equipment can hardly be regarded as income
repatriated by English capital invested in nitrate.

In my more recent estimate, the distribution of nitrate revenues
between 1880 and 1924 amounted to 6.9 billion gold pesos of 18 pence.
One-third accrued to government (and Chile's Center), one-third
involved the cost of production, and one-third was earned by capitalists, Chilean and foreign. The amount of nitrate revenues leaking
abroad—foreign profits, amortization, and so forth—was also 33 percent, or 7 percent of GDP if offsetting capital inflows are ignored.
However, it was only a small or negligible amount if these induced
inflows are considered.[25]

Foreign ownership in nitrate is said to have had negative effects in
two principal ways according to this widely accepted argument. First,
foreign nitrate capitalists coalesced with other Chilean interest groups
to prevent the only Chilean president who had ambitious reform plans
before 1930 from pursuing them. In particular, foreign nitrate capital
prevented President José Manuel Balmaceda from implementing programs that would have drastically changed the international dimension
of the resource distribution process. Second, foreign ownership in
nitrate was the major force behind the massive transfer of resource
surpluses from Chile to the developed nations.

The modern left-wing interpretation of the fall of Balmaceda em-
phasizes economic factors. His efforts toward structural reform of the
economy, especially in distribution, would have jeopardized the private
interests in nitrate and improved the Chilean share of nitrate resources.
The large landowning families, the bankers, the large commercial
entrepreneurs, and the national and foreign miners of the Great North
did in fact object to them. But Balmaceda relied heavily on the industrial bourgeoisie, the middle classes, and the proletariat.[26] According

24. Ibid., pp. 92–94. The cost estimate cited by Ramírez was prepared by the nitrate
inspector of the Ministry of Internal Revenue and was for 1888.

25. See Mamalakis, "Nitrate," pp. 192–95.

26. Ramírez, *Balmaceda*, pp. 192, 202–12. See also Ramírez, *La Guerra Civil de 1891,*
Antecedentes Económicos (Santiago: Editorial Austral, 1951), with introduction by

to the traditional interpretation his fall can be attributed to his methods, means, and political strategy rather than to his objectives. Yet neither account alone can explain the events completely, since Balmaceda's objectives were those of many Chilean governments, though for some they may have existed just on paper.

The intrusion and negative impact of British imperialism was allegedly compounded by the German and North American imperialistic penetration.[27] United States penetration is closely linked to a dramatic increase in its Chilean investments from $5 million in 1900 to $200 million in 1914. Of this fortyfold increase,[28] more than $150 million was destined to revive copper exports by establishing large-scale mining. Such a feat was far beyond Chile's capacity and was bound to contribute vast and indispensable riches, especially after the disappearance of nitrate in the 1930s.

It is inaccurate to fault this investment for all Chile's problems and to ignore its major contributions. When American capital came to the rescue of a languishing nitrate and a totally stagnant copper sector, it attempted to prevent nitrate extinction and to stimulate copper revival in view of growing international competition. Events reflected Chile's state of development rather than a deliberate policy by any one capitalist, labor, or governmental group.

The alleged inequalities in the international distribution of Chile's export resources, surpluses, and income provoked recommendations that were partially implemented in subsequent years. Luis Aldunate, who opposed in Congress the sale of the nitrate mines, recommended in 1893 nationalization of nitrate within the limits of the law, special privileges to Chileans within the nitrate sector, public works to promote private wealth, reduction of taxes, the obligatory formation by govern-

---

Guillermo Feliú Cruz. Hereafter cited as *Guerra Civil*. Harold Blakemore distinguishes between the "constitutional" and "economic" interpretations of the Balmaceda revolution and believes that "economic factors were much less significant than Ramírez suggests and that personal and political allegiances within the governing class were the principal determinants of conduct." See Harold Blakemore's extremely careful study "The Chilean Revolution of 1891 and Its Historiography," *The Hispanic American Historical Review*, 45, no. 2 (August 1965): 418, 420.

27. See Ramírez, *Historia del Imperialismo en Chile* (Santiago: Empresa Editora Austral, 1960). Hereafter cited as *Imperialismo*. For views similar to those of Ramírez see also Julio Cesar Jobet, *Ensayo Crítico del Desarrollo Económico-Social de Chile* (Santiago: Editorial Universitaria, S.A., 1955), and Marcello Segall, *Desarrollo del Capitalismo en Chile, Cinco Ensayos Dialécticos* (Santiago: Editorial del Pacífico, S.A., 1953).

28. Ramírez, *Imperialismo*, pp. 216–17.

ment of a large fund of national reserves, and the use of extraordinary nitrate revenues for equally extraordinary government expenditures.[29] Two decades later Francisco Rivas Vicuña made some far more drastic and radical recommendations: that means of production be nationalized, that extractive industries and those transforming national raw materials be heavily protected, that Chile become independent of foreign transport by nationalizing railroads and creating a national merchant marine, and finally, that Chile centralize and reorganize national credit.[30]

THE EXPORT GAP AND THE INTERNATIONAL DISTRIBUTION
OF INCOME

To measure the amount of resources that left Chile as a consequence of the presence of foreign capital and labor, the international dimension of resource distribution must be examined. The importance that contemporary scholars assign to this factor in explaining Chilean growth performance seems justified at first sight by the size of the resource in- and outflows presented in table 3.2. Considered identical to the export or import surplus, these flows are used as an unadjusted measure of the intercountry distribution of income. Adjustments and discussion of the limitations of this measure provide a more accurate picture of the direction and magnitude of this resource transfer.[31]

Chile transferred resources abroad both before and after 1880, but the average size of the export surplus after 1880 increased at least tenfold over its 1844–80 volume. However, distinct subperiods appeared before as well as after 1880. Chile was a net recipient of resources with a substantial import surplus during the 1844–60 period of spectacular export growth and prosperity, but it turned into a net donor during the 1860–80 period, which was marked by the War with Spain, the War of the Pacific, and relative stagnation.[32]

---

29. See Luis Aldunate, *Desde nuestro obsevatorio, estudio de actualidad* (Santiago: Imprenta Cervantes, 1893), and *Indicaciónes de la Balanza Comercial* (Santiago: Imprenta Cervantes, 1893). The recommendations cited in the text are found on pp. 99 and 137 of the former monograph and pp. 211–17 of the latter monograph.

30. See *Política Nacional* (Santiago: Imprenta Universitaria, 1913), pp. 35–36.

31. Capital inflows and repatriated profits and capital measure specific balance-of-payments flows.

32. Since the figures of table 3.2 are expressed in current U.S. dollars, the real value of the resource flows during the earlier years are underestimated by a degree related to the U.S. price index.

The outflow of resources during 1880–1900 was relatively stable and not much higher than that during 1860–80. After 1900 it became extensive, rising first to an average of $16 million a year during 1901–10 (three times its 1891–1900 size), then to $41.2 million during 1911–20, and finally to $57.6 million annually during 1920–30. A total of more than $1.1 billion worth of resources left Chile during the first thirty years of the twentieth century. Between 1875 and 1930 Chile had an import surplus in only six years, whereas in the much shorter 1840–75 period it enjoyed import surpluses during fifteen years.[33]

The quantitative significance of the resource transfers stands out even more if compared to the value of exports and indirectly to gross domestic product (GDP). From 1844 to 1850 the import surplus equaled 12 percent of exports, but it fell to 3 percent during 1851–60. The pattern was reversed subsequently, with the export surplus accounting for 16 percent of exports during 1861–70 and 13 percent during 1871–80, for an average of 9.3 percent for the 1844–80 period.

Table 3.2. Resource Transfer to (−) from (+) Chile to (from) abroad, 1884–1930
(In thousands of U.S. dollars)

Period	Total	Annual average
1844–50	− 6,400.4	− 914.3
1851–60	− 3,879.9	− 388.0
1861–70	+ 48,100.6	+ 4,810.0
1871–80	+ 38,249.6	+ 3,825.0
1881–90	+ 73,878.3	+ 7,387.8
1891–1900	+ 51,451.5	+ 5,145.2
1901–10	+ 160,967.4	+ 16,096.7
1911–20	+ 412,363.0	+ 41,236.3
1921–30	+ 576,035.6	+ 57,603.6
1844–1930	+ 1,350,765.7	+ 15,494.5
1844–80	+ 76,069.9	2,055.9
1881–1930	+ 1,274,695.8	25,493.9

Source: Calculated from information found in the following tables or sources listed therein: Mamalakis, "Historical Statistics," vol. 3, part IIE, tables IIEle1 and IIEle2, pp. A-562–568. The same statistics are found in C. Humud, "El Sector Público Chileno entre 1830 y 1930" (Santiago: Universidad de Chile, 1969), p. 100.
Note: Export (+) or import (−) surplus.

33. The long-term trends of the export or import gaps are the same whatever the statistical information we rely upon. However, the figures for individual years can vary as can be seen by comparing the work of Carlos Humud, "Sector Público", p. 100 with that of Daniel Martner, *Historia de Chile, Historia Económica* (Santiago: Balcells and Co., 1929), vol. 1, pp. 261, 273, 313, 359. Martner does not give the source of his statistics.

The export surplus ranged between 15 and 20 percent of exports during 1881–1910 but rose to 27 percent during 1911–20 and to 29 percent during 1921–30, thus bringing the average percentage value of the export surplus to 25 percent of exports during the 1880–1930 period. Assuming that exports had an average value of 30 percent of GDP, the export surplus was close to 2.5 percent of GDP before 1880 and approached 7.5 percent during the 1880–1930 period. Furthermore, had the export surpluses not existed and the respective resources been used for investment, the investment coefficient, which ranged from 15 to 20 percent of GDP, could have increased by the possibly critical amount necessary to achieve a self-propelling transformation.

The figures on the export surplus may overestimate the actual loss of resources to Chile. Imports are more likely to have been underestimated than exports, and if payments for services were included on both sides, the gap would be smaller. Chile used part of its export proceeds to pay for personnel employed in virtually every sector, and the contribution of such human resources was partially responsible for the export gap. But even after adjustment for these relatively minor factors, the export gap remains.[34]

Full analysis of this question must consider the various components of the balance of payments, the behavior that promoted it, and the structural and other forces that led to a pattern of real and monetary flows generally regarded to be detrimental to Chile. With respect to specific flows there is evidence on government borrowing and, on a rather crude basis, on some key balance-of-payments items for the 1925–30 period (presented in table 3.3). Insofar as the structural characteristics and forces are concerned, there exists evidence concerning foreign and immigrant ownership and price level and foreign exchange stability as well as the rather cursory evidence on the distribution of income among labor, land, and capital.

The export gap first assumed major proportions, though only temporarily, during 1878–84, when foreign exchange devaluation was dramatic in both speed and size.[35] Contrary to expectations, orthodox export surpluses became associated with weakness in the foreign

34. Historical balance-of-payments statistics would have to be prepared before a more accurate picture can be obtained. This research topic, which begs for callers, has not yet been touched because of the magnitude of effort and variety of skills required to execute it.

35. Martner, *Historia de Chile, Historia Económica* (Santiago: Balcells and Co., 1929), p. 359. The Chilean peso lost 30 percent of its value within the four-year period 1877–80 (ibid., p. 469).

exchange markets and with devaluation. Fortunately, after 1885 exports and imports remained relatively stable and almost equal until 1897. Both spurted upward between 1897 and 1913, while a massive export surplus developed between 1897 and 1906.[36] In the 1920s Chile once more developed a huge export surplus, which finally evaporated in 1930.[37]

Chile's ability to maintain an import surplus, and thus to derive net benefits from its trade balance, was extensively affected by internal monetary stability and sound public finances.[38] The general mixture of internal institutional transformation with price and exchange stability determined the attractiveness of Chile to capital. Yet even complete ownership and control by nationals and government could not guarantee that there would be no in- or outflows of speculative capital. Although transformation and modernization progressed substantially during the ninety-year period, fiscal, monetary, and foreign exchange stability deteriorated. The war against underdevelopment was slowly won in the areas of education, health, welfare, and institutional change, but this progress was accompanied by retrogression in price stability, government finances, and foreign exchange. As the need for funds to pursue internal transformation grew more urgent and the dependence on the export sector as a source of these funds increased, more and more instability was introduced into the system. This was the result not only of the decreasingly diversified base of tax revenues but also of the slow development, and difficulties in introduction, of institutional reform in the monetary field.

Measurement of the outflow of resources and its causes during the 1925–30 period lends partial support to the customary argument that an excess of exports over imports is caused by income and amortization payments to foreign capital. Payments to foreign capital were indeed massive, ranging between 31.5 and 55.1 percent of total revenues during 1925–30, as shown by columns 3 and 6 of table 3.3. However, since these payments were substantially lower than the export gap during the same period, other items must have offset this leakage. The major offsetting item was capital inflows, which, according to columns 4 and

36. *Resumen de la Hacienda Pública de Chile Desde 1833 Hasta 1914* (London: Spottiswoode and Co., 1915), p. 92.

37. Mamalakis, "Historical Statistics of Chile," tables IIE1e1 and IIE1e2, pp. A-562–63, 567.

38. Agustín Ross, *Chile, 1851–1910, Sesenta Años de Cuestiones Monetarias y Financieras y de Problemas Bancarios* (Santiago: Imprenta Barcelona, 1911), pp. 245–46.

Table 3.3. Key Balance-of-Payments Statistics, Chile, 1920–30
(In millions of U.S. dollars in 1961 prices)

| | Exports and other current revenues | Total imports | Payments to foreign capital | Capital inflows | Imports as % of current revenues | Payments to foreign capital as % of current revenues | Capital inflows as % of current revenues | Capital inflows as % of payments to foreign capital |
| | | | | | (2)/(1) | (3)/(1) | (4)/(1) | (4)/(3) |
	(1)	(2)	(3)	(4)	(5)	(6)	(7)	(8)
1920	572.7	334.3	—	—	58.4	—	—	—
1921	504.7	442.7	—	—	87.7	—	—	—
1922	389.4	278.0	—	—	71.4	—	—	—
1923	612.5	370.6	—	—	60.5	—	—	—
1924	702.5	420.4	—	—	59.8	—	—	—
1925	687.4	446.9	216.7	102.4	65.0	31.5	14.9	47.3
1926	625.2	488.0	297.2	435.6	78.1	47.5	69.7	146.6
1927	669.1	424.1	369.0	221.9	63.4	55.1	33.2	60.1
1928	767.6	506.9	412.6	374.7	66.0	53.8	48.8	90.8
1929	911.7	642.6	357.7	220.4	70.5	39.2	24.2	61.6
1930	581.4	612.8	233.5	167.3	105.4	40.2	28.8	71.6

Source: Original data in current U.S. dollars are found in "Mining, International Transactions, Money and Banking, and Government and the Public Sector," in Mamalakis, "Historical Statistics," table IIE2a2, pp. A-580–A-583.

Note: Income plus amortization payments to foreign capital [col. (3)] and long-term capital inflows [col. (4)] have been converted to 1961 prices from original data in 1950 prices.

8 of table 3.3, either partially or totally compensated for the factor payments. Thus, although gross factor payments from 1925 to 1930 were $1.886 million, the net outflow after taking into account capital inflows of $1.523 million was only $363 million. As a consequence, the real net outflow on this account was only 20 percent of the unadjusted gross outflow.

The excess of exports over imports was $2.121 million during the 1925–30 period. If the net outflow of $363 million is deducted, $1.758 million left the country for reasons other than foreign ownership. The primordial role played by factors other than foreign ownership can be seen by observing the year 1926, when capital inflows reached an astonishing level of 69.7 percent of Chile's foreign exchange revenues and exceeded payments to foreign capital by almost 50 percent (cols. 7 and 8). In spite of such vast capital inflows, however, imports were only 78 percent of current foreign exchange revenues.

Among the factors responsible for the persistence of the export gap, the first was an underestimate of imports because of smuggling and underinvoicing. This underestimate is likely to have caused as much as 10 to 15 percent of the measured gap. Moreover, payments for imported services, travel, and so forth may account for an average of 50 percent of the gap. Finally, the remaining 35–40 percent of the gap was caused by the movement and flight of capital out of Chile, primarily by Chileans.

The implications of these tentative estimates, which I believe come close to reality, are important. Factor payments abroad were indeed substantial during 1880–1930, but because they were largely offset by capital inflows, they were neither the major nor the exclusive cause of an unfavorable international distribution of resources. Hence, the international exploitation hypothesis receives at best only partial support. Furthermore, the use of a significant amount of foreign exchange for transport, insurance, services by foreign professionals, and travel— all of which contributed to Chile's development—can hardly be regarded as a unilateral transfer. Finally, the largest part, if not all, of the remaining net resource outflow was undertaken by Chileans and was caused mostly by monetary, price, fiscal, and foreign exchange instability.

Although the 1925–30 experience may have been representative of the whole 1880–1930 period, it is impossible at this time to judge exactly how typical it was. In any case it undoubtedly casts a serious cloud on the exploitation theory and lends support to the thesis that monetary and fiscal factors were a primary cause for Chile's less than adequate performance. Despite its relatively high capacity to attract foreign capital, and even to assimilate it in some sectors, it showed only a limited capacity to keep Chilean capital within the country.

THE HETEROGENEOUS LABOR SHARE

In spite of the important selective role of foreigners in the increasingly efficient and modern production system, the bulk of labor inputs was contributed by sui generis, heterogeneous Chileans.[39] The income share of labor fluctuated within the low range of 40–50 percent of the total product, both because labor demand never became strong enough to lead to scarcity and nationwide unionization and because education and skills of local labor remained low.[40] As a consequence of the inability of government to establish more rapidly a broad primary and an intermediate technical education and the sustained abundance of low-skilled labor, real wages and living standards for a major segment of the labor force increased only moderately.[41]

The degree of labor's contribution to the country's development was shaped by idiosyncracies that evolved during 1840–1930 and were strengthened during 1930–70. One of the crucial developments was the formation of a white-collar labor group consisting largely of employees in the service sectors, including government. The labor union movement among white-collar workers, initiated after some powerful blue-collar syndicates had been formed, had its first success when the social laws of 1924 established the contract of private salary earners and the Caja de Previsión. In 1937 this group obtained laws that enacted the vital salary, annual adjustments for cost-of-living increases, seniority salary raises, and the family allowance. These measures set them apart from blue-collar workers by raising their real income and weakening the labor movement among them.[42]

---

39. A very informative description of the hetero- as well as homogeneity of the Chileans is found in Hernán San Martín, *Geografía Humana de Chile, Nosotros Los Chilenos No. 17* (Santiago: Editora Quimantu, 1972).

40. For a concise history of Chile's labor movement and its accomplishments see Jorge Barría Serón, *Breve Historia del Sindicalismo Chileno* (Santiago: Instituto de Administración de la Universidad de Chile, 1967). Hereafter cited as *Sindicalismo*.

41. For a history of the labor movement and its accomplishments in the state railroads see Armando Sepúlveda, *Historia Social de los Ferroviarios* (Santiago: Imprenta Siglo XX, 1959). This monograph illustrates the social and labor problems in a stagnant sector.

42. Barría, *Sindicalismo*, pp. 30–31, 37.

The special status gained by the white-collar workers found expression in high and rising salary–wage differentials. In 1937 the monthly salary of the average white-collar worker in trade was at least three times higher than the monthly wages of the average blue-collar worker.[43] In agriculture, administrators of estates, who comprised the upper layer of the white-collar class, earned at least four times as much in 1925 as the better-paid sharecroppers.[44]

In addition to the widespread (occasionally even exorbitant) salary–wage differentials, wage earnings differed substantially among sectors. For example, in 1921 the average wage for a landless agricultural worker was 2.73 pesos[45] and ranged from 2.15 pesos in the winter to 3.18 pesos during the harvest. In contrast the average wage in mining in 1921 was 8.29 pesos.[46] Copper workers earned a maximum of 8.96 pesos a day, nitrate workers 8.27 pesos, and iron ore miners 5.55 pesos.[47] Industrial wages showed a wider range but an average level similar to that in mining.[48] Workers in gas and electricity, who were classified as industrial workers in 1922, earned the maximum of 10.95 pesos per day, while clothing workers were at the bottom with 4.63 pesos per day.[49]

However, wages in mining and industry were only twice as high as those in agriculture despite much higher average productivity differentials. This relationship implies that wages were determined by marginal productivity, which was pushed to low levels even in mining because of the abundant labor supply elsewhere in the economy. Small privileged groups and/or powerful labor unions did arise early among blue-collar workers, not only among but also within such sectors as copper, sheep raising in Magallanes, and the gas and electrical in-

43. See Dirección General de Estadística de Chile, *Censo Industrial 1937*, pp. xxx–xxxi.

44. *Boletín de la Oficina del Trabajo No. 24, Año 1926*, Anexo LXXXVIII.

45. Ibid., *Núm. 21, Año 1923*, Anexo XIII, p. 123.

46. Extensive information on wages and salaries in various sectors and jobs is found for the years since 1911 in the various issues of *Boletín de la Oficina del Trabajo* published by the Ministerio de Industria i Obras Públicas. The outstanding characteristic of these data is the difference between laborers and the more skilled carpenters and stewards. Stewards earned 2–4 times the earnings of laborers and about 2 times the earnings of carpenters (ibid., pp. 276–77, 283). See also ibid., *No. 4, Primer Semestre de 1912, Año II*, pp. 232–320.

47. Ibid., *Año 1923*, p. 120.

48. Information on industrial wages is found in the various issues of the *Estadística Industrial* for the various provinces published by the Sociedad de Fomento Fabril since 1895.

49. *Boletín del Trabajo, Año 1923*, p. 120.

dustries. The agricultural workers clearly fared worst. The wage differentials among sectors seemed to be generally greater than the salary differentials, suggesting greater fragmentation and lack of unity among blue- than among white-collar workers. For example, in 1937 average salaries in industry exceeded average salary in trade by at least 25 percent, while average wages in industry surpassed those in trade by at least 40 percent.[50]

Regional differences in salaries and wages were also substantial. For instance, the average industrial salary in Tarapacá in 1937 was at least three times that of Aisén, while the average industrial wage in Magallanes was at least triple that of Chiloé.[51] Some of the income differences may have been fictitious. Although wages of nitrate workers in the interior of the provinces of Atacama, Coquimbo, and Aconcagua were higher than elsewhere in the country, real income, considering the high prices charged by the company stores and the extremely adverse climatic conditions, may not have been superior to that in other regions.[52] It is also of interest to note that in 1925 women earned less than half the wages paid to men and children only one-fourth.[53]

Two more labor groups stand as separate entities. Professionals, because of education, family background, or high earnings, formed an elite that had more ties with the capitalists, employers, and landowners than with the workers. Also, a quasi-lumpenproletariat was composed of the landless, migrant agricultural workers and the transient laborers slowly accumulating around major cities.

Under these circumstances a meaningful discussion of the labor group as an aggregate force becomes impossible. Labor as a whole lacked the common interests, the common goals, or even the common adversaries that could provide the basis for unity. One segment, the white-collar workers, had common transsectoral interests and was somewhat united. But this was the exception not the rule. For most segments of labor sectoral inequalities outweighed class ties. As a consequence, class struggle involving labor on a national scale was inconceivable and did not take place.

The uneven introduction of capitalistic modes of production into the various sectors led to an unequal degree of confrontation between capitalists and workers. In large-scale copper, in nitrate mining, in

50. See *Censo Industrial 1937*, pp. xxxxiv–xxxxv.
51. See ibid., pp. xxxxiv–xxxxv.
52. See Galdámes, *Jeografía, 1911*, pp. 128–30.
53. *Dirección General del Trabajo, Boletín No. 24, 1926*, p. 141.

the Magallanes sheep-raising *estancias* (ranches), and in the Lota–Schwager coal mines of Concepción the struggle between labor and the capitalists over the whole spectrum of income and working conditions was continuous, frequently bitter, and occasionally fraught with profound social and ideological implications. But the capacity of this struggle to either unite the labor force or set national goals that would collectively favor either labor or the poor remained low. The contribution of labor to the overall transformation of the Chilean economy was confined primarily to its role as a production input and was to only a lesser degree a social catalyst or source of new ideas and objectives.

Discussion of labor's contribution to progress would be incomplete without some reference to the accusation by Marxist and other Left theorists that the middle classes in Chile did not identify with the common man and the laborer and did not break away from the political, economic, and ideological leadership of the feudal crust. Thus the middle classes failed to meet the historical challenge of carrying out the struggle for economic and social improvement of the masses. Bourgeois democracy could have been introduced by the antifeudal, anti-imperialist, and antimonopolistic forces, as it had been in Western Europe.[54]

This argument is misleading. The challenge actually confronted all elements of the nation: the middle classes, landlords, the working class, urban capitalists, and white-collar workers. Chile needed to create a common social ethos as a base for the nation by assimilating and integrating employers and workers, immigrants and creoles, and the diverse workers of the desert pampas, the rich farms, the wind-swept estancias, the Cordillera, and the sea. When Chile was exposed to the merciless forces of international competition, foreign capitalism, and Western imperialism, the people who would comprise the middle

---

54. Paul A. Barán, "On the Political Economy of Backwardness," in *The Economics of Underdevelopment*, ed. A. N. Agarwala and S. P. Singh (London: Oxford University Press, 1958), pp. 75–92, esp. pp. 78–79; Claudio Véliz, "Introduction," in *Obstacles to Change in Latin America*, ed. Claudio Véliz (London: Oxford University Press, 1965), pp. 1–8. As Robert L. Bennett, who reviewed the *Obstacles to Change in Latin America*, edited by Veliz, for the *American Economic Review* 56, no. 5 (Dec. 1966): 1295–96, correctly points out, "The essays, and particularly the Introduction, largely support the model, advanced more than a decade ago by Paul Barán, of the new industrial middle classes joining the landowners in a coalition of property owners who resist the institutional changes which are necessary for rapid economic development" (ibid., p. 1295). See also Aníbal Pinto, "Political Aspects of Economic Development in Latin America," in *Obstacles to Change in Latin America*, pp. 9–46, and Osvaldo Sunkel, "Change and Frustration in Chile," in *Obstacles to Change in Latin America*, pp. 116–44.

classes today were still very heterogeneous. Facing unprecedented events and forced to develop original solutions, they performed remarkably well. Such immigrants as the Edwards's, McIvers's, Tomics, Sumars, Freis, Teitelboims, Subercaseaux, and Brauns became an integral and indistinguishable part of the social and economic fabric. Spaniards, Italians, British, Germans, Arabs, Jews, Yugoslavs, Americans, and French meshed with the creole elite. However, major segments of labor or the population on farms, isolated islands, the deserts, the Andes, and the urban misery belts remained underprivileged and neglected, with little or no access to the state educational, health, and administrative services that were necessary to break down class rigidities through upward mobility. Most appalling was the abandonment of rural areas that were not particularly remote.

It is undoubtedly true that the benefits from the nitrate boom and overall growth were shared unequally by the various population segments. But more importantly, all groups (though to unequal degrees) demanded immediate benefits. These benefits penalized investment, a factor that is largely responsible for inadequate social and economic integration and the growing income inequalities within labor. As a consequence of these forces Chile failed to make full use of its very intelligent, talented labor at a major cost in terms of aggregate welfare. More specifically, the government reduced welfare for this low-income, inadequately employed labor.

The low-income share of the working classes was also a negative factor since it shifted demand away from standardized, basic industrial products locally available to more selective purchasers. Even the luxury products that were demanded by the middle- and upper-income groups were either imported or had a very high import component. Thus it was probably in the distribution process that the least amount of progress was achieved. Sometimes the developments were even negative as sectoral, class, and regional inequalities increased and a substantial share of domestic resources left Chile.

4

Capital Accumulation

Although the statistical information pertaining to the speed, shape, and continuity of transformation in Chile's capital formation is limited, it is clear that accumulation occurred in both human and physical capital after 1840. Quantifiable evidence exists only for physical investment. It is therefore necessary to use the progress of education as an indicator of investment in human, social, and institutional capital.

The statistical evidence on physical investment includes the capital formation estimates for 1925–30 by the United Nations Economic Commission for Latin America (UNECLA) and the time series on capital goods imports and developmental government expenditures. UNECLA's investment estimates, although imperfect, are sufficiently accurate and consistent to provide a picture of the investment pattern during 1925–30 and to permit comparisons with the 1930–35 depression years and the 1945–49 period of relative expansion.[1] The evidence concerning the three major agents in capital formation—the Chilean government, the national business and household sector, and the

1. The UNECLA information has to be used very cautiously because some statistics are erroneous. As an example, a major mistake exists in the estimate of the export and import values during 1925–30. In table 6 A, p. 281 of the publication, United Nations, Economic Commission for Latin America, *Economic Survey of Latin America, 1949* (E/CN. 12/164/Rev. 1, 11 Jan. 1951) (hereafter cited as UNECLA, *Economic Survey, 1949*), import values are shown as exceeding export values in each year when in reality the reverse is true in all years except 1930. The error is the result of an indirect estimation procedure. The correct estimates based on official statistics are either presented or used in tables IIE1e1, IIE1e2, IIE1b2, and IIE1b3 of my "Historical Statistics of Chile, 1840–1965."

foreign-owned business sector—is uneven. It is best for government, but marginal and indirect for the other two.

The UNECLA coefficient of capital formation averaged 19.5 percent, or almost one-fifth of production during the 1925–30 period, plummeted to 3.9 percent in 1933, and fluctuated between 10 and 14.5 percent during the 1935–40 period.[2] "Investment" in this instance is defined to include only domestic production of iron, steel, and cement and imports of capital goods. "Production" includes agriculture, industry, building, and mining but excludes all sevices. Thus the coefficient can be regarded as a good estimate of the relationship between investment in machinery and equipment and commodity production.

Estimates of investment in construction and public works are also provided by UNECLA, but unfortunately only for the 1928–30 period.[3] The statistics suggest that domestically produced capital goods ranged from 75 to 90 percent of machinery and equipment investment.[4] If the domestic component of capital formation were combined with machinery and equipment investment and value added in services with commodity production, both the investment coefficient and the overall picture of capital formation during the 1925–30 period would still remain unchanged.

Internally produced capital formation is further subdivided by UNECLA into public works, investments in corporations and limited liability companies, and private building.[5] Whereas public works were phenomenally high in 1930, accounting for almost 60 percent of internally produced capital formation, business investment was the largest category in both 1928 and 1929, contributing between 35 and 40 percent to total investment.

The evolution of capital goods imports during the 1840–1930 period reflects some significant changes in capital accumulation. Before 1883 such imports were generally minuscule. During the 1844–83 period, for example, the value of all types of machinery and equipment imports fell short of the individual value of imported hats, alcoholic beverages, or tobacco and was less than 20 percent of the value of sugar imports.[6] This may reflect a preference for consumption, but it also reveals Chile's

2. UNECLA, _Economic Survey, 1949_, table IIA, p. 293; table IIB, p. 294.
3. Ibid., tables 12 and 13, pp. 294–95.
4. Excluding cement, iron, and steel production.
5. UNECLA, _Economic Survey, 1949_, table 14, p. 295.
6. Chile, Superintendencia de Aduanas, _Estadística Comercial de la República de Chile_, Año 1883 (Valparaíso, Chile: Imprenta del Universo, 1884), pp. xxv, xxvii, xxi.

internal capacity to produce machinery and equipment and to provide most inputs required for construction. A variety of studies and primary sources shows that between 1850 and 1910 a highly advanced producer's durables sector engaged in the production of railroad, mining, and other heavy equipment.[7] During 1906–07 construction and machinery and equipment production, employing 11,000 persons, accounted for 24 percent of industrial establishments, 13.5 percent of production, and 22 percent of the industrial labor force.[8]

From 1900 to 1910 the state railroads began to place major orders for locomotives and other equipment with European producers. Because prompt delivery, proved high quality, low prices, uniformity, and easy availability of spare parts are usually cited as the reasons for this shift,[9] it can be inferred that locally produced railroad equipment was not uniform, lacked high and improving quality, was not always delivered promptly, and was costlier. Technical progress in Chile was not keeping up with that in Europe and the United States. The final shock came with World War I, which made necessary the suspension of much domestic machinery and equipment production because of the inability to obtain vital parts from Europe.[10] Coupled with the other problems, this

7. See J. Fred Rippy and Jack Pfeiffer, "Notes on the Dawn of Manufacturing in Chile," *Hispanic American Historical Review* 28 (May 1948): 292–303; Jack B. Pfeiffer, "Notes on the Heavy Equipment Industry in Chile, 1800–1910," *Hispanic American Historical Review* 32 (Feb. 1952): 139–44. The presence, competitiveness, and efficiency of a railroad-building sector can be seen by its offers to construct such equipment for the railroads. See, e.g., Ferrocarriles del Estado, *Actas de las Sesiones del Consejo Directivo de los Ferrocarriles del Estado, 1888*, (Santiago: Imprenta Victoria, 1888), pp. 13–14, 18, 33–34, 53–54, 63–70. The two major companies that seem to produce every type of equipment for the state railroads are Balfour, Lyon i C.ᵃ and Lever, Murphy i Cᵃ. The wide variety of locomotives, rolling stock, bridge building, and so forth undertaken by one or both of these companies is cited in *Boletín de Servicio de los Ferrocarriles del Estado*, Santiago, *1892*, pp. 599, 768; *1893*, pp. 850, 1045; *1894*, p. 167; *1896*, p. 109; *1899*, p. 379.

8. These figures are from Sociedad de Fomento Fabril, *Resumen General de la Estadística Industrial* (16 provinces) (Santiago: Sociedad de Fomento Fabril, 1908).

9. Empresa de los Ferrocarriles del Estado, *Boletín de Servicio* 16, no. 2 (1905): 494–95. Special mention is made of the fact that all locomotives imported will have interchangeable parts and that only the A. Borsig Company of Berlin could make such a promise.

10. Balfour and Lyon suspended the delivery of locomotives in 1915, and the Sociedad de Maestranzas y Galvanización had to suspend the construction of locomotives in 1917 for reasons derived from the European war. Balfour and Lyon delivered 18 locomotives between 1910 and 1914, and the Sociedad de Maestranzas delivered 72 during 1910–17, with a peak of 15 in 1911 (see *Ferrocarriles de Chile, Historia y Organización*, ed. Emilio Vassallo Rojas and Carlos Matus Guiterrez (Santiago: Editorial "Rumbo," 1943), p. 217).

suspension led to the end of locomotive production in Chile.[11]

Imports of capital goods rose after 1880 both in absolute value and as a share of imports. From then until 1930 competition from imports, lack of internal demand, and low protection slowly but steadily destroyed the internal producers' durables sector, which was displaced by imported machinery and equipment. The very rapid, cyclical, and often erratic changes in the size and composition of capital goods demand also contributed to this process of displacement—import desubstitution—which was facilitated if not accelerated after 1880, when nitrate became the quasi-capital goods sector. The required capital goods could not always be provided by an economy unable to shift from artisan to manufacturing production at the necessary speed. The producers' durables sector ultimately shrank as demand was increasingly satisfied by imports.

During the 1880–1914 period imports of machinery and equipment averaged 10–20 percent of total imports. This share reached its peak in 1889–94 and 1906–09, rising occasionally to one-fourth of total imports. Railroad equipment comprised the overwhelming majority in both instances. Imports of minerals and metals climbed dramatically after 1901 but did not exceed food and textiles, which remained the most important group, or raw materials imports, which followed immediately.[12]

According to UNECLA, during the 1925–30 period capital goods (of two types) accounted for an average of 37 percent of total imports.[13] Machinery and equipment averaged 22 percent and materials 15 percent of the total. Since the ratio of imports to production, as defined earlier, was 50 percent during 1925–30, the ratio of imports to GDP must have fluctuated between 25 and 35 percent, assuming that services contributed 40–50 percent of GDP.[14] With imports at an average of 30 percent of GDP, total capital goods imports were 10–12 percent and producers' durables imports only 6 percent of GDP. In contrast the ratio of imports to GDP had fallen by 50 percent during the 1930–49 period.[15]

According to another estimate based on official statistics (which,

11. Local producers were confined to the production of the less sophisticated equipment.

12. Mamalakis, "Historical Statistics," table IIE1a3, pp. A-546–47.

13. UNECLA, *Economic Survey, 1949*, table 17, p. 302; table 26, p. 312.

14. Ibid., pp. 281–82.

15. Ibid., table 6A, p. 281.

however, does not include under capital goods imports materials used for domestic capital formation), capital goods imports during 1920–30[16] ranged from 10 to 20 percent of export revenues or from 3 to 6 percent of GDP, a value almost identical to that during 1940–58.[17] Furthermore, as already noted, exports consistently exceeded imports.

Although Chile was able to satisfy its needs for machinery and equipment through imports, its nature as a quasi-complete system had a variety of drawbacks. As in the case of locomotives the imported supply of critical parts for capital goods was not continuous and smooth. Besides, once investments with high import components were worn out, their contribution to growth had ended. Had the investment goods been produced internally and efficiently, they would have augmented the domestic capital goods sector and its capacity for technological modernization and transformation.

GOVERNMENT INVESTMENT EXPENDITURES

Between 1888 and 1930 the government's developmental expenditures rose at a rate of 4.0 percent per year,[18] but these expenditures fluctuated. They reached their highest value in 1918 and declined rapidly afterward until 1930. Absorbing an average of 30 percent of total government expenditures, they started at 27.3 percent in 1888, passed 35.8 percent in 1890, hovered around 28 percent during 1895–1905, and fell to 20.5 percent in 1930.[19]

At first (1830) investment expenditures were heavily concentrated in the building of customs facilities. About 1850 they shifted to the construction of railroads and later, during 1910–30, to the building of roads and ports.[20] Physical investment by government was directed predominantly toward those sectors that changed the location, quantity, and time dimensions of goods and services among and within population centers and abroad. The golden era was between 1905 and 1920, when the annual growth rate of government investment expendi-

---

16. Mamalakis, "Historical Statistics," table IIE2a2, p. A-580.
17. See M. Mamalakis, "Public Policy and Sectoral Development, A Case Study of Chile, 1940–1958," in M. Mamalakis and C. Reynolds, *Essays on the Chilean Economy* (Homewood, Ill.: Richard D. Irwin, 1965), chap. 1.
18. Calculated from information found in Carlos Humud, "El Sector Público Chileno Entre 1830 y 1930 (Santiago: Universidad de Chile, Memoria de Prueba, 1969), table A-6.
19. Ibid., p. 191.
20. Ibid., p. 193.

tures was 10.5 percent for the whole period, 16.6 percent for 1910–20, and 23.0 percent for 1915–20. However, only in 1928 was a general plan of public works developed and investment expenditures removed from the current budget.

In view of the importance assigned to the nitrate-generated resource surplus in capital accumulation, we attempt now to determine the magnitude of government investment financed out of these proceeds. Between 1901 and 1914 expenditures of the ministry of industry, public works, and railways, which can be considered bona fide investment, were the largest of any ministry, accounting for 29 percent of total government expenditures. The biggest outlay was by the department of railways, accounting for 24 percent, and was followed by public works with 3.5 percent and the department of industry with a meager 1.1 percent.[21] Since between 50 and 80 percent of railway expenditures were financed out of railway revenues, the government support of railroads actually fluctuated between 4 and 12 percent of total expenditures. Even if the shares of the departments of public works and industry are considered, the evidence suggests that (at least during the fifteen-year period under consideration) the government share of nitrate resource surpluses was used primarily for consumption, including investment in human capital. Only a negligible amount—15 percent of government expenditures—was devoted to physical investment.

After 1914 the share of railroad expenditures covered by revenues declined secularly. These deficits and other types of investment were financed in part from the nitrate taxes, presumably to an extent proportional to the contribution of these taxes to gross revenues. The extremely low level of social, institutional, and educational capital of Chile during the 1840–1930 period probably forced government to emphasize expenditures in nonphysical capital formation. This did in fact occur, although the efficiency of the program cannot be tested. In any case, government was overwhelmingly dependent on one source of revenue, and with a more balanced base it might have contributed substantially more to all processes of capital accumulation.

EDUCATION

Accumulation of human and social capital is difficult to measure, but

---

21. See *Summary of the Finances of Chile from 1833 to 1914* (London: Spottiswoode and Co., 1915?), p. 64.

improvements in educational opportunities do give some indications of the allocation of resources in this area. Chile's educational base in 1842 was negligible. Only 1 percent of the population was enrolled in primary schools and only 0.2 percent in secondary institutions.[22] Progress was made early in most major subject areas with significant quantitative and qualitative results. By 1930 enrollment in primary schools had risen dramatically to 15 percent and in secondary schools to 1 percent of the population.[23]

Between 1840 and 1930 primary education was successively transformed from nonexistent to minimal and then to extensive, and from selective to general. The first teacher's college was founded in 1843, and by 1921 six such institutions for men and nine for women were functioning throughout the republic. Also by that year, 3,729 primary schools, of which 430 were private, had been established and more than 430,000 children were enrolled in them.[24] However, primary education did not become obligatory until in 1920, at least 100 years later than in most of Europe.[25] War against ignorance through primary education became the motto of enlightened intellectuals inspired by Miguel Luis and Gregorio Victor Amunátegui, Andrés Bello, José V. Lastarria, and Domingo F. Sarmiento and provided the impetus toward popular primary education from 1840 to 1880.[26] The literacy of the population rose from 13.5 percent in 1854 to 56.1 percent in 1930, but even so, illiteracy and analphabetism remained relatively common.[27]

The Chilean educational system before the War of the Pacific was indigenous but lacked teachers, methods, schools, and instruments. It was a "miserable,"[28] but a Chilean effort. The decade of 1880–90 was characterized by a departure from tradition, whereas the last decade of the century was marked by complete "foreignism" as teachers and programs from Europe and the United States were introduced every-

22. Amanda Labarca, *Historia de la Enseñanza en Chile* (Santiago: Imprenta Universitaria, 1939), p. 132.

23. The figures given by Labarca, ibid., p. 132, are for 1935 but her discussion in chap. 10 and 11 suggests that for 1930 the figures were at least the same, if not higher, than those for 1935.

24. Chile, *Geografía Económica*, ed. Alfonso Lastarria (Santiago: Imprenta Cervantes, 1923), p. 120.

25. Miguel Luis Amunátegui and Gregorio Victor Amunátegui, *De La Instrucción Primaria del Chile: Lo Que Es, Lo Que Debería Ser* (Santiago: Imprenta del Ferrocarril, 1856), p. 102, and Alfonso Lastarria ed., Chile, *Geografía Económica*, p. 119.

26. Labarca, *Enseñanza*, pp. 135–77.

27. Mamalakis, "Historical Statistics," table IIA1h6.

28. Labarca, p. 209.

where. By 1900 the system was national, centralized, and uniform but lacked organic unity.

By 1930 primary education was still beset by a variety of critical problems. The majority of the children attending school abandoned it at the end of the second year, and a class of semiliterate citizens was created.[29] Furthermore, major segments of the rural population and of the cities' poor remained on the fringes of the educational system because of lack of schools, isolated living areas, extreme poverty, or inadequate enforcement of obligatory education in marginal areas of Santiago and the countryside. There was also a lack of continuity between primary and secondary education, which had a different base and orientation.

In spite of substantial government outlays, the public primary schools were caught in a vicious circle. They remained poor, were often deprived of materials, and were relatively neglected because they were destined for the needy classes. Their material conditions and intellectual environment, far from attracting the middle classes, estranged them. Private primary schools with a parochial or ethnic base were created by the middle classes and immigrant groups to attain quality standards comparable to the European ones and provided the base for the lyceums (high schools). According to Amanda Labarca and others the major problem of the Chilean educational policy in 1930 was the elimination of dualism in primary education, which was leading to an undemocratic and uproductive ostracism of public schools.[30]

Secondary and university education were also developed but retained a high degree of selectivity. The University of Chile, incorporated in 1842 with Andrés Bello as its rector, expanded continuously but served a small part of the population, which automatically became an elite. The core of secondary education was the lyceum, which had as its model the French lycée before 1880 and the German gymnasium afterward. Such secondary education, principally its humanistic section, attracted in relative terms most of the resources and attention of the middle classes, government, the ruling elites, and immigrants. It emerged as the most successfully developed segment of the Chilean educational system by 1930.

The stimulus to such education came from a nucleus of an educated minority not from the governing classes or the people. The efforts of

29. Ibid., p. 278.
30. Ibid., p. 305.

foreigners, especially the Germans, were crucial in the reform and progress of public education.[31] The success of their efforts was determined mainly by the availability of nitrate-generated resources and, to a far lesser though not insignificant extent, by the cooperation of the government.

The debate over education never subsided during this period. The need for complete and massive primary education had become clear by the middle of the century.[32] The controversy over secondary education grew heated around the turn of the century. The argument evolved that Chilean secondary education had as its objective to instruct rather than educate, that it was transformed to serve higher education[33] and the professionals rather than the masses, and that it was an alien transplant in basic antinomy with the needs of the Chilean economic organism.[34] The real challenge was to develop institutions that spontaneously emerged within Chile and served Chilean needs. Although vocational education had been introduced early in many locations, it had never assumed even the modest, let alone massive, proportions that would have endowed it with the capacity to provide the variety of technical skills needed in agriculture, mining, industry, trade, and other pursuits.

Although all the improvements in educational opportunities reflect the revealed preferences of the state and the private sector, specific evidence suggests that this boom of investment in human capital was financed largely by the export-generated resource surplus. The vast benefits derived by education from the nitrate boom are illustrated by the rapid growth of the educational budget between 1890 and 1930 and by its abrupt decline between 1930 and 1935. Relatively stagnant during 1890–1900, the budgetary allocations rose from 137 million pence in 1900 to 935 million in 1930 in constant prices, doubling almost every ten years. They fell by 75 percent to 252 million pence in 1935, a value only slightly exceeding that in 1905[35]. This reduction exposed the dependence of educational investment upon the nitrate-created riches. Overall, education enjoyed long-term expansion but suffered major setbacks chiefly during the War of the Pacific, the revolution of

31. Moisés Vargas, *Bosquejo de la Instrucción Pública en Chile* (Santiago: Balcells and Co., 1908), p. 11.

32. See Miguel Luis Amunátegui and Gregorio Victor Amunátegui, *De La Instrucción Primaria en Chile.*

33. Labarca, *Enseñanza* p. 212.

34. See Julio Saavedra M., *Reformemos Nuestra Enseñanza Secundaria* (Santiago: Imprenta Universitaria, 1912), pp. 1–19.

35. Labarca, pp. 272–75.

Balmaceda, the chaotic political years of 1924–30, and especially the Great Depression.

The balance sheet in 1930 shows that Chile's unsatisfied, urgent needs were not in humanistic secondary education but in public primary schools. Above all, what was missing in 1930 was the general organization, the superintendency that could closely examine, evaluate, coordinate, harmonize, and satisfy Chile's educational needs, didactic efforts, and resources. This would have permitted maximum efficiency and the best service of the community by the educational system. Reform and progress were substantial, but they had been achieved without an integrated educational policy.

SUPPLY OF SAVINGS

The statistical data suggest that the capacity and willingness of the Chilean economic system to save and invest during the 1925–30 period were high, possibly accounting for close to 20 percent of GDP. With capital formation consisting heavily of capital goods imports,[36] its direct dependence on the developed nations was great. There was even a high degree of indirect dependence, for public works were supported largely by government revenues from nitrate and by loans from Europe and the United States. Of the three components of domestically supplied capital goods, only public works—previously financed from nitrate revenues—remained at a level below one-fifth of their 1930 values as late as 1937,[37] when both business investment and private building had surpassed their pre-1930 values.

In an ironic twist the 1930 depression brought about a change in the government's role in the capital accumulation process. Before 1930 the government had direct and major impact because the massive, single-source nitrate tax contributions allowed it to exercise unparalleled control over the sectoral resource-transfer process. It also shared in capital formation through its public works and the expenditures that augmented the country's human, institutional, and social capital. After 1930 the government's direct role in controlling the resource transfer and capital formation processes diminished as the depression drastically reduced the resources it could appropriate from one sector and directly or indirectly transfer to the rest of the economy.

36. Ibid., and UNECLA, *Economic Survey, 1949*, table 12, p. 294.
37. But 50 percent of their 1928 value.

The internal capacity of the system to generate savings was high. Chilean investors prospered in the nitrate provinces before they were acquired by the Chilean government and they also continued to prosper in Bolivia.[38] The banking system was sufficiently advanced during the 1880–1930 period to collect private savings and make them available to investors.[39] Even foreign investors were able to use Chilean capital for investment purposes. Robert Harvey and Thomas North became the "kings" of nitrate by acquiring large shares of the nitrate certificates issued by the following oficinas (mines): Primitiva, Peruana, Ramírez, Buen Retiro, Jaspampa, Virginia, and others. Harvey and North gained them through the use of inside government information, speculation, and above all Chilean capital, which they obtained from the Banco de Valparaíso with the assistance of its director, Dawson.[40]

Chile's continuous and huge export surplus during 1880–1930 arose of speculation and instability, limited internal investment opportunities, and payments to foreign factors of production. For a long period, credits were extended for consumption or nonproductive purposes, as the credits of the Banco Hipotecario to the landowning class seem to indicate.[41] Even government used its share of the massive resource surplus largely for wages and salaries rather than for investment, thus creating a heavy demand for consumer goods (including imported ones) rather than for capital goods. The extreme inequalities in sectoral incomes may have partially forced it to follow this path. However, the limited statistical evidence available concerning saving by households seems to suggest that blue-collar workers who dissaved outnumbered

38. Santiago Macchiavello Varas, *El Problema de la Industria del Cobre en Chile y sus proyecciónes Económicas y Sociales* (Santiago: Imprenta Fiscal de la Penitenciaría, 1923), pp. 109–11. According to Macchiavello, Chilean savings and capital existed but left the country because of the higher returns they could earn elsewhere, especially Bolivia. These ideas and data were originally developed and are found in Santiago Marín Vicuña, "La Industria del Cobre i el Mineral de Potrerillos," *Boletín Minero de la Sociedad Nacional de Minería, Enero de 1920*, 32 (Nov. 24, 1920): 32–34.

39. The availability of savings and loanable funds in banks was high and rising as demonstrated by the credits and deposits of the various savings banks. For a description of the advanced level of the mortgage and saving banks see Luis Barros Borgoño, *La Caja de Crédito Hipotecario*, 2 vols. (Santiago: Imprenta Cervantes, 1912). This highly legal and institutional treatise shows at the end of vol. 1 all mortgage issues in 1911, and at the end of vol. 2 all mortgages issued between 1856 and 1912 by the Caja de Crédito Hipotecario, the leading mortgage bank.

40. Guillermo E. Billinghurst, *Los Capitales Salitreros de Tarapacá* (Santiago: Imprenta El Progreso, 1889), pp. 49, 48.

41. On this see the indirect evidence given by Frank Whitson Fetter, *Monetary Inflation in Chile* (Princeton: Princeton University Press, 1931), pp. 86–87, 101–02.

those who saved whereas among better paid (white collar) workers savings were positive. On balance, workers' savings seem to be negligible.[42]

Since the export sector was the major source of an investable surplus and since this surplus was divided in relatively equal parts between foreign capitalists and the Chilean government, the *propensity* of the government to *invest this surplus* was a major determinant of growth. Although government allocated part of its revenues to public works and education,[43] the share of its expenditures allocated to human and physical capital was not substantial or at àny time extraordinarily high.[44] The vast literature of this era contains an almost unanimous condemnation of the government for misusing the export-generated revenues without due consideration of either the country's needs or the very real possibility that such a windfall could evaporate almost overnight. Not merely government but all of Chile was accused of imprudence, weakness, and a deplorable relaxation of the strong spirit of saving that was traditional in public administration. The fact that nitrate taxes were considered normal and ordinary revenues was regarded as inexcusable and detrimental as their use for consumption.[45] The following statement is typical and only slightly exaggerated:

In that period not even an attempt was made to solve some of our great problems. The surplus value which the nitrate revenues represented, was not utilized to alphabetize the population, or to stabilize the currency, or to develop a plan of economic promotion, and not even to put in order our public finances. However, there were voices—not numerous but carrying weight—that prognosticated that the wealth originating from nitrate would stop flowing

42. See the very informative budget studies by the labor office. *Boletín de la Oficina del Trabajo,* no. 2, Año I, 2nd trimester 1911, pp. 22–23, 68–69; no. 3, Año I, 2nd trimester 1911, pp. 20–22, 32–33; no. 4, Año 2, 1st semester 1912, pp. 82–83, 234–35. However, postal savings are positive and rising in the nitrate provinces ibid., pp. 203–09. See also ibid., no. 18, Año XII, Año 1922, pp. 90–97. In addition, see the informative budget study indicating zero savings for a worker's family by Guillermo Eyzaguirre Rouse and Jorge Errázuriz Tagle, *Monografia de Una Familia Obrera de Santiago* (Santiago: Imprenta Barcelona, 1903), esp. pp. 38–58.

43. See Mamalakis, "Historical Statistics," table IIG3a2, pp. A-711–A-713.

44. See also Carlos Humud, "El Sector Público Chileno entre 1830 y 1930" (Santiago: Universidad de Chile, 1969).

45. See Luis Aldunate, *Indicaciónes de la Balanza Comercial* (Santiago: Imprenta Cervantes, 1893), p. 217. See also the discussion in the section on the distribution of income.

one day and that it was necessary to adopt a policy of foresight in order to guarantee the future existence of the nation.[46]

Unlike other historical experiences, in which both investment funds and reinvestment opportunities existed in the same sector (frequently industry), in Chile the resource surpluses originated from one sector, nitrate, and reinvestment occurred in practically all other sectors of the economy, which boomed. Even though investment opportunities in the export sector were ample, they could not absorb more than a fraction of the nitrate surplus. And when major mining investments were made, as in the case of copper, they were not financed out of the abundant nitrate surpluses but by the New York capital markets. Again unlike other historical experiences, it was not agriculture but the mining sector that stood out as the primary source of investment funds. The export bonanza benefited the agricultural hinterland, which found a prosperous market for its products, received heavy injections of the nitrate-generated investment funds, was linked with the urban centers and ports by an elaborate, partially nitrate-financed, railroad network, and carried a small and decreasing tax burden. Important, if not unique, in the Chilean experience between 1880 and 1930 were the extensive codependence of agriculture, construction, industry, government, trade, and other services on the resource surpluses of one sector, nitrate mining, and the use of those resources to reduce their own contribution to the country's capital fund. Their own sacrifices and efforts were thereby reduced rather than maintained or augmented.

The nitrate saving funds proved to be insufficient for a permanent and rapid transformation and modernization of agriculture, services, industry, and so forth only because their injection was offset by a diminished internal contribution and reduced effort toward progress and change. Thus the low propensity of government to reinvest nitrate resources had its counterpart in the private household and business segments of all sectors, with saving and investment rates out of internal income falling as external sources of funds became available. The belief that nationalization of nitrate, even as limited as the one projected by President José Manuel Balmaceda, would have provided the investment funds needed for achieving a permanent, self-propelling state of growth overemphasizes the income distribution aspect. This Marxist approach places inadequate emphasis on the paramount issue of the capital

46. Carlos Keller, *Un País al Garete* (Santiago: Editorial Nascimiento, 1932), p. 9.

accumulation or division of resources between investment and consumption.[47] It also overlooks two crucial facts: investment in Chile was below the potential and optimum level, and with higher internal investment levels both the need for foreign capital and the outflow of resources due to instability and low investment opportunities would have been substantially lower.

The regional element played a vital role in capital formation. Northern Chile, which directly or indirectly supplied most of the government revenues, financed a major part of public works, most educational expenditures, and almost all capital goods imports. If Central and urban Chile (the net beneficiaries of this situation) had been taxed more heavily, government revenues could have increased and all investment expenditures, including those for social, institutional, and other capital, might have been augmented, thus assisting income growth and economic transformation. Whereas before 1880 most of Chile's investable resources originated and were allocated in the Central Valley, subsequently they originated predominantly in the nitrate North and were allocated to Central Chile. This transformation created a pattern of regional dependence that had repercussions for all aspects of economic growth.

The lack of a well-defined capitalist group was as significant as Chile's nature as a quasi-complete system. Employer and employee were normally indistinguishable in unincorporated medium- and small-scale agriculture, mining, services, and artisan industry. The main goal of enterprises was survival, not expansion, and sectoral links completely outweighed class links. Furthermore, the landowning capitalist class performed many functions beyond accumulating capital and achieving economic development, such as serving the public, entering government, and using its resources for the arts, the poor, and public service. However, it was not an investing but a partially egocentric class engaged in consumption for the public welfare.

In industry and the export sector the lack of a solidly unified capitalist community and esprit was even more evident.[48] At one extreme the

47. A detailed presentation of the Marxist–communist version explaining Chilean underdevelopment is found in Hernán Ramírez Necochea, *Historia del Imperialismo en Chile* (Santiago: Empresa Editora Austral, 1960), pp. 99–293.

48. According to the Marxist Marcello Segall, Chile's growth was hindered, first because of the class struggle between the bourgeoisie and the proletariat, and second because of the social struggle between the three capitalist groups of miners, industrialists and landowners. See Marcello Segall, *Desarrollo del Capitalismo en Chile, Cinco Ensayos Dialécticos* (Santiago: Editorial del Pacífico, S.A., 1953), pp. 22–23. Although Segall is

foreign speculators in mining were interested in quick, spectacular returns; at the other extreme the Chilean nitrate owners, many marginal, were bound to Chile and normally reinvested part of their profits in the country. Another group of foreigners who had permanently left their countries (France, Yugoslavia, Germany, Russia, Greece, and so on) stayed in Chile as immigrants only as long as business conditions and the financial climate were favorable. Many American and British operators had not come to stay, were interested in maximum earnings, and repatriated most of their profits. Finally, the mammoth modern corporations of the Guggenheims, Anaconda, and Kennecott decided their actions on the basis of multinational operations and interests. The state was perhaps the only capitalist entity that presumably had the interests of Chile exclusively in mind.

Each group of capitalists was subject to different motivations, but for no single group was the investment motive great. Government, unincorporated capitalists, and Chilean nitrate and landowner capitalists had either massive consumption commitments or were under constant pressure to finance consumption from profits. Although there was no open struggle, the lack of unity and the absence of common goals and objectives hindered cooperation among and within classes in solving the country's idiosyncratic problems in both the distribution and capital accumulation processes. In turn, these differences in goals, interests, and policies derived from differences in sectoral base and resulted in different sectoral orientations.

Low-productivity sectors made consumption demands upon the nitrate-generated resource surplus, and low-income groups demanded immediate consumption. Moreover, the government-associated service sectors that were directly or indirectly supported by the nitrate-generated prosperity continually adjusted their subsistence or minimum consumption expenditures upward, thus automatically reducing the government resources available for investment. Foreign capitalists in the nitrate and copper industries and even in agriculture in Magallanes were judged by their peers in terms not necessarily of their investment

---

one of the few Chileans to notice some of the internal sectoral conflicts and contradictions that were formalized in my theory of sectoral clashes, he is unable to depart from the Marxist approach and insists that "in fundamental lines the history of civilization [from the beginning of the formation of the state] is the one of the class struggle" (ibid., p. 22). See also Marcello Segall R., "Las luchas de clases en las primeras décadas de la República 1810–1816," *Anales de la Universidad de Chile, Año CXX*, Primer trimestre de 1962, no. 125, pp. 175–218.

programs but of the short- and long-term profits sent to the mother companies in the developed West. Thus considerable profits never became available to Chile for either consumption or investment.

Although the obvious coalition was with the export sector, the parallel and equally real coalition joining government, foreign capitalists in the export sector, the landed oligarchy, and an urban plutocracy led to increased consumption by government, the urban masses, and the landlords and an exodus of resources through greater repatriated profits by foreign capitalists.

The last, but not least important, leakage was caused by monetary instability, which cast doubt and distorted investment opportunities. The net effect was an outflow of capital and savings. Furthermore, since there was no domestic machinery and equipment sector to lobby with government and other capitalists in favor of investment goods purchases, the pressures for more consumption had an edge. The lack of an organized, widespread, and modernizing capital-goods sector hindered the development of a lobby to promote the type of extensive vocational education that would have benefited this as well as most other sectors.

A coalition between government and the export sector could not easily favor the capital goods sector, and whatever favorable treatment mining received, the repercussions on investment and growth were indirect. Thus, the impact of the government–export-sector coalition upon investment could hardly be positive because, due to the heterogeneity of the capitalist group in terms of functions, this group did not shape the coalition to its advantage. This was true because the heterogeneity and incompleteness of the capital goods sectors did not allow them to augment investment by becoming dominant and also because of the numerous bottlenecks emerging between the saving (or resource surplus creation) and investment processes.

Transformation and fluctuations in the external–internal composition of demand were reflected, however, in the investment–consumption composition. A relative rise in export demand was usually followed by a comparable rise in investment in gross domestic product. The export sector generated most of the internal investable resource surplus, permitted induced capital inflows, created internal sectoral investment opportunities that attracted investment, and established a quasi-complete system by making available to the economy capital goods that were not locally produced. In turn, the power of the export sector to influence growth through its effects on investment was directly linked to external demand.

The capital accumulation process was also negatively affected by the instability introduced into the system by the export–government coalition, which freed agriculture, services, and industry from direct taxation and made the highly volatile nitrate taxes the primary source of government revenues. Price stability suffered because the foreign exchange market became thin, readily mirrored all changes in nitrate fortunes, and was subject to repeated devaluation. Even with the nitrate revenues, the government continued to borrow in Europe and the United States, which turned speculators to the peso, an easily manipulable currency of a small nation.

The monetary instability also diverted the governments, from Pinto to Alessandri, away from efforts to achieve economic development and augment investment by creating the need for convertibility and price stability and by demanding the governments' energies in reestablishing them. Even more important, expectations of foreign exchange devaluation and price rises contributed to massive outflows of funds and resources and established the astonishing export gap.

The instability in monetary and fiscal affairs, the uncertainty of investment opportunities, the wild fluctuations of the nitrate investment fund, the heterogeneity of the capitalist class, the lack of a producer durables sector, and the immense pressures for increased consumption by government, services, and the cities were capital formation defects that reduced investment and impeded growth. Chile had its golden opportunity to achieve self-sustained growth before 1930. It succeeded in propelling the economy to new and higher levels of development, to historically unique levels of investment during 1920–30, but it failed in relative terms to achieve a permanent state of self-propelling dynamism through even greater levels of accumulation of physical, educational, institutional, and social capital. The unprecedented collapse that followed the depression of 1930–33 and the partial but rapid recovery from 1933 to 1940 provided a mirror image of the areas of continued achievements and the areas where Chile still remained weak, underdeveloped, and dependent.

PART 2   THE STRAINS OF CHANGE: 1930–1973

5

Retreat, Recovery, and Growth: 1930–1973

There is nothing intrinsic in the mentality of the Chilean people, in the nature of its territory and its resources, in its geographical location, or in any other of its permanent characteristics, that may make it impossible to build in this area a society that can function without hatred, without shameful misery, and with opportunity for all.[1]

Jorge Ahumada C., 1958

No other shock has affected the Chilean process of transformation and modernization so visibly and so strongly as the Great Depression of the early 1930s. Indeed, no event before or since the depression has so clearly demonstrated the extensive dependence of Chile's Center upon the combined nitrate and copper mining sector of the North. Overnight, the very forces of capitalism that had turned the desert nitrate pampas of the Chilean North into a source of gold for Central Chile as well as the developed West discovered that they themselves had lost momentum and were being dissipated. Chile's subsequent sufferings were related as much to the nitrate collapse per se as to the inability to develop immediately a new frontier that could serve as a substitute source of income and exports and that could provide a resource surplus and employment.

Nevertheless, by 1930 Chile had undeniably gained the capacity to determine its own destiny. It has recovered rapidly from or bypassed such formidable external or internal shocks as the Great Depression, the disappearance of nitrate, World War II, the government's anti-copper and antiagriculture policies of 1940–55, cyclically accelerating inflation, and Salvador Allende's transformation policies of 1970–73.

1. *En Vez de la Miseria*, 5th ed. (Santiago: Editorial del Pacífico, S.A., 1965, pp. 50–51.

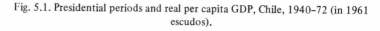

Fig. 5.1. Presidential periods and real per capita GDP, Chile, 1940–72 (in 1961 escudos).

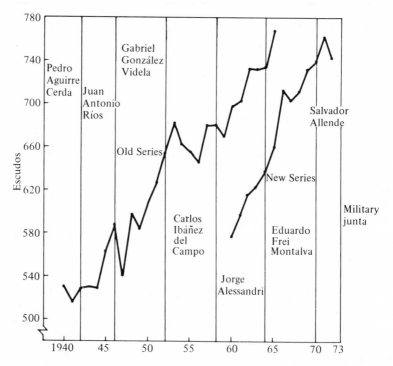

Source: Table 5.1.

The growth of per capita income by 1.4 percent per annum during 1940–60 and by 2.6 percent during 1960–70 (see fig. 5.1 and table 5.1) was a Chilean achievement with only a limited net contribution from foreign resources. It seems even more remarkable when one considers the sudden and dramatic rise in the rate of population growth.[2]

The collapse of international demand for Chile's mineral products, especially nitrate, during the worldwide depression of the 1930s spread misery, hunger, and unemployment to its cities, ports, the arid nitrate

2. The ODEPLAN national accounts estimates raised the growth rate of per capita income since 1960 but lowered its absolute level. Overall, the new estimates have adjusted downward the long-term performance of the Chilean economy. Income in service sectors was reduced and the estimate of construction investment was increased.

pampas, and even the rural sector.[3] The import-substitution policies of most nations involved synthetic nitrate, and the derived negative trade-multiplier effects swept over Chile's entire economy like a devastating tidal wave. The convulsions, distortions, and conflicts between 1930 and the present were largely delayed shock waves from the initial upheaval. President Arturo Alessandri (1932–38) responded rapidly to restore confidence, demand, employment, and income through monetary, fiscal (public works as well as other deficit financing), and other relief policies. Although aggregate demand increased, its external component never regained its pre-1930 significance.

The negative impact on sectors was mostly transitory. The industrial sector, after a severe crisis, a temporary halt, and crawling progress between 1930 and 1936, finally resumed its long-term expansion. Fishing, forestry, and trade, which had languished while ships moored idle and inactive in the ports, recovered. Agriculture, after its worst crisis of declining prices and diminishing markets and though still

Table 5.1. Total and Per Capita Real Gross Domestic Product
and Rates of Growth, Chile, 1940–72

| | Gross domestic product (In millions of escudos) | | Per capita GDP (Escudos) | |
	Old Series (1961 prices) (1)	New Series (1961 prices) (2)	Old Series (1961 prices) (3)	New Series (1961 prices) (4)
1940	2,676		529	
1945	3,125		564	
1950	3,690		608	
1955	4,431		655	
1960	5,364	4,426	698	576
1965	6,691	5,755	765	658
1970		7,201		741
1971 (official Allende)		7,542		763
1971 (official junta)		7,539		762
1972 (official junta)		7,482		744

3. See Arturo Alessandri, *Mensaje leído por S.E. el Presidente de la República, 21 de Mayo de 1933* (Santiago: Presidencia de la República, 1933); see also the *Mensajes* for 1934, 1935, and 1936.

Table 5.1 (contd.)

	Gross domestic product (Rates of growth in percentages)		Per capita GDP (Rates of growth in percentages)	
	Old Series (5)	New Series (6)	Old Series (7)	New Series (8)
1940–45	3.1		1.3	
1945–50	3.4		1.5	
1950–55	3.7		1.5	
1955–60	3.9		1.3	
1960–65	4.5	5.4	1.8	2.7
1965–70		4.6		2.4
1970–71 (official Allende)		4.7		2.9
1970–71 (official junta)		4.3		2.5
1971–72 (official junta)		−0.8		−2.5
1940–50	3.3		1.4	
1950–60	3.8		1.4	
1960–70		5.0		2.6
1940–70	4.0		1.8	

Sources: For GDP, Old Series, Mamalakis, in "National Accounts", "Historical Statistics," pt. I, table IA5, pp. A-65–A-67. The data for GDP, New Series, at 1961 prices, were calculated utilizing the information provided by ODEPLAN, *Cuentas Nacionales de Chile, 1960–1971* (Santiago: ODEPLAN, 1973), pp. 24–25, 49–50. GDP, New Series, at 1961 prices, for 1971–72, was calculated using the information provided in ODEPLAN, *Cuentas Nacionales de Chile, 1965–1972* (Santiago: ODEPLAN, 1973), table 10, p. 29; table 16, p. 37. The implicit population series are those used by CORFO and ODEPLAN in estimating per capita income.

Note: The figures for GDP, New Series, are available at current and 1965 prices. The conversion to 1961 prices was done as follows: (1) GDP at current prices was divided by GDP at 1965 prices to obtain the implicit price index (with base 1965 = 1.00); (2) the implicit price index was converted to base 1961 = 1.00 by dividing each year's index by that of 1961; (3) GDP at current prices was then divided by the implicit price index (with base 1961 = 1.00) to obtain GDP at 1961 prices. The rate of growth of GDP for 1940–70 was obtained as the simple average of the rates corresponding to 1940–50, 1950–60, and 1960–70, the data for the last decade belonging to the ODEPLAN Series.

saddled with the disguised unemployed who had fled from the mines to the farms, continued to expand. Only in mining, especially nitrate, were the partial loss of external demand and the change in the composition of aggregate demand permanent. Even though nitrate blue-collar employment was successfully raised to 25,000 in 1938 from a level of only 11,100 in 1933, its glamour was gone.

Despite subsidies and a large network of bilateral agreements, mining (indeed all exports) never recovered its pre-1930 importance.[4] By 1940, when the first complete national accounts were being prepared, the economy as a whole and all sectors except nitrate had achieved a high degree of normalcy. The major part of the mining production apparatus was rendered valueless, and after the external pull had vanished temporarily, the internal fiscal and monetary push became even more imperative. The need to guarantee compensatory expansion of the nonexport sectors became dominant and was no longer a matter of choice.[5]

Each president's economic policies had some unique features, but they all forged solid links in the closely interwoven chain of progress, errors, defects, booms, and recessions. Arturo Alessandri had to lift the economy from the depths of the Great Depression, and his response was rapid and effective. Yet, although the crisis offered a unique opportunity to implement long-overdue economic and social reforms, Alessandri failed to grasp it. Instead of asking all members of the society to make the sacrifices—in particular to accept the tax burden —required for the effective pursuit of the development goal, he confined himself to highly successful orthodox but limited antidepression measures. Even though between 1933 and 1938 the Caja de Colonización Agrícola subdivided more than 400,000 hectares of agricultural land and education, health, and welfare were improved, dissatisfaction and anxiety were widespread.

Direct planning and extensive government intervention were the responses of the Popular Front (composed of radicals, socialists, and communists) and of radical Presidents Pedro Aguirre Cerda (1938–41) and Juan Antonio Ríos (1942–45) to the pressing popular demands for

4. See Arturo Alessandri, *Mensaje leído por S.E. El Presidente de la República en la apertura de las sesiónes ordinarias del Congreso Nacional 21 de Mayo de 1938* (Santiago: Presidencia de la República, 1938), p. 221. This *Mensaje* provides a summary of the Arturo Alessandri years.

5. A general treatment of the major components of the Chilean economy during the the 1925–52 period is found in UN, CEPAL, *Antecedentes sobre el Desarrollo de la Economía Chilena, 1925–52* (Santiago: Editorial del Pacífico, S.A., 1954). This book gives the impression of being an extension of the earlier and more comprehensive study, UNECLA, *Economic Survey of Latin America, 1949* (E/CN. 12/164/Rev. 1, 11 Jan. 1951), New York, 1951, pp. 263–390. Both these publications provide an extensive description of the events before, during, and after the Great Depression. The subsequent issues of UNECLA's *Economic Survey* offer little information that cannot be found in the "Historical Statistics of Chile, 1840–1965," prepared by the present author. For a description of the events between 1929 and 1942 see also P. T. Ellsworth, *Chile, An Economy in Transition* (New York: Macmillan, 1945).

higher and better-distributed income, price stability, and a favorable balance of payments. Industrialization, especially in iron, steel, electricity, and consumer goods, became the immediate instrument for attaining growth. Inflation accelerated, and agrarian reform efforts came to a standstill, contrasting unfavorably with Alessandri's efforts because of their preoccupation with industrialization and the shortage of funds to expropriate farms.[6]

More than ever before, the government pursued ambitious plans without having or trying to obtain the needed resources equitably. While the foreign-owned copper sector was singled out to make special sacrifices, all other sectors waited for copper to become the new golden goose, postponing the inevitably larger tax burden required for accelerated growth. Both economic and social policies created tension because most benefits and privileges accrued to the rich, those employed in state enterprises, white-collar workers. The poor urban, agricultural, and many other blue-collar workers fell behind. Per capita income, which had been stagnant during 1940–44, rose sharply between 1944 and 1946 but collapsed in 1947 when the war-accumulated foreign exchange was exhausted (see table 5.1 and fig. 5.1).

The objective of President Gabriel González Videla (1946–52) was to "begin the conquest of economic independence of the Nation" through a "profound economic transformation...in order to transform our ruling regimen of Political Democracy into one of Economic Democracy." He sought vigorously to suppress every characteristic of a semicolonial economy by regaining control and freedom of distribution of the country's resources and surpluses and by making it independent of the "great international monopolies."[7] Whereas the primary goals of economic policy during 1932–38 had been full employment, maximum exports, and achievement of an industrial production level equivalent to that of 1927–29, González Videla rein-

6. A solid view of the plans and accomplishments of the Frente Popular can be obtained by reading Pedro Aguirre Cerda, *Mensaje de S.E. el Presidente de la República en la apertura de las sesiónes ordinarias del Congreso Nacional 21 de Mayo de 1939* (Santiago: Presidencia de la República, 1939), and Juan Antonio Ríos, *Mensaje de S.E. el Presidente de la República Don Juan Antonio Rios en la apertura de las sesiónes ordinarias del Congreso Nacional 21 de Mayo de 1945* (Santiago: Presidencia de la República, 1945). It was under Aguirre Cerda that CORFO (the Chilean Development Corporation) was established, the activities of which are discussed in chapter 12.

7. Gabriel González Videla, *Mensaje de S.E. El Presidente de la República don Gabriel González Videla al Congreso Nacional al Inaugurar el Período Ordinario de Sesiónes, 21 de Mayo de 1952* (Santiago: Presidencia de la República, 1952), (hereafter cited as *Mensaje 1952*); the quotations are from p. iii.

troduced the elusive objective of economic independence. The means of achieving this goal were modest; the three pillars of Gabriel González's policy of economic independence were industrialization, improved use of agricultural land, and establishment of a complete and efficient network of transportation and communication.[8] But the government lacked the resources to pursue even these modest objectives.[9] Matters became worse as it pursued conflicting policies of rigid exchange rates, relatively low income taxes on all but the large-scale copper enterprises, and subsidies coupled with spotty price controls. The government's role expanded, and the share of fiscal expenditures rose from 15.5 percent of the national product in 1945 to 18 percent in 1950.[10] Per capita income grew sharply from 1949 to 1953, but in 1954–55 Chile started paying the price: there were an intolerable acceleration in the rate of inflation, a diminution of production incentives in export mining and agriculture, a copper crisis aggravated by lower prices after the Korean War, and further deterioration in the fortunes of nitrate. As the economy stagnated, it appeared that the cure of the patient was bringing it close to death.

Upset and frustrated by the inability of the political parties to introduce unselfish, lasting solutions to the pressing economic problems, the people responded—in an Era of Protest—with the "Ibáñez earthquake." They reelected apolitical general Ibáñez, the former dictator who was now being hailed as the General of Hope.[11] The presidency

8. Industrialization encompassed development of an iron and steel industry and the founding and manufacturing of copper, petroleum, cellulose, heavy chemicals, fisheries, shipping, and electrification enterprises. Agricultural development included mechanization of farming, accelerated completion of irrigation plans, diffusion of scientific technical progress, and an increase in credit extended to agriculture with state control over this credit. The transportation plans involved an extension of the road system and an increase in terrestrial, maritime, and aerial transport to facilitate rapid movement of industrial and agricultural exports to consumption centers and for export (see *Mensaje 1952, ibid,* p. iv).

9. A description of economic events between 1940 and 1963 is found in two monographs of the Institute of Economics of the University of Chile. The title of the first is Instituto de Economía, *Desarrollo Económico de Chile,* 1940–1956 (Santiago: Editorial Universitaria, S.A., 1956), and Statistical Appendix, tables A-1–A-59. The title of the second is Instituto de Economía, *La Economía de Chile en el Período 1950–1963,* 2 vols. (Santiago: Universidad de Chile, 1963), the second volume being a compilation of statistics. The volumes were written largely either under the supervision of or by Joseph Grunwald and Aníbal Pinto themselves.

10. González, *Mensaje 1952,* p. xl.

11. See Sergio Molina, *El Proceso de Cambio en Chile* (Santiago: Editorial Universitaria, S.A., 1972), pp. 27–29.

of Carlos Ibáñez del Campo (1952–58), which was characterized by a partial return to economic orthodoxy, signified the end of one era and the beginning of another. The dominance of industry was reduced, the New Deal copper law ended the discrimination of the American-owned companies (leading to the 1958–70 expansion), incentives to the previously disfavored agriculture were partly restored, and the monosectoral (industrialization) emphasis of 1940–55 gave way to a healthy, balanced multisectoral orientation. Also, more than any other president either before or after, Ibáñez assigned maximum priority to price stabilization. With the guidance of the Klein–Saks mission, he pursued that goal relentlessly during 1955–57. As inflation was drastically stopped, it triggered the worst short-term recession since the Great Depression and provoked public outcries. Gross and per capita income fell sharply. The heterogeneous structuralist school began with attacks on the anti-inflationary monetary measures as a temporary alleviation but no permanent cure. The price stabilization measures were regarded as heavy doses of an alien remedy to a patient suffering from the highly idiosyncratic disease of structural bottlenecks—specifically, an antiquated land tenure system, export dependence, government revenue instability, and labor market distortions. By 1957 the "stop" had been succeeded by the "go" phase of Chile's post-1939 inflationary cycles; inflation was irreversibly exposed as an inseparable part of the economic fabric.

A new era dawned as the voices asking for a drastic transformation of income distribution and ownership patterns became louder and more numerous.[12] Until 1955, growth was largely a recovery to the pre-depression levels, with the net industrial gains offset by the nitrate losses. From 1955 onward major net gains were achieved.

Jorge Alessandri's narrow victory in 1958 over Christian Democrat Eduardo Frei and Marxist Salvador Allende on a wide-ranging progress platform led to a remarkable inflationary pause and complete openness in 1960–61 and six years of uninterrupted prosperity (the annual per capita income increase was 2.7 percent during 1960–65).

---

12. For a description of the development strategies during the 1952–58 period see Carlos Ibáñez del Campo, *Mensaje de S.E. El Presidente de la República don Carlos Ibáñez del Campo al Congreso Nacional al Inaugurar el periodo ordinario de sesiónes, 21 de Mayo de 1958* (Santiago: Presidencia de la República, 1958). Among other important achievements or events during the Ibáñez regime are the establishment of a minimum agricultural wage (1953), family allowances for blue-collar workers (1953), creation of the State Bank (1953), the Housing Corporation (1953), the Committee on Foreign Investments (1954), and the Copper Department (1955). See Appendix to ibid.

However, it also produced a host of lasting problems.[13] A well-conceived housing plan, extensive public works, the reconstruction effort after the devastating 1961 earthquake, and financial assistance from the United States, Europe, and international agencies raised the investment coefficient to unusual levels exceeding 13–15 percent of GDP. Direct and indirect linkages with the developed West gained unprecedented momentum, peaking in 1961. As all sectors expanded, industry grew at 6.6 percent per annum between 1958 and 1963.[14] Nutrition and education were emphasized, but except for the establishment of the Agrarian Reform Corporation (CORA) and promulgation of land reform laws, no transformation was attempted in the means of production ownership and income distribution.

By the second half of 1961 the balance of payments had suffered a drastic deterioration. There was a strong inflationary relapse, a rise in public debt, a return to a semiclosed status, and devaluation. The masses of the poor were even more disillusioned with the persisting inequities. The links with Europe, the United States, foreign private capital, and multinational corporations were regularly attacked by the Left and scrutinized and reassessed by the Christian Democrats. By 1964 most observers agreed that Chile was in desperate need of drastic changes in agriculture, mining, education, housing, and distribution.

When the Christian Democrats assumed control of the government on November 4, 1964, President Eduardo Frei Montalva adopted an approach of structural orthodoxy. He slowly but firmly reshaped production, distribution, ownership, and capital formation. Orthodox measures, stressing incentives and market forces, included flexible foreign exchange rates, inflation-proof bonds, export tax rebates, and favorable pricing of selected agricultural products. Structural measures modifying or eliminating the power, rules, or symptoms of antiquated noncapitalistic modes of production included land reform, regional development policy, fiscal reform, and others. Among the progressive

---

13. See Jorge Alessandri, *Exposición Hecha por S.E. el Presidente de la República, Don Jorge Alessandri Rodríguez ante el Congreso Nacional, al Inaugurar el Período Ordinario de Sesiónes el 21 de Mayo de 1964* (Santiago: Imprenta del Servicio de Prisiones, 1964). This is a summary exposition of the highlights of Alessandri's reign. A detailed, well-documented presentation of the achievements of his presidency is found in Jorge Alessandri, *Mensaje de S.E. El Presidente de la República don Jorge Alessandri Rodriguez al Inaugurar el Período Ordinario de Sesiónes, 21 de Mayo de 1963* (Santiago: Imprenta del Servicio de Prisiones, 1963). The annual messages of the President to the Congress provided a vivid picture of both progress and problems.

14. Ibid, p. 20.

structural measures was the copper mixed enterprise approach.[15] An important pillar in the government's production strategy involved improved primary and secondary education.[16]

Under Eduardo Frei it became evident that the system's low capacity to convert internal and external resources into physical, human, and institutional capital remained the foremost bottleneck to growth and economic independence. The transformation policies required increased national savings, sacrifices, and investment. Neither Eduardo Frei's policies toward this end nor the response to these policies by the people was of a magnitude close to the one needed for success. By 1970 Chile's population had increased to 9.78 million, with 74.2 percent being urban.[17]

President Salvador Allende attempted to achieve within three years what Chile's previous presidents had failed to pursue or achieve in almost a hundred years: maximum growth and economic independence through a revolutionary but bloodless redistribution of income. The primary emphasis during 1971 was on the destruction of the national and foreign maxicapitalism in mining, agriculture, industry, and banking and the transfer of its income to labor and the poor. He succeeded remarkably well. All capitalist groups surrendered peacefully, either because they totally lacked a united spirit of a capitalist–employer class or because Allende was too strong for them. Temporary price stabilization was achieved through a massive internal and external decapitalization—borrowing from the past—that was as shortsighted

15. For a summary of the government's economic policies during 1964–70 see Eduardo Frei Montalva, *Sexto Mensaje del Presidente de la República de Chile don Eduardo Frei Montalva al inaugurar el período de Sesiónes Ordinarias del Congreso Nacional, Ministerio de Hacienda* (Santiago: Presidencia de la Republica, 1970). For a more complete account see the mammoth document, *Sexto Mensaje del Presidente de la República de Chile don Eduardo Frei Montalva al inaugurar el período de Sesiónes Ordinarias del Congreso Nacional*, 2 pts. (Santiago: Presidencia de la República, 21 de Mayo de 1970). See also Molina, *El Proceso de Cambio en Chile*, pp. 40–124.

16. Teaching materials were completely revised and updated, the curricula were changed, the number of teachers was increased, and a massive program of teacher improvement was introduced. There is no indication, however, that university education was improved. To the contrary, it seems to have deteriorated drastically, especially at the University of Chile, where politics was the primary concern of both faculty and students. Technical training and technical assistance for farmers, small-scale miners, housewives, and others were also increased but not to an extent commensurate with the needs of Chile. The humanistic orientation of education grossly outweighed the more important technical and vocational orientation.

17. See CORFO, *Perspectivas de Crecimiento de la Población Chilena, 1970–1985* (Santiago: CORFO, 1970), p. 15.

and catastrophic as the Klein–Saks price stabilization of 1955–56, when the price was paid by the poor, and Alessandri's of 1960–61, when price stability was financed by the rest of the world and future generations.[18]

The full employment, price stability, and income redistribution policies brought about a utopia of "consumption socialism." By 1972 however, the losses in capital accumulation had again unlocked inflation, external dependence, strikes, black markets, food shortages, and poverty. Allende's brand of socialism failed to recognize Chile's most important idiosyncracy: an inadequate, distorted, inefficient, noncapitalistic capital accumulation process. His battle cry for the achievement of the six social freedoms—employment, health, culture, housing, social security, and recreation for *all*—was noble by any standard and close to the goals of the advanced private capitalist societies.[19] But it failed to realize that the goals of economic democracy and social freedoms could not be pursued without an efficient, modern system of capital accumulation. The ownership transformation policies of 1971–73 had deprived Chile of its inherited, principal, private arteries of capital formation without replacing them by new state institutions.

URBANIZATION

Urbanization in Chile had already reached a high level by 1930, when 49.4 percent of the country's population was located in urban areas.[20] Between 1940 and 1960 all population increments were absorbed by the urban segment for the first time since 1840. Furthermore, the trend toward an increase in the percentage of the total population in the Santiago area continued but weakened between 1952 and 1960.[21] A tendency also developed toward population dispersions within the urban areas.

Although Santiago has persistently filled the role of the Chilean metropolis, it has not yet developed into a megalopolis in terms of size

18. See Salvador Allende, *Primer Mensaje del Presidente Allende ante El Congreso Pleno, 21 de Mayo de 1971* (Santiago: Presidencia de la República, 1971). See also chap. 10 of the present monograph.

19. Salvador Allende, *Mensaje del Presidente Allende ante el Congreso Pleno, 21 del Mayo de 1972* (Santiago: Presidencia de la República, 1972), pp. vii–xcix.

20. See Mamalakis, "Historical Statistics," table IIAlf2, p. A-89.

21. Carlos Hurtado, "Population Concentration and Economic Development: The Chilean Case" (Ph.D. thesis, Harvard University, 1966), p. 139.

Fig. 5.2. Percentage of urban population in Chile and in the provinces of Santiago, Magallanes, and the North (Tarapacá, Antofagasta, and Atacama), census years 1930-70.

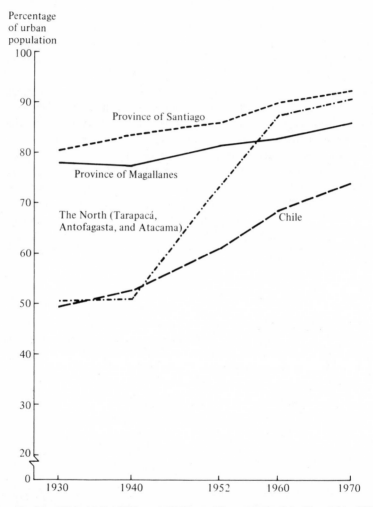

Sources: For 1930, 1940, 1952, and 1960, see "Demography," in Mamalakis, "Historical Statistics," table IIA1F1, pp. A-84–A-88. For 1970, CORFO, *Perspectivas de Crecimiento de la Población Chilena, 1970-1985* (Santiago: CORFO, 1970), table 5, p. 47.

or of industrial, technological, or architectural achievements. It has been a large but by no means a giant, overwhelming city. With its eleven communities Gran Santiago seems a conglomeration of smaller cities, a multicity or a "polypolis." Although there is no doubt that the community of Santiago has some unique characteristics that make the remaining communities dependent upon it, communities such as La Cisterna, Barrancas, and Conchalí function as independent cities and have the same features as numerous other urban areas in Chile.

The recent major progress in the city and province of Concepción and the growth of Valparaíso seem to represent a multicentered urbanization process. Gran Santiago cannot and will not become the primary center of all activities. Although some cities will always lack the ability or capacity to determine their own destinies in a distinct manner, many of them appear willing and able to become the center for some aspect of Chilean political, economic, and social life.

According to a rather popular theme, urbanization was both stimulated and required as the economy passed from its early stage of producing raw materials for exports to its second stage of import substitution and finally to its export diversification phase.[22] This trend could have been stemmed or reversed by a major overhaul in the structure of the rural segment and agricultural sector.

By 1970, as can be seen in figure 5.2, the percentage of urban population had risen to 74.2. The whole population increment of 3.78 million between 1950 and 1970 was absorbed by the cities. While rural population was stagnant, that of urban areas doubled between 1950 and 1970.[23] Throughout the years from 1930 to 1970 the nation's income, wealth, and investment resources were distributed in favor of the urban centers. The resulting rural–urban production, distribution, and capital formation imbalances have been reinforcing existing inequalities and retarding overall growth.[24]

22. Ibid., pp. 7–26. Hurtado discusses in detail what he considers the major forces behind the urban concentration of the Chilean population.

23. CORFO, *Perspectivas de Crecimiento de la Población Chilena, 1970–1985* (Santiago: CORFO, 1970), p. 15.

24. See Mamalakis, "Services in The Contemporary Latin American City: The Case of Chile," paper presented at The Rome, September 3rd–9th Urbanization Symposium of the 40th International Congress of Americanists, 1972.

6

Monetary and Fiscal Policy

THE DEPENDENT AND SHIFTING NATURE OF MONETARY POLICY

The primary objective of monetary policy under Arturo Alessandri in 1932 was to stem the depression and restore full employment. Monetary authorities sought to accomplish this directly through credit expansion and low interest rates and indirectly by supporting a deficit-spending fiscal policy. Although by 1938 income and employment had reached almost full capacity (except nitrate), the public sector continued to depend on Central Bank inflationary credit because, as a result of the defective tax structure, expenditures exceeded revenues.

Although nitrate is not mentioned in the literature as a major cause of Chile's long-term inflation since 1939, it was the pre-1930 nitrate-induced freedom from taxation of sectors and classes in Central Chile and the necessity after 1930 for the Center to assume greater fiscal responsibility that created the need for inflationary credit. Government recourse to inflationary credit and subordination of monetary to fiscal policy became inevitable once the machinery of the Center had to be supported by the people living in the region. The government was unwilling and unable to use taxation to cover its operating and investment expenditures even though some taxes were raised significantly. The door of foreign and internal noninflationary borrowing was mostly closed, and expenditures could not be reduced. Hence the government had to rely on printing money through its partner, the Central Bank. This subjugation of monetary to fiscal authorities, caused by the post-1930 struggle between sectors and income groups to maintain or improve their standard of living, would hardly have been necessary had aggregate income not greatly shrunk because of the export collapse. A structural cause, the nitrate sector instability, thus initiated the new inflationary process.

Inflation was mild but rising in the 1940s, accelerated to its pyrotechnic pre-1972 apogee between 1953 and 1955, subsided during 1956–57, 1959–61, 1965–67, and 1971, strongly rebounded in most other years, and became explosive (the worst in Chile's history) in 1972 and 1973. The money supply, the cost-of-living index, the wholesale price index, and gross domestic product in current prices moved upward together in a seemingly endless way (see figs. 6.1 and 6.2). Chilean inflation became almost as celebrated as German hyperinflation, although the two trends have had few, if any, aspects in common.[1] Chile's has been described as rampant, recurrent, cost-push or structural, demand-pull or monetarist,[2] as a hyperinflation, and so forth.

The chief nominal goal of monetary policy during the era of the Popular Front, under Pedro Aguirre Cerda and Juan Antonio Ríos, was to provide the public sector, and CORFO (Corporación de Fomento de la Producción, or the Chilean Development Corporation) in particular, with the financial resources required to pursue the policies of industrialization based on import substitution of consumer goods without greatly jeopardizing price stability. Inflation fluctuated between 9 and 26 percent from 1938 to 1945. In effect, monetary policy facilitated an income redistribution that favored industry, its workers and capitalists, and other urban sectors (mainly services) and caused

1. The Chilean inflation has been studied from different angles by Harberger and Hirschman. See Albert O. Hirschman, "Inflation in Chile," in *Journeys Toward Progress* (New York: Doubleday and Co., 1965), chap. 3, pp. 215–96. See also the extremely good studies testing the relative importance of demand-pull (monetarist) and cost-push (structuralist) factors by Arnold C. Harberger, "The Dynamics of Inflation in Chile," in *Measurement in Economics*, Studies in Mathematical Economics and Econometrics in memory of Yehuda Grunwald, by Carl Christ et al. (Stanford, Calif.: Stanford University Press, 1963).

2. A summary of the structuralist school of inflation and a list of the key articles propounding this hypothesis can be found in Markos Mamalakis, "Public Policy and Sectoral Development: A Case Study of Chile 1940–1958," in M. Mamalakis and C. Reynolds, *Essays on the Chilean Economy* (Homewood, Ill.: Richard D. Irwin, 1965), pp. 195–200. Hereafter cited as "Public Policy." This monograph also analyzes the relationship between inflation and growth in Chile between 1940 and 1950. The dean of the structuralist school was Aníbal Pinto Santa Cruz, Chile's most prolific and popular contemporary economist. Pinto's best monograph is *Chile, Un Caso de Desarrollo Frustrado* (Santiago: Editorial Universitaria, S.A., 1962). For the structuralist views, see esp. pp. 107–21. Events since 1955 and new ideas are developed in Aníbal Pinto, *Chile, Una Economía Difícil* (México, Distrito Federal: Fondo de Cultura Económica, 1964). A polemic, structuralist treatment of the Monetary Fund views on inflation is found in Aníbal Pinto S. C., *Ni Estabilidad Ni Desarrollo, La Política del Fondo Monetario* (Santiago: published privately by the author, 1960).

Fig. 6.1. Gross domestic product, total money supply, cost-of-living index, and wholesale price index, Chile, 1940–73.

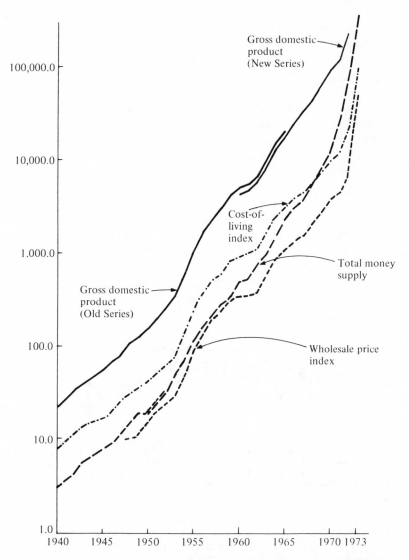

Sources: The data for gross domestic product, Old Series, are found in "National Accounts," in Mamalakis, "Historical Statistics," table IA1, pp. A-50–A-54; the data for gross domestic product, New Series, are found in ODEPLAN, *Cuentas Nacionales de Chile, 1960–1971* (Santiago: ODEPLAN, 1973), pp. 18–19; gross domestic product, New Series, for 1972 is found in ODEPLAN, *Cuentas Nacionales de Chile, 1965-1972.* (Santiago: ODEPLAN, 1973), p. 17. The data for general wholesale price index are found in "Agriculture, Industry and Trade," in Mamalakis, ibid., table IIC2b1, pp. A-396–A-397, for 1947-64; in ODEPLAN, *Antecedentes sobre el Desarrollo Chileno, 1960-1970* (Santiago: ODEPLAN, 1971), p. 39, for 1965-70; and in Instituto Nacional de Estadísticas, *Síntesis Estadística, August 1972* (Santiago: Instituto Nacional de Estadísticas, 1972), p. 7, for 1971; general wholesale price index, New Series, for 1972 and 1973 is found in Ministerio de Hacienda, Dirección de Presupuestos, *Exposición sobre el Estado de la Hacienda Pública* (Santiago: Ministerio de Hacienda, Oct. 1974), p. 68. The data for cost-of-living index are in "Agriculture, Industry, and Trade," in.Mamalakis, ibid., table IIC2c2, p. A-399, for 1940-64; in ODEPLAN, *Antecedentes, 1960-70,* p. 39, for 1965-70; and in Instituto Nacional de Estadísticas, ibid., p. 7, for 1971; cost-of-living index, New Series, for 1972 and 1973 is found in Ministerio de Hacienda, Dirección de Presupuestos, p. 67. Finally, the data for total money supply are found in "Mining, International Transactions, Money and Banking, and Government and the Public Sector," in Mamalakis, ibid., table IIF1a1, pp. A-625–A-632, for 1940-52, table IIF1a2, pp. A-633–A-641, for 1953-62, and in Banco Central de Chile, *Boletín Mensual,* various issues, for 1963-74.

Notes: Gross domestic product (Old and New Series) and total money supply are in millions of Escudos and in current prices. General wholesale price index base 1947 = 1,000. Cost-of-living index base 1961 = 1,000. The data for total money supply (which is in two series, 1940–52 and 1950–1971) are the figures corresponding to December of each year. Total money supply is defined as currency plus demand deposits.

a loss in real income for both agricultural workers and agriculture.[3] Monetary policy was not only dependent on fiscal policy and subordinate to CORFO but also an integral element in the government-sponsored sectoral coalition. The industrial consumer goods sector was dominant, and agriculture and mining suffered discrimination.

Although inflation reached its pre-Allende apogee during 1953–55 and was already considerable in 1940–45, it became permanent during the 1946–52 presidency of Gabriel González Videla. At first sight this condition seems the combined result of the disequilibrium in public finances, expansion of banking credit, excessive wage and salary increases, development of speculative spirit and behavior, and rises in

3. M. Mamalakis, "Public Policy," pp. 144–45. For further elaboration of the Mamalakis hypotheses for this period, see André Günder Frank, "La política económica en Chile-Del Frente Popular a la Unidad Popular," *Punto Final, Documentos,* supple. no. 153, *Punto Final,* March 14, 1972, Santiago, Chile, pp. 2–3.

Fig. 6.2. Gross domestic product, private consumption expenditure, and gross domestic fixed capital formation, Chile, 1940–72 (in millions of escudos, current prices).

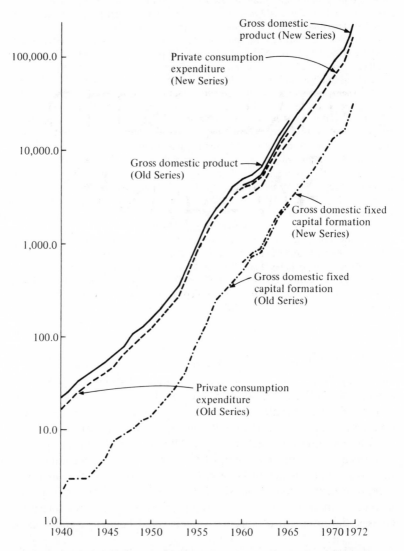

Sources: The data for 1940–65, Old Series, are found in "National Accounts," in Mamalakis, "Historical Statistics," table IA1, pp. A-50–A-54. The data for 1960–71, New Series, are found in ODEPLAN, *Cuentas Nacionales de Chile, 1960–1971*

(Santiago: ODEPLAN, 1972), pp. 18–19. The data for 1972, New Series, were obtained from ODEPLAN, *Cuentas Nacionales de Chile 1965-1972* (Santiago: ODEPLAN, 1973), table 2, p. 17.

Notes: Gross domestic product Old and New Series, private consumption expenditures Old and New Series, and gross domestic fixed capital formation Old and New Series are in millions of escudos in current prices.

prices of imported goods.[4] Despite the multitude of studies of Chilean inflation since it became a cause célèbre, few have matched the early, balanced view of the apparent inflationary causes presented by President González Videla himself.

The apparent goal of monetary policy continued to be support of import-substituting industrialization with a new emphasis on intermediate products and basic industries (steel, petroleum, electricity). The years 1946–52 saw the reaction. The sectors, classes, and regions that had suffered absolute or relative income losses because of income redistribution during 1938–45 rebelled. Their tolerance exhausted, they demanded and frequently received compensatory wage, salary, price, tax, subsidy, and transfer adjustments. The government and monetary authorities, committed to further industrialization and to the industrialization-linked income distribution pattern, opted to permit the upward price adjustments that maintained income distribution benefiting industry, services, and the urban population. Monetary and credit policy was used to reconcile the 1938–45 gains of the privileged with the demands of the losers and those falling behind; the tax, income, and relative price structure had become too labyrinthine to allow growth without continual adjustments through inflation.

Between 1952 and 1958, during the presidency of Carlos Ibáñez del Campo, it was demonstrated more strongly than ever before that monetary policy was totally subordinate to government's policies on income, distribution, and sectoral preference. These policies maintained industrial dominance, and a return to an independent monetary policy was too costly in terms of income and employment forgone. Although price stabilization efforts had been pursued before, the calamitous decline in investment, workers' income, and the growth rate during the 1955–57 Klein–Saks mission stabilization policies almost permanently shelved the arguments for the desirability of autonomous monetary

4. Gabriel Ganzález Videla, *Mensaje de S.E. El Presidente de la República don Gabriel González Videla al Congreso Nacional al inaugurar el período ordinario de sesiónes, 21 de Mayo de 1948* (Santiago: Presidencia de la República, 1948), p. vii.

policy.[5] Throughout 1930–57 monetary policy failed to raise saving and investment to the extent necessary for growth levels.

Monetary policy during the 1958–64 presidency of Jorge Alessandri was noninterventionist in nature. The belief was that, under neutral monetary policy and with substantial foreign capital inflows, the incentive system would permit the private sector to greatly accelerate growth. Since neither monetary nor fiscal policy—nor inflation, for that matter —had been neutral during 1940–58, the price stabilization policies and stability of 1959–61 and the massive capital inflows only temporarily contained and supported an explosive, distorted, and inequitable status quo. With the safety valve of almost unlimited imports closed in 1961, the system burst into a frenetic round of inflation that lasted until the second half of 1964. While the Klein–Saks stabilization schemes led to grave income–employment loss, the remarkable price stability along with growth achieved under Alessandri generated an onerous rise in foreign debts. The price of pursuing an independent, neutral monetary policy in both instances was too high.[6] Saving and investment rose significantly to more than 13.5 percent of GDP.

Monetary policy under President Eduardo Frei was aimed, officially, at containing the inflationary process, promoting a substantial increase in saving, and orienting those savings toward maximum fulfillment of the economic and social development programs.[7] The monetary authorities recognized that a price stabilization policy would have to be gradual and free of additional foreign debt burdens, a regressive redistribution of income, increased unemployment, and a decline in the growth rate. Once more, the inherited past could not be reversed even gradually, and inflation, after falling from 27.1 to 18.3 percent during

5. For a description of the Klein–Saks program, see *El Programa de Estabilización de la Economía Chilena y el Trabajo de la Misión Klein and Saks* (Santiago: Ministerio de Hacienda, May 1958). See also the informative study of inflation by Eduardo García D'Acuña, "Inflation in Chile. A Quantitative Analysis" (Ph.D. thesis, Massachusetts Institute of Technology, 1964).

6. For an analysis of the process of inflation see the following: Rolf Lüders, "A Monetary History of Chile: 1925–1958" (Ph.D. diss., University of Chicago, 1968), a systematic treatment of the monetary aspects of Chilean economic development since 1925. In certain respects this thesis has been updated by the recent article of B. Arbildua and R. Lüders, "Una Evaluación Comparada de Tres Programas Anti-Inflacionarios en Chile: Una Década de Historia Monetaria: 1956–1966," *Cuadernos de Economía* 14 (Apr. 1968): 25–105. This article contains an extensive statistical appendix and methodology.

7. See Jorge Marshall, "Introduction," in Banco Central de Chile, *Estudios Monetarios* (Santiago: Banco Central, 1968), p. 8.

1964–67 rebounded in 1968–70.[8] Once again, monetary policy became the victim of the fiscal deficit, the distribution-related wage and salary adjustments, and the inelasticity of food supplies induced by government neglect.[9]

Frei's monetary policy scored a major success in openly acknowledging the links between inflation and saving. Although never officially recognized until the Frei years, a major de facto tool of monetary policy since the beginning of the inflationary process in 1939 was administration of a system of subsidies by extending credits at low, zero, or negative real interest rates. The primary beneficiary was industry. The correct, though belated, reaction during 1964–66 was to change the spectrum of such subsidies in a manner promoting the government's development program and to reduce the margin between the nominal and real rate.[10] By 1966 the Central Bank had gained authority to determine money interest rates, which previously had adhered rigidly to predetermined ranges.

In spite of these efforts the effective, real interest rate charged on credits fluctuated between −19.9 and 30.3 percent during 1958 and 1969 and led to either excessively high rates or subsidies. Neither of these developments was actually planned by the monetary authorities.[11] Regardless of this distinct failure of monetary policy to either stabilize the real interest rate or sustain it at reasonable positive levels, some have alleged that the return to orthodox stabilization policies during 1965–69, when rates were low but positive, contributed to the weakening of the growth process.[12]

8. A discussion of all or part of Frei's monetary policy can be found in ODEPLAN, *Antecedentes sobre el Desarrollo Chileno, 1960–70* (Santiago: ODEPLAN, 1971), pp. 400–11 (hereafter cited as *Antecedentes, 1960–70*; Francisco Garcés G., "Fase de Transición: Economía y Finanzas de Chile 1964–1966," in Banco Central de Chile, *Estudios Monetarios* (Santiago: Banco Central, 1968), pp. 23–58. The most detailed institutional background in English concerning monetary and banking policy for the 1952–69 period is Ricardo Ffrench-Davis, "Economic Policies and Stabilization Programs: Chile, 1952–69" (Ph.D. diss., University of Chicago, Dec. 1971), chap. 5, pp. 111–58. This informative report, which resembles too much a Central Bank one, is greatly handicapped by the almost complete lack of references, the minimum degree of analysis, and occasional errors in statistical material. See also Jorge Cauas Lama, "La Política de Estabilización en el Caso Chileno," in Sergio Molina, *El Proceso de Cambio en Chile* (Santiago: Editorial Universitaria, 1972), Anexo, pp. 210–20.

9. Garcés, *Estudios Monetarios*, p. 29.

10. Marshall, "Introduction," in ibid., p. 8, and Daniel Tapia de la Puente and Eduardo Olivares Gajardo, "Tasas de Interés (1958–1969)," in Banco Central de Chile, *Estudios Monetarios II* (Santiago: Banco Central, 1970), pp. 101–20.

11. Tapia and Olivares, "Tasas de Interés (1958–1969)," pp. 110–14.

12. ODEPLAN, *Antecedentes, 1960–70*, p. 22.

In order to reorient the composition of credit utilization the Central Bank introduced a variety of measures. The most important were the budget credit lines, popular credits, and credits for the construction of small houses and for the purchase of national capital goods, exports, industrial transformation, and agriculture. This selective credit policy aimed to supplement (redistribute) household incomes in order to strengthen the housing and producers' durables components of aggregate demand.[13]

Probably the most effective use of monetary policy in pursuing the government's broad goals was made by President Salvador Allende's Popular Unity in 1970–72. Never before had the monetary authorities been called upon to cover such astronomical deficits, and thus they had never been so subordinate to the fiscal authorities. The Marxist-controlled government was determined to destroy the inherited social and economic order and used monetary policy to prevent price increases in the private enterprises that were to be nationalized. Forced to grant whopping wage increases, these industries were soon ripe, through induced insolvency or bankruptcy, for government takeover, intervention, confiscation, and so forth. A combination of selective price stabilization and monetary-credit policies and selective incomes policy brought about a massive redistribution of income in favor of labor, public or intervened enterprises, and government employees. Credit policy became the pivotal instrument in irreversibly changing the ownership pattern in favor of the state by providing CORFO with the financial resources required to transfer ownership to government. The publicly owned segments of sectors emerged as the dominant, preferred partners of government and monetary policy.

The short-term economic costs were too significant and pervasive to be ignored, even in terms of the political goals. Production was grossly dislocated, and voluntary decapitalization (disinvestment) was the worst in Chile's history. The most massive, pent-up excess demand since independence was accompanied by price, wage, and sectoral disequilibria and led to widespread black markets and pilferage by workers in state enterprises. Despite a new onerous debt dependence on socialist countries and Minister Vuskovic's efforts to obtain credits from Canada, Japan, and other countries by "taking advantage of the

---

13. Francisco Garcés, *Estudios Monetarios*, p. 32. Activities with a high social rate of return promoted by the Development Plan were also favored with credits.

contradictions of the capitalist world," there was a severe balance of payments crisis.[14] By 1972 the dome of artificial strings used by the Popular Unity to control prices during 1971 caved in, and the worst inflationary wave in Chile's history was unleashed.

The transformation in the sources of money creation between 1969 and 1971 reflects the structural changes as much as the new orientation of monetary policy. In 1969 Central Bank operations with the Treasury contributed 39.3 percent of new money emission; 55.7 percent originated from foreign exchange operations and 5.0 percent from internal credit. By contrast these operations contributed 55.1 percent of new emission in 1970[15] (36.5 percent due to internal credit) and 92.1 percent of money emission in 1971.

The pre-1930 dependence on nitrate, so totally idiosyncratic to Chile, and the collapse of the 1930s shaped the nature of the monetary policy. It remained captive to fiscal measures and was never autonomous in the sense of providing the instruments of transactions needed by sectors to perform their functions consistent with price stability. It supported fiscal policy by supplying the additional resources required by the public sector to fulfill its multiple and changing roles in production (financing deficits, shaping aggregate demand, offering special incentives to industry), distribution (facilitating ownership transfers, administering subsidies, changing the international, class, public–private sector, and sectoral distribution), and capital accumulation (introducing escalator clauses, changing interest rates, and financing capital goods purchases). Inflation was the safety valve released when too many goals were pursued simultaneously, when they were pursued in a conflicting manner, or when they could not be pursued for political factors under orthodox financial procedures.

Monetary policy did provide the quantity of money and credit essential for normal production throughout 1932–73 (with minor exceptions). It specifically and preferentially assisted the industrial sector, but failed to provide the quantity or quality of credit and to introduce the institutional reform needed for efficient performance of the food, quantity, time, location changing, and quality maintenance and im-

14. For a recognition of many of these problems by the government itself and the quotation, see *El Mercurio*, Monday, June 5, 1972, pp. 17, 22.

15. The detailed figures are given by the Central Bank and are also found in *El Mercurio*, Thursday, May 16, 1972, p. 3. El Mercurio provides also an excellent analysis of the causes that led to strong shifts in the demand for money during 1969–72.

provement functions. Capital accumulation suffered during 1930–58, and 1970–73, and distribution remained highly inequitable during 1930–70.

FISCAL POLICY, THE PUBLIC SECTOR, AND GOVERNMENT

Throughout 1930–73, certainly long before Allende's road-to-socialism policies, the main determinant of Chile's economic destiny was government. Its direct and indirect role as a producer, consumer, employer, and agent shaping distribution and capital accumulation grew almost continuously and irrevocably as its policies on taxation, expenditure, transfer, incomes, trade and balance of payments, ownership, and other matters affected almost every aspect of economic life.

The scope of the public sector's role was widely, though cautiously, broadened after 1939, when autonomous state enterprises were launched in critical bottleneck sectors. It was selectively and carefully expanded during 1964–70, when government became partner to existing enterprises and accelerated the process of institutional transformation.

Finally, it was spectacularly expanded during 1971–73, when President Allende's Popular Unity spearheaded government seizure of all large, key enterprises in a deliberate, totally open effort to destroy the previous social, economic, and political order. The Allende transformation was planned to precipitate a massive loss restricted to the opposition and the private sector.

This transition in the scope of government goals and policy determined the relationship among its three components. The central government, which included the central administration, had as its original goal the maintenance and improvement of the quality of life. The general government, which included the Central government plus the University of Chile, the State Technical University, the National Health Service, the municipalities, and the social security system, had the additional goal of improving the quality of all forms of capital and life and displayed a surplus in its current account. In addition, the public sector encompassed the general government and autonomous semistate enterprises and incorporated to changing degrees the goal of performing all functions needed to satisfy the economy's needs; it always operated with rather shocking deficits.[16]

16. The latest institutional composition and coverage of the public sector and its components are found in "Informe Financiero," *Finanzas Públicas*, Oct. 1971, no. 14, pp. 134–38.

Taxation underwent significant changes starting in 1924–32, when the sharp decline in nitrate revenues led to a system of direct taxes (external trade taxes fell to an average of only 3.7 percent of total revenues during 1950–60.[17]) During 1933–47 the tax rates gradually increased and new indirect taxes were introduced. Between 1948 and 1958 tax rates were raised considerably, income tax brackets were defined as multiples of the basic salary (*sueldo vital*), and more new indirect taxes were introduced. From 1958 to 1970 taxes became partially inflation proof as the payment lag was eliminated and tax liabilities were subjected to a cost-of-living adjustment.[18] Finally, an extremely progressive and uniform income tax was introduced in January 1973. As can be seen from figure 6.3, government revenues increased unrelentingly due to inflationary income increases. Only corporate profit taxes stagnated and government enterprise and property revenues fell sharply during Allende's presidency.

The outstanding characteristic of the government's revenue system was the number and magnitude of leakages. The worst arose from no or low income taxes and persisted as late as 1972. Frei raised direct income taxes from 27 percent of fiscal revenues in 1960 to 38.4 percent in 1970 and those on personal income from only 5.5 percent in 1960 to an extraordinary 18.3 percent.[19] Nevertheless, direct taxes in 1970 were not much higher than the 36.8 percent reached in 1956[20] and never exceeded 19 percent of public sector revenues. Personal income taxes almost always accounted for less than 2.5 percent of GDP when total public sector revenues ranged from 37 to 48 percent of GDP.[21] Within this group of taxes, the worst fault was the low tax burden of high-income households. Only Allende's manifold impositions and tax reforms of 1970–72 appreciably reduced this leakage.

17. Wally Meza San Martín, La Participación del Sector Público en la Economía Nacional," Memoria de Prueba para optar al Grado de Licenciado en Ciencias Económicas y al Título de Ingeniero Comercial (Santiago: Universidad de Chile, 1962, typewritten), p. 49. Hereafter cited as Meza, "Sector Público."

18. See Ministerio de Hacienda, Dirección General de Impuestos Internos, Oficina de Estudios Tributarios, *El Sistema Tributario Chileno*, 2 vols. (Santiago: Talleres Gráficos, "La Nación," 1960), Ministerio de Hacienda, Departmento de Estudios Financieros, *Cuentas Fiscales de Chile, 1925–1957* (Santiago: Talleres Gráficos "La Nación," 1959); and Kenneth G. Ruffing, "The Effects of Inflation on the Yield and The Structure of The Fiscal System in Chile" (Ph.D. thesis, Columbia University, 1971), pp. 11–145. (hereafter cited as "Inflation and The Fiscal System").

19. ODEPLAN, *Antecedentes, 1960–70*, p. 390.

20. Meza, "Sector Público," p. 47.

21. *Antecedentes, 1960–70*, table 299. See also E. Lee Ward Cantwell, "Consolidado del Sector Público: Metodología y Aplicación," Memoria en Economía (Santiago: Universidad de Chile, 1963), mimeo, p. 2.

Fig. 6.3. Sources of central government revenues, Chile, 1940–72 (in thousands of escudos, current prices).

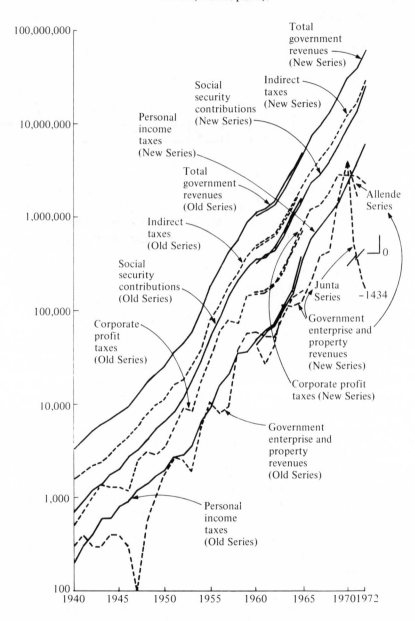

Sources: For Old Series, see "National Accounts," in Mamalakis, "Historical Statistics," table IC1, pp. A-86–A-91. For New Series, see ODEPLAN, *Cuentas Nacionales de Chile, 1960–1971* (Santiago: ODEPLAN, 1972), table 8, pp. 34–35; for 1971 and 1972, New Series, see ODEPLAN, *Cuentas Nacionales de Chile, 1965–1972* (Santiago: ODEPLAN, 1973), table 8, p. 26.

Perennial tax and other revenue evasion was a general malaise[22] that increasingly afflicted indirect taxes especially those paid by small and medium-sized unincorporated enterprises. Indirect taxes rose from 2.3 percent of the GDP and 16.4 percent of general government revenues in 1940 to 5.7 and 26.3 percent, respectively, in 1964. Taxable income was widely underreported, particularly in some service sectors; heavy leakage also occurred in social security contributions, which by 1962 amounted to 7.8 percent of GDP and 32.2 percent of general government revenues.

Other loopholes and leakages reduced the real value or distorted the relationship between revenues and expenditures or acted as disincentives. There was a leakage of regional revenue in 1953, when Arica gained free port status with generous tariff and tax exemptions. Revenue was also lost indirectly through smuggling of luxury imports. Further regional leakages occurred in 1956, when the provinces of Chiloé, Aisén, and Magallanes were declared free trade zones, and in 1958, when three provinces in the North were given export subsidies, a 90 percent reduction on most taxes, and selected tariff exemptions.[23] Another leakage was caused by the fact that, paid in nominal terms and with varying time lags, taxes lost real value depending on the speed of inflation. According to Kenneth G. Ruffing, the real value of direct taxes was reduced 1 percent for each 1 percent increase in the price level until 1965, when the one-year payment lag was eliminated. If measured as percentages of GDP, however, target collections of direct taxes were maintained by regularly raising the rates of taxation. Moreover, if we deduct from the estimated 1.6 percent of GDP government revenue derived from the issue of new money—inflationary tax on cash balances—between 1929 and 1969 the loss due to inflationary erosion

22. See Carlos Ibáñez del Campo, *Mensaje de S.E. El Presidente de la República don Carlos Ibáñez del Campo, 21 de Mayo de 1955* (Santiago: Presidencia de la República, 1955), p. xxii.

23. See "Puerto Libre y Plan Arica, 1953," in Carlos Ibáñez del Campo, *Mensaje de S.E. El Presidente de la República don Carlos Ibáñez del Campo al Congreso Nacional, 21 de Mayo de 1958* (Santiago: Presidencia de la República, 1958), Appendix. Hereafter cited as *Ibáñez Mensaje 1958*.

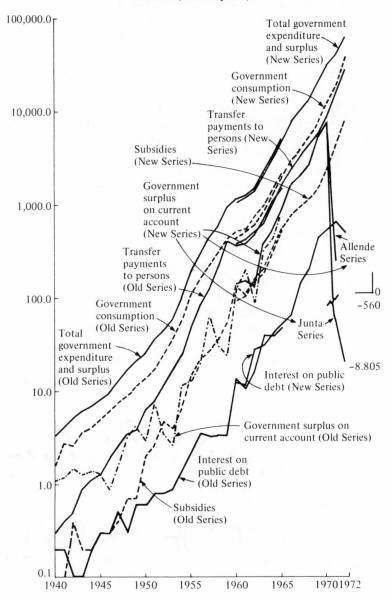

Fig. 6.4. Central government expenditures and surplus, Chile, 1940–72 (in millions of escudos, current prices).

Sources: For Old Series, see "National Accounts," in Mamalakis, "Historical Statistics," table IC3, pp. A-95–A-103. For New Series, see ODEPLAN, *Cuentas Nacionales de Chile, 1960–1971* (Santiago: ODEPLAN, 1972), table 8, pp. 34–37; for 1971 and 1972, New Series, see ODEPLAN, *Cuentas Nacionales de Chile, 1965–1972* (Santiago: ODEPLAN, 1973), table 8, pp. 26–27.

of direct, internal tax revenues, the Chilean government captured a maximum of .95 percent of GDP and at a minimum may have suffered a loss of − .35 percent of GDP.[24] Foreign exchange overvaluation also caused a revenue leakage by reducing income taxes on export concerns and duties on undervalued imports.

The weakness of the tax and revenue structure did not lie in the presence of these leakages. In spite of them general government receipts rose from 13.9 percent of GDP in 1940 to 24.1 percent in 1964 and to 33 percent in 1970.[25] Furthermore, this labyrinth provided the safety valves against overtaxation, but its regressiveness established unnecessary disincentives and distorted rather than promoted production.

CENTRAL AND GENERAL GOVERNMENT AND PUBLIC SECTOR EXPENDITURES

Statistical information concerning government expenditures has persistently been most precarious and for the 1930–50 period is almost nonexistent. Government consumption expenditures hovered around 10 percent of GDP throughout 1940–70[26] and the public sector generated directly between 12.7 and 14.1 percent of GDP during 1960–69.[27] If we use as an indicator of governmental role public sector expenditures, which include current operational expenditures, transfers, and capital expenditures, the role emerges as far more significant. These ranged between 37 and 48 percent of GDP during 1960–69.[28] With relatively minor cyclical fluctuations, almost all types of government expenditures (as can be seen in fig. 6.4) moved upward, propelled by inflation, real income rises, and changes in the tax structure. The

24. See Kenneth G. Ruffing, "Inflation and The Fiscal System," pp. 125–27.
25. Mamalakis, "Historical Statistics of Chile, 1840–1965," table IC1, pp. A-86–A-91. ODEPLAN, *Cuentas Nacionales de Chile, 1960–1970* (Santiago: ODEPLAN, Nov. 1971), Cuenta del Gobierno General, table 8, pp. 34–35.
26. See Mamalakis, "Historical Statistics," table IA1, pp. A-50–A-52.
27. *Antecedentes, 1960–70,* p. 372.
28. Ibid. pp. 391, 397–99.

only exception was the government surplus on current account, which plummeted to increasingly negative deficit levels in 1971 and 1972.

The subsectors maintaining the quality of life—police, defense, and central administration—received the bulk of public sector revenues (40 percent of gross revenues during 1950–60 and 38.3 percent or 5 percent of GDP during 1960–70.[29] The quality of police services in Chile has not only been exceptionally high by any standard but has also consistently improved. Along with the armed forces, the police with their renowned esprit de corps have constituted a segment of exceptional integrity, impartiality, and efficiency. In contrast the central administration has been plagued by bureaucratic inefficiency, rigidity, over-centralization in Santiago, and inadequate response to the needs of the rural and urban misery belt segments.[30] Constant administrative reform, especially under Eduardo Frei, wiped out some of the most notorious inefficiencies.

If educational, public health, social, and labor assistance and social security and pension payments are added, at least one-third of central government expenditures served to maintain the quality of life. The flow of health services may have suffered during 1950–60, when the health expenditures share fell from 13.3 percent to a dismal 5.6 percent and showed no appreciable recovery in the 1960s.[31] Although the flow of educational services increased without stint, the quality of this flow did not improve significantly.

At least one-third of both central and general government expenditures during 1960–70 was used for transportation, housing and urbanization, energy, and those industrial subsectors that preserved and improved quality and changed the location, quantity, and time dimension of goods and people.[32] The urban middle classes were the primary beneficiaries of these expenditures.

Within the public sector, state enterprises gained in secular significance during the effort to increase efficiency through decentralization and deconcentration—from 25.8 percent in 1950 to 30.3 percent in 1960. Within the autonomous public segment, transport and communications enterprises were the most important during 1950–60. They

---

29. Meza, "Sector Público," p. 33; *Antecedentes, 1960–70*, pp. 372, 397.
30. The problems plaguing Chile's central administration are described by Arturo Hein C. and Jaime Contreras V., *El Funcionario Público Caso: Ministerio de la Vivienda y Urbanismo* (Santiago: INSORA, 1971), pp. 91–96.
31. Meza, "Sector Público," p. 33.
32. *Antecedentes, 1960–70*, pp. 382–83, 394.

absorbed more than 33 percent of all state enterprise expenditures, followed by those in industry, electricity, and construction.[33] The autonomous public enterprises emerged as Chile's dominant feature during the 1970–72 nationalization policies. But the state enterprises have not proved their superiority over the private ones except as an instrument of income redistribution.

All Chilean presidents added to the expansion of the welfare state through a complex system of spectacularly rising transfer payments and subsidies. Transfers rose cyclically from 1.4 percent in 1940 to 10 percent in 1959, 7.3 percent in 1965, and 13.2 percent of GDP in 1970, and subsidies increased from 0.5 to 3.5 percent in 1965.[34] The heavy increments of social security contributions and part of the rise in indirect taxes financed Chile's pre-1970 "capitalistic" (private) welfare system, which consisted of social security payments of 60 percent, family allowances of 30 percent, and miscellaneous other transfers to private or public entities.[35] The redistributive impact was very limited before 1970 because the Chilean welfare state remained predominantly directed by and for the middle classes.[36]

President Allende's reforms transformed the welfare state into a socialist-based, labor-oriented system. Income was redistributed among the insured, but major segments of the uninsured young, old, unemployed or unemployable, indigent, and poor were neglected. Those in perennial need of maximum protection still fail to receive it.

33. Meza, "Sector Público," p. 33.
34. Mamalakis, "Historical Statistics," table 1C1, pp. A-86–A-91; ODEPLAN, *Cuentas Nacionales de Chile, 1960–1970*, table 8, p. 37.
35. *Antecedentes, 1960–70*, p. 399.
36. Meza, "Sector Público," p. 33.

7

The Agricultural Paradox:
Unfulfilled Functions amidst Rising Needs

"Chile is essentially an agricultural country," wrote George McBride in1936, and the multitude of scholars who have accepted this premise would also agree with another of his statements:

> Chile's people live on the soil. Her life is agricultural to the core. Her government has always been that of farm owners .... Her Congress is made up chiefly of rich landlords. Social life is dominated by families whose proudest possession is the ancestral estate.[1]

The traditional, primary, and basic role of agriculture is to produce enough food to satisfy the rural and urban population. While performing this function, agriculture also creates employment, can become a source of taxes, savings, and foreign exchange, and develops a market for industrial, service, construction, and mining products. Although before 1930 the quantitative employment role played by agriculture in Chile was unquestionably great, neither its overall income, food production and surplus, employment, market size, and related contributions nor its qualitative performance during 1840–1973 justifies the simplistic description of Chile as an agricultural economic structure and society.

THE AGRICULTURAL BOOM (1840–1880) AND DECLINE (1880–1930)

The golden era of domestic agriculture, when it satisfied the nutritional needs not only of the growing rural population—much of which had

1. See George McCutchen McBride, *Chile: Land and Society* (New York: American Geographical Society, 1936), p. 15.

very low consumption standards—but also of the urban population and at the same time generated an export surplus, continued for almost half a century after independence.[2] An unprecedented euphoria prevailed during the 1840–80 boom in wheat exports. As the railroad and maritime transportation revolution expanded world trade frontiers, the demand for Chilean wheat exports rose substantially.[3] Central Chile, like the East Coast of the United States, developed early. The famous eighteenth-century Peruvian market for the Central Valley's surplus livestock, wheat, and other agricultural products was reinforced or replaced by the nineteenth-century wheat trade with Europe, mainly England, with California during the gold rush, and even with Australia. Toward the end of the nineteenth century the latifundio–minifundio combination emerged as large-scale commercial production induced the previously floating population to settle at the fringes of the large estates. By 1875 the rural population had reached a level of 1.35 million, accounting for 65 percent of the total population and approximately equal to the Indian population in 1675.[4] However, in 1875—or for that matter even in 1840, when the rural segment comprised more than 70 percent of the population—agriculture may have generated at best only 50 percent of the gross domestic product.

By the end of the present period the society and economy were as much rural as they were urban. If the population criterion is used, the rural population was 50.6 percent of the total in 1930.[5] The rise in world population, trade, technological progress, and cultivable land put in motion the forces that generated the rise of the rural sector as well as its decline. As the immensely larger and richer Argentine pampas were opened up from 1840 to 1900, the role of Chilean agriculture as a dynamic, strategic sector with an export surplus passed on to Argentina permanently.[6]

2. The changing role of agriculture during the nineteenth century is described by Gonzalo Izquierdo F., *Un Estudio de las Ideologías Chilenas, La Sociedad de Agricultura en el Siglo XIX* (Santiago: Universidad de Chile, 1968). Hereafter cited as *La Sociedad de Agricultura en el Siglo XIX*. See also his bibliography on pp. 195–99.

3. The rise and fall of Chilean wheat is eloquently described by Sergio Sepúlveda G., *El Trigo Chileno en el Mercado Mundial, Ensayo de Geografía Histórica* (Santiago: Editorial Universitaria, S.A., 1959). Hereafter cited as *Trigo Chileno*.

4. For an interesting and detailed discussion of the substitution of the Indian by the "white" element and the demographic problem see Miguel Cruchaga's *Estudio sobre la Organización Económica y la Hacienda Pública de Chile* (Madrid: Editorial Reus, S.A., 1929), Vol. 1, pp. 457–540. For the statistics see my "Historical Statistics," p. A-89.

5. Mamalakis, "Historical Statistics," table IIAlf2, p. A-89.

6. See Francisco A. Encina, *Nuestra Inferioridad Económica* (Santiago: Editorial Universitaria, S.A., 1955), pp. 19–33, esp. p. 21.

The eclipse of agriculture from the international scene and from the soutern tip of the continent brought an end to Chile's era of great food prosperity and surpluses. Its international decline was matched after the spectacular 1882 nitrate bonanza by an internal transfer of growth functions to industry, services, and especially mining that together

Table 7.1. Indices of Total Agricultural Production and Capital Inputs and Their Annual Rates of Increase, 1910–32

Agricultural production

Period (1)	Crops (2)	Wine (3)	Livestock (4)	Total (5)
A. Indices of production (1933–37 = 100)				
1910–12	54.8	49.1	56.0	54.6
1913–17	62.4	80.2	71.7	68.9
1918–22	63.9	57.7	78.9	69.8
1923–27	71.6	70.8	73.2	72.1
1928–32	88.8	95.4	95.9	92.9
B. Annual rates of increase or decrease (In percentages)				
1910–12 to 1918–22	1.7	1.8	3.9	2.8
1918–22 to 1928–32	3.8	5.2	2.0	3.1
1928–32 to 1933–37	2.4	1.0	0.8	1.5

Agricultural capital inputs

Period (1)	Land (2)	Vineyards (3)	Livestock (4)	Machinery and equipment (5)
A. Indices of capital inputs in agriculture (1933–37 = 100)				
1910–12	44.9	58.8	61.8	82.9
1913–17	55.7	68.9	74.9	95.0
1918–22	59.3	76.6	78.3	99.5
1923–27	68.9	77.0	71.8	103.8
1928–32	85.1	90.8	92.9	111.9
B. Annual rates of increase or decrease (In percentages)				
1910–12 to 1918–22	3.1	3.0	2.7	2.0
1918–22 to 1928–32	3.7	1.7	1.7	1.2
1928–32 to 1933–37	3.3	2.0	1.5	−2.6

Source: Marto Ballesteros, "Desarrollo Agrícola Chileno, 1910–1955," *Cuadernos de Economia* 2, no. 5 (Jan.–Apr. 1955): 13, 21.

gradually replaced agriculture as the major employer and source of income, savings, government revenues, foreign exchange, and intersectoral input–output linkages.

Relatively accurate production statistics, which are available only since 1910 and are presented in table 7.1, show a rather respectable but by no means spectacular rate of growth (between 2.8 and 3.1 percent) during the 1910–32 years of moderate demographic growth and continuing urbanization. Crop, wine, and livestock production climbed between 1910 and 1930 with the biggest gain, a cyclical one, experienced by wine.

Although the agricultural sector became increasingly monetized, specialized, and commercialized between 1840 and 1930, it continued to satisfy a vast variety of internal needs—for water, light, transportation, trade, and industrial consumer goods. The total welfare enjoyed by the combined agrorural population greatly exceeded that suggested by either agricultural production or its income contribution, which, as shown in table 1.3, amounted during 1907–30 to a meager 14 percent of total income.

The agricultural labor force, which may have accounted for as much as 50 percent of the total labor force and 40 percent of the rural population in 1840, increased throughout 1840–1930 along with most other inputs. Assuming a rural population/labor force participation rate of 35 percent, the agrorural labor force must have increased from approximately 455,000 in 1865 to 760,000 in 1930.[7] However, according to Ballesteros the agricultural labor force was only 488,000 or approximately 25 percent of the rural population of 1.991 million in 1920, and it grew by only 14,000 as of 1930.[8] Capital inputs, which include land, vineyards, livestock, machinery, and equipment, appear to have risen throughout 1840–1930, with a definite increase registered after 1910. The agricultural frontier was expanded (in part through German colonization[9]) to include the wet and inhospitable Lake Region, the

---

7. Based on information in my "Historical Statistics," p. A-89. The implicit participation rate of the rural population in the agricultural labor force in 1920 in Ballesteros–Davis estimates of the labor force is only 30 percent. See Marto A. Ballesteros and Tom E. Davis, "The Growth of Output and Employment in Basic Sectors of the Chilean Economy, 1908–1957," *Economic Development and Cultural Change* 11 (Jan. 1963): 176.

8. See Marto Ballesteros, "Desarrollo Agrícola Chileno, 1910–1955," *Cuadernos de Economía*, Año 2 (Jan.–Apr. 1965), p. 16.

9. Concerning the incorporation of the agricultural South into the production system see Jean Pierre Blancpain, "La Tradición Campesina Alemana en Chile," *Boletín de la Academia Chilena de la Historia* 81 (1969): 81–139; see also two related publications:

Fig. 7.1. Map of regions of Chile.

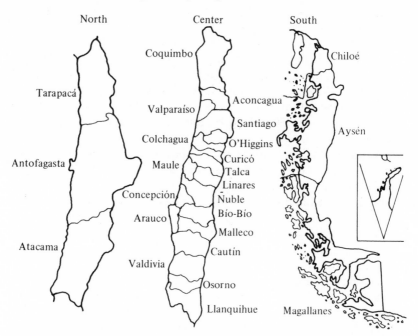

Source: Dirección de Estadística y Censos, *IV Censo Nacional Agropecuario, Año Agrícola 1964–65* (Santiago: Dec. 1966), p. xv. Designations "North," "Center," and "South" are mine.

Frontera preserves of the Araucanians, the canal region of Aisén, and the sheep-raising estancias of the land of Magellan (all shown in fig. 7.1). The land area planted with crops more than doubled between 1910–12 and 1938–42, and the number of hectares occupied by vineyards rose from 55,000 during 1911–12 to 102,000 in 1938–42.[10] The livestock index, which is defined in a special way by Ballesteros, climbed from a value of 61.8 in 1911 (using 1935–36 as base period) to 100.0 in 1935–36, and the stock of capital goods rose from $33 million in 1927 prices to $34 million in 1938–42.[11]

Louis Dorte, *El Porvenir en Chile de los Emigrantes Europeos* (Santiago: Imprenta de la República, 1884), and V. Pérez Rosales, *Ensayo Sobre Chile* (Santiago: Imprenta del Ferrocarril, 1859), esp. chap. 8.

10. See Marto Ballesteros, "Desarrollo Agrícola Chileno, 1910–1955," *Cuadernos de Economía*, Año 2, Jan.–Apr. 1965, table 9, p. 18.

11. See Ballesteros, ibid, tables 4, 10, and 11, pp. 12, 18–19, and table 7.1 of this book.

The use as well as the quality of land was improved through irrigation, a shift from natural to artificial pastures, the conversion from extensive livestock to intensive crop production and orchards, and controls over product quality. Irrigated land, the main improvement found in the Central Valley and the transversal valleys of Coquimbo and Aconcagua, was served by a vast and efficient canal system built before 1900 through the free labor time of migrant or semiserf tenant farmers within the hacienda–latifundio system.[12]

Agriculture, like Chile as a whole, was aristocratic in social and economic structure, political influence, and values throughout 1840–1930. But the *fronda aristocratica* (political elite) that presided over Chile during the nineteenth century was not exclusively agriculture based—nor, indeed, even agriculture oriented. It was a composite, multisectoral oligarchy that included most owners of large estates but also most large bankers, miners, and industrialists.[13]

The Chilean aristocracy was almost always urban and never became totally landed and agricultural. When a major segment of it branched out to agriculture during the colonial and early independence years, it was out of necessity. The resource surplus from the estates, managed mostly by hired administrators, supported its urban functions. Since 1840 many landowners have diversified into industry, mining, and services while maintaining the socially and politically valuable foothold on land. At the same time, as a remarkable intersectoral human and financial capital mobility prevailed, the rich and successful merchants, miners, bankers, industrialists, politicians, and so forth—by definition an oligarchy—sought and obtained through marriage or land acquisition an agricultural base.

As a *patrón*, the landowner aristocrat cared for the health, education, housing, social security, and political affiliation of his illiterate or semiliterate, highly dependent tenants.[14] Paternalism, stratification, and dualism within the encomienda–latifundio social order (which

12. For a 1907–55 index of per capita agricultural capital stock see Tom E. Davis, "Capital y Salarios Reales en la Economía Chilena," *Cuadernos de Economía*, Año 3, no. 8 (Jan.–Apr. 1966), pp. 94–95.

13. One of the most balanced treatments of the agricultural sector in the nineteenth century is found in Arnold Jacob Bauer, "Chilean Rural Society in the Nineteenth Century" (Ph.D. diss., University of California, Berkeley, 1969), pp. 185–87.

14. The aristocratic background of the agricultural sector is strongly pointed out by Gonzalo Izquierdo, *La Sociedad de Agricultura en el Siglo XIX*, pp. 159–65. See also the classic study by Mario Góngora, *Encomenderos y Estancieros, Estudios acerca de la Constitución social aristocrática de Chile después de la Conquista 1580–1660* (Santiago: Universidad de Chile, Sede de Valparaíso, 1970), and the works cited by him.

by no means dominated all agriculture) reflected the supremacy and de facto apotheosis of an aristocratic private sector, not of the competition associated with private laissez-faire capitalism. The Chilean land tenure system, mostly because of the Spanish Crown's inability to control its distant colonies, gave the private, decentralized sector authority, control, and power over law, order, education, health, and welfare.

Although this private control and dominance have gone largely unnoticed, their implications have been analyzed and the landowner has been turned into the villain responsible for retardation and backwardness. As McBride explains it:

> On the territorial encomiendas, where a settled district had constituted the grant, the status of the Indian had been gradually changing from that of a mere ward with obligations to render certain services to his guardian into that of a serf attached to the soil, with no liberty to engage in other pursuits than those on the owner's property, and obliged to spend his life in labor for a master, much as the case on the encomiendas established over the sedentary peoples of Mexico and Peru. The very dependence of the Indian upon the soil in such encomiendas has resulted in virtual ownership by the Spaniard of both the Indian and his land, the two constituting inseparable elements of a single property.

This, in turn, gave rise to a "unique agrarian society characterized by an extreme land monopoly and a sharply marked social stratification."[15] According to McBride, not only was the Chilean society historically divided into two sharply differentiated classes, but the nation's entire life was molded in relation to the land. The landholding aristocracy, well educated, widely traveled, and highly cultured, became the upper class of the patrón, the Master, "Don Fulano." The lower class, composed of the permanent tenants of the rural estates (*inquilinos*) and the floating rural population (*afuerinos*) became the servant, the laborer, "Zutano." The negative impact of the highly stratified rural society was broad and pervasive:

> ... The land system gave its "cast to the nation" and permeated the whole social structure of the country with the psychology of Master and Man. When Don Fulano became a mine operator or

15. George McCutchen McBride, *Chile: Land and Society*, pp. 116, xvi.

an industrialist, Zutano became a laborer.... The negative attitude of Master and Man, on which a feudality was originally based, was applied to the mass of the country. A negative economy, a negative education, and a negative political system were the result.[16]

The erroneous assignment of complete power to landowners leads to further untested ramifications of this powerful and popular sociological hypothesis. In terms of class struggle exploitation, the landowner's shadow is cast upon the urban middle classes:

... The middle class came to life contaminated with the stigma of the *patrón* system. First it was inspired by a desire to emulate and blend with the aristocracy. It was a class in transit towards the privileged caste.

The theme is complete when the ruling elites are accused of misusing their power within the system.

The chief accusation that could be made against the landowners and political bosses is not that they succeeded in perpetuating a system in which all the advantages were on their side, but that they made such poor use of it .... They established an "order," but certainly not such as was deserved by the centuries of loyalty, humility, and self-denial of the Zutanos.[17]

This view of patrón–servant dualism, exploitation, and domination is more fiction than reality, however, especially after the nitrate bonanza of 1882. The Chilean agricultural population has been heterogeneous, flexible, and open. The prevalent myth of a uniform landlord class is shattered by the fact that the landlord group included big corporations with thousands of stockholders;[18] absentee landlords residing in provincial capitals, Santiago, or Paris; industrialists, miners, merchants, bankers, and agronomists who bought farms for prestige, speculation, profit, or for transformation into model dairies, breeding

16. See Carlos Dávila's introduction to McBride's *Chile: Land and Society*, p. xvii.
17. See Carlos Dávila's forward in ibid., pp. xvii, xviii.
18. Typical of this category are the sheep-raising corporations in the province of Magallanes; see Fernando Durán, *Sociedad Explotadora de Tierra del Fuego* (Valparaíso: Litografía Universo, S.A., 1951), pp. 1–78. This company had 73 stockholders in 1894, 1,237 in 1906, and 6,923 in 1963. See *Sociedad Explotadora de Tierra del Fuego, 70ª Memoria Anual, 1963*, Valparaíso, 1963, p. 20.

centers, and other enterprises; the tenacious German, Italian, Jugoslav, and other immigrants; the impoverished *minifundistas;* and others. The interest in and attachment to land displayed by these groups were equally uneven. There is no evidence either that this heterogeneity has been reduced or that the landlords' ties to land have been changed during 1960–73, when a variety of cooperative, communal, or state ownership patterns replaced most large-scale private farms. The post-1960 revolutionary change in land ownership patterns has thus not revolutionized the relationship between men and the land.

There is no evidence that the agricultural worker class, which cannot always be separated from the owners, was less heterogeneous. It included the militant, highly unionized, and well-organized workers of Patagonia's estancias; the well-off resident workers (inquilinos) of the Central Valley; the great mass of landless, floating, often vagabond and colorful afuerinos, who changed *fundos* (agricultural estates) almost as easily as countries; the rich managers and administrators; the white-collar agronomists; and others. Class consciousness arose neither in the past nor very recently. And the issue of land reform, of badly needed social justice for much of the rural population, came from outside—from the universities, the intellectuals, the urban-based land tenure specialists from the United States, international organizations, and Chile, politicians, and, during 1970–73, from the urban Movimiento Izquierda Revolucionaria (MIR)—but not from within.

Although the rural population was an important segment of the national social and economic fabric, its economic base was too weak, its social structure too heterogeneous, the scope of its political power more imaginary than of the real size necessary for the complete domination of Chile's destiny assigned to it by McBride, the structuralists, the Alliance for Progress, the Christian Democrats, or the Marxist groups.

THE RISING FOOD CRISIS OF 1930–1973

As mining collapsed during the Great Depression, population growth accelerated and income recovered, and it appeared briefly that agriculture could once again achieve the adequacy of its pre-1880 performance. The prospects of domestic food shortages were real, and an internal solution to the agricultural food problem emerged as a sine qua non for accelerated growth.

Agriculture found itself in a very precarious situation in 1940. As can be seen in table 7.2, its share in GDP was a meager 14.9 percent,

Table 7.2. Relative Income (GDP) and Employment in Agriculture,
Chile, Selected Years, 1940–71

	Percentage of agricultural			Relative productivity	
	Income		Employment	(1)	(2)
	Old Series	New Series		(3)	(3)
	(1)	(2)	(3)	(4)	(5)
1940	14.9		37.3	0.40	
1945	13.0		34.7	0.37	
1950	13.2		32.2	0.41	
1955	13.0		30.5	0.43	
1960	11.3	(11.8)	30.7	0.37	(0.38)
1965	9.8	(9.9)	27.9	0.35	(0.35)
1970		(9.2)	23.2		(0.40)
1971		(9.2)	23.9		(0.38)

Sources: The original data used to calculate income figures, Old Series, are found in "National Accounts," in Mamalakis, "Historical Statistics," table IF3, pp. A-171–A-176. The original data used to calculate income figures, New Series, are found in Presidencia de la República, Oficina de Planificación Nacional, *Cuentas Nacionales de Chile, 1960–1971* (Santiago: ODEPLAN, 1973), table 14, pp. 49–50. And, finally, the original data used to calculate employment figures are found in "Demography," in Mamalakis, ibid., table IIA2a6, pp. A-160–A-165, for 1940–55; in ODEPLAN, *Población Ocupada por Sectores Económicos, 1960–1970* (Santiago, ODEPLAN, 1971), table 1, for 1960–70; and in ODEPLAN, *Analysis of the Economy in 1971* (Santiago, ODEPLAN, 1972), table 6, p. 24, for 1971.

Notes: The figures of income, Old Series, correspond to gross domestic product, market prices, in 1961 prices. The figures of income, New Series, correspond to gross domestic product, market prices, in 1965 prices. New and old series are not comparable due to changes in estimating methodology. The employment percentages correspond to the ratio of population employed in the sector to total employment (total employment = active population − unemployment).

which further declined secularly to a low of 8.6 percent in 1970. Even within Latin America during 1950–65, its income share was the second lowest after Venezuela and only one-half the Latin American average.[19] Because of its overall extreme state of poverty, a major saving, government revenue, market, foreign exchange, or technological contribution was impossible. As can be seen from table 7.3 the growth rate of

19. See my "Urbanization and Sectoral Transformation in Latin America, 1950–65," in *Urbanización y proceso social en América* (Lima, Peru: Instituto de Estudios Peruanos, 1972), table 1, pp. 295–98.

Table 7.3. Indices of Total Agricultural Production and Capital Inputs
and Their Annual Rates of Increase, 1933–55

Agricultural production

Period (1)	Crops (2)	Wine (3)	Livestock (4)	Total (5)
A. Indices of production (1933–37 = 100)				
1933–37	100.0	100.0	100.0	100.0
1943–47	108.7	94.7	124.9	114.2
1953–55	121.7	115.5	142.2	130.1
B. Annual rates of increase or decrease *(In percentages)*				
1928–32 to 1933–37	2.4	1.0	0.8	1.5
1933–37 to 1943–47	0.8	−0.6	2.3	1.3
1943–47 to 1953–55	1.3	2.2	1.4	1.5

Agricultural capital inputs

Period (1)	Land (2)	Vineyards (3)	Livestock (4)	Machinery and equipment (5)
A. Indices of capital inputs in agriculture (1933–37 = 100)				
1933–37	100.0	100.0	100.0	100.0
1943–47	98.7	104.1	106.1	83.2
1953–55	102.4	112.2	114.8	169.7
B. Annual rates of increase or decrease *(In percentages)*				
1928–32 to 1933–37	3.3	2.0	1.5	−2.6
1933–37 to 1943–47	−0.1	0.4	0.6	−1.7
1943–47 to 1953– 55	0.4	0.8	0.9	6.9

Source: Marto Ballesteros, "Desarrollo Agrícola Chileno, 1910–1955," *Cuadernos de Economía* 2, no. 5 (Jan.–Apr. 1955): 13, 21.

agricultural output, which was close to 3.0 percent during 1910–32, fell sharply to 1.5 percent during most of the 1930–55 period. Agricultural production increased by an astonishing 21 percent between 1955 and 1956 and by almost 40 percent between 1955 and 1963.[20] The growth rate of gross agricultural product was 2.6 between 1960 and 1969, slightly surpassing the rate of population growth.[21]

These figures conceal the true dimensions of an always impending food crisis. While industrial agricultural products, primarily oil and fibers, increased remarkably from a base of 100 in 1939 to 570 in 1964[22] (often at a high social cost[23]) and production of fruits and vegetables grew substantially, output of cereals and root products hardly kept up with internal demand. The performance in animal production was highly uneven; there was a significant expansion in poultry and dairy products but a dismal growth in internal "meat," that is, livestock supply. Although domestic agricultural output rose at an average yearly rate of 2.2 between 1940 and 1973, demand increased by approximately 4.0 percent (2.5 percent due to population and 1.5 percent due to income growth). The gap between internal demand and supply was filled by imports as the mining export sector, foreign credits, United States aid, and the P.L. 480 program (under which the United States donated surplus food) were increasingly called upon to act as quasi-agricultural sectors and indirectly perform the food producing function. Chile's trade deficit in food, water, and forestry products rose from $45.6 million in 1956 (9 percent of nonagricultural exports), to $110.6 million in 1963 (22.2 percent of nonagricultural exports), to $110.9 million in 1965 (17.3 percent of nonagricultural exports).[24] Food imports had climbed to approximately $300 million in 1972 (more than 30 percent of nonagricultural exports) and were expected, according to one estimate, to exceed $500 million in 1973.[25] Whatever gains in economic independence that Chile seemed to achieve through industrial growth and import substitution it lost through agricultural import desubstitution. The low-income share and relative productivity, shown

20. See my "Historical Statistics," table IIBla2, p. A-217.
21. See ODEPLAN, *Antecedentes, 1960–70*, p. 2.
22. "Historical Statistics," table IIBlal.
23. In a study by Ernesto Fontaine it was demonstrated that Chile was suffering a net loss in its sugar beet production due to gross inefficiency and a misallocation of resources. See Ernesto R. Fontaine, "La Industria de la Azúcar de Remolacha en Chile. Un Análisis de Costos y Beneficios," *Cuadernos de Economía*, Año 3, Jan.–Apr. 1966, no. 8, pp. 9–81.
24. Calculated from or found in information of Banco Central de Chile, *Boletín Mensual*, no. 462, Aug. 1966, p. 1291.
25. See Alberto Valdés E. and Rodrigo Mujica A., *Producción e Importaciónes Agropecuarias en 1973* (Santiago: Universidad Católica de Chile, 1973), p. 31.

in table 7.2, suggest that the capacity of agriculture to supply an investable resource surplus or to provide a market for industrial products was very limited. Agriculture earned less than one-tenth of total income in 1970 but had to support a rural population that was almost one-third of the total.

The 1940–73 pattern was one of rapidly rising internal demand for food, slowly rising internal food supply, and an increasing share of food needs satisfied through imports. The competitive model, in which industrial service growth would pull agriculture through expansions in demand and prices, was inoperative. In its place developed a perverse model, in which rising nonagricultural growth led to stagnation of agriculture and greater food import deficits. One group of specialist scholars blames chiefly the status-seeking rather than output-raising behavior of the landowners for the crisis, whereas another finds profits too low and risk and uncertainty too high. My attempt to explain it will examine the behavior of inputs.

THE POST-1930 LABOR INPUTS

Agricultural labor force statistics, which are subject to a significant margin of error, show a remarkable stability between 1940 and 1970. The labor force of 655,000 was the same in 1940 and 1970.[26] In agriculture proper, the labor force reached a high of 715,000 in 1967 before declining sharply to only 607,000 in 1970. The labor force in forestry and hunting increased from 25,400 in 1963 to 28,000 in 1970, while that in fishing increased from 17,000 in 1963 to 19,500 in 1970. The mere behavior of labor inputs provides no base for expecting a growth in output.[27] Within the agricultural labor force 88 percent had received only five or fewer years of primary education in 1960, compared to an economy-wide average of 59.7 percent and France's economy-wide average (1954) of 6.7 percent.[28] Furthermore, there is no evidence of any significant, rapid, or revolutionary rise in the quality of the agricultural labor force, which was the least qualified of all sectors.

In addition, ample evidence suggests that the labor force was not

26. For the 1940 figures see my "Historical Statistics," p. A-160, and for the 1970 figure see ODEPLAN, *Población Ocupada por Sectores Económicos, 1960–1970* (Santiago: ODEPLAN, 1971), table 4. Hereafter cited as *Población Ocupada, 1960–1970*.

27. See ODEPLAN, *Población Ocupada, 1960–1970*, table 4.

28. See Agustín Alberti S. and Guillermo del Campo C., *El Desarrollo de los Recursos Humanos para la Industrialización en Chile* (Santiago: INCAP, 1966), Appendix, p. 13.

always productively employed. Agriculture has been exposed to open, seasonal, and disguised unemployment. Open unemployment, which in 1960 was only 3.0 percent and the lowest among all sectors,[29] was sui generis in that those openly unemployed would tend to drift to urban nonagricultural occupations. Between 1967 and 1970 the rate of open countrywide agricultural unemployment fluctuated between 1.1 and 2.0 percent.[30]

Seasonal unemployment has plagued all segments of agriculture. According to the 1964–65 census, 23 percent of the agricultural labor force worked less than six months, while as much as 15 percent worked less than three months.[31] Moreover, open seasonal unemployment varied with size and tenure system. According to the CIDA study, sponsored by the OAS (Organization of American States) under the Alliance for Progress, workers in subfamily units worked an average of only five months, those in family units seven, those in medium multifamily units eight, and those in the large multifamily farms nine months in a year.[32] In the livestock province of Magallanes 59 percent of the blue-collar workers who were engaged in sheep-raising, most of them migrants from Chiloé or urban areas, worked a maximum of six months at this activity. Although all seasonally unemployed livestock workers sought employment elsewhere, half of them (i.e., 30 percent of the total) remained completely unemployed during the rest of 1969.[33] Thus, although seasonal, agricultural blue-collar unemployment amounted to 60 percent, only 30 percent remained truly seasonally unemployed, that is, without any work during the rest of the year. It is possible that for all of Chile as much as 40 percent of the agricultural labor force is seasonally unemployed as much as six months during each year. Therefore, this is the most serious form of unemployment. During the seasonal harvest peaks, the shortage of labor may be as much as 20 percent of peak employment.

29. See ibid., Appendix, p. 5.

30. Instituto Nacional de Estadísticas, *Evolución de la Mano de Obra Chilena, Marzo 1967 a Diciembre 1970* (Santiago: Instituto Nacional de Estadísticas, 1971), p. 7.

31. Estimates are based on República de Chile, Dirección de Estadística y Censos, *IV Censo Nacional Agropecuario, Año Agrícola 1964–1965, Resumen del País* (Cifras-preliminares) (Santiago: Dirección de Estadística y Censos, 1966), tables 23–25, pp. 26–31.

32. CIDA (Comité Interamericano de Desarrollo Agrícola), *Chile, Tenencia de la Tierra y Desarrollo Socio-Económico del Sector Agrícola* (Santiago: CIDA, 1966), p. 152. Hereafter cited as *Tenencia de la Tierra.*

33. See Emilio Klein, *Mano de Obra Agrícola en Magallanes* (Magallanes: ICIRA/ ORPLAN, 1970), pp. 41–45.

Disguised unemployment in the Robinsonian sense (the forced movement of workers from high- to low-productivity sectors because of a decline in effective demand[34]) emerged between 1930 and 1940, when the agricultural labor force increased by 117,000, or 97,000 more than what the historical rate of increase would imply.[35] Although the quality of the 1940 census does not permit us to say with confidence that 80 percent of the labor force increment was disguised unemployment, it must have been positive and significant, declining slowly in subsequent decades.

The national accounts and labor force statistics for the 1940–70 period suggest either absence of or no increase in disguised unemployment in the Lewis–Ranis–Fei sense. The wage rate does not seem to exceed the marginal product, which must have generally increased if it followed the net value added per agricultural wage earner. This net value, in 1961 prices, rose from $E^o 814.3$ in 1940 to $E^o 1042.9$ in 1953 to $E^o 1085.8$ in 1957 before falling to $E^o 1009.8$ in 1964.[36] However, there is evidence of disguised unemployment in fishing, whose labor force quintupled between 1940 and 1964, while net real domestic product barely increased by 20 percent. During the post-1950 rush into fishing, the allegedly hidden sea gold mine, the facilities were grossly duplicated while fish retreated or disappeared, causing a worker (including employers) net productivity decline from $E^o 2480.0$ in 1940 to $E^o 547.4$ in 1964.[37]

However, according to CIDA, open and disguised agricultural unemployment in 1955 was 214,000, or more than one-third of an active labor force of 577,000.[38] The estimate, which assumed a non-seasonal agricultural production and a perfect intertemporal and interfarm labor force mobility, supplied at best an approximate measure of seasonal rather than disguised unemployment.

34. "It is natural to describe the adoption of inferior occupations by dismissed workers as *disguised unemployment*" [Joan Robinson, *Essays in the Theory of Employment* (Oxford: Basil Blackwell, 1947), p. 62].

35. See Marto Ballesteros, "Desarrollo Agrícola Chileno, 1910–1955," *Cuadernos de Economía*, p. 16, and Mamalakis, "Historical Statistics," table IIA2a6, pp. A-160–A-165. The maximum historical rate of labor force increase during 1930–40 was 20,000 if the 1940–65 pattern is considered. It would be less if we go up to 1970.

36. Calculated from information found in my "Historical Statistics," table IF3, pp. A-155–A-158 and table IIA2a6, pp. A-160–A-165. For the total agricultural labor force, i.e., including the salaried and self-employed, the average product increased continuously.

37. Calculated in the same fashion as agricultural average product.

38. See CIDA, *Tenencia de la Tierra*, pp. 27, 151–52.

Disguised unemployed labor appears to have been kept at a minimum as the structure of agriculture forced an exodus of surplus labor to the cities. Return was discouraged, and during harvest peaks migrant and urban recruits were heavily relied upon.

According to a study by Alberto Valdés in O'Higgins and Colchagua provinces, agricultural unemployment was quasi-Keynesian in the sense that the capital stock did not generate sufficient demand to absorb all labor and that institutional wages were not only high but also rigid downward. In part, the high level of wages resulted from a relatively inelastic supply of labor.[39]

The qualitative labor–land relationship stands out as a major growth obstacle. At least 50 percent of the agricultural labor force during 1950–60—the blue-collar workers—was not attached to land but to the landlord, who could be an individual, the church, the military, a corporation, or the new super-patrón, the state. The complex and permanent attachment to land existed among the self-employed owners of medium-sized farms, who may have comprised at best only 15 percent of the labor force.[40] Many of the approximately 10,000 landowner-employers, possibly the majority, were attached to the estate, the fundo, not to the land. Their precipitous expulsion during 1970–73 left a vacuum of leadership that was not filled at a satisfactory speed because of the upheaval and repeated changes brought about by further seizures, expulsion of new owners, and title, social, legal, and political uncertainty. The shaking of the foundations of rural and agricultural areas may have been so bloodless and complete partly because for many landowners it meant simply a loss of capital, not of an irreplaceable land-based mode of life and a land creating a unique flow of utility.

There is barely any evidence as yet that the sweeping and irreversible land ownership changes of the 1966–73 period are shaping a new labor–land relationship that can extract from Chile's fertile fields the food its population so desperately needs. Unless the government not only acts as a guardian in establishing cooperatives, providing extension facilities, hospitals, schools, credits, and so forth but also develops a workable incentive system, Chile may remain confused by a state and/or

39. See Alberto Valdés E., "Costos, Ingresos y Diferenciales de Salarios en Dos Provincias Agrícolas," *Cuadernos de Economía*, Dec. 1967, no. 13, pp. 1–30.

40. Between 1960 and 1970 the self-employed farmers made up approximately 25 percent of the agricultural labor force, but they were predominantly minifundistas. See ODEPLAN, *Población Ocupada, 1960–1970*, table 4.

private ownership combination grossly alien to its idiosyncratic, polymorphic, rural setting and its uniquely productive man–land relationship.

INVESTMENT, PROFIT MAXIMIZATION, AND SUPPLY ELASTICITIES

The obvious inability of human-paced agricultural growth to satisfy a rapidly rising demand for food did not preclude the successful generation of an agricultural food surplus for cities and exports through a yield-increasing investment program. Such a program could conceivably have turned the capital–land relationship into the pivotal link between land and the new capital- and technology-paced food production. In reality, however, the rate of increase of output per unit of input fell to -0.2 during the period between 1928–32 and 1933–37, to 0.5 percent between 1933–37 and 1943–47, and to 0.4 percent during 1943–47 to 1953–55. The post-1932 reduction in productivity gains, which reflected in part the reduced importation of technical progress from the United States to Chilean agriculture, compared very unfavorably with the respectable pre-1932 cumulative annual rate of increase in output per unit of input of 1.4 percent from 1910–12 to 1918–22 and 1.6 percent from 1918–22 to 1928–32.[41]

The problem here is the relationship among investment, incentives, and agricultural supply elasticities. There is ample evidence that Chilean farmers have been acutely sensitive to market signals and incentives affecting production of individual products.[42] Production of sugar beets, sunflower, wheat, milk, broilers, and numerous other products has changed significantly and often, but not always swiftly, as changes in *product incentives* led to product substitution in acreage cultivated

---

41. See Marto Ballesteros, "Desarrollo Agrícola Chileno, 1910–1955," *Cuadernos de Economía*, Jan.–Apr. 1965, no. 5, table 14, p. 22, 25–26. The rate of productivity increase in agriculture in the United States was below Chile's before 1937 but substantially above the maximum gain experienced by Chile after 1937.

42. See on this point the evidence presented by M. Mamalakis, "Agriculture: The Neglected Sector" (chap. 3 of "Public Policy and Sectoral Development: A Case Study of Chile"), in M. Mamalakis and C. Reynolds, *Essays on The Chilean Economy* (Homewood, Ill.: Richard D. Irwin, 1965), pp. 117–48. Hereafter my study will be cited as "Public Policy"; James O. Bray, "Demand, and the Supply of Food in Chile," *Journal of Farm Economics* 44, no. 4 (1962): 1005–20; Jeannine Swift, *Agrarian Reform in Chile* (Lexington, Mass.: D. C. Heath, 1971), pp. 23–32. Swift, who distinguishes clearly between individual product and total agricultural supply curve elasticities, argues that "the long-run price elasticity for area of wheat with respect to the expected price of wheat is strong, but that the time needed for the actual area planted to reach the desired area is rather long" (ibid. p. 28).

and to highly elastic supply curves for the individual products. Although this evidence refutes the hypothesis that Chilean farmers are unresponsive to market signals and incentives because of the tenure system,[43] it sheds little light on the major issue of investment responsiveness to *production incentives* that determine the aggregate supply elasticity of farm products. The incentives, which affect only one or a few commodities, can stimulate a prompt operational response with or without only minimal investment. Thus they differ from the "production" incentives, which require major yield-raising investments, willingness to undertake greater risks, availability of capital goods, and so forth before they can elicit a significant augmentation in output.

However, the data concerning the aggregate agricultural supply curve are less definite. In his excellent econometric study Jere Behrman found that agriculture was "responding to long run product and factor market conditions in profit maximizing ways, especially in comparison to the other Chilean sectors."[44] Although this-evidence clearly contradicts the structuralist premise that the domestic food supply curve is totally inelastic and that landowners are prestige- rather than profit-maximizers[45] and confirms the earlier findings by Bray and myself,[46] it does not adequately explain the widening gap between domestic demand and supply and the apparently different supply elasticities for livestock and nonlivestock farm products.

Even if we assume that investment determines the long-term supply elasticity, the 1930–73 statistical evidence of what went wrong is not clear cut. Investment incentives did indeed fall after 1930, and during 1940–55 in particular, as output prices were controlled—in part through subsidized imports—and those of inputs raised. However, the domestic per capita production of principal crops, generally increased from 1940 to 1959, with the exception of 1950–52, because of

43. See CIDA, *Tenencia de la Tierra*, pp. v–vi. The CIDA report is an excellent polemic document in which the reader will find a list and summary of the writings of all those who share the view that the land tenure system is responsible for practically all ills plaguing either Chile or Latin America.

44. See Jere R. Behrman, "Aggregative Market Responses in Developing Agriculture: The Postwar Chilean Experience," Discussion Paper no. 165, Department of Economics (Philadelphia: University of Pennsylvania, 1970), p. 12.

45. The literature concerning the structuralist argument of an inelastic agriculture supply curve is reviewed by Jere Behrman, ibid., p. 1, and Mamalakis, "Public Policy," pp. 120–21,198.

46. Both these authors have presented statistical evidence in support of the hypothesis of an elastic aggregate supply curve.

an aggressive government policy designed to increase output through such measures as freight subsidies on agricultural products from distant provinces, subsidized credits to farmers, subsidized fertilizer as well as duty-free imports of agricultural machinery, and marked progress in the completion of the Pan American Highway. The significant and delayed output rise between 1955 and 1964 occurred in spite of falling crop prices from an index level of 125 in 1952 to 76 in 1959.[47]

The picture changes when one considers livestock production, in which the rate of return and actual investment certainly matter more. Output languished between 1930, when already low prices deteriorated even further, and 1952. In spite of continued subsidized credits and technical and other assistance by CORFO, expansion was stifled by the offsetting impact of subsidized Argentine cattle imports, inefficiency and monopoly power in distribution and slaughtering, and inflation-related risk and uncertainty. Poultry and pig production, which ample incentives and investment made superbly machine regulable boomed and cattle output recovered during 1955–70.[48] Meat supplies definitely increased in 1971 but decreased in 1972 as an unprecedented meat crisis developed because of the demand effect induced by redistribution policies. In a pattern somewhat reminiscent of the 1945–50 years, when war-accumulated reserves financed a buying spree of imported meat, slaughtering of imported cattle climbed by 52 percent during January–October 1972 while that of national cattle fell by 35 percent during the same period.[49]

The inadequate responsiveness of the livestock subsector is related to the long gestation period of the required investments and the growing risk and uncertainty associated with post-1930 social, political, and economic developments. Potential and actual land reform, which after 1960 absorbed an increasing amount of government investment resources, had a debilitating effect.

INSTITUTION-CHANGING INVESTMENTS

Political, social, and economic pressures for changes in the land ownership patterns increased almost exponentially between 1930 and 1972. The promulgation of the 1925 constitution, which severely restricted

47. See Bray, "Demand, and the Supply of Food in Chile."
48. See Mamalakis, "Public Policy," pp. 123–30.
49. See Valdés and Mujica, *Producción e Importaciónes Agropecuarias en 1973*, p. 40

private ownership rights, permitted the formation in 1928 of the self-financing Caja de Colonización Agrícola (Agricultural Colonization Bank). This institution had as its goal the subdivision of large estates, but it lacked the power to expropriate property. The great majority of the bank's land purchases and distributions—often to persons with no agricultural experience or training—occurred before 1940 during Arturo Alessandri's presidency. After 1940, as inflation wiped out the bank's assets and government emphasized import-substituting industrialization, its activities came to a standstill. Approximately 1 percent of Chile's families in agriculture in 1960 had received from the *Caja* parcels (i.e., family-sized economic units) or *lotes* (larger units that, for technical reasons, were not subdivided).

Because the farms in most new colonies were too large to be handled by one family, most of the *colonos* (settlers) became administrators who hired labor, much of it resident, to work their farms. Major changes were introduced after 1960, beginning in the latter part of Jorge Alessandri's presidency.

In 1960, as increased output and improved living conditions of agricultural workers became the central objectives of land reform, the *huerto*, which was equivalent to a house and a garden plot, was introduced and granted to the resident laborers who had often been bypassed previously. The *Caja* was changed in 1962 to the Agrarian Reform Corporation (CORA) and given limited power to expropriate private property.[50] Voluntary land reform was introduced by the Catholic Church on its holdings, which were meager because expulsion of the Jesuits in 1767, confiscation of church land by Freire in 1824, and persistent anticlericalism held church power in check. This reform led to extraordinary income and consumption for the new owners and generally increased the labor-absorption capacity of land.[51] The momentum of land reform entered a period of controlled acceleration during the 1964–70 rule of the Christian Democrats. A new land use form, the *asentamiento*, involving transitory cooperative ownership of an expropriated estate until final transfer of the land to its workers, was introduced.

50. A detailed examination of the direct land redistribution programs during 1929–64 is found in CIDA, *Tenencia de la Tierra*, pp. 248–67; for the early land reform programs under Frei see Swift, *Agrarian Reform in Chile*, pp. 36–71.

51. See the very interesting study by William C. Thiesenhusen, *Chile's Experiments in Agrarian Reform* (Madison: University of Wisconsin Press, 1966), pp. 56–172, and for summaries, pp. 108–10, 136–37, 169–72.

During President Frei's first-year pursuit of "Revolution in Freedom," more latifundios were expropriated than in the previous twenty years, the minimum agricultural wage was given parity with the industrial, the family allowance to farmers was doubled, and 44,000 small landowners received supervised agricultural credit, compared to only 12,000 the year before.[52]

Direct redistribution of land reached a crescendo with the election of Salvador Allende, who had as his goal complete and irreversible eradication of the large private estates and the mode of life of latifundismo. From assuming office until April 25, 1972, the Popular Unity coalition government expropriated 2,678 farms covering 4.25 million hectares.[53] In 1971 the Marxist coalition introduced two new forms of land exploitation, the Centers of Production (*Centros de Producción*) and the Centers of Agrarian Reform (CERA).

The production centers, a total of 18 with 141,000 hectares established in 1971, were strictly state enterprises. They were introduced either because the expropriated farms were true agricultural businesses with modern technology—breeding farms, model dairies, or ranches of fine cattle—or because the farmers "in response to their high social conscience and in the national interest" requested it.[54]

Although the CERA were not explicitly state owned they were heavily modeled along the lines of the Soviet bloc communes. They aimed at maximum production, establishment of the Internal Investment and Communal Development Fund, incorporation of all men and women above age 16 into the labor force, and elimination of unemployment. These giant corporations, created by reallocating and concentrating the hitherto dispersed workers, were served by polyclinics, schools, social security, cultural and entertainment projects, and capital goods. The corporations hoped to release and then harness Chile's abundant land riches by establishing a multifaceted labor–capital–land–output relationship through maximum, large-scale education, welfare, capital investment, and concentration of farmers.[55]

---

52. See *Un Programa en Marcha*, an 8-page pamphlet distributed by the Christian Democrats in 1966. No date, no publisher.

53. S. Allende, *Mensaje del Presidente Allende ante el Congreso Pleno, 21 de Mayo de 1972* (Santiago: Presidencia de la República, 1972), p. 277. Hereafter cited as *Mensaje 1972*.

54. Allende, ibid., p. 230.

55. See ibid., pp. 227–29.

Although 25 CERAs were formed in 1971—with an average of 2,500 hectares and 40 families each—past experience shows that unless strong incentives (rewards as well as penalties) are introduced, the CERAs may degenerate into inefficient, technologically backward, and resource-deficit state or cooperatively owned super-latifundia.[56] The short-term 1970–73 picture is admittedly bleak. The growing gap between increasing food demand and rigid or falling domestic supply (it partially recovered in 1974), which was filled in part by imports and also fostered black markets, rampant inflation, and shortages, was so large that it could not be corrected through internal production rises. Whereas supply increases were conceivably the major necessary step in reaching equilibrium before 1970, the post-1970–73 correction will necessarily have to come primarily through a painful downward adjustment of the grossly inflated demand.

President Allende's Popular Unity did indeed initiate an integrated process of rural development and used drastic changes in the land tenure system and in the resource control of income distribution, commercialization, and credit to provide real support "to the struggle of rural workers for a new economic, political and social organization of our agriculture."[57] However, mechanization, fertilizers, and credit facilities have existed without interruption at least since President Aguirre Cerda.[58] During 1971–73, however, agricultural machinery was imported from Rumania, the Soviet Union, and Czechoslovakia rather than from the West.[59] Direct redistribution of land under Frei experienced far less anxiety but only modest success.

A barrier apparently common to Chile's agricultural development and aggregate supply elasticity derives in part from the issue of the sector's "fair" income share and in part from the priority given to agricultural policy and investment within an increasingly tight national

56. Ibid., p. 229.

57. Ibid., p. 223.

58. Mechanization of agriculture was as popular in the late 1940s and 1950s as electrification and industrialization. The efforts of CORFO and other organizations raised tractor imports from 3,787 during 1945–49 to 8,641 during 1950–54 and the total stock from 14,200 in 1955 to 22,300 in 1964–65. Imports of threshing machines, harvesters, mowers, bale packers, and so forth also went up. See Dirección de Estadística y Censos, *III Censo Nacional Agrícola Ganadero*, vol. 1, *Resumen General del País* (Santiago: Dirección de Estadística y Censos, 1960), table 89, p. 123, and my "Historical Statistics," table IIB4b3, p. A-305a.

59. Allende, *Mensaje 1972*, p. 247.

budget constraint. Unless agriculture is given the highest priority, its admittedly low income share [60] will not increase to a level that permits, through greater consumption and yield-raising investment, an adequate performance of the food-producing function and a positive aggregate rather than product supply response. Although the share of agriculture in domestic income rose from 7.2 percent in 1970 to 8.4 percent in 1971,[61] such a priority was unlikely even under Allende because of the pressures from mining and the urban sectors. I find it difficult to comprehend why Allende, who was so conscious of the welfare of the people, the poor, and workers, pointedly declared the preeminence and governmental support of six social freedoms— employment, health, culture (education), shelter, social security, and recreation[62]—but failed to mention the primordial social freedom for food and drink. All governments, and Chilean society in general since independence, have been heavily but not exclusively agriculturally based, though never agriculturally oriented. Thus, the Popular Unity government may have been the first that was not even agriculturally based. The post-September 1973 military junta has adopted a positive price policy for agriculture.

The perennial flight of the declining agricultural surplus capital to the cities and abroad, which turned into a stampede when the 1970–73 opening of the revolutionary floodgates of land reform caused most assets capable of liquidation to be removed or sold, has been stopped. But this halt does not provide a solution. Habitual neglect has left the sector with such a low endowment of physical, human, and institutional capital that either an unlikely technological miracle or a significant influx of resources from mining, industry, and services will be needed to restore the balance required for accelerated growth.[63]

The lessons from Chile's agricultural failure—admittedly relative rather than absolute—are simple. The assignment of an inferior role of neglect, penalty, and investment starvation to agriculture is as erroneous as the view that industrial growth (i.e., satisfaction of industrial needs) is sufficient for accelerated growth. The basic human needs

60. Allende, *Mensaje 1972*, p. 223.
61. See ODEPLAN, *Distribución del Ingreso y Cuentas de Producción, 1960–1971* (Santiago: ODEPLAN, 1973), p. 25.
62. Allende, *Mensaje 1972*, p. xviii.
63. The theme that agriculture was a sector neglected by the government is central to my sectoral clashes framework, see Mamalakis, "Chapter 3, Agriculture: The Neglected Sector," pp. 117–48.

for food as well as those for clean air and water and an open and free environment can be neither replaced nor bypassed by other needs. Furthermore, although such quasi-agricultural sectors as copper, iron, industrial exports, foreign aid, and credits can supplement domestic agricultural supplies, permanent replacement of agriculture by them would constitute an excessively dangerous dependence. Although a fair agricultural income share may be a necessary condition for growth, a continued accumulation of human, institutional, and physical capital with flexible incentive mechanisms must also be present.

8

The Industrial Physiognomy

Industry, which was small, rudimentary, and noncapitalistic in 1840, had by 1973 become large and highly diversified. Its major components were modern, efficient, and capital intensive. Manufacturing grew significantly and almost without interruption throughout 1840–1973, partly at the expense of the artisan segment.[1] Whereas industrial growth was dominated by foreign and immigrant entrepreneurs until 1940, the role of the state as owner and manager increased markedly after 1939 and became supreme during 1970–73. Clustered in the urban centers of Santiago, Valparaíso, and Concepción, industry emerged as a producer of consumer and intermediate goods. Machinery and equipment production remained limited.

Industry, heralded as the primum mobile of self-sustained growth and the base of military might and international recognition, was considered the last-resort sector for development-hungry Chile. Expected to become a principal source of technical progress and modernization and the equalizer of income distribution, it was also viewed, through its profits and capital goods production, as a catalyst in the saving and capital accumulation process.[2] Chileans had high hopes for industry. Many of them were fulfilled, but not all.

THE ARTISAN BEGINNINGS

Artisan shops, primarily in the lines of textiles, baking, shoes and

1. Industry is composed of manufacturing, which includes industrial establishments employing five or more persons, and artisan production, with four or fewer persons.
2. The importance assigned to industry in the various theories of economic development is carefully examined in the excellent piece by Howard S. Ellis, *The Applicability of Certain Theories of Economic Development to Brazil* (Milwaukee: Center for Latin America Studies, University of Wisconsin, 1968).

leather, wine distilling, construction materials, armaments, and others, existed in 1840. Most of them elaborated agricultural, forestry, and mineral raw materials with the assistance of very rudimentary tools. Household production was also common. Almost all the large haciendas were partially self-sufficient units; the farmers and their wives produced cloth, primitive instruments, and construction materials and processed food and drink.[3] The small and fragmented urban markets led to noncapitalistic, diversified, and often luxury-oriented production.

Industrial expansion between 1840 and 1930 displaced some artisan production. At the beginning cheap imported textiles wiped out much of the traditional rural production. When domestic manufacturing was subsequently established, it destroyed many of the small-scale urban artisans. According to the first industrial census of 1927, 155,000 persons, or 67 percent of the total industry labor force of 230,000, were employed in establishments with four or fewer persons.[4]

Employment in handicraft industries as a percentage of total industrial employment declined sharply from 70.7 percent in 1925 to 46 percent in 1960. Nevertheless, artisan production remained indisputably strong, and employment, which had declined precipitously during the 1930s, recovered almost all its losses in the 1950s and had reached 207,000 in 1960.[5] As late as 1957 almost half of industrial employment and 8 percent of total labor was in the 70,000 small establishments. Clothing and shoes accounted for more than 40 percent of artisan employment and income. In the mechanical industries—metallic products, transport material, electrical equipment, and other machinery—artisan exceeded manufacturing employment.[6] Artisan employment, which according to a broader CORFO definition included establishments with 0–9 persons, had fallen by 1968 to 180,000, or 34.2 percent

3. See Oscar Alvarez Andrews, *Historia del Desarrollo Industrial de Chile* (Santiago: Imprenta y Litografía La Ilustración, 1936), pp. 92–97.
4. The artisan employment estimate was made by deducting manufacturing employment in 1927, given in O. Muñoz G., *Crecimiento Industrial de Chile, 1914–1965* (Santiago: Instituto de Economía y Planificación, 1968), p. 173 (hereafter cited as *Crecimiento*, from the total industrial labor force given by Max Nolff, "Industria Manufacturera," in CORFO, *Geografía Económica de Chile*, condensed text (Santiago: CORFO, 1965), p. 511. Hereafter cited as "Industria."
5. UN Economic and Social Council, *The Process of Industrialization in Latin America,* Statistical Annex (Santiago: UN, ST/ECLA/Conf. 23/L.2, 19 Jan. 1966), tables I-16–I-18, 16–18.
6. Nolff, "Industria," p. 525.

of the industrial labor force. It was heavily concentrated in clothing, shoes, construction of transport material, and food.[7]

Inflation, insulation from foreign competition, easy entry, ample labor supply, the high demand for custom-made goods, and other factors explain the abundance of artisan shops in the 1960s. They catered to the tastes of the Chilean population. The demand for tailored rather than ready-made clothing, for example, coupled with the relative scarcity of capital and abundance of labor, led to the proliferation of repair shops for shoes, clothing, and consumer durables. These shops made a major employment contribution, but their income growth potential was limited because they served small, fragmented markets and used productivity-raising inputs, such as electricity and capital goods, sparingly. The outstanding weaknesses of the artisan sector were its almost total lack of export orientation, its low capitalization (it possessed less than 15 percent of the industrial capital stock in 1957[8]), and its inability to enter, with the exception of the mechanical group, into such modern areas as electronics, transistors, and radios.

THE RISE OF MANUFACTURING

Large-scale manufacturing production making maximum use of labor division and specialization, capital equipment, and energy was almost nonexistent in 1840 but developed rapidly. Its first major boom occurred during the decade of Manuel Montt's term (1850–1860), which saw the acceleration of economic development that divides "colonial" from "modern" Chile. As railroad construction began, commercial and mortgage banks were opened, the Civil Code and important legislation were promulgated, new foreign agricultural markets were found, and investment rose significantly.

Manufacturing expanded around Santiago, Valparaíso, and Concepción. Santiago was dominant, though Concepción almost as early developed manufacturing based on agriculture, forestry, and mining. Development of the coal mines of Lota in 1837, of Lirquén in 1843,

7. See vol. 2, pp. 67–70 of the highly informative analysis of past industrial growth and future strategies by CORFO, *Estrategia Industrial*, vol. 1, *Bases de Una Estrategia de Desarrollo Industrial para la Década del 70* (Santiago: CORFO, 1970); vol. 2, *Políticas Específicas Comunes A Todo el Sector Industrial* (Santiago: CORFO, 1970); vol. 3, *Políticas de Desarrollo Industrial por Areas de Actividad* (Santiago: CORFO, 1970). Hereafter cited as *Estrategia Industrial* with appropriate volume number.

8. Nolff, "Industria," p. 527.

and Schwager in 1874 gave birth to a manufacturing nucleus of glass factories, clay product plants, a copper smelter, and a foundry in the area during the 1860s.[9] By 1930 the region contained the leading or one of the leading national suppliers of cotton and woolen textiles, ceramics, refined sugar, and glass as well as fish- and whale-processing plants.

CORFO's post-1940 industrialization plans, which envisaged Concepción as Chile's Ruhr Valley, established the pivotal Pacific Steel Company in 1950. The company's Huachipato iron and steel complex led to extensive horizontal and vertical integration, and peripheral industries sprang up in steel wires, ferrous alloys, zinc and tin recovery plans, electrical equipment, and tools and machinery. By 1950 the Concepción area had been transformed into "one of the most significant and dynamic centers of manufacturing in Latin America."[10] It accounted for more than 50 percent of the national value of basic metals production and contained 37.7 percent of the nation's investment in plant and equipment, although it possessed only 4.6 percent of the industrial establishments.[11] The high capital intensity of this heavy industry reduced its labor absorption capacity, with the result that Concepción employed only 9.2 percent of the industrial labor force in 1960.[12] Some severe constraints have also been present. The region's coal resources are average to poor and, because they are primarily under the sea and in narrow veins, mining involves increasing costs. Even iron ore has to be transported from northern Chile. By 1973 this metallurgical complex had come under state or mixed ownership and was expected to provide iron, steel, and machinery not only for Chile's road to socialism but also for exports to other Latin American nations. In addition it would permit improvement, expansion, and rationalization in the production of white-line consumer durables (refrigerators, stoves, and so forth) and in shipyards and engineering firms.[13]

9. For a detailed description of manufacturing in Concepción up to 1958 and analysis of its growth potential see Joseph H. Butler, "Manufacturing in the Concepción Region of Chile, Present Position and Prospects for Future Development" (Washington, D.C.: National Academy of Sciences–National Research Council, 1960), typewritten copy of Office of Naval Research, Report no. 1.

10. Ibid., p. 10.

11. Ibid., p. 46.

12. See M. Mamalakis, "Historical Statistics of Chile, 1840–1965," mimeo, table II C3b6, pp. A-435–A-436.

13. CORFO, "La Política Industrial," in *El Pensamiento Económico del Gobierno de*

However, Santiago remained the industrial and manufacturing giant of Chile. It employed 52.3 percent of the industrial labor force and contributed 48.5 percent of gross value added in 1960. If the neighboring port province of Valparaíso is added, these figures become, respectively, 62.2 and 66.4 percent. The provinces outside the three industrial nuclei had a declining labor force (from 31.9 percent in 1952 to 28.7 percent in 1960) and gross income share (from 22.9 percent in 1952 to 20.8 percent in 1960).[14] Santiago was endowed with the markets, the government bureaucracy, the educational institutions, and the social, cultural, and intellectual attractions. The regional and metropolitan concentration in Central Chile was caused by and in part explains its distinct lack of export orientation. It also explains the general lack of integration between the mineral export and industrial sectors and their reliance on separate, expensive infrastructures.

AGRICULTURE-BASED MANUFACTURING

The introduction of new, imported, or domestic products and larger markets and the increased specialization within agriculture as well as in urban areas led to a decline of "in agriculture" industrial activities and a rise of industry proper. The major early beneficiaries were agriculture-based handicraft and manufacturing, industries that transform raw agricultural, forestry, and fishing food and materials into intermediate products or final consumer goods. This segment is defined here to include the categories of food, beverages, tobacco, wood, paper, and leather. The unusual combination of extremely favorable flour and wheat export prices and demand (strong stimuli originated primarily from external trade), abundant land and wheat production, and easy access to modern plants and technology brought on the unique spurt of agriculture-based manufacturing during 1840–60.

The spectacular but short-lived flour export boom of 1840–60 led to the development of large, modern, mechanized mills. (The Unión mill, built by Juan Antonio Pando in 1847, was the largest in South America.) Capital intensive, efficient, and benefiting from economies of large-scale production, they slowly replaced many of the small

---

Allende, ed. Gonzalo Martner (Santiago: Editorial Universitaria, 1971), pp. 121–24. Hereafter cited as *Pensamiento de Allende*. Salvador Allende, *Mensaje del Presidente Allende ante el Congreso Pleno, 21 de Mayo de 1972* (Santiago: Presidencia de la República, 1972), pp. 369–72.

14. See my "Historical Statistics," pp. A-435–A-436.

inefficient mills usually located on the estates or in provincial towns. As a consequence, whereas there were 1,271 mills in 1843 and 1,484 in 1858, apparently only 519 remained in all of Chile in 1882.[15] The marketing system and the capital that enabled this new flour-milling industry to flourish were supplied by the merchant houses of Valparaíso.

The drop in flour exports after 1860, the rise of Santiago as an organized banking and credit center and urban market, and the pattern of the railroads led to the decline of Talca and Tomé and a gradual concentration of the milling industry in the capital city. The agriculture-industry interactions were fragmented and unequal. Although the milling industry boomed by exploiting agriculture's forward linkages, investment opportunities in numerous related lines remained unexploited. Thus, there was complete or heavy dependence on imports; almost all sacks and equipment were imported.[16] The outward flow of goods from agriculture was rarely matched by an offsetting inward flow of industrial and construction goods and services. The agricultural surplus was largely transferred to the cities, and cash wages and salaries provided a relatively small market for industrial goods, many of which were imported.

Until 1930 agricultural-based manufacturing was quantitatively the most important segment. As late as 1938, as can be seen from table 8.1, it generated more than 60 percent of total manufacturing income and employed 46.7 percent of manufacturing's labor force.[17] By 1970 agriculture-based artisan and manufacturing employment had fallen to 30 percent of the industrial labor force, even though it had increased in absolute numbers to 170,000.[18]

15. See Arnold Bauer, "Chilean Rural Society in the Nineteenth Century" (Ph.D. diss. University of California, Berkeley, 1969), pp. 105, 106, 113.

16. Ibid., pp. 112, 109.

17. The most detailed examination of the various branches and overall manufacturing income, employment, and long-term trends is found in Oscar E. Muñoz, "Long-Run Trends in the Manufacturing Industry in Chile Since 1914" (Ph.D. thesis, Yale University, 1967). Hereafter cited as "Long-Run Trends." An abbreviated version of this thesis appeared as Muñoz, "An Essay on the Process of Industrialization in Chile since 1914," *Yale Economic Essays* 8, no. 2 (1968): 137–84. Hereafter cited as "An Essay on Industrialization." Finally, an extended version with a chapter on the determinants of productivity changes in manufacturing appeared in Spanish as Muñoz, *Crecimiento.* Since this study omits the artisan segment, the reader is warned not to apply indiscriminately all its findings to industry as a whole.

18. See ODEPLAN, *Población Ocupada por Sectores Económicos, 1960–1970* (Santiago: ODEPLAN, 1971), table 6k. Hereafter cited as *Población Ocupada, 1960–1970.*

Table 8.1. Sectoral Gross Income Shares in Agriculture- and
Mining-based and Autonomous Manufacturing
(In percentages and Current Prices)

	Income			*Employment*		
	1915	*1938*	*1961*	*1915*	*1938*	*1961*
A. Agriculture based						
1. Food	31.9	30.4	16.8	21.5	20.0	16.6
2. Beverages	6.2	6.3	5.7	5.5	3.5	3.0
3. Tobacco	7.4	5.8	4.0	4.5	2.0	0.6
4. Wood	5.3	5.4	3.5	8.8	8.3	7.1
5. Paper	7.7	8.4	7.7	7.2	8.6	4.7
6. Leather	6.1	3.9	3.5	5.5	4.3	3.0
Total	64.6	60.2	41.2	53.0	46.7	35.0
B. Mining based						
7. Nonmetallic products	2.2	5.7	6.8	4.3	8.8	5.6
C. Autonomous						
8. Textiles	2.9	12.1	11.6	4.8	16.3	18.2
9. Clothing	16.9	5.6	5.6	23.2	11.4	10.7
10. Chemicals	5.7	8.4	11.8	5.3	5.1	5.7
11. Metallic	7.7	8.0	23.0	9.4	11.7	24.8
Total	33.2	34.1	52.0	42.7	44.5	59.4
Grand Total	100.0	100.0	100.0	100.0	100.0	100.0

Source: All basic data are found in Oscar E. Muñoz, "Long-run Trends in the Manufacturing Industry in Chile since 1914" (Ph.D. diss., Yale University, 1967), table 3.1,
p. 60; table 3.3, p. 65.

At least in part, its diminishing relative significance has been caused
by an inadequate performance in satisfying existing needs rather than
by declining or inelastic market demand. Its food component has been
unable to meet either the internal or external demand: export demand
for raw or processed Chilean fruit, seafood, oils, wine, and so forth is
almost unlimited. Although industrial food exports almost quadrupled
between 1960 and 1969—$7.5 million to $29.1 million—more than
80 percent of the increment is accounted for by fish meal, with the
remainder contributed by seafood exports. In the nonfood categories
of tobacco and leather, exports and imports are negligible. In the
forestry-based categories of wood, paper, and cellulose, where international demand is also literally unlimited for reasonably priced
Chilean surpluses, exports more than quadrupled between 1960 and
1969—to $34.5 million—surpassing the exports of food as well as of

semiprocessed iron and copper, which were highly volatile.[19] Although the base of this predominantly consumer goods sector is agriculture, and thus by inference traditional, its products, markets, technology, potential growth, and efficiency have not been and need by no means be stagnant, inefficient, or backward. The premature and inaccurate designation as traditional, and thus by inference not open to rapid growth, may have caused in part the relative deemphasis of this sector within Chilean industrial policy.[20]

Import substitution, which was a crucial growth determinant for some agriculture-based industry, was neither uniform nor the only force in operation. High import substitution in the pivotal categories of food, beverages, and tobacco products during 1914–38 was succeeded, as can be seen in table 8.2, by import desubstitution during 1937–72.[21] Similarly, import substitution for forestry-based wood products, the second highest for any subsector during 1914–27, diminished during 1927–53 and turned negative during 1952–64. In a distinct pattern the negative import substitution in paper, printing, leather, and rubber products before 1927 and during 1937–53 became positive and significant during 1927–38 and 1952–64. Although four of the six agriculture-based subsectors grew at less than 1 percent during 1960–69, paper and cellulose production—with an annual rate of increase of 22.8 percent) grew more quickly than any other industrial subsector.[22] Expansion of most agriculture-based manufacturing, although dependent on demand factors, faced its most critical problems on the supply side. A rapid uninterrupted growth could not materialize without previous or simultaneous expansion of the complementary and prerequisite agricultural production. When this did not occur, primarily because of the absence of an integrated agriculture–manufacturing policy, agriculture-based manufacturing was forced to gradually reduce its domestic agriculture base and to accept a socially onerous dependence on agricultural imports as well as less rapid growth.

Modernization, efficiency, and heavy capitalization did sweep

19. CORFO, *Datos Básicos Sector Industrial Manufacturero Período 1960–1968* (Santiago: CORFO, 1970), pp. 11–13.

20. The distinction between traditional and dynamic industrial subsectors, which is fraught with conceptual difficulties, is widely used in the literature. See Instituto de Economía, *La Economía de Chile en el Período 1950–1963* (Santiago: Instituto de Economía, 1963), vol. 1, pp. 110–12.

21. Alberto Valdés E. and Rodrigo Mujica A., *Producción e Importaciónes Agropecuarias en 1973* (Santiago: Universidad Católica de Chile, 1973), p. 33.

22. CORFO, *Estrategia Industrial*, 1: 93.

Table 8.2. Coefficients of Import Substitution

Industrial groups	*From* 1914–15 / *To* 1927	1927 / 1937–38	1937–38 / 1952–53	1952–53 / 1963–64	1914–15 / 1963–64
1. Food, beverages, and tobacco products	.388 (.029)	.455 (.025)	−.145 (.030)	−.017 (0.35)	.154 (.051)
2. Textiles	.482	.788 (.396)	.570 (.362)	.120 (.270)	.586
3. Clothing and footwear	.333 (.145)	2.261 (.106)	.105 (.089)	.540 (.067)	.623 (.188)
4. Wood products	1.314 (.109)	.043 (.092)	.101 (.094)	−.038 (.082)	.336 (.176)
5. Paper and printing	−.235 (.271)	.385 (.221)	−.168 (.215)	.327 (.169)	.328 (.393)
6. Leather and rubber products	−.715 (.356)	.869 (.288)	−.521 (.259)	.714 (.197)	.116 (.462)
7. Chemical products	1.636 (.388)	.644 (.348)	.248 (.341)	.330 (.302)	.885 (.550)
8. Nonmetallic mineral products	.817 (.192)	.955 (.145)	.269 (.134)	.077 (.082)	.821 (.251)
9. Metallic products	.470 (.585)	.907 (.522)	.529 (.493)	.216 (.360)	.774 (.753)
Total[a]	.431 (.194)	.730 (.171)	.150 (.184)	.145 (.153)	.410 (.297)

Note: Coefficients have been computed with the formula $\dfrac{(u_0 - u_1)Z_1}{X_1 - X_0}$, where u is the import proportion in total supply, Z is total supply, equal to the value of domestic gross output plus the value of imports, and X is the value of domestic gross output. The real values are those calculated by Oscar Muñoz, *Crecimiento Industrial de Chile, 1914–1965* (Santiago: Instituto de Economía y Planificación, 1968), table 4.2, p. 82. The normal values found in parenthesis are those estimated by Hollis Chenery and are also found in O. Muñoz, ibid., p. 82.
[a] The total has been computed by aggregation of the partial components.

through most agriculture-based manufacturing after 1940. But none of these events could conceal a basic segregation between domestic industry and agriculture. Industry, which had never been agriculture oriented, failed to exert an expansionary impact upon it. Most of its linkages with domestic agriculture were deliberately weakened, whereas those with imports were strengthened. The inability of agriculture to expand its supplies to industry must be largely explained by and attributed to the same factors that prevented industrial expansion from transmitting itself to agriculture: overvalued exchange rates, subsidized imports, price controls, low level of education, and lack of institutional reform.

MINING AND MANUFACTURING

The abundance of mineral raw materials nourished exuberant hopes for prosperous mining-based manufacturing. This segment, which includes the nonmetallic products category, transforms mineral raw materials into intermediate products or final consumer goods. As can be seen from table 8.1, its income share, which tripled between 1915 and 1961, had reached only a meager 6.8 percent in 1961. Its employment share, which doubled between 1915 and 1938, subsequently declined by almost 40 percent to 5.6 percent in 1961. If a correct estimate could be made of the portions of other subsectors (e.g., metal products) that belong to mining-based rather than autonomous manufacturing—which unfortunately is impossible at this moment—the income and employment shares would undoubtedly increase. Nevertheless, for many reasons real growth fell short of expectations.

Mining–industry interactions, which underlie the minerals theory of growth, were weaker, narrower, and more transitory than the interactions in the celebrated staples pattern used to explain early growth in Canada, Argentina, and Australia.[23] Unlike the continuously rising demand for wheat and other staples, the demand for Chilean nitrate skyrocketed with industrial technical progress between 1880 and 1930 but thereafter almost vanished as cheaper, synthetic nitrate replaced it. During the boom the impact was pervasive: export and aggregate

23. See Melville H. Watkins, "A Staple Theory of Economic Growth," *Canadian Journal of Economics and Political Science* 29 (May 1963): 141–58; Carlos F. Díaz Alejandro, *Essays on the Economic History of the Argentine Republic* (New Haven: Yale University Press, 1970), pp. 1–66.

demand and income expanded, the composition of aggregate demand shifted in favor of exports, and government revenues, expenditures, and derived demand for industrial products flourished. Nitrate also offered Chile the choice of using its export revenues for competitive consumer goods (primarily agricultural, industrial, and service) or complementary intermediate and capital goods imports. Nitrate functioned before 1930 as a quasi-industrial, -agricultural, and -service sector but was far more a competitive quasi-consumer than a complementary quasi-capital goods sector. During the nitrate bonanza much of the derived demand for industrial products spilled over to imports. The consequent increase in imports and total supply raised total income and welfare but also hurt industrial growth. The growth of mining-based manufacturing was modest and domestic oriented. During the nitrate collapse export demand, aggregate demand, government revenues and expenditures, income, investment, and other factors plummeted. But the collapse of the capacity to import also led during 1930–33 to the greatest forced short-term import-substituting industrialization in Chile's history.[24] Both before and after 1930 Chile lacked the technological capacity and the social desire to export nitrate, copper, iron, silver, gold, and other mining products in anything but their raw form.

As can be seen in table 8.2, import substitution in nonmetallic mineral products was very high during 1914–64: .821. This was principally because of its high level during 1914–38: the import substitution coefficient was .817 (compared to .192 predicted by Chenery) during 1914–15 to 1927 and .955 (compared to the Chenery estimate of .145) during 1927 to 1937–38. After 1938 it was minimal. Chile's comparative advantage produced early and rapid import substitution. After 1936 growth followed developments in the domestic market as the almost unlimited export demand was left untouched. A special, enduring relationship between mining and either mining-based or mining-oriented industry, which would have generated the technical progress so necessary for reaching the international market frontiers, failed to develop.

The post-1930 mining–industry relationship underscores some key issues and dilemmas of contemporary development. Mining not only failed to provide employment relief but indirectly multiplied and

24. See Alvarez, *Historia del Desarrollo Industrial de Chile* pp. 322–26.

strengthened the employment-absorption pressures affecting industry. Between 1940 and 1970 mining failed to absorb any of the 1.06 million new entrants to the labor force. Its employment now is stagnant at 100,000, and it shares with agriculture the dubious distinction of "zero employment growth."[25]

Table 8.3. Relative Income (GDP) and Employment in Mining and Quarrying, Chile, Selected Years, 1940–1971

	Percentage of mining			Relative productivity	
	Income		Employ-ment	$\frac{(1)}{(3)}$	$\frac{(2)}{(3)}$
	Old Series	New Series			
	(1)	(2)	(3)	(4)	(5)
1940	8.6		5.7	1.5	
1945	5.8		5.4	1.1	
1950	5.7		5.0	1.1	
1955	4.1		4.7	0.9	
1960	6.4	(10.0)	4.0	1.60	(2.50)
1965	6.8	(9.9)	3.6	1.89	(2.75)
1970		(10.0)	3.5		(2.86)
1971		(9.7)	3.2		(3.03)

Sources: See table 7.2.
Notes: See table 7.2.

The losses in relative mining employment (its share in the labor force declined from 5.7 percent in 1940 to 3.2 in 1971, as can be seen from table 8.3) are caused by the demise of nitrate and the growth of large-scale copper and iron as "superindustrial" sectors. Highly specialized and capital intensive, copper and iron were dependent on the costly and constantly renewed technology that saves both capital and labor and were dominated by the technological relationship between capital and raw materials that determines output. They also reflected the rise of a bitter class struggle between hard-driving, pioneer, foreign capitalists and a well-organized, well-paid, highly skilled, ambitious national proletariat. These sectors overshadowed the less efficient small- and medium-scale mining.

25. For the 1940 statistics see Mamalakis, "Historical Statistics," table IIA2a6, p. A-161, and for 1970, see ODEPLAN, *Población Ocupada, 1960–1970*, table 1.

Generating 10 percent of GDP both in 1960 and 1970 (i.e., more than agriculture) but employing less than one-sixth of the agriculture labor force throughout 1940–70, mining created substantial resource surpluses. However only a small fraction was used for industrial investment; the majority leaked out of Chile as repatriated profits, supported consumption by the central government, or was used to subsidize imports.

Unlike the growth pattern in Montana, Arizona, and New Mexico, mineral riches were not invested in the socially desirable mining- and industry-related engineering, geological sciences, and chemistry schools. Without such specialized education, Chile was unable to compete with the developed nations, which favored raw material imports but discriminated against processed manufactured ones. Even if we accept that foreign multinational firms encouraged processing abroad, domestic national processing and manufacturing could not be expanded—if and when mining were nationalized, as it was in 1971 —without specialized national technicians.

A policy of integrating mining and industry into a metals and non-metallic minerals complex was totally absent during 1940–55. In fact, discrimination against mining was so intense that it caused mining to stagnate. When government policy treated mining and industry as adversaries rather than partners in growth, the neglected and oppressed mining sector underperformed in almost all respects. It also displayed the highest sectoral excess capacity (14 percent) during 1945–65, with a forgone production "equal to five years of the mean actual production."[26] Most important, it fell short in its performance as a quasi-producer of capital goods and raw materials. As a consequence, there was intermittently a capital goods and raw materials asphyxiation of the industrial sector.

Intermediate mining demand for goods and services was successfully diverted in favor of Chile after 1956, when first the Copper Department and later the Copper Corporation actively encouraged a "Buy Chilean" policy. In addition to increasing copper's returned revenues, this policy strengthened the mining sector's ties to industry.[27]

26. See Jere R. Behrman, "Cyclical Sectoral Capacity Utilization in a Developing Economy," discussion paper no. 156, University of Pennsylvania, Philadelphia, pp. 7, 11.

27. See my "Contribution of Copper to Chilean Economic Development, 1920–67: Profile of a Foreign-Owned Sector," in Raymond Mikesell and Associates, *Foreign Investment in Minerals and Petroleum* (Baltimore, Md.: John Hopkins Press, 1971), pp. 410–11.

AUTONOMOUS MANUFACTURING

Autonomous manufacturing makes its most significant, though by no means exclusive, contributions to growth by producing technology-rich consumer goods, primarily durables, for which the income elasticity of demand can be almost infinite; by producing intermediate products, such as cement, steel, chemicals, and fixtures, that are indispensable ingredients in the construction of dwellings, public works, and other areas; and finally, by producing primary (i.e., capital goods producing) and secondary (i.e., consumer goods producing) capital goods for mining, agriculture, construction, services, and itself.[28] As shown in table 8.1, autonomous manufacturing includes consumer goods (textiles, clothing, and part of metallic), intermediate goods (chemical and part of metallic), and capital goods (part of metallic products). This subsector was expected to enhance the transformation and modernization capacity of Chile's production system and to harness its abundant human and natural resources by discovering, generating, implementing, and disseminating to other sectors new commodities, raw materials, and techniques. The technological relationship among capital, labor, and output dominates this sector, and there is no discernible, direct functional relationship between raw materials and output.

Autonomous manufacturing fulfilled some of the high expectations for it by becoming the most rapidly expanding industrial subgroup during 1915–72. As can be seen from table 8.1, its relative income contribution within manufacturing rose from 33.2 percent in 1915 to 52.0 percent in 1961, while its employment share increased from 42.7 percent in 1915 to 59.4 percent in 1961. Its employment share had climbed to 66 percent by 1970.[29]

Starting in 1960 autonomous manufacturing, with almost relentless ambition, expanded remarkably the production of such producer durables as television sets, radios, washing machines, refrigerators, floor polishers, automobiles, and so forth, making this the fastest growing segment.[30] Automobile production climbed by 11.4 percent annually

---

28. For a more detailed examination of these terms and issues, see my "Public Policy," pp. 149–68.

29. ODEPLAN, *Población Ocupada, 1960–1970*, table 6k.

30. ODEPLAN, *Antecedentes sobre el Desarrollo Chileno, 1960–70* (Santiago: ODE-PLAN, 1971), p. 159. Hereafter cited as *Antecedentes, 1960–70*.

during 1960–70. Annual production of television sets increased by 64.0 percent during 1963–68, that of refrigerators by 26 percent, and that of auto engines by 28 percent during 1960–67.[31] The variety and quality were impressive. Chile, a country of fewer than 10 million inhabitants, had more auto assemblers or producers—ten producers[32] in 1967— than the giant United States. It also led to heavy royalty, license, and fee payments abroad. The formidable underlying technical base was borrowed, imported, consumer oriented, erected behind massive protective walls, and strongly anticompetitive. Although the average participation of foreign capital in all anonymous manufacturing corporations in 1967 was 16.55 percent, it was 48.9 percent in the manufacturing of electrical machinery, apparatus, appliances, and supplies, which in Chile centered on producer durables.[33]

Chile became a unique consumer paradise. A huge variety of consumer goods was produced or assembled simultaneously in Chile— exclusively for domestic markets—and in the originating developed nations. This situation was unique because artifically high prices largely restricted the market before 1970 to the upper- and middle-income groups.

Growth of output and variety of consumer durables were impressive under both Presidents Alessandri and Frei. However, it became increasingly apparent that the social cost of excessive diversification might be too high for Chile. Allende assumed the presidency in an almost universal climate of skepticism about the nature of industrial growth, and he struck a deliberate blow against the phenomenon of many firms with excess and duplicate capacity producing small quantities of slightly differentiated products.

In spite of the astonishing growth in automobiles, electrical appliances, and other consumer durables, the most important consumer goods segment within autonomous manufacturing remained that textiles and clothing. As the textiles subsector expanded (its employment share within manufacturing rose from 4.3 percent in 1915 to 18.2

31. The figures for these and other producer durables are found in Muñoz, "Crecimiento industrial, estructura del consumo y distribución del ingreso. Análisis de la década de 1960," in *Proceso a la Industrialización Chilena*, ed. Oscar Muñoz (Santiago: Centro de Estudios de Planificación Nacional, 1972), p. 18. Hereafter cited as "Crecimiento industrial."

32. CORFO, *Estrategia Industrial*, 1: 56.

33. CORFO, *Participación del Capital Extranjero en las Sociedades Anónimas Industriales* (Santiago: CORFO, 1970), p. 3. Hereafter cited as *Capital Extranjero*.

percent in 1961), that of clothing shrank from a 23.2 percent industrial employment share in 1915 to only 10.7 percent in 1961. The combined textiles–clothing employment share remained highly stable at 28.0 percent in 1915 and 28.9 percent in 1961, while their combined income share declined mildly from 19.8 percent in 1915 to 17.2 percent in 1961. Their combined employment of 164,400 in 1970 was 29.0 percent of total industrial employment, whereas their combined income share in 1968 was slightly below 20 percent of the industry total.[34] Although import substitution in both textiles and clothing had been carried to its limit, with imports being minuscule, exports were also zero during 1960–69, indicating some gross anomaly.[35] The undisputed elegance of Chilean textiles and clothing, in a variety combining the best of French, American, German, and Italian fashions and products, improved the welfare of the great majority of Chileans, though to unequal degrees. Because it remained unable to develop an autochthonous quality and product mix, however, the textiles–clothing segment remained captive to the external sources of innovation and inspiration and to its own domestic orientation.

The second segment of manufacturing that experienced an impressive growth was that of intermediate products. This included not only part of the autonomous but also most of the nonmetallic products segment, that is, mining-based and some of the forestry-based manufacturing. A major portion of these intermediate products was used by the industrial consumer goods subsector, but an even greater part was used by the construction sector. An intimate, two-way relationship was thus created between construction—primarily of dwellings but also of offices, roads, airports, and other public works—and industry. Among the manifold characteristics of these interactions, several stand out. The bulk of intermediate industrial products was an input in capital accumulation. In turn, this capital formation created largely though not exclusively a service output in, for example, housing, transportation, education, government, and gas, water, and electricity. Industrial production was thus establishing the conditions for an efficient performance by the service sectors of their functions: time, location, and quantity transformation and quality maintenance and improvement. Most of the quality improvements, however, emanated

34. ODEPLAN, *Población Ocupada, 1960–1970*, table 6k; CORFO, *Datos Básicos Sector Industrial Manufacturero Período 1960–1968* (Santiago: CORFO, 1970), p. 9.
35. CORFO, ibid., pp. 11–12.

from housing and thus affected consumer welfare without necessarily revolutionizing productive efficiency and ingenuity.

Industrial commodity production emerged as a joint input with and prerequisite for the performance of the quality-maintenance, location-transformation, and other service functions. With the livelihood of both dependent on the ultimate demand for housing, transport, and other services, construction and supportive urban modern industry boomed and declined together.

Table 8.4. Relative Income (GDP) and Employment in Construction,
Chile, Selected Years, 1940–71

	Percentage of construction			Relative productivity	
	Income		Employ-ment	$\dfrac{(1)}{(3)}$	$\dfrac{(2)}{(3)}$
	Old Series	New Series			
	(1)	(2)	(3)	(4)	(5)
1940	2.3		3.5	0.66	
1945	2.7		4.0	0.67	
1950	2.4		4.7	0.51	
1955	2.4		5.8	0.41	
1960	2.4	(5.2)	5.6	0.43	(0.93)
1965	3.3	(5.6)	7.0	0.47	(0.80)
1970		(4.6)	6.3		(0.73)
1971		(4.8)	6.3		(0.76)

Sources: See table 7.2.
Notes: See table 7.2.

Pivotal complementary roles emerged in employment. Much of intermediate industrial production was large scale, high in productivity, and capital intensive—as, for example, in cement, iron and steel, chemicals, and so forth. Construction, the sector dependent on them, was low in productivity, as can be seen in table 8.4, and was labor intensive. It succeeded in absorbing 10 percent of the total labor force increment between 1940 and 1970, with its employment almost tripling from 61,000, or 3.5 percent of the labor force, to 177,500, or 6.3 percent.[36]

36. See my "Historical Statistics," p. A-160, and ODEPLAN, *Población Ocupada, 1960–1970*, tables 1, 7.

Certain subsectors, (construction, intermediate products industry, and housing services) entered into a powerful symbiosis that transcended ownership patterns, derived its appeal as much from providing a highly needed consumer service as from making a contribution to multisectoral employment, and led to mass production of goods and services. However, because the orientation of this relationship was internal, urban, and proconsumer, it failed to provide the benefits of exports of copper in Chile or of textiles during the British Industrial Revolution.

Industry involves more than specialization, large-scale mass production, capital intensity, and heavy use of electrical, fuel, or other power. Industry can create technology, machinery, and equipment that give the nation an autonomous, autochthonous transformation and modernization capacity. It performs the strategic function of quality improvement in production.

The performance of this function, which improved cyclically over time, nevertheless remained weak. Few secondary instrumental goods for agriculture, mining, or industry were produced, and almost no primary ones. By 1971 the domestic share in total machinery and equipment supply was 25 percent.[37] Also, even though some technical progress originated from within Chile, most of it was an adaptation or transplantation of foreign developments. The growth contribution made by an indigenous technology appears vastly different from that of a quasi-technology sector, that is, an export one permitting purchase of foreign technology. Though autarky is patently inefficient in a medium-sized market economy such as Chile, a critical minimum internal *and* national technology as well as capital goods production (i.e., a largely complete system) are necessary for regular quality improvement and self-sustained, accelerated growth.

OVERALL INDUSTRIAL AND MANUFACTURING GROWTH

Reliable statistics for the growth rate of overall industrial output are found mainly in the national accounts estimates for the 1940–71 period. Reliable statistics for the growth rate of the manufacturing segment of industry exist since 1914. In addition to Oscar Muñoz,

37. ODEPLAN, *Cuentas Nacionales de Chile, 1960–1971* (Santiago: ODEPLAN, 1972), p. 52.

Ballesteros and Davis[38] and the United Nations Economic Commission for Latin America[39] have prepared time series providing long-term trends of manufacturing value added. Although valuable for understanding manufacturing growth, these studies have some common drawbacks. They are unable to indicate how much of the observed manufacturing income growth rate is the result of a decline in handicraft income and how much represents an overall industrial gain. Furthermore, since they exclude artisan industry, these manufacturing statistics are not comparable to industrial value added series in the post-1940 national accounts, which include the artisans. My discussion of manufacturing growth is based on Oscar Muñoz's work because it contains the longest time series and is the only one for which the methodology of the estimates has been revealed.[40]

Manufacturing growth averaged close to 4.3 percent per annum during the half-century between 1914 and 1964. This rate is neither spectacular nor insignificant. Gross domestic product grew at approximately 3.6 percent per year. During the same period, on a per capita basis gross manufacturing value added grew at 2.4 percent per year, while per capita income grew by only 1.6 percent.[41] It is not known how much of this manufacturing growth resulted from a shift of handicraft production and enterprise to manufacturing.

As can be seen from table 8.2 import substitution, which augmented the demand for domestic manufacturing products, contributed 41 percent of total manufacturing growth between 1914–15 and 1963–64. But this contribution was highly variable during several subperiods. Import substitution was a far more important growth factor before 1927, when it contributed 43 percent of the manufacturing growth, than after 1937, when it contributed only 15 percent between 1937–38 and 1963–64. Its 73 percent contribution to output growth between 1927 and 1938, which was as remarkable as it was short lived, demon-

38. Marto A. Ballesteros and Tom E. Davis, "The Growth of Output and Employment in Basic Sectors of the Chilean Economy, 1908–1957," *Economic Development and Cultural Change* 11, no. 2 (Jan. 1963): 152–76.

39. UNECLA, *Economic Survey of Latin America, 1949* (New York: E/CN.12/164/ Rev. 1, 11 Jan. 1951), table 8A, p. 287. Also UNECLA, *The Process of Industrialization in Latin America*, Statistical Annex (Santiago: E/CN.12/716/Add. 2, 19 Jan. 1966), table I-1.

40. Muñoz has used a variety of deflators to prepare three different sets of gross value-added time series and has examined and tested a variety of hypotheses concerning the role and pattern of manufacturing growth.

41. Muñoz, *Crecimiento*, table 2.1, p. 26.

strates that most of the import substitution was confined to the interwar years.

The golden era of industrialization allegedly dawned with the birth of the Chilean Development Corporation (CORFO) in 1939. As subsidized credits, imported machinery and equipment, raw materials, and other advantages were bestowed upon it, domestic industry replaced foreign imports, which were kept out through a complex system of quotas, foreign exchange controls, licenses, tariffs, and complete ostracism. But the unprecedented continued governmental favoritism, which brought industry into dominance, was a mixed blessing: in each of three successive decades there were five prosperous years followed by five lean years. During the World War II years of radical presidents Pedro Aguirre Cerda and Juan Antonio Ríos (1940–45), industrial output climbed by a formidable 9.3 percent per year. Helped by war-induced shortages, rising demand, and CORFO-sponsored import substitution, the CORFO-estimated income share of industry jumped by more than 33 percent from 16.7 percent of GDP in 1940 to 22.4 percent in 1945. With only minor subsequent increases, this share rose to 26.1 percent in 1971. The meager 2.9 percent annual growth during the five postwar years reduced the rate for the 1940s to 6.1 percent— still the highest for 1940–70.[42] During 1950–55, which includes the last two years of radical president Gabriel González Videla, the Korean War, and the first three years of nonpartisan president Carlos Ibáñez del Campo (the "General of Hope"), industry grew at 5.4 percent per year.[43] The lean years of 1955–60, when the industrial growth rate fell to −0.4 percent, were dominated by the crippling Klein–Saks stabilization policies and the recession of 1955–57, which broke the back of the 1953–55 superinflation. It is the 1950s, with their meager industrial annual growth rate of 2.5 percent, that has prompted some economists to expound a long-term stagnation hypothesis for Chile.

During the 1960s the Alessandri boom of 1960–65, with its 7.3 percent annual industrial growth rate, was followed by a low growth rate under Christian Democrat Eduardo Frei (3.6 percent during 1965–70). Even so, the Frei years emerge with the best growth rate in the second

42. The growth rates throughout this section refer to GDP in real terms and at market prices. The underlying time series are found as follows: For the 1940–60 period, Mamalakis, "Historical Statistics," pp. A-171–A-176; for the 1960–71 years, ODEPLAN, *Cuentas Nacionales de Chile, 1960–71*, pp. 49–50.

43. See Sergio Molina, *El Proceso de Cambio en Chile* (Santiago: Editorial Universitaria, S.A., 1972), pp. 27–29.

half of a decade since 1940. Industrial booms, which largely coincide with but are not identical to the aforementioned five-year periods, were achieved at a high social cost. That of 1940–45 led to the inception of permanent inflation. Sectoral conflicts, growth-impeding unequal sectoral growth, uncontrolled inflation, and a major recession were part and consequence of the 1950–55 industrial euphoria. An ominous rise in foreign indebtedness leading to a severe balance-of-payment crisis was left behind by the Alessandri prosperity. In terms of the relationship between social benefits and costs, the Christian Democrats must be credited with the best performance.

In an ironic twist of history the successful, orthodox, middle-of-the-road, frugal Christian Democratic policies permitted Socialist president Salvador Allende and his Popular Unity coalition to embark in 1971 on a spectacular and populistic spree of short-term industrial consumer goods. Industrial income spurted by 12.9 percent in 1971;[44] the index of physical manufacturing output rose by 14.6 percent from 104.0 in 1970 to 119.3 in 1971. Approximately two-thirds of this gain reflected a recovery to the 1968 peak, when the index had risen to 115.2.[45] Nevertheless, the price for this achievement was the highest ever paid by Chile: a drastic decline in productive capacity, the worst inflation, and the use of the export sector as a quasi-consumer goods sector with almost no regard or respect—the message of Marx's *Das Kapital* was apparently lost—for its role as a quasi-capital-goods sector. Industrial production grew by only 2.8 percent in 1972 and started falling after September 1972, with sharp declines of 7.1 percent registered in the early months of 1973.[46]

Herculean efforts—both social and private—will be needed to disentangle the current labyrinthine complex of production relationships and turn them into a growth-promoting set. The shadow hanging over Chile's industrial growth is one of partial policies partially implemented and then partially replaced by new partial ones. Although the industrial growth rate of 4.7 percent during 1940–70 exceeded the 3.6 percent rate of GDP—both a far cry from stagnation—neither was outstanding or

44. ODEPLAN, *Cuentas Nacionales de Chile, 1960–1971*, pp. 49–50.

45. As in practically all instances, the figures found in *El Mercurio* and President Allende's *Messages* coincide. See *El Mercurio*, Apr. 30–May 6, 1973, p. 2, and Salvador Allende G., *Mensaje del Presidente Allende ante el Congreso Pleno 21 de Mayo de 1972* (Santiago: Presidencia de la República, 1972), pp. liv–lv (hereafter cited as *Mensaje 1972*).

46. *El Mercurio*, international ed., May 7–13, 1973, pp. 2, 1.

indicative of accelerated self-sustained growth, especially in view of the 2.2 percent annual population increase.

The role of industry as an employer was even less decisive than that as an income generator. Its employment share, already a respectable 17.4 percent in 1940, climbed to 19.3 in 1950, with no significant changes subsequently. Total industrial employment almost doubled from 307,000 in 1940 to 563,000 in 1970[47] and absorbed approximately 25 percent of the labor force increment.

Table 8.5. Relative Income (GDP) and Employment in Industry
Chile, Selected Years, 1940–71

	Percentage of industrial			Relative productivity	
	Income		Employ- ment	(1)	(2)
	Old Series	New Series		(3)	(3)
	(1)	(2)	(3)	(4)	(5)
1940	16.7		17.4	0.96	
1945	22.4		18.4	1.22	
1950	21.9		19.3	1.13	
1955	23.7		19.1	1.24	
1960	19.2	(23.3)	17.8	1.08	(1.31)
1965	18.6	(25.4)	19.5	0.95	(1.30)
1970		(24.2)	19.9		(1.22)
1971		(26.1)	19.2		(1.36)

Sources: See table 7.2.
Notes: See table 7.2.

Industrial employment increased by 33 percent during 1940–50, then remained stationary until 1960, and rose sharply by 36 percent during 1960–70. The argument that Chilean industrialization is an offspring of the Great Depression of the 1930s seems refuted by the employment statistics, which show that industry employed 320,000 in 1920 but only 307,000 in 1940.[48] Events both before and after 1930 suggest a strong positive relationship between export prosperity and industrial employment–income growth. The negative impact on industry of export

47. See my "Historical Statistics," p. A-160, and ODEPLAN, *Población Ocupada, 1960–1970*, table 1, no page numbers.
48. Dirección General de Estadística, *Censo de Población de la República de Chile, Levantado el 15 de Diciembre de 1920* (Santiago: Sociedad Imprenta y Litografía Universo, 1925), p. 406.

contraction/collapse/stagnation during 1920–40 and 1950–60 seems to reinforce the belief that the constellation of forces that is propitious to the export sector and balance of payments is also propitious for industry. Indeed, it may be the only necessary favorable factor. The 1970–80 industrial employment growth may thus be determined by the fortunes of the export sector along with foreign credits. In this view the Marxist ownership and income transformation policies are almost inconsequential. The broad contours of the industrial physiognomy of Chile are shaped far more decisively by its linkages and interactions with export mining, food agriculture, and the housing sector than by the economically, but not politically, alien model of class struggle, income redistribution, and state ownership. Industrial socialism can survive in Chile, but in order to succeed it must fully take account of and adjust to the nation's idiosyncratic intersectoral relationships.

Industrial employment growth must be viewed in relation to employment in the commodity and services sectors as well as in the economy as a whole. Within the commodity sectors industry, with its 2.0 percent annual employment growth rate between 1940 and 1970, is flanked on one side by zero growth in mining and agriculture and on the other by the rapid employment growth (3.6 percent per year) in construction. Surprisingly, as can be seen in table 8.5, relative industrial labor productivity declined in each successive decade. Industrial employment grew slightly faster than the aggregate rate but slightly slower than services, which grew at 2.5 percent per year. Because growth in urban industry and construction could not offset the below-average performance of hinterland agriculture and mining, the combined commodity sectors employment growth was a disappointing 0.9 percent during 1940–70 as can be seen in table 8.6. Although commodity sector employment had fallen from 54 percent of the active population in 1960 to 49.7 percent in 1970, it still comprised more than half of the employed population, which was 92.9 percent of the active population in 1960 and 93.9 percent in 1970.[49]

This stagnation of industrial employment came despite Chile's high urbanization, inflation, import substitution, and a revealed worker's preference for industrial employment.[50] The lack of labor absorption by industry has been recognized by the Chilean authorities and corrective strategies have been suggested.

49. See ODEPLAN, *Población Ocupada, 1960–1970*, table 1.
50. See CORFO, *Obreros Industriales Chilenos* (Santiago: CORFO, 1970), p. 15.

Table 8.6. Growth Rates in Commodity Sector Income, Employment,
and Labor Productivity, Chile, 1940–70

	1940–50 (2)	1950–60 (3)	1960–70 (5)	1940–70 (1)
Agriculture				
GDP	1.8	2.3	2.4	2.2
L	0.5	0.3	−0.8	0.0
GDP/L	1.3	2.0	3.2	2.2
Mining and quarrying				
GDP	−1.0	5.1	5.0	3.0
L	0.7	−1.4	0.7	0.0
GDP/L	−1.7	6.5	4.3	3.0
Industry				
GDP	6.1	2.4	5.4	4.6
L	3.0	−0.1	3.2	2.0
GDP/L	3.1	2.5	2.2	2.6
Construction				
GDP	3.8	3.8	3.8	3.8
L	5.0	2.7	3.1	3.6
GDP/L	−1.2	1.1	0.7	0.2
Electricity, gas, and water				
GDP	3.9	3.2	5.8	4.3
L	6.1	−5.7	0.9	0.4
GDP/L	−2.2	8.9	4.9	3.9
Total commodities				
GDP	3.4	2.8	4.6	3.6
L	1.6	0.2	1.0	0.9
GDP/L	1.8	2.6	3.6	2.0
All sectors				
GDP	3.3	3.8	5.0	4.0
L	1.9	0.8	2.0	1.6
GDP/L	1.4	3.0	3.0	2.4
Investment	5.2	3.3	5.4	4.6

Sources: The data for GDP for the period 1940–60 are found in Mamalakis, "National Accounts," in "Historical Statistics," pt. 1, table IF7, pp. A-171–A-174; the data for GDP for 1960–70 are found in ODEPLAN, *Cuentas Nacionales de Chile, 1960–1971* (Santiago: ODEPLAN, 1973), table 16, p. 54; the data for employment for 1940 and 1950 are found in Mamalakis, "Demography," ibid., pt. 2, table IIA2a6, pp. A-160–A-165; and, finally, the data for employment for 1960 and 1970 are found in ODEPLAN, *Población Ocupada por Sectores Económicos, 1960–1970* (Santiago: ODEPLAN, 1971), table 1.

Notes: "All sectors" includes electricity, gas, and water. GDP stands for gross domestic product, market prices, in real terms, while L stands for employment (active population = employed population + unemployed population). Investment refers to the sum of gross fixed domestic capital formation and increase in stocks.

THE QUEST FOR AN EXPLANATION

The paradox of apparently plentiful stimuli to industry and a meager, fragmented response has invited a multitude of explanations. In order to describe and scrutinize them, industrial performance can be judged by the three efficiency criteria for a successful industrial strategy suggested by CORFO. Industry must have technical efficiency to obtain maximum productivity from resources used, economic efficiency to achieve maximum output with the total resources available in the economy, and social efficiency to ensure that the country's priority needs are satisfied and that the production apparatus it gives rise to is compatible with national objectives.[51] None of these criteria had been fully satisfied, according to most scholars, either in 1970 or by 1974.

Industry has made inefficient use of resources, as witnessed by extremely high prices, the perpetual need for protection, and the heavy dependence on imports and limited exports.[52] Technological backwardness coincided with and was integral to a dependence on techniques generated in the capitalist or socialist centers. Moreover, economic efficiency has not been attained. The major symptoms of the failure to satisfy this second criterion include production disequilibria whereby surplus and inadequate capacity coexist, excessive diversification of firms and products and lack of specialization, and widespread monopolistic practices.[53] The greatest shortcomings are in the fulfillment of the social efficiency criterion. Unable to raise labor demand sufficiently to create scarcity and augment the wage share, industry failed to correct the deformed class, regional, or sectoral distribution of income. Although it contributed to capital formation through its reinvested profits, industry never succeeded as either a capital goods or a technology sector. As a consequence, on the production side it catered to urban, predominantly well-to-do consumers.

Although such pre-1970 outcasts as the urban and rural marginals were given a larger industrial output share during 1970–73, Allende's change in the short-term distribution pattern of consumption benefits carried in part the price of lower saving and investment. Although

---

51. The three criteria are listed in *Estrategia Industrial*, 1: 6.
52. CORFO, "La Política Industrial," p. 116.
53. The excessive diversification theme has been very popular in recent years. See Muñoz, "Crecimiento industrial," pp. 42–43; ODEPLAN, *Antecedentes, 1960–70*, p. 153.

industry must be considered a successful producer of consumer goods, it has not succeeded at quality improvement, through either technology or the production of capital goods.

The social efficiency criterion was also not satisfied, according to an increasingly vocal group of economists, because domestic industrial output growth was achieved by the indiscriminate and unnecessary surrender of economic (and by inference political) independence to foreign capital and capitalists. Foreign capital in 1968 accounted for 16.74 percent of all capital in anonymous manufacturing corporations but for 57 percent in tobacco, 44 percent in rubber, and 42 percent in electrical machinery and equipment.[54] Thus, it allegedly exerted a disproportionate influence on economic policy, discouraged exports, repatriated high profits, and made only a small contribution to employment and saving. Greater concentration of power in large multinational firms operating in Chile and subordination of the productive structure to the developed nations' consumption patterns reduced autonomy and increased technological dependence. If Chile seeks long-term control over its own destiny, an integrated strategy of foreign investment and technology is viewed as indispensable.[55]

According to one historically and politically very relevant school of thought, almost everything plaguing Chile, including unbalanced and distorted industrial development, had its origin in private ownership of the means of production, especially land, capital, and mineral resources. The two natural consequences of private capital were monopolism and imperialism. With impressive consistency the Marxist argument singles out the level and composition of aggregate demand as the dominant growth constraints. In turn, demand deficiency is directly linked to the unequal class distribution of income caused by monopolism and imperialism.

Antimonopolism and anti-imperialism thus naturally emerged as the two pillars of Salvador Allende's extremely loose industrial strategy.[56] In practice the strategy of the Popular Unity, under the broad goal of

54. CORFO, *Capital Extranjero*, p. 4.
55. CORFO, *Seminario de Estrategia de Desarrollo Industrial para la Década del 70, Informe de Comisiónes* (Santiago: CORFO, Publicación 22a, 1969), pp. iii-1–iii-11. Hereafter cited as *Seminario de Estrategia*.
56. For a very lucid, pro-Allende description of the 1970 election and related events see Richard E. Feinberg, *The Triumph of Allende, Chile's Legal Revolution* (New York: New American Library, 1972), pp. 108–09. Surprisingly, industry is the only major economic sector for which Allende does not devote a section in either his first or second *Mensaje* to Congress.

independence and social liberation, has had a variety of facets. As an immediate corrective it redistributed income in favor of the industrial workers during 1970–73. In order to divert the sector's motivation away from private profit to the serving of social needs, it introduced an ownership transformation whereby social, mixed, and private enterprises would coexist. All strategic, monopolistic, and foreign-owned enterprises were to form part of the social or mixed ownership area, thus "destroying the dictatorship of private monopoly" and replacing the powerful symbiosis of large foreign and internal capitalists by a new labor–state coalition.[57] The social area was conceived in its structure and orientation as the embryo of a future socialist economy.

In order to ensure mass participation of workers in all levels of the production process, President Allende's government created the Committees for Sectoral Development, intermediate state structures for the direction and application of policies under the supervision of CORFO, and the Committees of a Firm. The last-mentioned group, composed of executives of the firm designated by the government and representatives of workers designated by the workers themselves, was made responsible for the coordination and fulfillment of the targets assigned to the firm by the government.[58] Furthermore, in order to create "real democracy" by transferring decision-making power from the capitalists to the workers, an elaborate system of participation was introduced. In one-plant firms that are totally state owned, there are the workers assembly, the administrative council, production committees, and a workers' coordinating committee. In multiplant firms the administrative council delegates authority to a specially created plant organization. In the private segment labor unions and the newly created vigilance committees are entrusted with making sure that private owners use the firm's productive apparatus in a manner consistent with the government's social goals.[59]

The argument that markets for mass-produced industrial commodities did not expand sufficiently because labor and the poor received a disproportionately low income share (less than 50 percent of GDP) was tested after 1970, when labor's income share rose to 64 percent of GDP in 1971, and was found, at least in part, wanting. The industrial

57. Allende, *Mensaje 1972*, p. xiii.
58. CORFO, "La Política Industrial," pp. 118–21, and *Mensaje 1972*, pp. 360–62. As Allende himself points out, some labor participation in enterprise management had been achieved under Eduardo Frei, ibid., pp. lxvii–lxix.
59. See Allende, *Mensaje 1972*, pp. lxix–lxxiv.

income share estimated by ODEPLAN (Oficina de Planificación Nacional de la Presidencia de la República) did indeed rise from 24.2 percent in 1970 to 26.1 percent in 1971, but the employment effects were minimal. As can be seen from table 8.5, the employment share of industry, which after the post-1930 recovery and the unceasing industrialization efforts of the 1940s had reached 19.3 percent in 1950 and 19.9 percent in 1970, declined to 19.2 percent in 1971.

An alternative hypothesis has placed primary emphasis on autonomous or induced supply bottlenecks. Partly because of the vicious circle of poverty and partly because of government-induced disincentives, Chile alternately or concurrently faced constraints in the supply of qualified labor, capital goods, raw materials, and intermediate products. The lackluster agricultural and export mining growth, mostly government induced, strongly contributed to inelastic supplies of major industrial inputs.[60] These supply constraints arrested industrial expansion even though aggregate demand was abundant and its composition favorable.

Much of the 1930–73 experience lends support to this hypothesis. The formidable 1936–52 industrial expansion, partly a recovery from and partly a gain over the 1930 peak, came to a halt during 1953–58. Economy-wide bottlenecks caused by agricultural and mining discrimination and stagnation first triggered extreme inflation in 1952–55 and subsequently invited the Klein–Saks policies. With production incentives partly or totally restored for mining and agriculture during 1955–60, the rise in exports, and unlimited imports during 1959–62, Chile experienced the spectacular Alessandri–Frei industrial boom of 1958–67.[61] Much of the slow 1967–70 growth must be explained by the Christian Democratic attempts to bring aggregate demand in line with an import supply supported by export proceeds rather than by burdensome foreign indebtedness. The industrial cycle of 1970–73 follows a similar pattern. An industrial boom in 1971 became possible as imports rose to $1.269 billion, capacity was fully utilized, and internal stocks were eaten up. Industrial output stagnated or declined between July 1972 and April 1973 because the even greater total imports of $1.495 billion in 1972 (with exports exceeding imports by

60. For the details of this hypothesis see the author's "Public Policy and Sectoral Development: A Case Study of Chile 1940–1958," in Markos Mamalakis and Clark Reynolds, *Essays on the Chilean Economy* (Homewood, Ill.: Richard D. Irwin, 1965), pp. 3–82.
61. ODEPLAN, *Antecedentes 1960–70*, pp. 151, 165.

$538.2 million) would not compensate for the reduction in internal output and stocks.[62] The income redistribution policies of 1970–72, although socially just in the short run and in many respects overdue, had a pervasive negative impact on aggregate domestic supply.

Strong empirical support of the view that the government treated sectors unequally, thus causing production inefficiencies, was provided by a study on the structure of protection for 1961. Although industry as a whole emerged as dominant and favored, not all subsectors fared equally well. Food processing, the making of leather products, textiles, beverages, clothing, and shoes—all of which were granted a net effective protection (or effective protection adjusted for overvaluation of the escudo) in excess of 100 percent—stand out as the superprivileged industrial subsectors. Also dominant, but with rates of net effective protection between 50 and 100 percent, were nonmetallic mineral products, furniture, and basic metals. Least protected were machinery and equipment production and a few subsectors producing intermediate products.[63]

According to CORFO an industrial strategy must focus on the sector's relationship to (1) external trade, (2) employment and technological advancement, (3) foreign investment, (4) structure of consumption, and (5) institutional organization.[64] Such a strategy would at least in part operate in a vacuum unless industry relates to the needs of the consumer—directly through its own consumer goods production and indirectly by providing not only intermediate but also capital goods inputs and technology to agriculture, mining, construction, and services that satisfy the food and service needs of society's members.

Although the consumer offers the ultimate orientation and justification for aggregate social production goals, they cannot be fulfilled without a simultaneous or even a prior orientation toward the producer. He either provides industry with its resource base—from agriculture, forestry, fishing, and mining—or maintains as well as improves the quality of the production apparatus and the final flow of goods and services. Having largely changed ownership patterns and established a prolabor income distribution between 1970 and 1972, the Popular

62. The trade balance statistics are found in *El Mercurio*, international ed. May 28–July 3, 1973, p. 2.

63. See Teresa Jeanneret, "The Structure of Protection in Chile," in Bela Belassa et al., *The Structure of Protection in Developing Countries* (Baltimore, Md.: Johns Hopkins Press, 1971), chap. 7, pp. 166–67 and table 7.10.

64. CORFO, *Seminario de Estrategia de Desarrollo Industrial para la Década del 70 Informe de Comisiónes* (Santiago: CORFO, Publicación 22a/1969), pp. i-1–v-11.

Unity government faced in 1973 the same dilemma that has plagued Chile since independence: namely, establishment of the production incentives that can harness latent productive potential and channeling of it toward welfare-raising technical progress and capital formation. State ownership is neither a more necessary nor a more sufficient condition for success than private ownership; what is needed are rules that reward efficiency and penalize incompetence by integrating and harmonizing production (effort), distribution (rewards), and capital formation on a regional, class, sectoral, international, and functional basis. Chile's moderate growth performance over 130 years reflects only moderate success in developing such rules. The challenge that Chile should set for itself is to discover and implement an amicable symbiosis between successful political and economic democracy. If and when this challenge is met, Chile will have succeeded in becoming one of the most advanced nations, economically as well as politically.

9

The Service Sector: Its Growth and Functions

DEFINITION AND FRAMEWORK

One of the most widely diffused and repeatedly refuted ideas has been Colin Clark's life cycle law.[1] This states that an economy in its infancy is engaged in primary activities, such as agriculture, fishing, and mining, grows with adolescence up to the specialized and technologically advanced secondary activities such as industry, and finally reaches an old age plateau where tertiary services become the affluent society's servant.[2] Allegedly, however, an anomaly arises in modern, less developed countries. The adolescent phase is totally or partially omitted from their life cycle, and old age arrives prematurely, as witnessed by heavily inflated governmental services, trade activities, and personal services. According to this untested hypothesis the tasting of the fruits of development is premature in the sense that the product sectors have not achieved a quantitative importance and level of productivity that will permit a large segment of the resources of the economy to engage in the leisure-catering service activities. Moreover, the benefits of economic development are often reaped on the principle of borrow now, pay later (with the assistance of developed nations).

For any economic sector, but particularly for services, an analysis of the stages and pattern of growth—the transitions from primary to secondary to tertiary activities—must consider simultaneously the sectoral distribution of the labor force and the sectoral income distribution.[3] One set of generalizations can be developed with respect to

1. Colin Clark, *The Conditions of Economic Progress*, 1st ed. (London: MacMillan, 1940), pp. 337–73.

2. The Colin Clark hypothesis was criticized among others by P. T. Bauer and B. S. Yamey, "Economic Progress and Occupational Distribution," *The Economic Journal* 61, (Dec. 1951): 741–55.

3. The existing literature, with the exception of Kuznets, is not clear or consistent on this matter. Although the shift from food to industrial goods to services is said to be

the sequence of final demand for food, industrial goods, and services by the consumer. Another set of generalizations can be formed about the sequence in which the relative or absolute magnitude of income is generated in agriculture, industry, and services. A distinct set of generalizations can be developed with respect to the relative and absolute employment in these three sectors. And, ultimately, a hypothesis of a composite nature can be developed with a set of generalizations relating to the ratio of relative income to relative employment in the service sector. Each generalization can be properly understood only in relation to the others.[4]

As discussed here, the service sector encompasses six categories from the income side (trade, banking, transport, government, personal services, and ownership of dwellings) and three categories from the employment side (commerce, transport, and personal services). All of them are described in greater detail in table 9.1. It is worth noting that no universally accepted definition of this sector exists in the economic literature. My classifications follow the so-called old System of National Accounts (SNA) and the old (1958) International Standard Industrial Classification of All Economic Activities (ISIC), since it is according to these standards that Chile prepared its income and employment statistics during 1940–72.[5]

---

dictated by demand factors and therefore all types of demand functions and elasticities are both hypothesized and tested, the controversy concerning the pattern of economic growth is restricted rather narrowly to the distribution of employment by sectors. The distinction between service income and service employment is rarely made because it is apparently assumed that both behave in the same fashion. For Kuznets's work, see Simon Kuznets, "Quantitative Aspects of the Economic Growth of Nations, II, Industrial Distribution of National Product and Labor Force," *Economic Development and Cultural Change* 5, no. 4 (July 1957): 5. This pioneering article distinguishes clearly between income generated by major sectors and employment in them. Kuznets included the major findings of this paper in his more recent *Modern Economic Growth, Rate, Structure, and Spread* (New Haven: Yale University Press, 1966). Although Kuznets includes ownership of dwellings in the definition of the service sector in his Yale book (pp. 143–44), the figures for percentage of value added generated in services appearing in it are either identical or too close to those appearing in the earlier article to account for the addition of ownership of dwellings. Thus, either the definition of services was changed but the income data were left unchanged, or the earlier definition did not reflect the information found in the tables. Furthermore, Kuznets included transport and communications in services in his 1957 work but excluded them from the definition found in this Yale book without explanation or theoretical justification.

4. These generalizations about the role of services in economic development and statistical evidence for nineteen Latin American countries during 1950–65 can be found in M. Mamalakis, "Urbanization and Sectoral Transformation in Latin America, 1950–65," in *Urbanización y proceso social en América* (Lima, Peru: Instituto de Estudios Peruanos, 1972), pp. 293–345. Hereafter cited as "Sectoral Transformation."

5. For the income categories and further information on them, see United Nations,

Table 9.1. Services

Income side[a]	*Employment side*[b]
A. 1. Wholesale and retail trade	A. 1. Commerce (Division 6 of 1958
2. Banking, insurance, and real estate	ISIC)
B. 3. Transport, storage, and	B. 2. Transport, storage, and com-
communications	munications (Division 7 of
	1958 ISIC)
C. 4. Public administration and defense	C. 3. Services (Division 8 of 1958
5. Services	ISIC)
D. 6. Ownership of dwellings	
Total Services	Total Services

[a]Categories according to *A System of National Accounts and Supporting Tables, UN 1964.*
[b]Categories according to *International Standard Industrial Classification of All
Economic Activities* (ISIC) *UN 1958.*

The service sector's dominant quantitative significance during 1940–
72 is unmistakable no matter which of the three definitions of total
services outlined in table 9.2 is considered. According to the first and
most complete one, which includes all subsectors, the overall sector
generated more than 54 percent of GDP in all selected years between
1940 and 1965—if the CORFO income estimates are considered.
Although the sector's CORFO income share was high and stable,
fluctuating between 54 and 60 percent of GDP, its employment share,
shown in column 7 of table 9.2, was lower but rising (from 35.5 percent
in 1940 to 46.7 percent in 1970). Even before 1930 the service sector
was a major employer, absorbing 34 percent of the labor force, or
468,400 persons, in 1920.[6]

Both the amazingly high income share of the service sector and its
unequal contribution to income and employment are strongly affected
by the inclusion of ownership of dwellings on the income side. Lacking

A System of National Accounts and Supporting Tables, Studies in Methods, ser. F, no. 2,
rev. 2, United Nations, New York, 1964, pp. 21, 38. For a description of the employment
categories see United Nations, *International Standard Industrial Classification of All
Economic Activities* ST/STAT/SER. M/4 Rev. 1) (New York: Statistical Office of the
United Nations, 1958), pp. 14–17. Information about the new System of National
Accounts (SNA) is found in *A System of National Accounts*, Studies in Methods, ser. F,
no. 2, rev. 3 (New York: 1968), United Nations, pp. 84–88, 166. The new SNA income
categories have been almost totally reconciled with the new employment categories of
the latest *International Standard Industrial Classification of All Economic Activity* (ISIC),
ser. M, no. 4, rev. 2 (New York: United Nations, 1968).
    6. See Dirección General de Estadística, *Censo de Población de la República de Chile*,
Levantado el 15 de Diciembre de 1920 (Santiago: Sociedad Imprenta y Litografía
Universo, 1925), pp. 407–08.

Table 9.2. Relative Income (GDP) and Employment in Total Services, Chile, Selected Years, 1940–71

	Percentage of total services								Relative productivity					
	Income						Employment							
			Excluding ownership of dwellings		Excluding ownership of dwellings, transportation, storage, and communications			Excluding transportation, storage, and communications	$\frac{(1)}{(7)}$	$\frac{(2)}{(7)}$	$\frac{(3)}{(7)}$	$\frac{(4)}{(7)}$	$\frac{(5)}{(8)}$	$\frac{(6)}{(8)}$
	Series													
	Old	New	Old	New	Old	New								
	(1)	(2)	(3)	(4)	(5)	(6)	(7)	(8)	(9)	(10)	(11)	(12)	(13)	(14)
1940	56.1		44.8		38.0		35.5	31.0	1.58		1.26		1.22	
1945	59.3		48.8		41.4		36.8	32.2	1.61		1.33		1.28	
1950	57.4		47.4		41.2		37.9	33.3	1.51		1.25		1.24	
1955	54.1		47.1		41.2		38.9	34.0	1.39		1.21		1.21	
1960	59.2	(50.3)	47.4	(46.0)	41.2	(42.9)	41.4	36.2	1.43	(1.21)	1.14	(1.11)	1.14	(1.18)
1965	58.5	(47.6)	50.9	(44.0)	43.1	(39.4)	41.5	35.8	1.41	(1.15)	1.23	(1.06)	1.20	(1.10)
1970		(46.8)		(43.7)		(39.3)	46.7	40.5		(1.00)		(0.93)		(0.97)
1971		(48.2)		(45.3)		(40.9)	47.0	41.1		(1.02)		(0.96)		(0.99)

Source: See table 7.2.

Notes: See table 7.2. Total Services includes: (a) health, education, and miscellaneous services; (b) general government; (c) wholesale and retail trade; (d) banking, insurance, and real estate; (e) transport, storage, and communications; and (f) ownership of dwellings.

an employment counterpart, this emerges as a unique, distorting sub-sector. Furthermore, since the drastic cut in the income estimate of ownership of dwellings explains more than 70 percent of the reduction of the service sector's income share by ODEPLAN in 1960 to 50.3 percent from CORFO's 59.2 percent, special treatment of this subsector seems advisable. If ownership of dwellings is excluded from the service sector, its income (CORFO) share is less than half of GDP in most years, rises rapidly during 1940–45 but stabilizes subsequently until 1960, and (according to ODEPLAN, which adjusted all subsector income estimates downward) declines between 1960 and 1970. However, employment remains intact, and the gap between the respective income and employment shares therefore declines. The employment share finally surpasses that of income by 1970. Stagnation and a drop in the sector's ODEPLAN income share between 1960 and 1970 do not prevent the seemingly inexorable employment rise to 46.7 percent of the labor force in 1970, and transformation of the sector from high productivity (with a relative productivity value of 1.26 in 1940) to low productivity and surplus labor by 1970 (with a relative productivity of 0.93 in 1970).

Even if transport, storage, and communications as well as ownership of dwellings are excluded, services emerge as the overall most significant sector in the economy in terms of income and employment contribution. Its income share either exceeds or is close to 40 percent—and thus is larger than for any other sector—and its employment share rises from 31.0 percent in 1940 to 40.5 in 1970.[7]

Services have been indispensable in satisfying a wide range of needs. They are generated jointly with or complement food, housing, mineral, or industrial production, leading to either consumption or investment, or are consumed directly and separately by households. Their quantitative presence and qualitative contribution to development depend on the rising and shifting need–demand pattern on the one hand, and the degree and form of the derived or autonomous supply on the other. As one of its other functions, the sector must satisfy the indirect human needs for food and industrial and other products at a specific time and location and in specific quantities. Thus, the time-transformation func-

7. Annual statistics for income and employment are found in an earlier and larger version of this study, which is available at the Yale Economic Growth Center. See "The Service Sector: Its Growth and Functions," in "The Structure and Growth of the Chilean Economy" (Milwaukee: Dept. of Economics, University of Wisconsin, 1971), pp. 372–464.

tion is the set of actions that transforms the time dimension of the stock and flow of goods and services and that bridges the time gaps between production and consumption patterns. The sectors performing this function have always been present, although frequently only in embryonic form, as secondary activities within other sectors. Similarly, the location-transformation function is the set of actions that alters the spatial dimension of stocks and flows of goods and services.

The quantity transformation function is the set of actions that alters the amount of the stocks and flows of goods and services. Services that change the time, location, and quantity dimensions of other goods and services are complementary to commodity or other service production in that they act as an automatic and necessary joint input in satisfying consumption or investment.

A further service function, quality maintenance, is defined as the set of actions that aims to maintain the quality of the human, physical, institutional, political, and social capital stocks and the flow of goods and services thereof. Unlike some functions that can be fulfilled exclusively by one or more service subsectors, quality maintenance can be performed by both the goods and service sectors. Thus, the quality of the stock of consumer durables has been preserved either through constant replacement of those durables in need of repair—a function of the goods-producing sector—or by use of the service sector to uphold quality through repair and maintenance. The magnitude of maintenance services has depended, at least partially, on the quality of available resources, the cost and possibility of replacing goods in need of maintenance, and the cost of using services for such maintenance.

The quality-improvement function is defined as the set of actions that improves the quality of the stock of physical, human, environmental, social, and political capital and the flow of services thereof.[8] The secret of the relationship between services and aggregate growth may lie in the strength of this function, which shapes the economy's ability to modernize and transform.

The service sector also operates to satisfy the needs for information, instruments of transaction and storage of wealth, and cultural and

8. The present analysis of the role of services in terms of functions was first developed in my "Sectoral Transformation in Latin America," pp. 326–34. Moreover, on the basis of these ideas I made recommendations for revisions and an extension of the United Nations national accounts in my "New Dimensions in National Accounting with Special Reference to Chile," Paris, Nov. 13–17 1972 meeting on *National Accounts and Development Planning in Low Income Countries* (Paris: OCED [Organization for Economic Cooperation and Development], 1974), pp. 1–19.

religious activities. The information-transmission function, fulfilled by communications and transportation, is the set of actions required to convey information concerning economic and noneconomic events in a society. The money function is the complex of actions performed by the banking and financial intermediation system in an exchange economy. Finally, the function of cultural and religious enrichment includes all actions necessary to balance and enrich the soul and spirit of society members.

The size, variety, and nature of the needs for services have changed with development. Much of this demand has been and still is satisfied through such free goods as clean air, water, wildlife, and forestry products. Another part is satisfied by the households themselves without market transactions—household transportation, trade, storage, education, and so forth. Value added in services has arisen only when the existing needs have been met by the various subsectors.

In some instances services are supplied to satisfy an existing demand need. In other instances, however, it appears that they emerge and create needs that they themselves subsequently satisfy. Some of the demand and supply forces seem to apply to all subsectors, whereas others have exclusively or primarily influenced the growth of a specific subsector.

Chile's early and high degree of monetization (conversion from a barter to money-exchange economy), specialization, and commercialization (separation of the consuming from producing units) was caused by the market-dependent, stratified, and hierarchical latifundio land tenure system, the speedy and pervasive incorporation of domestic production into international trade through export orientation, and early urbanization. Exchange and specialization prevailed in agriculture as the dominant large estates with their quasi-corporate structures emphasized mono- or oligo-cultivation, relied heavily on a seasonally floating, migrant labor force (afuerinos) receiving primarily cash payments, and were either urban- or export-market oriented.

From their very inception Chile's export sectors, as integral parts of the highly specialized international market system, diffused commercialization and specialization and caused an autonomous increase in the demand for services. The impact of urbanization on demand was even more pervasive. As the direct needs for services expanded greatly in the urban environment, specialization was stimulated further (generating increased service demand), and many needs previously met through "free" services were now satisfied through exchange. This development gave rise to value added.

In view of these considerations, it is understandable that services were concentrated in urban- and export-oriented provinces. The concentration of the sector was high in the urban Santiago–Valparaíso complex. The province of Santiago was 90 percent urban and had 53.4 percent of its labor force in services in 1960. The concentration of this sector was also high in the export-oriented urban North, which had 87.3 percent urban population and 53 percent of the Tarapacá labor force in services in 1960, and in the South (in Magallanes urban population was 77.7 percent in 1940, with 53.1 percent of the labor force in services).[9]

The demand for services was satisfied by domestic sectors, some partly foreign owned, by services imported from abroad, or directly by households without giving rise to national accounts value added. The supply or push forces that seem applicable to all rather than to a particular subsector included the demographic explosion of 1930–73, the inadequate expansion or capital intensive growth of the commodity sectors, and the rising urban–rural mobility.

TRANSFORMING THE TIME, LOCATION, AND QUANTITY DIMENSIONS:
TRADE, BANKING, REAL ESTATE, AND OWNERSHIP OF DWELLINGS

The demand for banking, trade, and housing services was strong throughout 1930–73/74 because these three subsectors—along with the time-, location-, and quantity-transformation functions they performed—were indispensable to the functioning and survival of the traditional production system. Banking, which performed par excellence the time-changing and money functions, captured surplus resources, centralized and concentrated them, and then channeled them to the deficit-investing units. Trade performed this same function indirectly. Housing and storage services were largely responsible for maintaining as well as improving the quality of life in Chile by permitting individuals to enjoy life in protected habitats.

The flow of banking, trade, and housing services underwent some critical quantitative and qualitative changes throughout 1930–73. The

9. These calculations are based on information found in "Demography," in M. Mamalakis, "Historical Statistics of Chile, 1840–1965," mimeo, table IIAlfl, pp. A-84–A-88; table IIA2al, pp. A-134–A-144; table IIA2a3, pp. A-148–A-156.

Table 9.3. Relative Income (GDP) and Employment in Trade and Banking,
Chile, Selected Years, 1940–71
(In percentages)

	Income generated by						Employ-ment		
	Trade		Banking						
	Old Series	New Series	Old Series	New Series	(1) + (3)	(2) + (4)		Relative productivity	
								(5)/(7)	(6)/(7)
	(1)	*(2)*	*(3)*	*(4)*	*(5)*	*(6)*	*(7)*	*(8)*	*(9)*
1940	18.1		4.1		22.2		10.1	2.20	
1945	19.3		3.9		23.2		10.4	2.23	
1950	17.4		3.8		21.2		10.6	2.00	
1955	20.5		3.0		23.4		10.5	2.23	
1960	19.8	(22.4)	3.2	(2.8)	23.1	(25.2)	11.2	2.06	(2.25)
1965	21.8	(20.9)	2.9	(2.3)	24.7	(23.2)	11.7	2.11	(1.98)
1970		(20.7)		(4.1)		(24.8)	14.7		(1.69)
1971		(21.3)		(4.5)		(25.8)	15.0		(1.72)

Sources: See table 7.2.
Notes: See table 7.2.

qualitative and quantitative roles of banking, which was far greater than the sector's income contribution to GDP during 1940–70 (between 2.3 and 4.1 percent, as shown in table 9.3) remained unfulfilled or even declined as the serious deterioration in the quality and quantity of its services during 1930–72 created a major bottleneck.

Chile's monetary system confined itself mainly to lending short- and medium-term credit. Most long-term credits authorized to various sectors originated from the development institutions.[10] The major deterioration in the amount and quality of financial services occurred between 1940 and 1954; it stabilized during 1955–59 and then partly recovered during 1960–70 as a consequence of the introduction or expansion of the saving and loan associations and the activities of the housing corporation.[11] Inflation and sectoral discrimination, coupled with obsolete and rigid usury laws, fell most heavily on the financial sector, whose mortgage banks and savings institutions became early

10. See Banco Central de Chile and Oficina de Planificación Nacional, *Estudio de Fuentes y Usos de Fondos Chile 1960–1964* (Santiago: Editorial del Pacífico, 1967), pp. 7–10. Hereafter cited as *Fuentes y Usos de Fondos.*
11. See Javier Fuenzalida and Sergio Undurraga, *El Crédito y Su Distribución en Chile* (Santiago: Editorial Lambda, 1968), pp. 12–17.

primary victims. Credits from mortgage banks decreased by 90 percent between 1940 and 1955, those from the State Bank by 33 percent, and those of private banks by 50 percent.[12]

This decline was almost fatal. The credit deficit, the best indicator of the gap between the quantitative demand and actual flow of financial services, grew in real terms from 98 million escudos in 1941 to 3.028 billion in 1965.[13] The ensuing credit asphyxy became increasingly acute during 1940–55 as the stock of institutional monetary capital suffered a net decumulation. After 1955, and especially during the 1960–70 presidencies of Alessandri and Frei, the quantity and quality of financial services improved significantly but suffered a new major setback during 1970–72.[14]

The decumulation of institutional banking capital affected different groups unequally. The distribution originally favored the private sector. The public sector's credit share fell from 12.3 percent in 1940 to 4.1 percent in 1951 but rose from 1952 onward to 43.4 percent in 1960 and stabilized at between 41 and 45 percent during 1960–65.[15] The strong regional concentration (whereby Santiago Province absorbed 68 percent of aggregate credit during 1960–70), the concentration of credit among few recipients (with 1.5 percent of the debtors receiving 44 percent of total credit), and the inadequate variety of credit instruments in terms of maturity, size, interest rates, readjustability, and so forth have only aggravated the shortage in the internal supply of loanable funds.[16] The substitute sources of funds were not only inefficient and inadequate but also socially and politically explosive.

Part of the deficit between rising internal credit and money demand and internal savings that was left unsatisfied was met by the growth of a parallel financial system, and part was countered by the influx of foreign capital, which assumed a strategic role in money creation and the financing of production and investment activities. The flow of external banking services from Western private capitalist nations had reached an upper limit by 1970—primarily because of the constraints imposed by the already high foreign indebtedness—when Chile's internal political shift fostered the rational strategy of making maxi-

12. Ibid., p. 21.
13. Ibid., p. 30.
14. Ibid., pp. 14, 17.
15. Ibid., p. 41.
16. *Antecedentes sobre el Desarrollo Chileno—1960–70* (Santiago: ODEPLAN, 1971), pp. 406, 407. Hereafter cited as *Antecedentes, 1960–70.*

mum use of the untapped lending power of the Soviet bloc and other social capitalist nations.

The internal performance of the money- and time-transformation functions was grossly inadequate throughout 1940–73, as measured by almost any standard: credit supply, aggregate or sectoral growth, or saving and investment level. The unnecessarily heavy reliance on foreign resources—credits, banks, and so forth—to satisfy these needs contributed to economically burdensome and politically explosive foreign indebtedness.

The principal, though by no means sole, responsibility of wholesale and retail trade is to change the quantity dimension of goods by purchasing goods in small (or large) quantities and selling them in large (or small) quantities. Thus, as it equalizes demand, trade also changes the location and time dimension of goods and undertakes packaging, payment of transfer or sales taxes, and so on. Chile's idiosyncratic territorial configuration, with nonoverlapping spatial distribution of productive resources and population and high levels of urbanization, inflation, protection, and so forth, has created an unusually high demand for the services of the trade sector.

Trade needs are almost unlimited for the northern mineral region that borders Peru and Bolivia, the mining–agricultural zone of Gabriela Mistral's Norte Chico, the agricultural, industrial, and service heartland of Santiago–Valparaíso–Concepción, the agricultural–forestry region from Arauco to Swiss-like Llanquihue, and the southern livestock–petroleum tip.[17] Most regions maintained direct trade links with abroad, giving rise to a major triangular, multilaterally offsetting pattern. The mining North's net export surplus to Europe and the United States (its ports of Arica, Iquique, and Antofagasta handled chiefly export cargo) and its much smaller import deficit with the Center were matched by the large import deficit of the Center (whose ports of Valparaíso and Talcahuano handled primarily import cargo) with Europe and the United States.

The remarkable pre-1930 export–import trade, first with Peru, then with California, Australia, and the rest of the United States, was largely a response to foreign demand facilitated by the railroad and shipping revolution. It collapsed during the Great Depression and never regained

17. For an early description of trade see Luis Galdámes, *El Comercio Interior de Chile* (Santiago: Sociedad Imprenta y Litografía Universo, 1909).

its old glory[18] as the unrestricted freedom of external trade decreed in 1811 came to an abrupt end.[19]

Most export trade and commercialization of nitrate, copper, iron ore, and other minerals were taken over by the state after 1970. For more than 100 years it had been in the hands of a small group of national and foreign firms—frequently the producers themselves—and state agencies. Wholesale export trade was more a passive response to foreign demand than a force that created or stimulated such demand.

Retail trade has been the subject of major controversy. According to one view commerce in general, and retail trade in particular, inhibited instead of stimulated domestic sectoral exchange and growth because an especially large number of widely dispersed firms were plagued by high costs resulting from disguised unemployment among superfluous personnel and from low sales. While consumers paid excessive prices because of inefficient commercialization, the producer's share of the final price was too low to provide continuous incentives for production growth.[20] Implicit in this hypothesis is the belief that the extremely great income share of trade was the result of inefficiency. According to table 9.3, this income share was 18.1 percent of GDP in 1940, 19.8 percent (CORFO) or 22.4 percent (ODEPLAN) in 1960, and 21.3 percent in 1971. It was very high, especially if compared to the comparatively low employment contribution of the combined trade and banking—which, according to table 9.3, was only 10.1 percent of the labor force in 1940 and 11.2 percent in 1960 but had risen to 15.0 percent in 1971.

The logic in this argument is by no means foolproof. A high degree of inefficiency should have contributed to increased employment and, through competition, to a smaller income share. But this alternative hypothesis argues not only that trade was very efficient in general but also that it performed much better than many other sectors. Admittedly, a distorted trade pattern did arise, but it was primarily because government provided distorted incentives. The relative productivity of the trade and banking sector had been extraordinarily high [2.20 in 1940

18. For a useful analysis of internal trade see Juan Crocco and Helio Varela [Carmona], "Comercio Interior," in CORFO, *Geografía Económica de Chile* (Santiago: CORFO, 1962), vol. 4, pp. 83–109. See also Helio Varela, "Comercio Interior," in *Geografía Económica de Chile, Primer Apéndice* (Santiago: CORFO, 1966), pp. 276–91.

19. Alfonso Lastarría Cavero, "Comercio," in *Chile, Geografía Económica* (Santiago: Imprenta Cervantes, 1923), pp. 235–50, esp. p. 235.

20. See Helio Varela, "Comercio Interior," in CORFO, *Geografía Económica de Chile,* condensed (Santiago: CORFO, 1965), p. 772.

and 2.06 (CORFO) in 1960] and declined only between 1960 and 1971 from 2.25 to 1.72 (ODEPLAN), as shown in table 9.3. It may be worth mentioning that this pattern—wherein commerce's normal income share of more than 20 percent of GDP is enjoyed by its only half as large normal labor force share of less than 10 percent—is not unique to Chile but has prevailed in most Latin American countries. Brazil, Colombia, Costa Rica, the Dominican Republic, Ecuador, El Salvador, Guatemala, Haiti, Honduras, Mexico, Nicaragua, and Paraguay are other examples.[21]

Chile's trade employment, among the highest in Latin America, was tied to urbanization (more than 50 percent was in the Santiago–Valparaíso urban trading and banking nucleus), as well as to the trade configuration and the nature of the employment. More than 80 percent of the employed were white-collar workers, employers, and members of unincorporated enterprises.

The large commerce income share was the result of lack of foreign competition due to almost complete protection, inflation-induced quasi-rents, and sectoral discrimination, which reduced the agricultural and mining income shares. However, trade was heterogeneous: a prosperous, highly diversified segment dealing largely in industrial, imported, high-quality products and dominated by immigrants and their offspring coexisted with the smaller number of farmer's markets dealing in food and second-hand or low-price products. In the latter, income was close to subsistence.[22]

The inherent weakness of trade reflected the distorted governmental stimuli that promoted internal and import trade but penalized export trade. In addition, the extravagant commerce quasi-rents and the discrimination against agriculture and mining channeled the energies and resources of foreigners and immigrants into the admittedly high-income but least necessary and productive activities, those that changed the quantity dimension of goods. Trade earned one-fifth of the country's income and supported only one-tenth of its population, while agriculture earned only one-tenth of the income but supported one-third of the population. Trade was not a bottleneck sector; its inadequate performance was induced.

The paradoxical coupling of a disproportionately high income share, compared to the labor share, with inadequate performance arose from

21. See my "Sectoral Transformation," table 7, pp. 320–21.
22. See Varela, "Comercio Interior," in CORFO, 1965, p. 788.

government policies that provided maximum incentives for this sub-sector, as measured by the ex-post income share. But these policies were both excessive for trade's relative contribution and sufficiently distorted to provide a distribution and composition of such services that did not match the country's needs. The unsatisfied gap between total demand and supply could have been corrected by a shift in the composition of the supply of these services. Even though trade and banking emerged as the most "productive" according to the income and employment accounts, their capabilities were not matched by a maximum efficiency in performing the time-, location-, and quantity-transformation and money functions. Export trade languished, banking services were rigid, and retail trade often operated under semimonopolistic conditions.

CHANGING THE LOCATION DIMENSION: TRANSPORTATION, STORAGE,
AND COMMUNICATIONS

With its extended, bean-like shape, geographic diversity, remoteness from the world's industrial centers, vast coastal shores, rich mineral deposits, and urban sprawls, Chile has provided fertile ground for prompt adoption of the numerous innovations that led to the successive revolutions in sea, land, and air transportation. Indeed, the transport-ing of people and goods played a central role in the development of the economy by shaping the demand as well as supply of resources. The country's needs were primarily satisfied by the transportation sector proper but also to a lesser extent by the trade, gas, water, and electricity, and personal services sectors (giving rise to corresponding value added in the national accounts) and by private ownership of automobiles and other vehicles, which increased utility but not value added. As late as 1973, door-to-door peddlers, modern jet aircrafts, and animal-drawn and motorized vehicles—there were 54,000 of the former and 63,000 of the latter in 1960—coexisted to satisfy Chile's transportation needs.[23]

Employment in transport, storage, and communications rose

23. A very good, general review of Chile's transportation sector during 1960–70 can be found in ODEPLAN, *Antecedentes, 1960–70* pp. 189–235. See also the very informa-tive description of its key characteristics found in Oscar Miranda, "Transportes," in *Geografía Económica de Chile*, vol. 4, pp. 1–75, and its bibliography. The information on vehicles is found on p. 6 of the current book.

Both the national accounts and the employment statistics lump together transportation with storage and communications. In this section I deal exclusively with transport both because the quantitative importance of storage and communications is comparatively small and because of lack of other sources of information.

Table 9.4. Relative Income (GDP) and Employment in Transportation, Storage, and Communications, Chile, Selected Years, 1940–71

	Percentage of transportation				
	Income		*Employment*	*Relative productivity*	
	Old Series	*New Series*		*(1)* / *(3)*	*(2)* / *(3)*
	(1)	*(2)*	*(3)*	*(4)*	*(5)*
1940	6.8		4.5	1.51	
1945	7.4		4.5	1.64	
1950	6.2		4.6	1.35	
1955	5.9		4.9	1.20	
1960	6.2	(3.1)	5.2	1.19	(0.60)
1965	7.8	(4.6)	5.7	1.37	(0.81)
1970		(4.4)	6.2		(0.71)
1971		(4.4)	5.9		(0.74)

Sources: See table 7.2.
Notes: See table 7.2.

secularly both in relative terms (from 4.5 percent in 1940 to 6.2 percent in 1970, as shown in table 9.4) and in absolute terms (from 78,508 in 1940 to 175,000 in 1970). The most rapid increase occurred during 1960–70.[24] Questions concerning the efficiency of this labor force become evident when the income share of the sector, shown in table 9.4, is considered. According to the old, CORFO estimates, transportation was relatively efficient. It generated more than 6 percent of GDP, with a relative productivity of at least 1.19, in the six years considered. ODEPLAN almost halved these income estimates, however, and lowered relative productivity to only 0.6 in 1960 by adjusting for the size of deficits, covered through government transfers, that were rooted in Chile's transport history.

When the steam engine revolutionized maritime transport as the wheat, copper, and nitrate export boom pulled Chile into the mainstream of world production and trade, the first transportation crisis hit. Export–import needs skyrocketed between 1850 and 1910, and the government built costly port and storage facilities. Nevertheless, Chile's merchant marine not only failed to expand correspondingly but was almost extinguished under the onslaught of foreign competition. By

24. ODEPLAN, *Población Ocupada por Sectores Económicos, 1960–1970* (Santiago: ODEPLAN, 1971), table 10j. Hereafter cited as *Población Ocupada, 1960–1970.*

1969 only 9.9 percent of export–import traffic was carried by Chilean ships, having fallen from 21 percent since 1960. Even coastal shipping, which had regained strength before 1930, was gradually replaced by truck and railroad transportation, although its long cargo hauls of minerals and fuels rose astonishingly between 1960 and 1969.[25] The ports, backward and deteriorating loading, unloading, storage, and related equipment and facilities (which made up more than 60 percent of transport expenditures), combined with inefficient management and corrupt unions, caused a stagnation that suggests that the maritime revolution was repulsed from Chile's coasts.[26]

The railroads descended upon Chile almost as early as the steamship. This rapid and early expansion (Chile built the first line in Latin America) between 1855 and 1913 was largely the remarkable achievement of William Wheelwright and Henry Meiggs and the Chileans Juan and Mateo Clark.[27] Stimulated by the export boom, private railroads sprang up in the nitrate North, the Concepción coal region, and the copper areas. These areas accounted for more than 50 percent of the railroad network before 1900.[28] Established in 1859, state railroads gradually assembled the longitudinal line that forms the artery between the Andes and the sea from Arica to Puerto Montt. Transversal branches now run from the coastal ports toward the mountains. Construction continued in spite of declines or only small rises in cargo and passenger traffic in the decades after 1910, and by 1971 there were 8,219 kilometers of railroad.[29]

As early as 1892, Chilean railroads had been singled out as the world's most inefficient by Augustín Ross (1844–1926), important politician, public figure, and writer. Operating costs absorbed 85 per-

25. ODEPLAN, *Antecedentes, 1960–70*, pp. 217, 219, 223.

26. Instituto de Economía, *Movimiento de Carga de Cabotaje 1950–1958* (Santiago: Instituto de Economía, Universidad de Chile, 1959), pp. 1–3. Also Instituto de Economía, *Eficiencia Portuaria en Chile* (Santiago: Universidad de Chile, 1960), pp. 3, 7.

27. For background information see the classic treatise on railroads, *Ferrocarriles de Chile, Historia y organización*, ed. Emilio Vassallo Rojas and Carlos Matus Guiterrez (Santiago: Editorial "Rumbo," 1943). Hereafter cited as *Historia Ferrocarriles*. This compendium of essays and articles deals with all aspects of growth and development of railroads from their beginning to 1943. (see pp. 25, 43–56).

28. See ibid., pp. 157–80. Indispensable for anyone interested in the state railroads are the *Memorias de los Ferrocarriles del Estado*, which are published annually.

29. *Antecedentes, 1960–70*, p. 202. The early traffic stagnation is described in *Historia Ferrocarriles*, pp. 37–38, 195, and in Martiniano O. Poblete, *Una Jornada Ferroviaria* (Recuerdos de 38 años de vida carrilana) (Santiago: Imprenta Universo, 1930), vol. 2, pp. 382, 386–87, 447.

cent of their gross revenues in 1889 and 82 percent in 1890, compared to a world average of only 62 percent.[30] Although state railroads had developed periodic deficits even during 1920–45, deficits assumed staggering magnitude during 1960–64, when they fluctuated between 1 and 4 percent of GDP.[31] The pre-1940 problems were created by the periodic transfer of ill-equipped and uneconomical lines to the state railroads, high repair costs because of heterogeneous rolling stock, routes parallel with the steamships, inefficient management, and habitual governmental neglect. These problems were subsequently compounded by the falling rates caused by fierce competition from motorized vehicles and the mounting costs resulting from early retirements, rising wages and employment, and further mismanagement. As national and foreign savings were diverted to the railroad deficits, the inefficient performance of the transportation sector (illustrated by the low relative productivity shown in table 9.4) was accompanied by a costly leakage of resources away from productive uses.

The revolution induced by the combustion engine had far greater impact and mass appeal. In spite of its high direct-import component— 39,000 motorized vehicles, or 62 percent of total supply, were imported in 1970—it launched a boom in national automobile production and assembly between 1955 and 1970. Domestic production accounted for 25,000 vehicles in 1970.[32] The spectacular improvement in intra- and intercity bus transportation until 1972 facilitated urbanization by providing unprecedented divisibility and flexibility in the labor and commodity markets. Maximum mobility was offered to a privileged class of car owners, but the transport needs of major population segments in Santiago's megalopolis were left partly or totally unsatisfied.

As a means of cargo movement, road transport was until 1971 the privileged subsector. It was completely free in movement, ownership, and setting of rates and enjoyed extremely low fuel prices and free use of the road network built and maintained by the general public. As trucking emerged as the most economical means of transport, its share in cargo traffic climbed to 33.5 percent in 1969—71.4 percent if minerals and fuels are excluded.[33] By replacing the steamship and railroad

30. See Agustín Ross, *Memoria sobre los ferrocarriles de Chile* (Paris: Imprimerie Paul Dupont, 1892), pp. X–XI.

31. José Luis Federici Rojas, *Tarifas, Entradas y Gastos de la Empresa de Ferrocarriles del Estado de Chile* (Santiago: Instituto de Economía, Universidad de Chile, 1965), pp. 3–8.

32. República de Chile, Instituto Nacional de Estadísticas, *Síntesis Estadística*, June 1972, p. 18.

33. ODEPLAN, *Antecedentes, 1960–70*, p. 192.

whenever it provided similar services (i.e., complementary to commodity production), its growth raised their deficits.

The high social cost of automobile production until 1970 was due to the industry's distant location in Arica, the large number of firms, the minuscule annual production, inflation-induced distortion, overvalued exchange rates, and other factors.[34] These problems, which often led to negative value added as well, were in part offset by intense utilization of public vehicles in urban areas. Allende's reform of production contemplated a reduction in number of firms to three (from more than twenty in 1964, ten in 1970, and six in 1971) with each confined to one of the specified three automobile submarkets.[35]

The air transport revolution, which was import- and capital-intensive, served only a small minority at a high social cost. It catered increasingly to international traffic, neglecting its unique potential role for long-distance internal movement.[36]

By 1975 Chile was still plagued by imbalance in the transportation sector. Many urban needs for spatial mobility remained unsatisfied—as witnessed by full or overutilization of roads and vehicles—while railroads, ships and seaports, planes and airports, and intercity highways displayed high but uneven degrees of excess capacity. Disguised unemployment, deficits, and duplication were typical. Although the need for the preparation and implementation of a global, efficient transport policy was always present, the ability to satisfy it escaped all governments. As a result, overall growth suffered.[37]

MAINTAINING AND IMPROVING QUALITY: THE CONTRIBUTION OF PUBLIC ADMINISTRATION, DEFENSE, AND PERSONAL SERVICES

The maintenance and improvement of the quality of human, physical, social, political, and institutional capital depend on the performance of

34. See Leland L. Johnson, "Problems of Import Substitution: The Chilean Automobile Industry, " *Economic Development and Cultural Change* 15 (Jan. 1967): 202–16.

35. Salvador Allende, *Mensaje del Presidente Allende ante el Congreso Pleno, 21 de Mayo de 1972* (Santiago: Presidencia de la República, 1972), pp. 380–82. Hereafter cited as *Mensaje 1972.*

36. *Antecedentes, 1960–70,* p. 195, 225–35.

37. Ibid., p. 194. Also Robert T. Brown and Carlos Hurtado R-T., *Una política de transportes para Chile* (Santiago: Instituto de Economía, Universidad de Chile, 1963), publication no. 59, pp. 1–99; Instituto de Economía, *Empresa de ferrocarriles del estado, Sistemas de costos y sus posibles modificaciones* (Santiago: Instituto de Economía, Universidad de Chile, 1963), pp. 1–17 plus appendexes; Carlos Hurtado and Arturo Israel, *Tres ensayos sobre el transporte en Chile* (Santiago: Instituto de Economía, Universidad de Chile, 1964), publication no. 67.

Table 9.5. Narrowly Defined Services Maintaining and Improving Quality

A. 1958 ISIC	B. 1968 ISIC	C. Present Classification
Division 8. Services	Division 9. Community, social, and personal services	Division 9. Services maintaining or improving quality
81. Government services	91. Public administration and defense	91. Of institutional and political capital: public administration and defense
82. Community services	92. Sanitary and similar services	92. Of social capital: business, professional, and labor associations; other social and related community services
83. Business services	93. Social and related community services	93. Of human capital: education, health, welfare, and research and scientific services; personal and household services
84. Recreation services	94. Recreational and cultural services	94. Of cultural and recreational capital: recreational and cultural services
85. Personal services	95. Personal and household services	95. Of international institutional and political capital: international and other extra-territorial bodies
	96. International and other extra-territorial bodies	

the generally misunderstood and neglected sectors that provide public administration and defense, health, education, and other personal services. These will henceforth be referred to as narrowly defined services and are presented in a variety of frameworks in table 9.5 In Chile the overall share of income and labor resources devoted to those sectors rose from 15.3 percent of GDP (CORFO) in 1940 to 20.0 percent (CORFO) in 1950. It declined to 18.1 percent (CORFO), or 17.7 percent (ODEPLAN), in 1960 and 14.3 percent (ODEPLAN) in 1970. As shown in table 9.6, the labor force share in such services rose from 20.9 percent in 1940 to 26.2 percent in 1965 before declining mildly to 25.8 percent in 1970. It would appear that their performance improved continuously between 1940 and 1970, even though the rewards were stable until 1950, but declined subsequently until 1970, when relative productivity fell to 0.55. Or alternatively, the poor and low productivity performance may have only deteriorated over time—relative productivity has been persistently below the countrywide average of 1.00. However, unless the role of these services in maintaining and improving the specific social, political, human, physical, and institutional capital forms is examined, not even an approximate judgment of efficiency can be made. Although my analysis is based on the United Nations classifications, I am recommending a new, simpler, and more consistent approach. Table 9.5 presents the new framework and compares it with the existing ones.

Public administration and defense have not only been entrusted with maintaining a high-quality flow of services affecting the political and social capital, they have also influenced the human and physical one. Some of the services have been excellent by any standard, especially those provided by the police, the military, and all those segments that guarantee constitutional freedoms and rights. Law and order have been preserved throughout 1930–70, although the government's conception of order altered radically between 1970 and 1973 to permit legal and institutional changes destroying private maxicapitalism and to shift the focus away from the middle and upper classes and toward labor and the underprivileged poor. Allende's loose pattern was reversed after September 11, 1973, by the military junta, which applied extremely strict and strong rules of law and order.

Nevertheless, beyond the narrow confines of law and order and the maintenance of political democracy until 1973, public services were mediocre. The stock of public administrative capital was grossly inadequate, as were efforts to maintain and improve it. Low efficiency, recognized by the public employees themselves, was attributed to

Table 9.6. Relative Income (GDP) and Employment in Narrowly Defined Services,
Chile, Selected Years, 1940–71

Percentage of

	Income generated by				Employ-ment	Relative productivity	
	Services		General government		(1) + (3)	(2) + (4)		(5)/(7)	(6)/(7)
	Old Series	New Series	Old Series	New Series					
	(1)	(2)	(3)	(4)	(5)	(6)	(7)	(8)	(9)
1940	10.4		5.4		15.8		20.9	0.75	
1945	11.5		6.8		18.3		21.8	0.84	
1950	11.5		8.5		20.0		22.7	0.88	
1955	9.5		8.3		17.7		23.5	0.75	
1960	9.7	(11.9)	8.4	(5.8)	18.1	(17.7)	24.9	0.73	(0.71)
1965	9.9	(11.1)	8.5	(5.1)	18.4	(16.2)	26.2	0.70	(0.62)
1970		(9.9)		(4.5)		(14.4)	25.8		(0.56)
1971		(10.5)		(4.6)		(15.1)			(0.58)

Sources: See table 7.2.
Notes: See table 7.2. Narrowly defined services include (a) health, education, and miscellaneous services, and (b) general government.

inadequate training, lack of motivation, and poor remuneration.[38] Corrupt customs officials and understaffed or underfinanced traditional services persisted because government continually moved into new areas rather than confining itself to expanding and improving the services that were already under its domain.

Those services that maintain and improve the stock of human capital—health, education, and welfare—were persistently emphasized. Employment in education and health rose by more than 80 percent from 115,900 in 1960 to 193,100 in 1970.[39] Employment in education increased extraordinarily during 1966–70 as part of the Christian Democrats' emphasis on social, human investment, while value added by the education subsector remained stable at slightly above 3 percent of GDP.[40]

38. See Arturo Hein C. and Jaime Contreras V., El Funcionario Público. Caso: Ministerio de la Vivienda y Urbanismo (Santiago: Instituto de Administración, Universidad de Chile, 1971), pp. 95–96.
39. See ODEPLAN, Población Ocupada, 1960–1970 tables 11, 11j.
40. ODEPLAN, Antecedentes, 1960–70, p. 296.

Even before Salvador Allende emphasized greater social freedom of access to culture through education,[41] the demand for and supply of more and better education had grown phenomenally, especially during 1964–70. The demand was determined by the increased knowledge, intellectual and cultural aspirations, and income level of the population as well as by the rising production needs for more and better labor inputs. The supply was shaped by public and private efforts at every level—preschool, primary, high school, university, vocational, and adult education—and was determined by the resources available to finance the wages and salaries of the teachers, the buildings, teaching materials, and so forth, and last but not least, the food and clothing of the schoolchildren. Although the expansion of the teaching staff can be termed successful, capital expenditures remained grossly inadequate (the capacity deficit in 1969 in public primary education was for 109,000 students, that for preschoolers 15,000[42]), and large socioeconomic differences resulted in an exorbitant dropout rate between ages 12 and 19. Although school participation rates surpassed 90 percent for the 8–12 bracket, this rate was only 14 percent for 19-years-old in 1970.[43]

Throughout 1940–73, but more strongly during 1965–70 and with an unprecedented impetus during 1970–72, the demand for educational services was increased when prospective students were provided with the resources to stay in school: food, clothing, loans, medical–dental assistance, student colonies, and so forth.[44] On the supply side, the number of schools rose, the universities opened regional branches, and two-year centers and vocational and adult courses increased. University enrollment grew by 185.7 percent from 25,000 in 1960 to 71,000 in 1969 and 100,000 in 1971; basic education enrollment rose from 1,162,000 in 1960 to 2,064,000 in 1970 and high school from 228,300 in 1960 to 292,900 in 1970.[45]

The educational effort was further strengthened under Allende. Enrollment in primary education became completely free, enrollment fees in secondary education were frozen at their 1970 level, and maximum attention was paid to preschoolers. If measured by enrollment, these efforts were successful. Basic education was provided to 97.9 percent of the school population between 6 and 14 years. Enrollment in the 12–

41. See Allende, *Mensaje 1972*, p. xx.
42. ODEPLAN, *Antecedentes, 1960–70*, p. 302.
43. Ibid., p. 300.
44. Ibid., p. 301.
45. Ibid., pp. 297, 304; Allende, *Mensaje 1972*, p. xx.

19 age bracket rose by more than 50 percent, and dropout rates were reduced. University enrollment advanced by 30 percent in 1971 over 1970. Vocational education, in both the Technical State University and the specialized institutes, was expanded. Nevertheless, because of the high dropout rate, inadequate intermediate vocational and technical education, distortions in the administration of education, and duplication or even triplication of higher education facilities, the flow of educational services still remains distorted in terms of Chile's needs.[46] The quality of education also continues to be a critical bottleneck in 1975.

Technical education is still primitive compared with the country's needs. Secondary and higher education in the sciences, engineering, agronomy, and other fields related to mining, agriculture, and industry have not succeeded in creating even a modest pool of internal technical progress and innovation. Overall educational quality suffered during 1972–73 because of strikes, political intervention, and polarization in the intermediate and higher-level educational institutions and did not improve significantly in 1974.

Health has been defined as a state of complete physical, mental, and social well-being or as the ability to resist disease and death.[47] Although the potential demand for preventive and curative health services is literally unlimited because it covers the complete life cycle, the actual demand depends on the level and distribution of income; the level of education, culture, and psychology, all of which determine the degree of perception of one's state of health; and on such related factors as nutrition, housing, clothing, and the complex of sanitary facilities and environmental factors.[48] Even though, according to Chile's constitution, the state has been obliged to provide public health and preserve the hygienic welfare of the population, health needs have also been fulfilled by the private sector and the households themselves. The overall level of health services has been high and is improving, as some statistics clearly indicate. The death rate fell from 32.9 per 1,000 in 1921

46. ODEPLAN, ibid., pp. 302–03, 305.

47. The first definition, which is found in *Antecedentes*, p. 308, was formulated by the World Health Organization: "Constitution of the World Health Organization, Annex I," *The First Ten Years of The World Health Organization* (Geneva: 1958). The second, by Ffrangcon Roberts, *The Cost of Health* (London: Turnstile Press, 1952) is cited by Victor Fuchs, "The Contribution of Health Services to The American Economy, in *Essays in the Economics of Health and Medical Care*, ed. Victor R. Fuchs (New York: National Bureau of Economic Research, 1972), p. 12.

48. For a discussion of public health in Chile see *Antecedentes, 1960–70*, pp. 308–21.

to 15.0 in 1950 and 8.56 in 1970.[49] Infant mortality fell from 338.0 per 1,000 live births during 1890–94 to 234.0 in 1930 and 77.52 in 1970,[50] though this must still be regarded as an intolerably high level.

The quality of life as well as health was in some instances not only maintained but improved as medical consultations in the principal public establishments rose by 50 percent between 1960 and 1969. The average annual immunizations during 1965–69 exceeded by 29 percent those of the 1960–64 period. The mortality rate from measles fell from 30.4 deaths per 100,000 inhabitants in 1964 to only 3.5 in 1969. Health expenditures per capita grew in real terms by 21.6 percent between 1960 and 1969.[51]

Even though most indices suggest an overall improvement, in some cases the quality of health or medical services remained the same or even deteriorated. The flow of health services increased proportionately to the rise in GDP, which fluctuated between 2.8 and 3.1 percent during 1960–69. The average hospitalization period remained stable at 1.2 days throughout 1960–69. Only 67.1 percent of the urban and 7.1 percent of the rural population received piped-in drinking water in 1964. A deterioration occurred as the hospital/inhabitant beds ratio fell from 1:217 in 1960 to 1:244 in 1968.[52] Dental and infant care services have remained extremely poor. The intake of animal protein improved constantly from 1934 to 1972 but has hardly been raised to the minimum desirable level, primarily because of discrimination against the agricultural livestock sector. The nutritional deficit has been a major cause of infant mortality but has also resulted in mental retardation, school absenteeism, low productivity, and the like.

Furthermore, the regional flow of health services is unequal. The number of inhabitants per physician (which declined nationally from 1,732 in 1961 to 1,606 in 1967) improved from a range of 906 in Santiago and 11,643 in Chiloé in 1961 to 938 in Santiago and 8,759 in Arauco in 1967.[53] The low-income rural and urban marginal populations had distinctly less access to health services than the workers and middle- and higher-income groups even under Allende, but to a lesser extent.

The social freedom to enjoy health had deeply preoccupied Salvador

---

49. Mamalakis, "Historical Statistics," p. A-72, and Instituto Nacional de Estadísticas, *Síntesis Estadística Agosto-Año 1972*, p. 1.
50. Mamalakis, ibid., p. A-71, and *Síntesis Estadística Agosto-Año 1972*, p. 1.
51. *Antecedentes*, pp. 312–13, 315.
52. Ibid., pp. 311, 315–16.
53. Ibid., pp. 314, 316.

Allende, a physician, since 1939, when he served as President Aguirre Cerda's minister of public health. After 1970 an integrated health policy was planned and partly implemented. External consultations rose by 15.3 percent in 1971 over 1970 and emergency treatments by 32.3 percent. The income redistribution during 1970–72 and the heightened health consciousness of the previously less privileged population strata largely explain the enormous increase in the demand for health services. The distribution of milk to the infant population and mothers was raised by 350 percent between 1970 and 1971. But although Chile needed 9,000 physicians and 11,000 nurses in 1971, only 6,000 physicians and 2,610 nurses were available.[54] Attempts during the Allende presidency to hire health personnel from the Soviet Union and other socialist countries met stiff domestic opposition, and even if they had materialized (they were discontinued in 1973 by the military junta), could have provided only a short-term palliative to the urgent need for a larger domestic flow of physicians, paramedics, and nurses. The short-term objective to put all government health institutions in the service of popular demand was generally accomplished.

Because it was believed that the social freedom of health was best attained through adequate early nutrition, a supplementary program, partly supported by the United States, was greatly expanded. As 48 million kilograms of dry milk were distributed to infants and mothers in 1971—a 350 percent increase over 1970—infant mortality continued the declining trend it had started under previous presidents. Other efforts were less successful. Although the production of some pharmaceuticals rose sharply in 1971, serious shortages developed in the open market during 1972 and early 1973. Even though the National Health Service increased its number of physicians in 1971 by 6.6 percent, dentists by 31.5 percent, and nurses by 17.6 percent, and even though medical–dental benefits were extended to many white-collar workers, medical services in smaller and remote areas remained extremely poor.

Chile's system of social security, among the most complete and advanced in the world, absorbed the formidable amount of 15 percent of GDP during 1970.[55] It covers almost all (except unemployment) risks and accidents and was probably the major contributor to the maintenance and improvement of Chile's high health, productivity, and

54. Allende, *Mensaje 1972*, p. xix.
55. *Antecedentes*, p. 336.

welfare standards. Social security improved throughout 1930–72. The percentage of population covered grew to 72 percent in 1971, up from 63 percent in 1960,[56] as a consequence of Allende's maximum use of social security as an instrument to redistribute income in favor of labor and insured segments of the community.[57] The coverage also improved as workers were continuously reclassified from the less desirable manual-worker category to the better insured white-collar group.

The major risks covered—maternity, unemployment, old age, death (with payments to widows and orphans), general health, and work accidents—differed greatly in terms of quality of services and qualification requirements, depending on the security institution to which the secured belonged. The family allowance ranged in 1970 from 45 escudos per month, if paid by the Social Security Service, to 210 per month for members of the Welfare Fund of the office workers of the Bank of Chile. The value of the family allowance paid by the Social Security Service ranged between 19.4 and 25.2 percent of the family allowance paid during 1960–70 by the Welfare Fund of the Central Bank of Chile.[58] The security system has remained sectoral and thus by definition discriminatory: rich sectors have surplus resources and provide excessive benefits while poor sectors run deficits even though they provide meager services. The social tensions created by these inequalities have plagued Chile ever since the funds were created, and the promise of equalization gained powerful political appeal in the hands of Salvador Allende.

The shifting intersectoral conflicts and tensions have been but one of the high social and economic costs of social security for Chile. Expansion of coverage of risks and population increased the cost to manufacturing employers in 1962 to 22.12 percent of wages and salary costs, compared to an average of less than 5 percent in Costa Rica, El Salvador, Guatemala, Honduras, and Panama in 1962, 11 percent in West Germany in 1960, and 37.3 percent in Italy in 1959. The resulting rise in labor costs has contributed to the adoption of labor-saving techniques and reduction in the labor-absorbing capacity of industrial investment. The majority of orthodox economists, and even the government-controlled National Planning Office (ODEPLAN), agree that the incidence of employers' social security contributions over remunera-

56. See Allende, *Mensaje 1972*, p. 874, and ODEPLAN, *Antecedentes*, p. 337.
57. Allende, ibid., pp. xx–xxi.
58. *Antecedentes*, pp. 350, 351.

tions had reached its maximum tolerance limit by 1970–71. Moreover, during 1960–70 the relation between the passive (benefit receiving) and active (cost carrying) secured population rose from 13.7 percent in 1960 to 21.4 percent in 1970.[59] This reflects not only the system's maturity but also its authorization of excessive benefits.

A particular problem was early retirement that does not fulfill the requirements. By appropriating an increasing share of the income of capital, employers, and the general public, the social security system was converted into a mechanism by which a privileged leisure class of ex-workers was supported by active members. During 1960–70 the secured population financed only 51.5 percent of the system's cost, while the rest of the population, which received no benefits, contributed 48.5 percent.[60]

The social security system's revenues were equal to 15 percent of GDP and 18 percent of domestic income, or 74.8 percent of tax revenues, 66.5 percent of fiscal expenditures, and 31 percent of public sector expenditures. The staggering magnitude of the system's costs not only indicates the size of resources dedicated to quality maintenance and improvement but also the rigidity in government expenditures and policy. The system surplus, which was mostly used to finance personal negative saving, fell from 12.9 percent of gross national saving in 1963 to 8.9 percent in 1968.[61]

Allende introduced major reforms in social security. Equalization of family allowances, which began in 1971, had by 1972 affected more than 80 percent of the beneficiaries, especially the blue-collar workers, farmers, armed forces, police, and public employees. Furthermore, the coverage of the social security system, which corresponded to 72 percent of the total population in 1970, increased to 90 percent with extension of social security to merchants, small industrialists and artisans, transporters, and miscellaneous independents.

Not only the persons covered but also the benefits granted were increased. Thus, the 4.253 million active or passive insured members of the population are protected, in the majority of instances and in addition to the family allowances, by medical, maternity, widowhood, and orphanage insurance. Furthermore, the minimum pensions for disability and old age were raised in 1972 to 100 percent of the minimum

59. Ibid., pp. 347, 346, 354.
60. Ibid., pp. 354, 360.
61. Ibid., pp. 342–44.

industrial wage. Since the ascent to power of the Popular Unity the real increase of these pensions in the social security system has been of the magnitude of 78.5 percent.[62]

Although Allende correctly reformed social security to ensure a more equitable distribution of benefits, no balance has yet been achieved between costs and benefits, even under the military junta. Unless welfare costs are brought into line with the economy's ability to carry them and also come closer to true welfare needs, the degree of social protection may suffer a decline in the very near future.

Some of the gains realized during 1971 and the first half of 1972 appeared to dissipate during the wartime-like inflation of June 1972–June 1973. In the long run, social protection depends on the growth of the productive apparatus. Even though equalization of benefits is desirable, conversion of an economy into a welfare state can be almost fatal, as the case of Uruguay has demonstrated. Social justice demands active and pragmatic altruism for the poor. Chile's phenomenon of selective income redistribution toward privileged groups has intolerably high social costs: it exaggerates the expectations of all secured, raises total and labor costs, reduces the active labor force, and may decrease the welfare of those paying by an amount equal to the welfare increase of the recipients. Complete coverage of the population is bound to diminish excesses.

Among the major coverages that could be eliminated are family allowances to spouses and children of middle- and upper-income families and full pensions for able persons below age 60. The use of social security surpluses for consumer loans should be prohibited. The widespread poor and uneven services, inadequate coverage, and excessive costs have been caused not by a lack of economic resources but by the misuse of existing ones. An unlimited amount of foreign aid and redistributed profits of private or nationalized concerns is used up by social security that is social pilferage. In reality, if only the contributions and receipts of those secured are included and special government contributions are excluded, the social security system operated with a deficit rather than a surplus.

The flow of housing services increased substantially throughout 1930–73 because of the cyclically rising net addition of homes. The declaration that the apotheosis of social freedom was to own a home, made by Salvador Allende in 1971, represented the climax of a process

---

62. Allende, *Mensaje 1972*, pp. xx–xxi.

that had begun as early as 1906.[63] The need for housing, already high in 1930, grew each year until 1973 as a consequence of demographic growth, urbanization, rural to urban migration, the rise in per capita income and aspirations, the repeated destruction of homes by earthquakes and to a lesser extent by fires and floods, expropriation, and the significant shifts in income distribution. The country's ability to provide an adequate supply of these services was superior also because of the availability of labor, intermediate products, capital goods, entrepreneurship, and so forth. Nevertheless, although both the quantity and quality of housing services were not only maintained but also improved throughout 1930–73, many of the needs remained unsatisfied because institutional factors prevented them from being expressed as or converted into actual housing demand. Many of the basic institutions that harmonized demand and supply, such as mortgage banks and household savings, had been corroded by inflation during 1940–56, and no appropriate substitutes were developed. As a consequence Chile developed a "deficit" of 406,000 homes in 1960 and 585,000 in 1970.[64]

However, the demand for and supply of housing services were so heterogeneous among regions and income and family groups that the notion of an easily identifiable housing deficit is grossly misleading.[65] The upper- and middle-income groups enjoyed a disproportionately privileged access to housing services, especially during 1958–65. Even though all governments were greatly concerned with improving the housing services for the poor and destitute, it was not until 1966–70, under the *operación sitio* (building sites program) and *operación callampa* (operation shantytowns), that special treatment of the poor was developed. Under Salvador Allende, the government first directed its attention and resources toward the poor by initiating the construction of approximately 80,000 urban and 7,000 rural dwellings in 1971— four times the 1967–70 annual average and the biggest effort in the country's history.[66] The remarkable improvement in the quality of all services inherent in more and better housing enjoyed since 1970 by Chile's former untouchables was only partly offset by the food shortages and black markets of late 1972.

---

63. See *Antecedentes*, p. 323, and Allende, ibid., pp. xxi–xxii.
64. *Antecedentes*, p. 333.
65. See the most interesting study by Charles A. Frankenhoff, *Hacia una Política Habitacional Popular: El Caso de Chile* (Santiago: CIDU, Universidad Católica), pp. 21–28.
66. Allende, *Mensaje 1972*, pp. xxi–xxii.

More people have been employed in domestic services, which include maids, gardeners, cooks, janitors, and other household servants, than in any other service category. However, the figure fell from 227,000 in 1960 to 204,000 in 1970 as the cost of such services rose, as household servants demanded more privileges and independence, and as higher- and middle-income groups shifted to commercial cleaning and related services. As a corollary, employment in cleaning, laundry, cosmetic, and beauty services increased sharply from 27,000 in 1960 to 70,700 in 1970.[67] Commercialization, specialization, and the social stigma often suffered by household servants also added to this trend.

The irreversible winds of emancipation and social liberation had shaken, weakened, or destroyed the old lord–servant relationship by 1970. The effective scarcity of household servants, especially in Santiago, is typical of more advanced, industrialized, urbanized nations.

Entertainment (theater, television, music, ballet, movies and so forth) and religious services have been relatively abundant and of high quality in Santiago but become limited or nonexistent as one moves toward the agricultural hinterland. Clergy have been persistently in short supply despite heavy immigration from Europe.

Recreation blends the mass entertainment provided by the press, television, radio, movies, and sports such as soccer with more selective activities such as skiing, theater, ballet, horseriding, and symphonic music. Portillo's superb ski facilities attract the world's best skiers and hosted the 1966 Winter Olympics, Gabriela Mistral was Latin America's first Nobel Prize winner in 1946, and when Pablo Neruda won Chile's second Nobel Prize, the country gained a special status in the world of arts. The variety and abundance of recreational services diminish sharply, however, as one moves from the large urban areas toward the agricultural hinterland.

The mass media are unmatched in variety, freedom, intellectual strength, and spirit in Latin America. *El Mercurio*, the oldest and most prestigious newspaper, is read as avidly by the sophisticates of the Center or Right as by its arch enemies of the Left. The communist, powerful, doctrinaire *El Siglo*, which in open Chile reflected views and style normally found in monolithic iron curtain countries, assumed a special role after 1970 by publishing governmental strategies or policy shifts even before *La Nación*, the state's traditional propaganda arm, announced them. *El Siglo* and all other pro-Allende newspapers were

67. ODEPLAN, *Población Ocupada, 1960–1970*, tables 11, 11j.

closed by the military junta on September 11, 1973. Many other satirical, pictorial, religious, or independent newspapers and magazines have been published, even during but not after the 1970–73 crisis of polarization that contained the seeds of internal conflict. The overall degree of cultural independence, identity, authority, and strength of the press until September 11, 1973, was remarkable.

Radio stations offered a range of entertainment and news, but because much of the earlier private support dwindled or disappeared between 1970 and 1973, their variety was reduced. The few television stations run by the universities and the state perform well, even though they depend strongly on imported programs. Between 1970 and 1973 Chile was unwilling or unable to pay for the latest films from the Western nations, while the government deliberately increased the supply of entertainment from the Soviet Union, Hungary, Bulgaria, China, East Germany, North Korea, North Vietnam, Cuba, and the other socialist nations. A shift in favor of mass-produced, low-cost, revolutionary, ideological, proselytizing, popular entertainment has been bolstered by extensive cultural exchange programs and the flow of artists to the socialist nations.[68] All these procommunist tendencies came to an abrupt end and were reversed by the military junta on September 11, 1973.

INCOME, PRODUCTIVITY, AND EMPLOYMENT GROWTH IN SERVICES

The great disparities in the rates of growth of output, employment, and labor productivity found in the commodity sectors are encountered to a much lesser degree in services. The sector is marked by an extraordinary degree of labor absorption. As total employment rose from 1.765 million in 1940 to 2.825 million in 1970, 63 percent of the 1.060 million increment was absorbed by services.[69] Their annual employment growth of 2.5 percent between 1940 and 1970, shown in table 9.7, is indeed exceptional compared to the meager 0.9 rate for the combined commodity sector.

However, the employment and productivity behavior of each service subsector is idiosyncratic. The government and personal services subsector absorbed 35 percent of the 1940–70 labor force increment. As a

68. Allende, *Mensaje 1972*, p. xviii.
69. Calculated from information found in my "Historical Statistics," vol. 2, "Demography," p. A-161, and ODEPLAN, *Población Ocupada*, table 3.

Table 9.7. Growth Rates in Income, Employment, and Labor Productivity
in Services, Chile, 1940–70

	1940–50 *(1)*	*1950–60* *(2)*	*1960–70* *(3)*	*1940–70* *(4)*
I. Government and personal services				
GDP	5.7	2.8	2.9	3.8
L	2.8	1.7	2.3	2.3
GDP/L	2.9	1.1	0.6	1.5
II. Trade and banking				
GDP	2.8	4.7	4.8	4.1
L	2.4	1.3	4.8	2.8
GDP/L	0.4	3.4	0.0	1.3
III. Transport and communications				
GDP	2.3	3.9	8.7	5.0
L	2.2	2.1	3.8	2.7
GDP/L	0.1	1.8	4.9	2.3
IV. Total (I + II + III)				
GDP	3.9	3.9	4.5	4.1
L	2.7	1.7	3.2	2.5
GDP/L	1.2	2.2	1.3	1.6
V. Ownership of dwellings				
GDP	2.0	5.5	1.9	3.1
L				
GDP/L				
VI. Total services				
GDP	3.5	4.1	4.3	4.0
L	2.7	1.7	3.2	2.5
GDP/L	0.8	2.4	1.1	1.5

Sources: See table 8.6.
Notes: See table 8.6.

consequence, whereas its labor force in 1940 was less than 60 percent of that in agriculture, it had become the largest for any sector by 1970. Its rate of productivity growth (which averaged 1.5 percent during 1940–70) declined sharply from 2.9 percent during 1940–50 to only 0.6 percent during 1960–70. Trade and banking experienced an extremely high employment growth during 1960–70 (4.8 percent) whereas their rate of growth of labor productivity was zero during the same period and negligible during 1940–50. They experienced extremely high productivity gains during the stagnation decade of the 1950s, however, when their employment grew the least. In transport and

communications income and productivity growth rates are rising in
each successive decade and employment has also risen significantly.

Services have always been important in Chile. I have attempted to
explain why this little-known, heterogeneous, polychromatic cluster
of sectors—which according to Colin Clark emerges only in rich and
old societies—has always been necessary and present. Services performed some functions (changing location, quantity, and time, maintaining quality, and providing entertainment) as soon as production
and consumption took place, sometimes, as in the case of transport
and trade, at a very high social cost. The autonomous quality-improvement and money functions, which determined Chile's ability to control
its economic destiny, were performed by banking and education inadequately or even in a deteriorating manner after 1930.

The factors determining income and employment in services (as
recorded in national accounts, censuses, and employment surveys) are
of a technical or statistical, economic, social, political, or institutional
nature. The technical or statistical factors refer principally to the
adequacy of statistical definitions adopted from developed, fully
monetized economies and consequently to the degree of coverage of
actual services. In this chapter I have discussed only the economic forces
that can now be grouped more systematically into those that affect
primarily the demand (pull) or those that operate predominantly on the
supply (push) side. The forces on the demand side pull labor into
services from commodity sectors, the unemployed, or the inactive
population. Forces operating on the supply side suggest that labor is
directly or indirectly pushed into services. The demand and supply
factors listed below determined the colossal presence of services at
least since 1900, if not earlier.

I . Demand factors
    A.   Complementarities in production between goods and services
        1.   Export orientation
        2.   Industrialization
        3.   Urbanization
        4.   Expansion of the service sector
        5.   Commercialization and specialization
        6.   Monetization
    B.   Complementarities in consumption
        1.   Population growth and the changing demographic char-
           acteristics

        2.   Increased claims for better health, education, and welfare
        3.   High inequality of income distribution among and within classes, sectors, and regions
        4.   Duplication and redundancy of services
   C.   Independent demand forces
        1.   The demonstration effect
        2.   Increased government employment
        3.   Higher per capita income
        4.   Multiple amenities of city life
        5.   Higher probability of obtaining good education or improving social status in cities
        6.   Rapid deterioration in environmental capital stock

II.   Supply factors
   A.   High and rising population growth
   B.   Insufficient growth of commodity sectors
        1.   Inadequate demand for goods
        2.   Artificially low profit rates in commodity sectors
        3.   Shortage of imported fuels and raw materials
        4.   Capital goods bottleneck
   C.   Increasing capital intensity and capital-intensive technological change
   D.   Labor unionization
   E.   A humanistic orientation of society
   F.   Increasing rural to urban mobility
   G.   The high and increasing degree of technical knowledge
   H.   The process of social liberation and emancipation of women

Chilean economic development has traditionally been examined either by contrasting a pre-1930 outward orientation with a post-1930 inward orientation or, alternatively, by dividing the economy into a subsistence segment (mainly agriculture), a highly productive export sector with uneven linkages to the rest of the economy and frequently foreign controlled, and a third, slowly growing industrial sector that, through import substitution, reduced the country's heavy dependence on exports. In neither case have services been considered.

An analysis of stages of development of the service sector is necessarily largely hypothetical. The criteria used in classifying stages encourage a variety of emphases. The origin of the stimuli to service expansion is the first. The initial stage of this orientation was marked by export expansion, which led to the establishment of a service

infrastructure consisting primarily of supportive, complementary production services. The collapse of the export sector in the 1930s was
followed by industrialization, which could not be achieved without an
advanced service infrastructure of education, banking, transportation,
storage, and so forth. Although the export-oriented services helped or
even stimulated industrialization, the industry's need for new services
provided an independent stimulus.

The usefulness of an export-oriented service infrastructure and its
conversion into an industry-oriented service infrastructure were limited
both because of differences in functions and because of the location of
the infrastructures. The facilities of the North could not be easily used
in the Center. The servicing of the export sector in terms of banking,
insurance, and transport had also been provided by developed nations,
a practice that the industrial sector attempted to reduce.

During the third stage, urbanization and service expansion exerted
an independent expansionary influence upon the service sector. It is
interesting to note that, while export orientation and dependence were
linked and associated with high productivity services, industrialization
and urbanization have been associated with declining or low-productivity service sectors.

In a different but related analysis of the service sector's stages of
development, the criterion used is the value of the relative income/
employment ratio. During the first phase, when Chile was predominantly agricultural and rural with low income and limited specialization,
both value added and employment in the service sector were small (in
the neighborhood of 5 to 10 percent) and gave rise to a value of close
to 1 for relative productivity. Such key subsectors as trade, banking
and finance, ownership of dwellings, and government, which loom
large in later stages, were insignificant, bartered, or offered free.

The second phase, one of transition, was characterized by the growing support given by export and industry to well-paid, modern segments
of the service sector and by a mild rise in service employment. The
unique characteristic of this phase is that relative productivity rose to
and even exceeded a value of 1.5 as service income increased more
rapidly than service employment. In Chile services were transformed
by European and American immigrants and concerns into a highly
efficient and modern sector with average incomes far above the
economy-wide average. However, the Chilean case may have been a
special one because of the unusual strength and influence of foreign
immigrants and concerns in both the export-dependent and other

Fig. 9.1. Relative importance of income and employment in services.

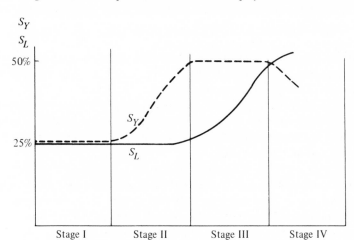

Note: S_Y = value added in services as a percentage of total value added (gross domestic or national product)

S_L = employment in services as a percentage of total labor force

service subsectors. The relative importance of the service subsistence sector is the same in the second as in the first phase.

The third stage will be achieved when relative income and employment are approximately the same and the value of relative productivity falls to the range of 0.8–1.2. A fourth stage could emerge as relative productivity falls below 0.8. The low-productivity service subsectors would become the buffer that absorbs the urban labor surplus.

The hypothetical behavior of services that emerges from the limited information available is presented in figure 9.1. These findings are extremely tentative, and one cannot verify all stages of this pattern for Chile.

As mentioned earlier, if the relative value added (S_Y) and relative employment (S_L) are used as criteria, the growth of services is expected to go through four stages. During the first stage of early development S_Y and S_L are approximately equal. During the second stage S_Y rises rapidly while S_L remains almost completely constant. By the end of Stage II, S_Y has already stabilized and remains approximately constant during Stage III. During Stage III, however, S_L starts rising and by the end of the period has caught up with S_Y. Because Chile has passed

Stage I and is currently at the end of Stage II or the beginning of Stage III, it is only possible to make conjectures about the pattern that will develop in Stage III.

Although the second stage is one of transition, the anomalies and problems it brings may be necessary to achieve the presumed competitive and equalitarian conditions of Stage III. The two sets of S curves observed in the development of the service sector reflect the unequal growth of its subsectors, the varying relative importance of the subsectors during the various stages, and the anomalies that could be the price an economy has to pay for achieving growth or that could be induced and unnecessary.

In the case of Chile a distorted incentive system bestowed significant riches upon such sectors as internal trade and transport while under-emphasizing or neglecting critical parts of banking, education, insurance, and welfare. Therefore, both growth and its relationship to services have been far below their potential. Massive riches generated by nitrate, copper, and even agriculture were used to support consumption-facilitating rather than investment- or production-promoting services. The imposing presence of services, in particular as a source of income but also as an employer, was not matched by an adequate performance of such crucial functions as quality improvement and financial intermediation. The qualitative role of services in improving production capacity through modernization and continuous change was far less than the desired one and definitely less than that suggested by its income level.

10

Distribution

The rising Chilean emphasis on distribution and on the derived transformation of production and capital accumulation is the outgrowth of latent forces of rising momentum and intensity that prevail throughout Latin America. After 1964, and especially since 1970, the transformation in distribution has been manifold and far reaching. Perennial skepticism and open criticism of foreign investment have brought strict control and limitations on foreign ownership—the primary source of resource leakages abroad—without creating a visible change in the international distribution. Aiming to change class, sectoral, and international distribution, the government entered all major industries. It assumed ownership of the extractive industries—the principal source of fabulous but often transitory resource surpluses. It nationalized the banking system—the main source of financial capital. It took control of and restricted private ownership of rural land, the alleged major source of political power and Ricardian rents. It also took over all large industrial enterprises, the alleged source of monopoly profits and power.

All these largely irreversible ownership transfers aimed at wiping out the control of Chile's riches by a few private individuals. And the list can go on. Elitist education, entertainment and health services, and excessive differences in wages, salaries, pension, insurance, health, and other social security benefits—sources of unequal accumulation of human capital by social groups and intralabor inequalities—were attacked, constrained, and reduced. The changes portend of events to come, possibly to be achieved by different means and with different intensity, elsewhere in the hemisphere and on the African and Asian continents. These changes and their effects on production were also primarily responsible for the fall of Allende on September 11, 1973.

THE INCOME SHARE OF LABOR

No other short-term objective was so important to President Allende's program in 1970 as the rise in the income share of labor. Virtually all the tools available were used to redistribute income and destroy the usurpers of labor's surplus value. The resulting short-term income redistribution was the most outstanding in Chile's history. The participation of wage earners in income, including contributions by employers, increased from 54.9 percent in 1970 to 65.8 percent in 1971 (see table 10.1).

With inflation artificially kept in bounds between January 1971 and May 1972 while nominal wages and salaries were strongly adjusted upward, real wages and salaries spurted by 28.4 percent.[1] Salaries rose faster than wages between October 1969 and July 1971, and between October 1970 and July 1971 the combined wage–salary index climbed

Table 10.1. Distribution of Domestic Income by Type of Compensation, Selected Years, *1940–71*
(In percentages)

	1940	1950	1960	1970	1971
Salaries	15.0	19.0	26.0	30.0	35.1
Wages	25.0	22.2	18.4	16.5	20.6
Social security contributions of employers	2.4	3.3	7.2	8.4	10.0
Remuneration of labor by white- and blue-collar workers	42.4	44.5	51.6	54.9	65.8
Other factor payments	57.6	55.5	48.4	45.1	34.2
Domestic income	100.0	100.0	100.0	100.0	100.0

Sources: For 1940 and 1950, CORFO, *Cuentas Nacionales de Chile, 1940–1954* (Santiago: Editorial del Pacífico, S.A., 1957), table 9; for 1960, 1970, and 1971, ODEPLAN, *Cuentas Nacionales de Chile, 1960–1971* (Santiago: ODEPLAN, 1972), table 11, pp. 41–42.

Notes: Information on the distribution of income can be found for the 1940–54 and 1960–71 periods. Publication of income distribution statistics for the 1955–59 years was suspended, allegedly because they revealed a marked deterioration in labor's income share. The main sources of information are: CORFO, *Renta Nacional, 1940–1945* (Santiago: Imprenta Universitaria, 1946), vol. 1, p. 157; CORFO, *Cuentas Nacionales de Chile, 1940–1954* (Santiago: Editorial del Pacífico, S.A., 1957), tables 7–11; and ODEPLAN, *Distribución del Ingreso y Cuentas de Producción, 1960–1970* (Santiago: ODEPLAN, Jan. 1972).

---

1. ODEPLAN, *Analysis of the Chilean Economy in 1971* (Santiago: ODEPLAN, Feb. 1972), table 11, p. 30. Hereafter cited as *Analysis 1971.*

by almost 100 percent in manufacturing and between 46 and 56 percent in the public sector but fell by 9.4 percent in mining.[2] The labor share also increased as unemployment was drastically reduced from 8.3 percent in December 1970 to 3.0 percent in September 1972 and 3.8 percent in March 1973 (as can be seen in table 10.2). The minimum daily wages for agriculture and industry were equalized and raised and Santiago's subsistence wage was brought back to its 1962 level. The minimum real wage experienced a spectacular increase of 39 percent, while the subsistence wage increased by 12 percent. Much of this relative redistribution of income in favor of labor resulted from almost complete appropriation of the GDP increment. Nonwage income maintained the same real value as in 1970.[3]

The 1970–73 events are the apogee of a transformation in distribution that has its roots in the 1930s. Official announcements notwithstanding, interclass redistribution of income in favor of labor, blue-collar workers, and the poor did not receive serious attention as a top policy goal—even though it was listed as such since 1930—until 1964.[4] Although cyclical fluctuations in the distribution of income between labor and capital have occurred (table 10.1 shows a rising trend for the labor share), the respective shares remained generally constant during 1940–54. The average value of labor's income share during 1940–54 was 44.7 percent according to the CORFO definitions, and 50.7 percent if the concept of social class more relevant to Chile is used.[5] The indirect

2. Ibid., table 10, p. 30.
3. Ibid., pp. 31, 32, 29.
4. For some insightful official announcements see Pedro Aguirre Cerda, *Mensaje de S.E. el Presidente de la República en la apertura de las sesiónes ordinarias del Congreso Nacional 21 de Mayo de 1939* (Santiago: Presidencia de la República, 1939), p. 4; *Mensaje de S.E. el Presidente de la República en la apertura de las sesiónes ordinarias del Congreso Nacional 21 de Mayo de 1941* (Santiago: Presidencia de la República, 1941), p. 4; and Juan Antonio Ríos, *Mensaje de S.E. el Presidente de la República Don Juan Antonio Ríos en la apertura de las sesiónes ordinarias del Congreso Nacional 21 de Mayo de 1945* (Santiago: Presidencia de la República, 1945). To a large extent the major objectives of economic policy and the tools to pursue them are similar and overlap between presidencies. The similarities stand out in the 1940–52 *Mensajes.*
5. See Helio Varela Carmona, "Estratificación Social de la Población Trabajadora en Chile y Su Participación en el Ingreso Nacional, 1940–1954," Memoria en Ciencias Económicas (Santiago: Universidad de Chile, Escuela de Economía, Nov. 1958), table 6, p. 80. Hereafter cited as "Estratificación Social." Varela's work represents an attempt to group persons into classes more homogeneous than those permitted under the United States Department of Commerce methodology originally employed by CORFO. Varela substituted the blue-collar, white-collar, employer distinction with one of a proletariat, middle class, and capitalist–employer class. The end product was a set of statistics showing a greater concentration of income among the capitalist–employer class than that for the employer class as defined by CORFO. The official information is presented in table 10.1.

Table 10.2. *Greater Santiago: Unemployment Rates, 1956–72*
(In percentages)

	Month	Unemployment rate		Month	Unemployment rate
1952	Census	4.0	1966	March	4.7
1956	October	6.7		June	6.0
1957	June	6.4		September	5.3
1958	June	9.5		December	5.4
1959	March	10.4	1967	March[d]	5.5
	June	7.4		March[e]	6.3
1960	April	7.3		June	5.9
	June	8.0		September	5.8
	September[a]	7.2		December	6.4
	September[b]	7.3	1968	March	5.6
	December	7.0		June	6.4
1961	March	7.6		September	6.7
	June	7.1		December	5.4
	September	6.9	1969	March	6.8
	December	5.0		June	7.1
1962	March	6.2		September	5.3
	June	5.7		December	5.4
	September	4.3	1970	March	6.8
	December	4.8		June	7.0
1963	March	5.5		September	6.4
	June	5.2		December	8.3
	September	5.2	1971	March	8.2
	December[c]	4.3		June	5.2
1964	March	5.1		September	4.8
	June	4.9		December	3.8
	September	6.2	1972	March	4.8
	December	4.8		June	3.7
1965	March	6.1		September	3.0
	June	5.0		December	3.6
	September	5.9	1973	March	3.8
	December	4.7		June	3.1
				September	—
				December	7.0
			1974	March	9.2
				June	10.3
				September	9.4

Sources: The figures for 1952 are found in "Demography," in Mamalakis, "Historical Statistics," table IIA2b1, p. A-171. The data for Oct. 1956–Sept. 1971 are found in Universidad de Chile, Instituto de Economía y Planificación, *Ocupación y Desocupación, Gran Santiago*, Publicación no. 132 (Santiago: Sept. 1971), table 21. The data for the remaining months are found in Universidad de Chile, ibid., Publicación no. 139 (Santiago, March 1972), table 1. The data for June 1972–March 1973 (estimated by the

Institute) are found in Banco Central de Chile, *Noticias Económicas*, no. 44, May 31, 1973, p. 14. The data for June 1973–Sept. 1974 are found in Ministerio de Hacienda, Dirección de Presupuestos, *Exposición sobre el Estado de la Hacienda Pública* (Santiago: Oct. 1974), p. 63, and Universidad de Chile, Departamento de Economía, *Ocupación y Desocupación en el Gran Santiago* (Santiago: Sept. 1974), table 7, p. 19; table 10, p. 24.
[a]Sample survey designed in 1956.
[b]Sample survey designed in 1960.
[c]Sample survey designed in 1963.
[d]Sample survey designed in 1963.
[e]Sample survey designed in 1967.

measures introduced by Eduardo Frei's Christian Democrats during 1964–70 to improve labor's income share had short-term beneficial effects during 1964–66 but were partly lost during 1967–70.[6] Unemployment also remained high.

Allende's emphasis on a more equitable distribution of income was so extreme that it became self-defeating. The astronomical inflation and almost chaotic economic conditions of the second half of 1972 and of 1973, which followed the redistribution-induced massive consumption increases of 1971, were jeopardizing labor's real income gains of 1971. The moving force behind the policies of 1970–73 was the desire to dismantle a distribution pattern in which 9 percent of the population controlled 43 percent of national income,[7] in which an even greater concentration of economic power existed in the financial, agricultural, mining, industrial, and communications media sectors,[8] and in which unequal distribution was identified in orthodox Marxist terms as exploitation of one social group by another. Abolition of private ownership of means of production and state control of financial capital had been given empirical support and theoretical justification in early studies on concentration of distribution.[9]

The income distribution figures of table 10.1 are somewhat misleading because they refer to pre-tax distribution rather than more accurate and

6. There exist two other important studies on income distribution. The first, covering the 1940–54 period, is by Roberto Jadue Saba, "Distribución Probable del Ingreso de las Personas en Chile, 1940–1954," Memoria en Economía, (Santiago: Universidad de Chile, 1959), mimeo. The second is a very solid statistical analysis by Francois Bouzguignon D. and Isabel Heskia V., "Análisis Estadístico de la Distribución del Ingreso Personal en Chile en 1967," *Análisis*, ser. B, no. 12, 1970.

7. Varela, "Estratificación Social," p. 80.

8. See Ricardo Lagos Escobar, *La Concentración del Poder Económico. Su Teoría. Realidad Chilena* (Santiago: Editorial del Pacífico, S.A., 1961). This study covered only the year 1958.

9. Ibid., pp. 171–73.

far less concentrated post-tax figures that also include subsidies. These figures also include in the employer–capitalist class all self-employed in unincorporated enterprises, who are really more part of labor than of capital, and fail to make clear that much of capitalist income, such as rents, accrues to the working classes. Thus, although the income share of labor as a factor of production fluctuated between 42 and 66 percent of GDP during 1930–72, the income or expenditure share of workers' households may have been higher and come closer to 50–80 percent of GDP. Very probably the Allende-induced redistribution did change workers' household real income level as much as it changed the sources of this household income.

The low measured income share of labor before 1970 does in part reflect an abundant labor supply, capital scarcity, and low labor demand. However, it also reflects the distorting impact of a large unincorporated sector whose income is classified with that of capital even though it is more part of an individualistic, diverse labor force.

TOWARD A ONE-COLLAR PROLETARIAT?

Gradual elimination of enormous discriminatory inequalities in intra-labor distribution of income was also attempted by President Allende's government during 1970–73,[10] but it met with only limited success. The goal of equal labor remuneration was emphatically and directly pursued during 1970–71: an obligatory minimum wage for workers of all ages, including apprentices, was introduced; the law permitting payment of less than one basic salary to those less than 18 and more than 65 years old was revoked; all legal dispositions permitting payment below the minimum wage or basic salary were eliminated;[11] and all wages and salaries were readjusted by 100 percent of the cost-of-living increase but the lowest ones by substantially more. Furthermore, a gradual equalization of family allowances was begun that aimed at a single uniform allowance, and low-income groups were liberated from taxes.[12]

10. See Salvador Allende, *Primer Mensaje del Presidente Allende ante el Congreso Pleno, 21 de Mayo de 1971* (Santiago: Presidencia de la República, 1971), pp. 105–06, 607–08; *Mensaje del Presidente Allende ante el Congreso Pleno, 21 de Mayo de 1972* (Santiago: Presidencia de la República, 1972), pp. 207–10, 872–74.

11. *Mensaje 1971*, pp. 607–08.

12. *Mensaje 1971*, pp. 105–06. The manual-worker family allowance was doubled, that of the public sector raised by 50 percent, and that of the military and the police by 112.5 percent compared to a 34.9 percent cost-of-living increase. See *Mensaje 1972*, p. 873.

The indirect instruments used by Allende to redistribute income in favor of low-income wage earners also exerted a powerful catalytic influence upon the old social order. Low-income workers, the retired, and the indigent were given a larger and improved share of health, housing, education, and welfare services; scarce food and other supplies were made preferentially available to low-income neighborhoods; so-called illegal takeovers of land, houses, apartments, and industrial plants were tolerated, if not encouraged; employment was practically guaranteed for all; housing loans to the poor became open giveaways as escalator clauses were eliminated amid the tidal inflation of 1972 and 1973.[13] In no other area has there been so strong a consensus about the desperate need for basic reform as that of inequality of compensation among workers. In no other area, however, did Allende's policies meet with so much resistance. The economy moved toward economic and political disaster and on September 11 Allende's era was violently ended and replaced by a military junta composed of General Gustavo Leigh Guzmán, junta president General Augusto Pinochet Ugarte, Admiral José Toribio Merino Castro, and General César Mendoza Durán, commander of the *carabineros*, the armed police.

The income inequalities among and within the working classes had become a cause célèbre between 1955 and 1970. CORFO's classic national accounts covering the 1940–54 period statistically demonstrated the privileged economic, and by inference social, status enjoyed by the *empleados*, the white-collar office employees.[14] Composing one-tenth of the labor force during 1940–54, they received 17.8 percent of national income. The manual workers (*obreros*) received only 23.8 percent of national income during that period even though they made up 56.9 percent of the labor force.[15] An abysmal, unbridgeable income gap separated manual from office workers. This occupational inequality was strengthened by unequal access to public services.

13. *Mensaje 1972*, pp. xix–xxii, 209–10. Free milk distribution to infants and mothers increased by 350 percent during 1970 (ibid., pp. xix).

14. CORFO, *Cuentas Nacionales de Chile, 1940–1954* (Santiago: Editorial del Pacífico, S.A., 1957), pp. 30–31, Appendix tables 7–38. See also the even more valuable, detailed statistical collection, República de Chile, CORFO, *National Accounts, Annex XI of Agriculture and Transport Development Program* (Santiago: CORFO, 1954), accounts I–VI, tables 1–65-B. Hereafter cited as *National Accounts*.

15. Varela, "Estratificación Social," p. 80. According to the CORFO statistics, blue-collar workers received 26.3 percent of the national nominal income during 1940–52 (CORFO, *National Accounts*, table 10-A) while they comprised 62.3 percent of the labor force (CORFO, *National Accounts*, table 44A). The CORFO statistics seem to exclude employers in incorporated enterprises from the labor force.

An even more unequal income distribution pattern emerged in Helio Varela's study, which divided the active population into three social groups. The proletariat, which comprised 77.7 percent of the labor force during 1940–54, received only 30.3 percent of real national income. The middle class, comprising 12.9 percent of the labor force, received 17.5 percent of real income. The employer–capitalist class, accounting for 9.4 percent of the labor force, received more than half the national income.[16] However, these statistics grossly exaggerated the income inequalities because they were pre- rather than post-tax-cum-subsidy figures and ignored the fact that much capital income accrued to labor households.

The sectoral aspect of intralabor income inequalities was brought into the forefront by my analysis of Chile's economy between 1940 and 1960. This showed that during 1940–54 white-collar workers increased their income superiority over manual workers, who fared highly unequally depending on their sectoral affiliation. Blue-collar laborers fared best in privileged subsectors of dominant industry and in mining, while in maltreated agriculture they suffered real income losses.[17]

Intra- and interlabor income inequalities persisted into the 1960s, as the statistics of table 10.3 illustrate. Nevertheless, income distribution between manual and office workers improved. Salary–wage differentials, which were often substantial (agriculture had the highest salary/wage ratio of 6.6 in 1970) declined in all sectors except agriculture during 1960–70. The economy-wide salary/wage ratio fell from 3.0 in 1960 to 2.5 in 1970. Salaries dropped below wages in construction (where the salary/wage ratio was 0.8 in 1969), in banking, insurance, and real estate (where the ratio fell to 0.7 in 1967) and in public administration. As the income distribution between manual and office workers improved, the salary/wage differentials disappeared in construction, electricity, trade, and banking and became negligible in transport, public administration, and services, but they persisted in agriculture, mining, and industry.

However, intersectoral income distribution within the highly heterogeneous blue-collar class deteriorated during 1960–70. Intersectoral wage differentials, with agricultural wages as a numeraire, were large, pervasive, and rising. In 1969 a small, particularly privileged group

16. Varela, ibid., p. 80.

17. See Mamalakis, "Public Policy and Sectoral Development: A Case Study of Chile, 1940–1958," in M. Mamalakis and C. W. Reynolds, *Essays on the Chilean Economy* (Homewood, Ill.: Richard D. Irwin, 1965), pp. 64–71, 143–47. Hereafter cited as "Public Policy."

Table 10.3. Sectoral Income Differentials with Agricultural Income as the Numeraire

	1960			1970		
	Wage	*Salary*	*Salary/ wage Ratio*	*Wage*	*Salary*	*Salary/ wage Ratio*
Agriculture	1.0	1.0	4.9	1.0	1.0	6.6
Mining	4.4	3.1	3.4	5.8	1.9	2.1
Industry	3.2	1.4	2.0	3.7	1.2	2.0
Construction	2.4	1.0	2.0	2.9	0.4	0.9
Electricity, gas, and water	5.6	2.6	2.2	11.4	1.9	1.0
Commerce	4.5	2.4	2.6	5.3	0.8	1.0
Banking, insurance, and real estate	3.7	2.5	3.3	14.8	2.3	1.0
Transport	4.4	1.3	1.5	4.5	0.8	1.2
Public administration and defense	8.1	1.7	1.0	9.0	1.6	1.1
Services	4.4	1.3	1.5	5.3	1.1	1.3
Average	2.5	1.5	3.0	2.9	1.1	2.5

Source: Calculated from unpublished information given to the author by ODEPLAN. Complete information is available for 1960–70 in an unpublished study by the author on *Employment–Unemployment in Chile.*

composed of manual workers in banking had earnings nineteen times those of their agricultural counterparts. Along with the blue-collar workers in electricity, public administration, defense, commerce, mining, and some personal services, who earned more than five times as much as agricultural workers, they had achieved middle-class status. Manual workers in agriculture, as well as those living in the urban misery belts, remained the backbone of the lumpenproletariat. Income concentration within the blue-collar class (measured by an index equal to the variance of income distribution divided by the square of the median of this distribution) declined from 0.65 in 1960 to 0.49 in 1966. The index has a value of zero for an equal distribution and rises to the extent that income concentration increases. A small but rapidly increasing proportion of blue-collar workers earned more than five basic salaries during 1960–66.[18] Although income distribution within the

18. See Patricio Millán S., "Estructura de Costos y Distribución del Ingreso en la Economía Chilena" (Santiago: Universidad de Chile, 1968, Memoria de Prueba), pp. 57–60. Hereafter cited as "Distribución del Ingreso." In the Braden Survey sample of manufacturing, mining, and construction, income differentials among skilled, semi-skilled, and unskilled manual workers were small and "substantially narrower than occupational differentials in other countries at early or intermediate stages of economic development" [P. Gregory, *Industrial Wages in Chile* (Ithaca, N.Y.: Cornell University Press, 1967), p. 89]. Hereafter cited as *Industrial Wages.*

manual worker group advanced during 1960–66, intersectoral wage differentials widened during 1960–70, declining until 1966 and rising during 1967–70.

The intraclass distribution of income among office workers was more unequal than that among manual workers but also displayed a tendency toward improvement between 1960 and 1965. The income concentration index rose from 0.70 in 1960 to 0.99 in 1962 before falling to 0.61 in 1965. In 1966 the 8.0 percent of office workers earning more than five basic salaries received 27.5 percent of all salaries.[19] Although the intrasalary income differentials exceeded those within wages, the intersectoral salary differentials were significantly below the intersectoral wage differentials.[20] The salary spread between sectors had narrowed significantly in 1970 (compared to earlier years of the 1960s), each sector's salary differential over agricultural salaries was highly stable, and the average salary differential (with agricultural salaries always as a numeraire) fell from 1.5 in 1960 to 1.1 in 1970. Agricultural white-collar employees, unlike their manual laboring co-workers, who were perennially victimized, emerged as equal partners within a relatively uniform and less heterogeneous class. Above the disintegrated, extremely heterogeneous, pluralistic blue-collar class stood, before 1970, a more integrated, relatively cohesive and homogeneous, salaried middle class with high education, intersectoral mobility, political participation, connections with the managerial class, and other advantages. In spite of its relative cohesion the white-collar group was sufficiently diverse to prompt the National Statistical Office to divide it into five separate categories: management personnel, technical personnel, office workers, salesmen, and miscellaneous employees.

Although practically all the information available shows that intralabor income inequalities were great, that interindustry wage relationships were highly volatile, and that there was an apparent lack of association with the functional role that wages are normally expected

19. Millán, "Distribución del Ingreso," pp. 63–68.

20. For the evidence concerning the 1940–52 period see Mamalakis, "Public Policy," pp. 68, 70, 144–46. Peter Gregory, in a study covering primarily industry during three years in the early 1960s, also found that "the range of interindustry differences for office workers is narrower than . . . for manuals" and that "salary relationships among industry groups have been much more stable than manual wage relationships were" (see *Industrial Wages*, p. 80). The same almost extreme income uniformity among white-collar workers employed in different sectors was also found to exist in 1967, which, peculiarly, came as a surprise to its finder. See Isabel Heskia Villanueva, *Análisis Estadístico de la Distribución del Ingreso Personal en Chile en 1967* (Santiago: Universidad de Chile, 1970), pp. 61–62. Hereafter cited as *Distribución en 1967*.

to fulfill,[21] it is almost impossible to explain these phenomena with certainty and to measure the relative contribution to their formation of such factors as education, inflation, price stabilization schemes, sectoral preferences of government, unionization, and changing labor demand and supply patterns.[22] To President Allende and his Popular Unity they were both a symptom and an effect of a backward, exploitive social order that had to be destroyed. In order to create a new social order, it was necessary to transform the polyglot, feuding, unequal, heterogenous but coexisting labor groups into a homogeneous, egalitarian proletariat imbued with unifying and binding class spirit and consciousness. Allende's actions on labor-income differentials were far more realistic and pragmatic than some of the Popular Unity's extreme rhetorics. Labor-income differences had been greatly reduced by 1972—85 percent of all workers earned between one and five basic salaries—but recipients of more than five basic salaries were permitted and continued to control a disproportionately high share of labor income. The sensible tax reform of 1972, which became effective in January 1973, reduces but by no means eliminates labor-income inequalities.[23]

THE INTERNATIONAL DISTRIBUTION OF INCOME: DIRECT RENATIONALIZATION OF THE EXTRACTIVE EXPORT SECTORS

A major unfulfilled dream of Chile's political Left before 1970 was a complete return to Chile of its mineral resources, which had been denationalized since 1882. Salvador Allende encountered no political difficulties in keeping this perennial campaign promise during his first year in office. A unanimous constitutional amendment passed Congress in July 1971, and the principal copper companies—El Teniente, Chuquicamata, El Salvador, La Exótica, and Sociedad Minera Andina—

---

21. It is also true as Gregory and others have pointed out that substantial economic rents were being paid workers in some firms (see *Industrial Wages*, p. 104).

22. Isabel Heskia Villanueva disagrees. Her analysis of income distribution for 1967 disclosed that "to a large extent the income inequalities are explained by differences in educational level, occupational situation and access to capital. Without belittling the explanatory character of the other socioeconomic variables considered in this study—i.e. sex, age, sector of economic activity and residential area—the aforementioned ones appear, during the first approximation, as the ultimate determinants" (see Heskia, *Distribución en 1967*, p. 5).

23. See the article on "Escasos Sueldos Altos en el País" in *El Mercurio*, international ed., Nov. 27–Dec. 3 1972, p. 5.

became an integral part of the socially or state-owned segment. Through the application of the so-called Allende doctrine of retroactive taxation of excess profits, the takeover amounted to confiscation. The program will demonstrate whether Chile has acquired since the Balmaceda years the internal modernization capacity that will permit it to extract from the mining sector the fabulous quasi-rents that European and American capitalists were able to create. It could have also shown whether Chile can internally augment production and appropriate the mining surplus without a new, more onerous, and possibly irrevocable dependence on the Soviet, Chinese, or other socialist republics, which, lacking such assistance by foreign or immigrant entrepreneurs, have levels of income lower than Chile's.

For many of Chile's intellectuals and politicians the nationalization was but the final step of the long march that led through the War of the Pacific to annexation of the Bolivian and Peruvian North. When during 1879–82 the government conquered foreign land to protect its nitrate capitalists, Chilean imperialism was supported by the strength of its arms. In 1970 Allende, aiming to correct the alleged injustices of the traditional oligarchy, completed the nationalization of nitrate by acquiring SOQUIM (Sociedad Química), the enterprise formed by merging Anglo Lautaro and Salitrera Victoria, and by placing under state management the Alemania firm. Finally, the government-owned Pacific Steel Company acquired the iron mines of the Bethlehem Steel Company. Along with the purchase of the Santa Bárbara and Santa Fe companies, this move brought 95 percent of iron under government ownership. The remaining 5 percent belonged to private Chilean interests.

Once copper, nitrate, and iron had been transferred to state or Chilean private ownership, the destiny of Chile became intimately linked with the productive capacity of a coalition between the central government and the mining sector. Now that the long-term, cyclically rebounding conflict is disappearing, it remains to be shown whether the new rules of the game yield higher returns than the previous policies of laissez-faire, excessive discrimination, mixed foreign–Chilean ownership, and so forth.[24] At least during Allende's 1970–73 reign, his rules of the game for copper production did not deliver the promised output increase. More than anywhere else in the economy Allende's

24. For background information see ODEPLAN, *Analysis 1971*, pp. 33–34; and ODEPLAN, *Informe Económico Anual 1971* (Santiago: Editorial Universitaria, 1972), pp. 30–31.

Popular Unity successfully destroyed foreign extractive capitalism, but the question was whether this immense source of real capital could be placed at the service of all Chile's people rather than be allowed to cater to the mining workers, the Communist party, and/or a small segment of the Santiago urban, bureaucratic elite. By May 1972 some of the Chuquicamata miners who had so vociferously asked in the past that the Gran Minería be saved from the "hands of the yanquis" were now demanding that it be saved from "the hands of the communists."[25]

INTERNATIONAL DISTRIBUTION OF INCOME:
THE CASE OF COPPER

The 1930–73 transformation in international distribution revolved strongly around copper. The government's primary objective was to retain for Chile the maximum share of the copper sector's production value. The transformation of distribution of copper resources between Chile and abroad can be observed most clearly by comparing the gross availability effect, which is measured by production value, with the net effect, which equals total domestic expenditures by the copper sector (i.e., the sum of the legal cost of production, mainly wages and salaries, direct taxes, investment and miscellaneous local expenditures), and with the net overall foreign exchange availability effect, which in addition includes copper-induced capital inflows. A comparison between the gross and the net overall availability effect is the most accurate measure of the international distribution of copper resources because it considers leakages abroad as well as *all* offsetting capital inflows induced by the export sector's foreign ownership.[26]

The net foreign exchange availability effect during 1930–64 added up to an extraordinary $5.598 billion, or 77 percent of a gross effect equal to $7.280 billion in 1961 prices.[27] Although prima facie the international distribution of copper's domestic resources appears unfavorable to Chile—$1.682 billion paid to all foreign inputs—if the induced capital inflows of at least $2 billion are considered, the net impact of the

25. See editorial "Costoso Fin de una Huelga" in *El Mercurio*, May 8, 1972.

26. For a detailed description of this theoretical framework and the underlying empirical analysis see M. Mamalakis, "Contribution of Copper to Chilean Economic Development, 1920–67: Profile of a Foreign-Owned Export Sector," *Foreign Investment in the Petroleum and Mineral Industries*, Raymond Mikesell and Associates, (Baltimore, Md.: Johns Hopkins Press, 1971), pp. 397–409. Hereafter cited as "Copper Contribution."

27. See ibid., table 120, cols. 1, 10.

foreign-owned copper sector on the international resource distribution is positive for Chile. Had the mining sector not been so heavily discriminated against during 1940–54, the magnitude of the net effect could have been even greater.

The international distribution went through cycles, as the difference between the gross and net effects indicates. Enormous and relatively stable during 1930–39, this difference not only shrank to zero but even became negative during 1940–54. Chile's policy of bringing the values of the two effects together was so successful, in fact, that it practically killed the goose that laid the golden eggs: the quantity of copper produced declined between 1944 and 1954, and the gross availability effect stagnated.[28]

The pattern was similar during 1965–70. The gross availability effect was $3.629 billion, the net $2.986. From the $910 million profits realized by the Gran Minería de Cobre during 1965–70, $502 million were reinvested. The foreign share in total copper revenues had a maximum value of $642.6 million, which included profits, amortization costs, and other payments abroad. The actual value of foreign revenues may have been close to $400 million since official figures of CODELCO (Corporación del Cobre) used in the present calculations do not give investment figures and the Chilean government profit and amortization share for 1970. Thus, the international distribution of the revenues of the mixed-ownership large-scale copper sector during 1965–70 gave a minimum of 83 percent of copper resources to Chile and a maximum of 17 percent to the foreign countries (including the American capitalists). This situation was almost ideal and provided no economic justification for Allende's nationalization, which was politically motivated. There is no evidence that distribution of the nationalized copper resources improved during 1970–73.[29] If international distribution is measured by comparing the gross with the net overall availability effect, Chile received more than 100 percent of copper resources during 1965–70 because of induced positive capital inflows and less than 100 percent upon Allende's election to office. This phenomenon has been described by Allende as

28. Mamalakis, "Historical Statistics," pt. 5; "Mining," table IID, p. A-498; and "Copper Contribution," table 120, col. 1, p. 418.

29. The above data, from Corporación del Cobre, Gerencia de Finanzas, Sección Estudios y Estadísticas, were given to the author in an official document 9/6/72. The cooperation of CODELCO in providing the basic data on which my calculations are based is gratefully acknowledged.

an American imperialistic boycott and by his opponents as pains from self-inflicted wounds and risk, augmented by economic mismanagement. Whatever the explanation, Chile has been worse off in terms of benefits derived from copper since President Allende declared his war against private foreign capital in November 1970.

The change in the international distribution of copper revenues was accomplished from 1930 to 1964 through the government's taxation, foreign exchange, and expenditure policies. After a taxation lull that lasted until 1939 the maze of taxes imposed on Gran Minería's resource surplus had spectacular results. Explicit government taxes (i.e., those recorded in the budget) climbed from 11.5 percent of production value in 1939 (expressed in 1961 prices) to an all-time high of 63.5 percent during 1953 before falling to between 25 and 30 percent during 1955–64. The impact on repatriated profits was as catastrophic as that on Chile's

Table 10.4 The CORFO dollar rate, the parity rate,
and the Chilex and Andes Company rates
(In pesos per U.S. dollar)

	CORFO dollar price	New dollar price (parity rate)	Chilex rate	Andes rate
1930	8	8.0	8.3	8.3
1932	14	8.5	12.4	12.4
1935	24	10.7	16.6	16.6
1940	25	15.1	19.4	19.4
1941	30	17.4	19.4	19.4
1942	30	21.9	19.4	19.4
1945	30	30.8	19.4	19.4
1950	51	76.8	19.4	19.4
1952	66	114.6	19.4	19.4
1955	181	433.5	109.8	109.8
1960	1,049	1,667.2	1,045.4	1,045.4
1964	—	4,312.4	1,775.0	1,775.0

Sources: The CORFO dollar price is from Mamalakis, "Mining," in "Historical Statistics," pt. 5, table IID, p. A-522. The parity rate was calculated by the formula: $P_t = P_{t-1} + P_{t-1}$ times the percentage variation between yearly averages of the cost-of-living index. The Chilex and Andes rates are the foreign exchange rates at which the respective companies could convert dollars into pesos. These rates have been obtained from the companies.
Note: The statistics for other years can be found in the author's "Copper Contribution," table 116, p. 404.

retained revenues was beneficial; the repatriated profits dived from $68.8 million in 1940 to $10.5 million in 1953 before recovering in the late 1950s and 1960s.

Foreign exchange policies, which gave rise to direct and indirect implicit taxes, affected distribution even more profoundly. Direct implicit taxes—defined as the difference between the government's buying rate for dollars from the American companies and the average selling rate—were estimated as the difference between the CORFO and the Chilex–Andes Company rates and are presented for selected years in table 10.4. They rose secularly after 1932, reaching a peak of 200 percent of the Chilex–Andes rate in 1952 and declining to zero in 1961.

The indirect implicit tax revenues—defined as the difference between the average selling rate and the equilibrium rate—were measured as the difference between the CORFO and the parity rate. With the peso undervalued until 1945, the copper companies received implicit subsidies from the government until 1942. Reaching a peak of 63 percent of the parity rate for Chilex and 66.5 percent for Andes in 1936, these subsidies strengthened the already existing leakages to Chile's disadvantage. Since 1941–42, when the parity passed the Chilex–Andes rate, and even more after 1945, when the parity also passed the CORFO rate, indirect implicit taxes rose and soon exceeded the direct implicit ones. These indirect taxes caused by the peso overvaluation led to a fierce struggle among the American investors and Chilean workers to maintain their respective income shares within the discriminated against, suppressed copper sector. Both lost. Labor's climbing dollar wages were not matched by rising real peso wages; worse, employment plummeted as the foreign companies combated discrimination by curtailing labor as well as capital inputs. Although foreign investors preserved positive profit margins through a reduction of the capital stock, their gross profits fell abysmally.

Only the income losses of foreign investors and Chilean labor arising from direct implicit taxes were appropriated by government. The more important income losses inherent in indirect implicit taxation were automatically converted into implicit import subsidies that made importers directly the foremost beneficiaries and winners. The redistribution of income from the Gran Minería's factors of production to importers, and occasionally consumers, greatly distorted production incentives against mining and agriculture and turned the underlying foreign exchange policies into the most powerful tool in the sectoral clashes prevailing between 1939 and 1973. The distortions diminished during 1955–68 but rose during 1968–73, assuming singular significance after the copper nationalization. With direct and indirect implicit taxes on copper rising to new heights in 1971, 1972, and 1973 while explicit taxes evaporated, a major segment thereof was converted into import subsidies to consumers. This shift was detrimental to the competing domestic sectors.

The goal of deriving maximum benefits for Chile from copper production was shared by all governments. Indirect tools, such as taxes, profit incentives, overvalued exchange rates, and so forth, were relied on in pursuing this goal between 1930 and 1964—frequently with spectacular short-term success. The direct tool of ownership transformation was added by President Frei, and the mixed Compañía Minera Exótica, S.A. (Sociedad Anónima, or Stock Corporation), and the Sociedad Minera El Teniente, S.A., were established during 1964–70.[30]

With minor exceptions, government efforts from 1930 to 1970 aimed to transform the international distribution of income by increasing the national and decreasing the foreign share of copper revenues, income, and resource surpluses. Claiming that all pre-1970 efforts had failed to unravel the Gordian knot—the problem of optimum national versus foreign shares—that blocked economic independence and strangulated growth, Allende declared Chile exclusive master of copper by directly cutting this knot with the knife of nationalization.

INDIRECT DENATIONALIZATION

Although direct foreign investment was always less than $1 billion, it fluctuated cyclically until 1970, when it was wiped out literally by decree. Nevertheless, indirect investment of foreigners in IOUs of the Chilean Government, Central Bank, autonomous government enterprises, and private firms increased by leaps and bounds until 1973. The indirect investment of foreigners, as measured by Chile's short-, medium- and long-term foreign debt, gave rise to a process of indirect denationalization and growing dependence that more than offset the benefits derived from the renationalization of all other direct investments. Although foreign debt in 1970 was very probably below Allende's estimate of $4.125 billion, it was massive, secularly growing, and accurately reflected the indirect denationalization. The relative signi-

---

30. For more details see Raymond F. Mikesell, "Conflict and Accommodation in Chilean Copper," in Mikesell et al., *Foreign Investment*, chap. 15, pp. 369–86.

ficance of the factors that led to this debt, and thus induced indirect denationalization, can be estimated quantitatively, albeit tentatively. Approximately $1.5 billion had to be borrowed in order to pay the dividends and profits of direct and indirect foreign investment; as Allende correctly pointed out, direct foreign investment can breed indirect foreign ownership or denationalization.[31] At least $1 billion, or 25 percent of the 1972 foreign debt, was needed because the CORFO-sponsored industrialization plans were financed by foreign credits rather than by national savings. Some $500 million was needed because most private or public national and foreign investment was import- rather than export-creating. At least $1 billion foreign exchange was lost because the mining and agricultural export sectors were discriminated against. And finally, borrowing was necessary to offset the loss of foreign exchange, which was due to a flight of capital caused by lack of confidence and political instability. Foreign debt led to heavy interest, profit, and amortization remittances, which contributed to an unfavorable international distribution by diverting export revenues away from imports.

Allende's and CORFO's reliance on foreign savings, combined with their mismanagement and/or severe discrimination against the agricultural, mining, and industrial sectors, their unwillingness to openly default on credits by the United States, the Bundesbank, and other lenders, and their active solicitation of more foreign credits, demonstrates that in the foreseeable future the structural causes for continued denationalization and partial, unfavorable international distribution will continue unabated. External debts remain high despite complete nationalization of direct foreign investment. Chile can default on but cannot nationalize its debts to foreign governments and institutions.

AGGREGATE MEASURES OF INTERNATIONAL DISTRIBUTION

International distribution of Chile's product was affected by all forms of direct and indirect foreign ownership, related financial and real flows, and other factors. The measures of the aggregate impact of the factors provide the following picture.

If international distribution is measured by the difference between domestic and national product, it was unfavorable to Chile throughout 1940–71. The domestic–national product gap, which is equal to net

31. Allende, *Mensaje 1972*, p. xiii.

factor payments abroad, reached a high value of 4.7 percent of GDP in 1942 but fell to less than 2.0 percent throughout 1949–65[32] before rising again to around 3 percent during 1965–69.[33] It fell to 2.0 percent of GDP in 1970 and to only 1 percent in 1971.[34] If the figures are interpreted literally, Chile's gross domestic product was divided, with nationals receiving 95–99 percent and interests abroad 1 to 5 percent.

The second measure of international distribution of income is the difference between domestic exports and imports. A domestic export surplus reflects an unfavorable distribution because part of domestic product constitutes what might be called unmatched exports. An import surplus reflects a favorable distribution; the economy disposes of more products and services than it produces. Consumption plus investment plus government expenditures, or what is often referred to as absorption, exceed GDP. The domestic export–import gap is in many respects the best measure of international distribution because it describes the net in- or outflow of resources resulting from monetary instability, foreign capital and labor, Marxist exploitation, aid, and so forth.

The domestic trade gap presented in table 11.3 was positive throughout 1933–56 (except for 1949), indicating an unfavorable international distribution. It became negative between 1957 and 1964 (with the exception of 1959), creating a favorable distribution; and became positive once more during 1965–70, accompanied by unfavorable distribution.[35]

Rather huge domestic export gaps developed in the 1940s, especially during the war years. Chile's domestic export gap or surplus in 1943 (9.4 percent of GDP in 1961 prices) substantially exceeded factor payments abroad, which were only 2.4 percent of GDP. This unfavorable distribution caused by war-induced import shortages, factor payments, debt services, and so on, which averaged more than 5 percent of GDP during 1940–50, became negligible during 1950–57, while factor payments abroad stabilized after 1945. The income distribution measured by the national accounts current account or export–import

32. See Mamalakis, "Historical Statistics," table IA5, pp. A-65–A-67.
33. ODEPLAN, *Cuentas Nacionales de Chile, 1960–1970* (Santiago: ODEPLAN, 1971), table 1, pp. 19–20.
34. ODEPLAN, *Cuentas Nacionales de Chile, 1960–1970* (Santiago: ODEPLAN, 1972), table 12, p. 44.
35. See table 11.3. Some minor changes in the sign and size of the export–import gap, depending on the use of current and constant prices, develop if national accounts statistics on exports and imports are used.

gap in 1961 prices became favorable during the mild import surpluses or gaps of 1960–65, although positive factor payments abroad suggest an unfavorable one. It returned to its unfavorable historical pattern of export surpluses during 1966–70, if measured by the current account of the balance of payments expressed in current U.S. dollars or by the national accounts export–import statistics in current prices.[36] If, however, the international distribution of resources is measured by the export–import statistics of the national accounts for 1960–71 in 1965 prices, it is favorable throughout 1966–71. The import gap ranges between 2 and 4 percent of GDP during 1969–71. The aggregate international distribution of income is favorable to Chile, according to any criterion, during Allende's three-year reign.[37] The abundance of socialist, Latin American and other non-American credits, and other factors enabled Chile to reach the highest import levels in its history in 1970 and 1972 as exports stagnated. However, the net international transfer of resources to Chile—a massive $460 million in terms of the trade balance and 74 percent of its 1972 exports—cannot offset the internal distortions and sharp reductions in output.[38]

According to this second measure the share of Chile in its total domestic product ranged between 90 and 104 percent during 1940–72. It fluctuated between 90 and 95 percent during 1940–50, between 97 and 101 percent during 1950–60 and 1965–70, and within 101–104 percent during 1960–65 and 1969–72. The rest of the world received in some years as much as 10 percent of Chile's GDP but also gave to Chile during other years as much as 4 percent of GDP. The positive export–import gap can be attributed to internal instability and flight of resources (as much as one-half), repatriation of profits and servicing of foreign debts (between 20 and 100 percent depending on the year), war-induced supply shortages (10 percent), and other factors.

Although the export–import gap gives the best measure of the actual international distribution of Chile's product, it either grossly conceals or even distorts some critical international distribution phenomena

36. For the statistics concerning national accounts based on the export–import gap see Mamalakis, "Historical Statistics," pp. A-65–A-67; ODEPLAN, *Antecedentes sobre el Desarrollo Chileno—1960–70* (Santiago: ODEPLAN, 1971), table 303, p. 413; and ODEPLAN, *Cuentas Nacionales de Chile, 1960–1971*, table 1, p. 19.

37. ODEPLAN, *Cuentas Nacionales de Chile, 1960–1971*, table 12, p. 44.

38. For a description of Chile's severe economic problems and of the reduction in some sectoral outputs during 1972–73, see Salvador Allende, *Mensaje, Presidente Allende ante el Congreso Pleno, 21 Mayo '73* (Santiago: Presidencia de la República, 1973), pp. xx–xxiv.

that have shaped Chile's growth. In order to describe these phenomena one can examine national exports, which are defined as domestic exports less all payments to foreign inputs. They are the net export earnings at Chile's disposal after the economy has met all its commitments to foreign capital and labor.

National exports, shown in part in figure 11.1 and table 11.3, fell short of domestic exports throughout 1925–70. As a percentage of domestic exports they reached a peak during 1925–31 (69 percent in 1931) fell to an average of less than 20 percent during 1932–40, drastically rose to a high plateau (mostly above 60 percent) during the government's copper discrimination policies of 1941–57, and, reversing this trend, declined drastically during 1960–64, largely as a consequence of increased overall indebtedness. There is no evidence of a significant change in this pattern during 1964–70.[39] Factor and amortization payments abroad declined mildly in 1970 and sharply during 1971–72.

National exports can be used to measure the international distribution of Chile's income in two ways. The difference between them and domestic exports indicates the actual share of Chile's income appropriated by the rest of the world. This fluctuated between 1 and 12 percent of GDP during 1930–70.[40] Foreigners, including owners of foreign debt, received a large share of Chile's product because their direct or indirect ownership of much of Chile contributed to its development.

The national trade gap—the difference between imports and national exports—shows that foreigners returned to Chile much or most of, and sometimes even more than, what they earned in Chile, thus permitting its nationals to have expenditures far above their national income, defined here as income whose imports are equal to national exports. On the average, more than 80 percent of the foreigners' income share was redistributed back to Chile through unilateral transfers, credits, and other measures. It would not be an exaggeration to say that 100 percent or more would have been given back to Chile, had risk and uncertainty been not so high.

The flows that determine national exports and close the national export gap changed substantially in an offsetting fashion. Thus, as

39. ODEPLAN, *Antecedentes, 1960–70*, table 303, p. 413.

40. See table 11.3 here, my "Historical Statistics," table IA5, pp. A-65–A-67; table IA1, p. A-180, and ODEPLAN, *Cuentas Nacionales de Chile, 1960–1971*, table 1, pp. 18–19; table 12, p. 44. The reader is warned that the estimate will vary depending on whether the CORFO or ODEPLAN national accounts are used. The trends remain unchanged.

payments to foreign capital rose from 18.3 percent of current export revenues in 1942 to 80.4 percent in 1962 and 78.7 percent in 1964, capital inflows as a percentage of current revenues also rose from 2.2 percent in 1942 to 84.4 percent in 1961, 87.0 percent in 1963, and 76.0 percent in 1964. However, only after 1957, and until 1964, as both short- and long-term capital inflows increased spectacularly and exceeded payments to foreign capital, did Chile witness six historically unusual years of domestic import gap surpluses.

These relationships reveal an unmistakable dependence of Chile on foreign factors of production and continued, possibly rising, foreign capital inflows. Such complications appeared to an increasing number of Chilean leaders as a labyrinth within which Chile's economic and political independence had been permanently lost. Chile's growing nationalism, anti-imperialist rhetoric, copper nationalization, and balance-of-payments phobia can be properly understood only by examining the reasons for and implications of national exports. Although the aid and trade issues (increased exports) were always discussed, the dominant problem was that of national versus domestic exports. It was believed that unless the two types of exports were brought closely together, no lasting trade or aid policies could be formulated. This approach proved in part spurious since the beneficial effects on national exports of Frei's efforts and of Allende's drastic measures to curtail or eliminate foreign ownership in mining, banking, agriculture, industry, and trade have been greatly offset by the negative effects of relatively stagnant exports and relentlessly advancing dena- tionalization through foreign indebtedness.

THE INCOME SHARE OF CAPITAL

As illustrated in table 10.1, the income share of capital declined secularly from 57.6 percent of domestic income in 1940 to only 34.2 percent in 1971. Chile's growth pattern and governmental policies throughout 1930–1973 cannot be properly understood without a more careful examination of this share and the recipient classes.

The profit share is a mixture of earnings by inputs other than labor, or, as the national accounts office describes it, "other [i.e., non labor] factor payments."[41] The profit share includes rents, paid or inputed,

41. ODEPLAN, *Distribución, 1960–1970*, pp. 1, 4, and throughout.

interest rates, income of unincorporated enterprises, and corporate profits. The class of capitalists throughout 1930–1973 was remarkably heterogeneous. It included the barrel organists, street photographers, newspaper sellers, and kite makers as part of the unincorporated enterprises, the giant foreign corporations and state enterprises, the owners of dwellings, and those holding savings accounts at the multitude of banking institutions. Above all—and this indicates the most serious error in accounting practice and development theory—the profit share was at least 50 percent "income earnings to labor" in the unincorporated as well as the corporate sector.

The capitalists working on their own account constituted 23.8 percent of the labor force during 1940–52, 20 percent in 1960, and 23.6 percent in 1969.[42] The large majority received relatively modest incomes. As can be seen from table 10.5 they received one-fourth of the country's income during 1940–52. Almost 90 percent of their income reflected earnings of labor, not capital, which was used very sparingly in the unincorporated enterprises. According to this evaluation the profit share throughout

Table 10.5. Average Percentage Distribution of
National Real Income by Shares, 1940–52

	1940–45	*1946–52*	*1940–52*
Wages	27.1	24.4	25.6
Salaries	16.8	17.9	17.4
Social security contributions	2.6	3.3	3.0
Compensation of employees	46.5	45.6	46.0
Income of unincorporated enterprises	25.8	25.5	25.6
Proprietor's income	27.7	28.9	28.4
Rental income	10.7	12.0	11.4
Interest	0.8	1.2	1.1
Profits	16.2	15.7	15.9
Other factor payments	53.5	54.4	54.0
Total	100.0	100.0	100.0

Source: CORFO, *National Accounts, Annex XI of Agriculture and Transport Development Program* (Santiago: Republic of Chile, 1954), unpublished compilation of tables, table 11-A.

---

42. This share fell to 22.5 percent in 1970. See ODEPLAN, *Población Ocupada por Sectores Económicos 1960–1970* (Santiago: ODEPLAN, 1971), table 2. For the 1940–52 figures see CORFO, *National Accounts*, unpublished compilation of tables, table 44-B.

1940–52, and possibly 1953–70, is reduced from 54 percent of GDP to 34 percent, with a corresponding increase in labor income share to 66 percent. According to these calculations the income redistribution created by Allende raised the labor income share above 80 percent and strongly endangered the survival capacity of unincorporated enterprises. The ensuing "consumers' labor socialism" destroyed the traditional profit–reinvestment relationship. The resultant disruption of production led to social upheaval and the revolts in October 1972 and spring 1973 of the imperiled unincorporated businesses so closely identified with the middle classes and to the military junta of September 11, 1973.

Rents are another profit item fraught with conceptual and measurement difficulties. Whereas they accounted for more than 10 percent of GDP during 1940–52 according to the early CORFO accounts, table 10.5 shows that by 1970 they had been statistically reduced to zero and in 1971 to − 1.8 percent of the GDP.[43] The resulting changes in income distribution were obviously to a large extent spurious.

The incomes of employers and those working on their own account suffered a comparative decline; their relationship to average national income fell from 157.1 in 1960, to 127.3 in 1966. However, income concentration within the employer–capitalist class during 1960–65 was very great, especially if compared with that for blue- and white-collar workers. The economy-wide index of concentration, which was heavily influenced by the profit–wage differentials as well as income inequalities within the employer–capitalist class, dropped from 3.2 in 1963 to 2.1 in 1966. Nevertheless, only 9 percent of the population still possessed 39 percent of total income.[44] The capitalist–employer class had no monopoly over riches, however. The richest 20 percent in 1967 included 2.5 percent of all blue-collar workers, 47 percent of all office workers, 20 percent of those working on their own account, and 82.9 percent of all employers.[45] Although Allende frequently attacked all forms of private capitalism, his actions during 1970–73 concentrated primarily on dispossessing the small number of bankers, latifundistas, industrialists, and merchants.

43. ODEPLAN, *Distribución del Ingreso y Cuentas de Producción, 1960–1971* (Santiago: ODEPLAN, 1973), table 11, p. 25.
44. Millán, *Distribución del Ingreso*, pp. 82, 88. The richest 5 percent received 27.4 percent of total income in 1967 (Heskia, *Distribución en 1967*, p. 48).
45. Heskia, ibid., p. 49.

THE FALL OF THE PRIVATE BANKERS

The Marxists argued that private capitalism was identified with, linked with, and in practice based upon a banking system that catered especially to large corporations concentrated in the Santiago–Valparaíso region. In turn the post-1970 opposition parties used to derive their power from their associations with and control over the resources and income of the banking sector. Elimination of this source of power became an imperative instrument in the Popular Unity's program, which intrinsically maintained that under the old order the sector was unable to perform efficiently and equitably its functions of facilitating and promoting production, exchange, and distribution and of stabilizing economic flows. Small and medium-sized firms could obtain no or only limited credit and even paid interest rates higher than large firms, sometimes exceeding the statutory maximum.[46] The alleged monopoly or, more properly oligopoly, power was reflected in the fact that three banks shared 44.5 percent of total deposits and 55.1 percent of the profits (monopoly power), that 1.3 percent of borrowers used 45.6 percent of total bank credit (monopsony power), and that 70 percent of credit in September 1970 had been extended in the provinces of Santiago and Valparaíso (regional concentration).[47]

By buying out private shareholders and by making the Central Bank exclusively governmental without representation of private interests, the Allende regime hoped to establish not only a more equitable distribution of income but also greater efficiency, introduction of specialized credit services, a regional bank, conversion of CORFO into a true investment bank, lower interest costs, development banks, and elimination of speculative internal and external activities.[48]

The statization of the Chilean banks may not be sufficient to change the heavy regional, deposit, and credit concentration of banking services, which are dictated by the intense concentration of economic activity in Santiago and the admitted benefits of large-scale production. To the extent that profit margins and reinvested profits have declined in

46. See "Statement by Mr. Alfonso Inostroza, President of the Central Bank of the Republic of Chile. Monetary Policy," in *CORFO Chile Economic Notes*, March 1971, *Special Issue, Excerpts from the CIAP Meeting on Chile*, pp. 17–18. Hereafter cited as the *Inostroza CIAP Statement*.

47. *Inostroza CIAP Statement*, pp. 17–18.

48. Ibid., pp. 18–19.

the newly publicly owned oligopolies, these large enterprises have actually captured under government auspices an even greater share of total available credit than before. Thus, although the destruction of a vital pillar of private capitalism has had an immediate effect, credit monopoly by the state has led to friction with small industrialists and artisans, who have claimed discrimination against them rather than favorable treatment by the Popular Unity.[49] Furthermore, the promised effects on efficiency, concentration, savings, and so forth cannot be observed during 1970–73 and may fall significantly short of expectations.[50] Private ownership gave maximum flexibility to the banking sector in developed nations; its demise in Chile provides no guarantee for success so long as it is not allowed to develop in consonance with Chile's idiosyncratic economic physiognomy.

Allende gave assurances that the Central Bank's de facto policy of supervising a subsidy program whenever it extended credits at negative interest rates would benefit mostly the publicly owned part of the economy. Although the Central Bank had redistributed income ever since nominal and real interest rates differed because of inflation-induced lags in money rates, the effective redistribution and income subsidies were more widespread before than after 1955. They occurred at the peaks of the inflationary cycles: between 1958 and 1969. Subsidies through negative real interest rates were provided primarily during 1961–64, but subsidies due to low but positive real interest rates were more prevalent. The real losers or beneficiaries have never been clearly identified.[51]

THE DEMISE OF PRIVATE AGRICULTURAL LATIFUNDISTAS

With the reduction of agriculture's income share to a dismal 7.5 percent of GDP in 1969,[52] its revival may have become as difficult as it is necessary. The impact of the 1966–72 governmental land reform policies on redistributing the income share of the latifundistas was thus

---

49. See *El Mercurio*, May 8, 1972, p. 25.

50. Massive deficits (3.000 million escudos in 1972) for the state enterprises were projected by Christian Democratic senator José Musalem. See detailed criticism and data in *La Segunda*, April 21, 1972, pp. 8–9.

51. See the author's "Public Policy," pp. 46–51, 184–94, and Daniel Tapia and Eduardo Olivares, "Tasas de Interés (1958–1969)," in Banco Central de Chile, *Estudios Monetarios II* (Santiago: Banco Central, 1970), pp. 111–20.

52. ODEPLAN, *Antecedentes, 1960–70*, p. 57, table 45.

relatively small, though the campaign against latifundismo had already reached climactic proportions during the ill-fated Alliance for Progress. Allende completed the task started by the Christian Democrats, when by April 1972 he expropriated more than 2,000 latifundios with more than 3 million hectares.[53] Although he was able to destroy the economic base of his past enemies in the cities and the mining sector with a degree of order and respect to the law that could be loosely construed as being in the Chilean tradition, he permitted (or instigated) a highly unstable situation in the rural agricultural areas. Illegal takeovers of farms mushroomed with only lip service in the government's efforts to stem them. Unlike the agrarian reform efforts in numerous developing nations, which led to small-scale, privately owned, individual farms, much of the Frei–Allende program moved toward replacement of private ownership by a potentially even more onerous state latifundismo. A program to restore small-scale private ownership in agriculture has been carried out since 1973 by the military junta.

President Eduardo Frei had already placed great emphasis on ownership transformation in agriculture. After 1965 large private estates were subdivided into smaller private farms under a program that the Left-wing extremists found too slow and that the Right-wing parties argued was ignoring the incentive ideas of production. Although a process of consolidation of smaller, inefficient farms was under way in Europe, the change in the size of private land ownership was being used in Chile to break down the political power of landowners and to destroy a rigid system of class stratification. More than 3 million hectares were expropriated by CORA between 1965 and February 1970, with a peak reached in 1969.[54]

The 1970–73 income redistribution improved the standard of living of agricultural workers, the former losers of intrasectoral clashes, at the old landowners expense but added practically nothing to the inadequate agricultural production incentives. The intra-agricultural redistribution of income was not accompanied by the more important industry–agriculture or general intersectoral redistribution of income that shaped sectoral terms of trade and incentives. The inter- and intraclass redistri-

53. ODEPLAN, "Informe de ODEPLAN sobre la Actividad Económica en el Primer Trimeste de 1972" (Santiago: ODEPLAN, Apr. 1972), mimeo, p. 1.
54. See *Quinto Mensaje del Presidente de la República de Chile don Eduardo Frei Montalva al Inaugurar el Período del Congreso Nacional, 21 de Mayo de 1969* (Santiago: Presidencia de la República, 1969), p. 365. Also *Mensaje 1970, ibid.*, pt. 2, p. 261.

bution did not solve the basic issues of a fair income share for agriculture for performing the food producing function of fair shares for its labor and capital.

THE STATE'S TIGHTENING GRIP OVER THE INDUSTRIAL LEVER

The dominant place in Allende's government's scheme to redistribute income, wealth, and power was reserved for the industrial sector. The vital segments to be nationalized included monopolies, semimonopolies, oligopolies, mono- or oligopsonies, the metal–manufacturing segment, and all firms that produced goods for popular consumption. The criteria used to define these categories were vague enough to allow takeover of almost any industrial firm.

As in all other instances the immediate political aim was to destroy the financial base of the opposition parties in the large industrial firms. Monopolistic or oligopolistic enterprises were defined as those "characterized by the use of largely mechanized technologies, underutilization of installed capacity, by a high concentration of income generated, control of prices and supplies, and the use of policies discriminating quality and types of products." To eliminate any doubt and expedite nationalization, all firms with a capital in excess of half a million dollars were defined as monopolies. Because they satisfied either the monopoly or popular consumption criteria or both, fourteen major textile enterprises, producing more than 50 percent of textiles, were promptly expropriated or intervened. Under the same guidelines and in order to ensure normal, continuous supplies threatened by abandonment by owners, bankruptcy, and the like, government takeovers took place in beer, and, outside industry, in coal, fishing, poultry, smoked pork or beef, and ninety other small enterprises.[55]

The most rapid and immediate statization involved the instrumental goods segment of iron, steel, and peripheral products industries. In March 1971 the Pacific Steel Company passed over to social ownership, and participation was guaranteed to this complex by ARMCO, INDAC, INDESA, PRODINSA, SOCOMETAL, INCHALAM, COMPAC, MADECO, NIBSA, SGM, EQUITEM, AZA, as well as by the intervention of two major cement firms and numerous construction materials enterprises. Either directly or indirectly, government assumed

55. See ODEPLAN, *Analysis 1971*, pp. 34–35.

almost total ownership or control over national machinery production and over those firms producing material or equipment necessary to fulfill the Popular Unity's ambitious construction plans.[56]

Some effects of these moves appeared in 1972 and 1973. With rigid output prices and extraordinary real wage increases, profit margins shrank to the point where reinvestment was minimal, firms were abandoned by frightened owners, or wage shares were so high that firms could not buy the raw materials needed to increase production. Supply bottlenecks began to arise everywhere. Furthermore, as the Popular Unity government deliberately reduced royalties, licensee fees, and other payments to foreign companies that had directly or indirectly lent know-how, new products, technology, and so forth to Chile, numerous basic pharmaceutical, health, and personal care products disappeared from the market or declined in quality. Industrial supply suffered most from the balance-of-payments effect of rising food consumption because of income redistribution. The crunch was felt on the imports of raw materials, and there was increased discrimination against agriculture, intermediate products, and capital goods. Allende's government had to choose between more butter, milk, meat, and sugar from New Zealand, Australia, Argentina, and Cuba or more imports for industrial expansion; it could not have both. When in 1970–72 the choice was made to continue discriminating against agriculture and to subsidize and increase the amount of competitive imports, the industrial supply shortage became a fact. Universal shortages developed during the first half of 1973 and black markets became rife.

BYPASSING THE PRIVATE MIDDLEMEN

Although the Marxist coalition aimed to destroy the foreign miners, aristocratic landlords, pioneer industrialists, and powerful bankers, only the middlemen were accused of receiving an income share "without contributing any effective service."[57] This return to the contention that distribution and commercialization services are unproductive openly implied that income distribution was grossly inequitable not only because commerce was earning quasi-rents induced by inflation, protection, or sectoral clashes but, more significantly, because it earned any income at all. The immediate goal of such income redistribution

56. Ibid., pp. 35–36.
57. Ibid., p. 36.

indicated more than a condemnation of the middlemen's allegedly inadequate pursuit of the location-, quantity-, and time-transformation functions. It incorrectly implied, in consonance with Marxist and medieval theory, that there are no costs involved or benefits derived from changing the quantity, location, and time dimensions of goods and services.

Reduction of the middlemen's income share was pursued indirectly as well as directly. By fixing or controlling prices to consumers and by raising the costs of product and labor in commercial enterprises, commercial profit margins were cut. Total commercial profits at the retail level were not reduced correspondingly during 1971 and the first half of 1972, when sales rose significantly. This implied a major gain in the battle against inflation, an income redistribution to the consumer, and no vital losses as yet for the commercial community.

More important in terms of present and forthcoming structural reform was the state's expanding role as an intermediary, especially at the wholesale level. Old state-owned commercial firms were strengthened, new ones were created, and private ones were purchased or absorbed. The government created the National Distribution Corporation (DINAC), the Agriculture Marketing Corporation (ECA), the National Poultry Firm (ENAVI), and the National Corporation for Fuel (ENADI). Also, the Chilean (State) Development Corporation purchased the brokerage houses of Duncan Fox, Gibbs, and Williamson Balfour and absorbed other firms.[58]

The government's policies had at least one major beneficial effect during 1971 and the first half of 1972. Industrial consumer goods markets expanded appreciably as a consequence of critical intersectoral income redistribution, which was long overdue but was nevertheless short-lived. This redistribution primarily involved trade, but also banking, transport, and some other services, which by earning inflationary quasi-rents had raised prices and diminished the market for industrial goods. With trade markups drastically reduced after 1970, industrial prices fell relative to the income of almost all sectors. Most significantly, the price of trade services declined compared to most other prices. As the cost of price paid for performing the quantity, location, and time transformation was decreased, not only did the real income of all other sectors grow but, furthermore, sectors that were previously affected most strongly by these intermediation costs, such as industry, experienced a real income increase. This positive effect on real demand

58. Ibid., p. 36.

and supply was more than offset by the negative effects mentioned earlier. But Allende unleashed forces that neither he was nor anyone else will be able to control or contain for years to come. Trade markups recovered sharply as inflation accelerated in 1972 and 1973.

THE ALLENDE-LED MARXIST SECTORAL COALITIONS AND CONFLICTS

The emerging coalition between Allende's Marxist government and state-owned segments of various sectors had powerful ramifications that went beyond the immediate and already successful income redistribution and destruction of direct foreign and national large-scale private capitalism. An elite privileged class of bureaucrats and technocrats gained immediate access over the whole governmental machinery. A direct coalition with and dependence of the Chilean state and state-owned segments on the socialist states of Russia, China, Rumania, Poland, East Germany, and so on was forged by consolidating and expanding the power of the Chilean state's segment of the economy and by eliminating the private. Support provided under this open coalition became most evident during 1970–73 in fishing, copper, transportation, agriculture, entertainment, and culture.

Under the 1970–73 coalition pattern the state-owned segment of mining (particularly copper) retained a much higher share of the copper-resource surplus than in the past. Thus the copper workers gained an unprecedented privileged position consistent with the theory of sectoral clashes but alien to socialist or communist theory. Besides, under the dominant coalition between government and the export sector, quasi-rents sharply declined through inefficiency, and the copper quasi-rents previously received by the foreign capitalists and not dissipated now accrued to the privileged copper workers rather than being invested in human and physical capital. Most of the reduced copper quasi-rents available for general government expenditures were dispensed in the urban areas under Marxist guidance, and virtually nothing trickled down to the perenially neglected rural areas.

Contrary to official pronouncements credit was channeled through the state banks to the state-owned segments of the economy. This procedure slowly but inexorably strangled the minority private sector. However, this overt clash between state-owned and privately owned segments conceals the equally if not more important internal coalitions and clashes within the state-owned segments. Some patterns can be clearly discerned; others can only be conjectured. Copper mining and the mono- or oligopolistic state-owned industrial enterprises involved in mass production of consumer goods, the metals machinery complex, and to a lesser extent fishing emerged as the dominant subsectors with privileged status and highly favored treatment in the sectoral income redistribution. Neglected or discriminated were agriculture, state commerce, state banking, some parts of education, and, very strongly, health. Construction, heavily state owned or controlled, held a neutral position between the privileged and discriminated against sectors or segments thereof.

Public health was ignored and neglected not only during the Allende years but throughout 1930–73 because of its low priority and severe budget constraints. Lacking the strong feedbacks and linkages of construction, it elicited no political support from other sectors. Even though it faced unlimited demand, the fact that it was a nonmarket service, offered free as a public good, deprived it of the political glamour of industry, airports, and other public works. More visible sectors and budget items, such as higher wages and family allowances, persistently edged it out in the selection process.

The 1970–73 Marxist-inspired coalitions and clashes led to balance-of-payments convulsions reminiscent of the Great Depression. The elimination of copper factor payments abroad was more than offset by a sharp decline of private capital inflows. With the cutoff of Western credits because of the prohibitive rise in risks, the Chilean government accepted any credit or trade deal, however uneconomical, from export-driving socialist countries. The arrangements for tractors were a prime example. Cuba's sugar was imported to penalize national sugar beet producers that were on strike. Australian and Argentinian food imports at artificially low escudo but high dollar prices further penalized agriculture, artificially augmented food consumption, and extended indirect foreign ownership in Chile by raising foreign debt. Those willing to export to Chile on credit emerged as a privileged class of foreigners enjoying returns far beyond those deserved realistically under competitive maket conditions. The sectoral clashes of 1970–73 illustrated once more that Chile's problems were in supply, not demand, and were intimately related to incentives and capital formation.

However, from October 1972 to September 1973 no other dimension of sectoral clashes had such a powerful impact as the undisguised economic and political warfare between the trucking transport subsector and Allende's government. The prolonged strikes by the truckers contributed to, as well as accelerated, the gradual disintegration of the production apparatus built by Allende. With agricultural output already sharply reduced during 1972–73, this clash further reduced food supplies to the cities, triggered a series of sympathy strikes and, along with the El Teniente copper strike and the semihyperinflation, led to the death of Allende and the rise of the military junta.[59]

The severe balance-of-payments constraint of 1973 was choking overall economic expansion and was severely damaging industry, transportation, and selected services. Throughout 1930–73 the pattern of income distribution was characterized by great, though diminishing, inequalities. The division of income between labor and capital was to a great degree a statistical artifact that produced a highly inflated profit share. The distribution of income was idiosyncratic in that inequalities within the employer, capitalist, and self-employed classes greatly exceeded the inequalities among the manual and office worker classes as well as those between the two major groups of classes. It was also idiosyncratic in that intersectoral income inequalities within the manual-worker class were much larger than those suggested by indices of concentration.

A pluralistic income distribution was characterized by the coexistence during 1930–70 of the superrich, the very rich, the upper middle, the middle middle, the lower middle, the moderately poor, the poor, the very poor, the marginal, and the submarginals. The range of income differences was too wide, the contrasts were too great, not only between the misery belts of the marginals and the golden living standards of the rich but also between the middle classes and the very poor.

Chile experienced a profound transformation in its distribution from 1970 to 1973. Much of the income of the small elite of private bankers, industrialists, merchants, landowners, and so forth had been transferred by 1973 to the state, laborers, and the poor, thereby boosting consumption and lowering investment. The range of income inequalities was quickly and sharply reduced. The underlying ownership transformation is largely irreversible. As much as socialization led to economic distortions and disequilibria, reduction of the previously highly unequal intralabor income distribution created a social upheaval. Allende's efforts to destroy the obvious urban lord–serf pattern by favoring the poor, laborers, and those living in slums appeared more successful than his weak efforts to reduce the pervasive urban–rural and interregional income differentials.

59. Allende fully recognized the forces and events leading to his downfall but appeared unable and unwilling to accept the compromises typical of Chilean tradition that would have saved him and the economy. See Allende, *Mensaje 1973*, pp. xix–xxiv.

11

Capital Formation

Capital accumulation suffered its worst setback since independence when saving and investment dropped to less than 5 percent of GDP in 1931–33. Its gradual rise, first to 9–11 percent during 1940–55—one of the lowest rates in Latin America—and then to 12–19 percent of GDP during 1955–73, marked a significant progress, compared to the debacle of the depression, but persistently fell short of the pre-1930 performance and the levels necessary for self-sustained growth. To the extent that a transformation did occur, it was inadequate in terms of needs as well as aspirations. Insufficient progress in capital formation (saving, investment, and the mechanisms linking them) remained the primary bottleneck to accelerated growth for many reasons. Each of the wide spectrum of partial hypotheses advanced to explain the physiognomy (progress, deficiencies, and distortions) of capital formation, which has combined the inherited pre-1930 features and some idiosyncratic characteristics acquired during 1930–73, provides valuable insights concerning the determinants of saving, investment, and the interactions between them.

SAVING

Gross saving increased in each successive decade, as can be seen in table 11.1, while net national saving, which was zero or negative during 1930–61, increased, though not strikingly, during 1962–70 and fell to zero and negative levels during 1971–72.[1]

The landowners, other national private capitalists, the households, the state, and the direct and indirect foreign capitalists who shaped

---

1. See ODEPLAN, *El Ahorro Bruto Monetario Generado por Agente Económico* (Santiago: ODEPLAN, July 1969), pp. 1–59. Hereafter cited as *Ahorro Bruto*.

saving and its components (shown in table 11.1) during 1930–73 retained much of their pre-1930 heterogeneity and volatility in terms of origin, motivation, and access to financial and physical capital. Each group has been partly responsible for the overall inadequate level of saving. In the meantime the role of sectors as a source of resource surpluses changed dramatically.

Table 11.1 Sources of Saving as Percentages of National Product, 1940–71

	Private saving	Public saving	National saving	External saving	Total saving
1940[a]	6.3	6.5	12.8	−1.3	11.5
1940[b]	4.5		11.0	.5	
1950[a]	6.7	4.6	11.3	−.3	11.0
1950[b]	4.4		11.0	.01	
1960	10.3	3.4	13.7	3.9	17.6
1961	9.4	3.4	12.8	5.7	18.5
1962	10.4	2.5	12.9	3.1	16.0
1963	9.7	4.6	14.3	4.5	18.8
1964	10.8	4.2	15.0	2.8	17.8
1965	12.4	4.8	17.2	1.3	18.5
1966	10.2	6.6	16.8	1.5	18.3
1967	7.8	6.4	14.2	1.7	15.9
1968	8.2	6.2	14.4	2.2	16.6
1969	8.1	8.4	16.5	0.7	17.2
1970	7.3	8.5	15.8	1.6	17.4
1971 (official Allende)	9.3	0.2	9.5	3.3	12.8
1971 (official junta)	13.3	−0.4	12.9	2.2	15.1
1972 (official junta)	.13.8	−3.9	9.9	6.0	15.9

Sources: For the early CORFO estimate, see CORFO *Cuentas Nacionales de Chile, 1940–1954* (Santiago: Editorial del Pacífico, S.A., 1957), tables 1, 51, 54; for the later UN-based CORFO estimate, see CORFO, *"Cuentas Nacionales de Chile, 1940–1962"* (Santiago: CORFO, June 1963), mimeo, table 4, p. 27; for 1960–71, see ODEPLAN, *Cuentas Nacionales de Chile, 1960–1971* (Santiago: ODEPLAN, 1972), table 5, p. 28, table 10, p. 40; for 1971 and 1972 (junta data), see ODEPLAN, *Cuentas Nacionales de Chile, 1965–1972* (Santiago: ODEPLAN, 1973), table 5, p. 22; table 10, p. 29.

Note: Public saving for 1940 and 1950 is defined by CORFO in a way that is not strictly comparable to the ODEPLAN definition applicable for 1960–69. The superscript a stands for early CORFO estimate and the superscript b for later CORFO–UN methodology-based estimate. According to early CORFO estimates, foreign saving was defined as the deficit or surplus of the trade balance; according to later CORFO and ODEPLAN estimates for 1940–65, it was measured by the deficit or surplus of the current account with abroad.

Landowner Capitalists and Agricultural Saving

Agriculture accounted for only a small amount of actual savings even
when it had a relatively high potential. The leakages included the flight
of agricultural capital to other sectors and the cities, the nonconversion
of free time of labor into investment, the high consumption–use of its
gross income, and the depletion of much of the agricultural credit for
seasonal production expenditures.

As a capitalist class the landowners—members of the so-called
traditional national oligarchy—disposed of a saving or investable fund
composed of the gross agricultural resource surplus received (rents and
profits), credits,[2] and actual or potential control over the free time of
laborers and tenant farmers. The first component of the gross saving
potential, which is measured here by nonlabor income, declined
secularly from 68.6 percent of agricultural value added in 1940 to 61.8
percent in 1960 to 52.8 percent in 1970 and 48.2 percent in 1971. It
accounted for a remarkable 12 percent of national income in 1940,
7.3 percent of GDP in 1960, and only a meager 3.7 percent of GDP in
1970 and 3.8 percent in 1971.[3] However, approximately two-thirds of
this nonlabor income was in reality employers' salaries. Thus only
one-third forms, according to the national accounts, the true net
agricultural surplus.[4] On the other hand since some simple production
functions of a small segment of agriculture indicate that the contribution of land to output ranged between 67 and 77 percent, much labor
income did in reality reflect rental income.[5] An exaggerated identification of all landowners with rich capitalists is evident: approximately
one-third of the agricultural labor force fell into the employer category
in 1940, and many of the employers were unincorporated small- or
medium-scale farmers. Whatever their ultimate source, the extremely
conservative estimate of employers' salaries suggests that even in 1940

2. For an excellent analysis of the distribution of credit and the share of agriculture
see Javier Fuenzalida and Sergio Undurràga, *El Crédito y Su Distribución en Chile*
(Santiago: Editorial Lambda, 1968), pp. 81–147. Hereafter cited as *Distribución del
Crédito*.

3. All estimates based on information found in CORFO, *Renta Nacional, 1940–45*
(Santiago: Imprenta Universitaria, 1946), vol. 1, pp. 152–53. vol. 2, p. 29 (hereafter cited
as *Renta*), and in ODEPLAN, *Distribución del Ingreso y Cuentas de Producción 1960–
1971* (Santiago: ODEPLAN, 1973), tables 1, 9, 11, 12, pp. 4–5, 20–27 (hereafter cited
as ODEPLAN, *Distribución 1960–1971*).

4. CORFO, *Renta*, 1: 167; 2: 29.

5. See Lillian Collyer, *Naturaleza, Significado y Uso de la Función de Producción y
Aplicación Práctica de la Fórmula "Cobb–Douglas" en la Provincia de Aconcagua*, p. 66.

the net direct internal agricultural investable resource surplus may not have exceeded 4 percent of GDP and that it dropped to less than 1 percent in 1970 and 1971.

To a very large extent the de facto highly discriminatory agricultural policy of government was responsible for this steep secular decline of landowners' Ricardian rents as well as for the flight of the agricultural investable surplus to the cities, other sectors, and abroad. The potential investable resources of the omnipresent and ever-expanding state capitalism were large throughout 1940–73 but once more were not directed or attracted to agriculture. Furthermore, at least until 1973 neither the incentives nor the mechanisms were created that would have permitted conversion of the free time of either the permanent or floating agricultural labor force into more and improved land, livestock, and physical capital. Low capital formation remained synonymous with low utilization of labor despite the spectacular institutional transformation under Salvador Allende.

The internal redistribution of agricultural income during 1967–73 almost totally wiped out landowners' surpluses. Therefore, future saving will depend on government saving, increased conversion of under- or unutilized agricultural labor reserves into capital formation, and more intensive cultivation of lands in addition to the monetary savings of the new fundos and their workers. If agriculture is to perform its food-producing function adequately, the trends of instability, secular decline, and low surplus reinvestment must be reversed. Not only a new agricultural incomes policy but also new mechanisms of capturing potential savings, such as an agricultural bank, are needed.

Industrialists, Merchants, and Other Private Capitalists

Profits by private nonagricultural capitalists were only partly converted into savings. A major share of these funds was also labor remuneration essential for consumption. They were also heavily taxed, and a portion of them was repatriated abroad. Finally, such profits went to a middle-class amalgam of heterogeneous entrepreneurs. Savings suffered becaused of consumption, tax, remittances abroad, and operating credit leakages from private investment funds. The capacity and willingness to save of the highly heterogeneous private, industrial, merchant, mining, construction, transport, and service capitalists were determined by the level and origin of their income, their legal status, their access to credit, their social and ethnic affiliations, and their links with interests abroad. The share of profits, which is traditionally

Table 11.2 Percentage Distribution of the Profit Share by
Economic Activity: 1940, 1960, 1970, 1971

	1940	1960	1970	1971
Agriculture	28.0	15.1	8.5	11.8
Fishing	—	0.6	0.7	1.0
Mining	7.0	11.5	17.0	6.9
Industry	22.0	29.8	38.0	36.0
Construction	0.8	4.3	3.3	6.3
Electricity, gas, and water	—	0.5	0.6	−0.4
Transportation	—	4.5	1.0	0.4
Trade	20.7	23.2	21.7	30.6
Banking	14.0	1.1	3.0	3.8
Ownership of dwellings	7.5	1.5	−0.3	−5.2
Public administration and defense	—	—	—	—
Services	—	7.9	6.5	8.8
Total	100.0	100.0	100.0	100.0

Sources: CORFO, *Renta Nacional, 1940–1945* (Santiago: Imprenta Universitaria, 1946), vol. 1, p. 167, for 1940; and ODEPLAN, *Distribución del Ingreso y Cuentas de Producción, 1960–1971* (Santiago: ODEPLAN, 1973), pp. 20–21, for 1960, 1970, and 1971. In some respects the CORFO figures are not strictly comparable with the ODEPLAN ones.

considered the key determinant of savings by the capitalist class, had some peculiar features.

A pervasive transformation of the sectoral distribution of profits between 1940 and 1971, which is illustrated in table 11.2, led to a substantial rise in the share of industrial profits and a dramatic decline of agricultural ones. This increasing importance of industrialists as potential savers, coupled with a dramatic recovery in the role of miners, which was in turn reversed during 1971, and a milder one among merchants, coincides with a doubling of actual saving between 1940 and 1970 as a percentage of GDP.

The heterogeneity of the profit share explains in part why all of it was not saved. At least half of the so-called profit share, or nonlabor income—that is, approximately one-quarter of net national income—consisted during 1940–43 of employers' salaries and reflected returns to human capital (education, training, and the like).[6] In the case of the merchant and service capitalists, employers' salaries accounted for almost half of their respective sectoral incomes.[7] For this employer class, composed of immigrants and their descendants who formed the

6. CORFO, *Renta*, 1: 157.
7. Ibid., p. 166.

national elite, education and related factors were the primary determinant of income. Their spending pattern was typical of the middle class. Seeking to maintain or improve the quality of life inherited or borrowed from Europe, they spent most of their income on educating their children in the best schools at home or abroad, on comfortable homes, on the best food, on health care and other services, and on travel, most of which were very expensive. Since a major segment of their income was also absorbed by taxes, support of the arts, the news media, political parties, and social causes, the saving surplus was far below that expected from puritanic capitalists. What set them apart from workers was not high savings but high reinvestment in education, which in turn yielded income levels that set them apart from low-education workers and placed them close to the capitalists. Moreover, the scarcity of their talents allowed them to earn labor quasi-rents.

The industrial capitalist group, which emerged so powerfully in 1970, received approximately 55 percent of sectoral value added during 1940–43 and close to 60 percent during 1960–70. In 1971 its income share had fallen to 46.3 percent, but of the 1940–43 income almost 60 percent consisted of employers' salaries.[8] Some of their profit share came from inflation- or protection-related quasi-rents. Only the banking financiers and mining capitalists earned a high (but shrinking) share of their income from profits, interest, and so on.[9] Only part of these were net resource surpluses available for internal investment because they were taxed away or repatriated abroad. More than 40 percent of mining value added during 1940–43, much of it quasi-rents, was taken by government.

Of the meager posttax surplus available, which ranged from 6.8 to 12.5 percent of sectoral income, much was repatriated abroad. The tax leakage of potential savings was thus aggravated by the profit leakage abroad.[10] Losses in rental housing rose sharply between 1970 and 1971.

Rents were another declining component of the profit share (9.5 percent of net income in 1940 versus 7.1 percent in 1943), and it can only be conjectured that the spending–saving pattern of the rentier class was not very distinct from the overlapping salaried employer class. Nevertheless, rents, along with profit and interest income, which ranged between 14.3 and 17.5 percent of net income during 1940–43,[11] pro-

8. Ibid., pp. 166–67; ODEPLAN, *Distribución, 1960–1971*, pp. 32–33.
9. CORFO, *Renta*, 1: 167.
10. Ibid., 2: 121.
11. Ibid., 1: 157.

vided the lion's share not only of tax revenues but also of aggregate investable resources, if they were not imputed ones. However, by 1970 the national accounts had reduced their estimate of rents to zero. Profits, which are regarded as the mainstay of private capitalism, hovered around 10 percent of income during 1940–43, which is by no means spectacular.

Stated in modern terminology, compensation of workers operating on their own account (profits of unincorporated enterprises) formed a major share of national income—21.8 percent in 1960 but only 14.3 percent in 1970—and money or imputed housing rents, government property income, and the like fluctuated mildly below one-tenth of national income. Net remuneration of owners and entrepreneurs ranged between 17.2 and 26.3 percent of national income during 1960–70.[12] Since per capita income of the minicapitalists working on their own account was substantially below that of salaried employees— less than half in 1969—and only marginally above that of workers, the very use of the term "nonlabor income" or "profits" is misleading, at least in terms of its potential saving capacity.[13]

Among industrial enterprises the principal source of funds has been retained profits, which have been used for investment as well as for current exploitation. For a sample of industrial enterprises, retained profits as a percentage of total net profits advanced from 29.8 percent in 1951 to 64.8 percent in 1959.[14]

Inflation had a strong negative impact on industrial profits available for reinvestment. Credit availability was cut so dramatically between 1940 and 1955 that a credit asphyxy was created, and industrial enterprises were forced to retain an increasing share of their profits. This was to be used not predominantly for reinvestment but to provide credit to customers. The general credit asphyxy, which was only partly reversed during 1955–65, was especially onerous for large industrial concerns because the distribution of total credit was simultaneously transformed in favor of the public sector on the one hand and small and medium-sized enterprises on the other. The response to these changes (namely, the emergence of large industrial enterprises as credit-extending institutions and their conversion into the foundations

12. ODEPLAN, *Antececentes sobre el Desarrollo Chileno—1960–70* (Santiago: ODEPLAN, 1971), table 29. p. 43. Hereafter cited as *Antecedentes, 1960–70*.

13. Ibid., table 33, p. 45.

14. See Instituto de Economía, *Formación de Capital en las Empresas Industriales* (Santiago: Instituto de Economía, Universidad de Chile, 1961), pp. 110–11.

of a parallel financial system) satisfied some of the country's credit needs, though at the cost of lower investment, employment, and growth.[15]

The Household Capitalist Class and Housing Investment

As monetary policy, captive to the fiscal restrictions, was called upon to finance part of the public sector's budget, an inflation-induced decumulation in institutional capital adversely affected private household savings. Savings deposits, time deposits, life insurance policies, and all types of fixed-price debts became unattractive forms of storing wealth since they provided low, zero, or negative real interest rates. The government's response to a drastic decline in savings and to the disappearance of time-honored instruments linking creditors with debtors was slow. Finally, during the late 1950s and the 1960s inflation-proof assets with cost-of-living escalator clauses were established.[16]

Households allegedly dissaved from 1.6 to 7.1 percent of GDP during 1960–67, while general government reported savings ranging between 2.4 and 7.4 percent of GDP during the same period even though the public sector had massive deficits. In spite of the negative personal savings, which are examined in chapter 13, households emerged as an important saving and capitalist group, especially in housing investment. Nevertheless, most indicators of private savings during 1960–67 showed increases only in 1961, 1966, and 1967.[17]

Slowly but unmistakably, households emerged as a powerful capitalist class in the area of housing saving and investment. The trend began in the late 1920s, when white-collar workers as a group, and some privileged individuals within this group, began receiving mortgage loans with no escalator clause from their health, pension, and social security associations. As inflation accelerated, these loans, plus the credits of the Housing Bank, which financed 70 percent of the dwellings built in 1952,[18] led to a scandalous accumulation of wealth by the predominantly salaried, middle-income groups. In response to public outcries and pressures by foreign missions and numerous economists,

15. Fuenzalida and Undurraga, *Distribución del Crédito*, pp. 27–31, 36–46, 66–70, 127–43.

16. See ODEPLAN, *Ahorro Bruto*, table 11, p. 36.

17. See ibid., table 3, p. 28; table 11, p. 36.

18. See Gabriel González Videla, *Mensaje de S.E. El Presidente de la República don Gabriel González Videla al Congreso Nacional al Inaugurar el Período Ordinario de Sesiónes, 21 de Mayo de 1952* (Santiago: Presidencia de la República, 1952), pp. xlvii-xlix, 733–34. Hereafter cited as *Mensaje 1952*.

inflation-proof mortgages were introduced in the early 1960s, thus reducing or eliminating their ability to redistribute income. As escalator clauses were attached to mortgages by the newly created dwellings corporation (CORVI) and saving and loan associations, housing savings boomed.[19] Further support for household dwelling purchases was provided by the social security system and various savings banks and by public indirect investment.[20]

The rise and spread of actual (or even potential) minicapitalist homeowners spawned a strong pressure group that could not be ignored by any government. Even though housing investment exerted a magnetic appeal, primarily on buyers, and the ultimate beneficiary was the private household as a dwelling owner, it operated most effectively through its impact on builders, the industrial sector, and all segments of the economy catering to it. Mortgage credit never lost its redistributive ability, however. In 1965 one of the officially stated goals of monetary policy was to administer the continuous redistribution of income inherent in inflation and negative real interest rates in favor of households purchasing dwellings.[21] In 1972 the escalator clause of housing mortgage units was eliminated with respect to owners of small dwellings and other special groups, thus fulfilling the Popular Unity promise to redistribute income in favor of the underprivileged.[22]

Savings for housing have thus become a major source of funds that has gone beyond a life cycle. Such inflation-proof assets, which, unlike gold, dollars, cars, and paintings, could promptly provide the amenities of a home, shaped the composition of investment. Most significantly, they have proved the best, if not the only, Marxist-proof form of asset during 1970–73. Salvador Allende not only publicly and repeatedly disclaimed any intention of his Marxist government to eradicate private homeownership but also made it a main goal of the Popular

19. See Fuenzalida and Undurraga, *Distribución del Crédito*, p. 21; Carlos Ibáñez del Campo, *Mensaje de S.E. El Presidente de la República don Carlos Ibáñez del Campo al Congreso Nacional al Inaugurar el Período Ordinario de Sesiónes, 21 de Mayo de 1958* (Santiago: Presidencia de la República, 1958), Appendix. The Corporación de la Vivienda was created in 1953 (see *Mensaje 1958*, Appendix). See also ODEPLAN, *Antecedentes, 1960–70*, p. 408.

20. ODEPLAN, *Recursos Financieros Asignados por el Sector Público al Sector Privado con Fines de Inversión* (Santiago: ODEPLAN, 1969), p. 34.

21. ODEPLAN, *Antecedentes, 1960–70*, pp. 401–02; Francisco Garcés G., "Fase de Transición: Economía y Finanzas de Chile, 1964–1966," in Banco Central de Chile, *Estudios Monetarios* (Santiago: Banco Central, 1968), p. 32.

22. See "Suprimida reajustabilidad de las deudas habitacionales," *El Siglo*, June 1, 1972, p. 13.

Unity to turn all Chilean households into proud owners of these inflation- and party-proof assets.[23] Homeowner minicapitalism has become a symbol of the standard of living. The immediate aspiration of almost all Chile's households, it was promoted by and coexisted with the economy-wide maxisocialism. During 1970–73 it was a force capable of shaping the country's path to socialism rather than being shaped by it.

Public Saving and State Capitalism

The gradual ascendancy of state capitalism since 1855, which was mildly accelerated after 1930 and reached a crescendo during 1970–73, has added to rather than reduced the heterogeneity of the Chilean capitalist class in general and of the state capitalist–employer group in particular. The performance of the state as a saver appears as weak as that of any other capitalist group and has constituted an equally significant bottleneck.

The relationships among Chile's major economic agents are so labyrinthine that the indispensable estimates of different types of savings must be used with extreme caution. According to the national accounts estimates presented in table 11.1, public saving represented more than half of total saving in 1940, fell secularly until 1962, and rose to more than a third of total saving during 1966–70. Public saving dropped to 0.2 percent of GNP in 1971 (Allende estimate) from 8.5 percent in 1970 and to − 3.9 percent in 1972. These could be considered both an over- and as an under-estimate.[24]

According to ODEPLAN, public sector savings have financed private investment through so-called indirect public investment, which accounted for 10.4 to 25.5 percent of private investment during 1961–67. If these indirect public investments are added to direct public investment, more than half of total investment was financed by public sector savings during 1961–67, and possibly even during 1940–70.[25] The public sector, as an indirect capitalist, funded private enterprise and household investment, with almost 50 percent going into private

23. Salvador Allende Gossens, *La Lucha por la Democracia Económica y las Libertades Sociales del Segundo Mensaje del Presidente Allende ante el Congreso Pleno, 21 de Mayo de 1972* (Santiago: Quimantú Ltda., 1972), pp. 64–65. Hereafter cited as *Segundo Mensaje 1972*.

24. General government allegedly supplied between 2.4 and 7.4 percent of GDP in savings, a highly suspect figure in view of the persistent public sector deficits (see ODEPLAN, *Ahorro Bruto*, table 3, p. 28).

25. See ODEPLAN, *Recursos Financieros*, pp. 27–29, 34.

254 *The Strains of Change: 1930–1973*

housing in the 1960s. In the same way that public savings financed private investment, foreign credits contributed a major segment— between one-forth and one-third during 1965–68—of the financing of public investment, primarily direct.[26] This support of fiscal policy by foreign credits remained one of the most deeply imbedded Chilean traditions, even during Allende's three-year reign.

Public sector savings originated from tax revenues of the general government, social security and other net revenues of the general government, and net surpluses of state enterprises. Tax revenues were rarely if ever sufficent to cover government expenditures. Although the state early became the dominant employer in public administration, education, health, and railroad transportation, its foremost concern as an employer continued to be the establishment of high and highly uneven incomes for various categories of public servants. Its role as a saver–investor was lesser or peripheral.

The most serious leakage as well as misallocation of resources occurred among state enterprises. Many of them were monopolistic, and they became more and more numerous during 1930–73. Between 1960 and 1962 more than two-thirds of them had deficits. Loses for the state railroads, airlines, ports, mining, sugar, and transportation were especially high at a time when generated profits should have been reinvested in general development. The large surpluses in petroleum and electricity were insufficient to bail out the other perennial losers,[27] partly because of CORFO's policy until 1970 of divesting itself from profitably operating enterprises. A major leakage of savings involved the railroads. For example, government transfers to the state railroads to cover their losses between 1959 and 1961 were equal to 87 percent of the increase in public debt in foreign currency during the same period.[28] During 1970–73 the entry of state capitalism into copper, farming, distribution, entertainment, industry, banking, and other areas did not radically change the investment motivations, the access to financial capital, or the differential treatment accorded to employees under private ownership. Although the overall investment motivation

26. See ODEPLAN, *La Utilización de Créditos Externos por Parte del Sector Público* (*Antecedentes Cuantitativos*) (Santiago: ODEPLAN, Sept. 1970), p. 9–11. Hereafter cited as *Utilización de Créditos Externos*.
27. E. Lee Ward Cantwell, "Consolidado del Sector Público: Metodología y Aplicación," Memoria en Economía (Santiago: University of Chile, 1963), table 4, pp. 155, 166, 176. Hereafter cited "Consolidado del Sector Público."
28. José Luis Federici Rojas, *Tarifas, Entradas y Gastos de la Empresa de Ferrocarriles del Estado de Chile* (Santiago: Instituto de Economía, Universidad de Chile, 1965), p. 3.

may not have declined, the ability to invest is likely to have suffered strongly as reduced profits, increased deficits, and smaller resource surpluses tilted the balance even more in favor of consumption than in the past. For example, as the banking sector's ownership was transferred from private capitalists to the state, its handsome profits of 1970 were replaced by whopping losses in 1971, greatly diminishing national and public savings. The traditional concern about the rate of profit reinvestment gave way to the far more ominous preoccupation of trying to minimize dissaving and disinvestment.[29] The third principal source of public saving was the surplus of the broadly defined social security system. The ODEPLAN national accounts estimates present this as the major source, but reliable and complete statistics are missing. The surplus of the social security system accounted for 13 percent of national savings in 1963 but decreased to a meager 6 percent in 1970. Approximately 25 percent of this surplus was used for consumption loans to members while the rest was used for mortgage credit. The declining trend in this surplus was expected to continue in the 1970s. Overall, the substantial income redistribution caused by the social security system increased consumption and sharply reduced profits, potential savings, and investment.[30] It may be repeated here that public saving according to the national accounts is defined and measured by the surplus of general government. However, if public saving is defined as the surplus of the public sector—that is, all current revenues less expenditures of the public sector—it was insufficient to cover direct public investment in any of the three years for which information is available. Throughout 1960, 1961, and 1962 it covered less than 50 percent.[31] A major part of the balance was financed out of domestic inflationary and foreign credits. Internal credits were equal to one-third of direct public investment.[32] The public sector surplus is reduced to a fraction of direct public investment if we deduct amortization of debt and personal assistance credits.[33] Furthermore, if the impact of inflation on the real value of revenues as related to expenditures is taken into account, it could be safely conjectured that during many inflationary years almost *all* public investment was financed by foreign or inflationary internal credits. Although ODEPLAN has argued that

29. See *Boletín Mensual*, Banco Central de Chile, no. 535, Sept. 1972, p. 1,134.
30. ODEPLAN, *Antecedentes, 1960–70*, pp. 242–45.
31. Ward, "Consolidado del Sector Público," pp. 148, 156, 167, 177.
32. Ibid., pp. 156, 167, 177, 147–48.
33. Ibid., pp. 156–57, 167–68, 177–78.

Lee Ward has underestimated the public sector's social security contributions, the size of this underestimate is not great enough to change
the basic conclusion that the public sector as a whole was repeatedly
not a net saver (even though general government was).

The Heterogeneous Foreign (and Immigrant) Capitalist Class and Foreign Saving

Foreign and immigrant investors constituted a large, heterogeneous
class of capitalists. At the one extreme the immigrant Spanish, Arab
(Syrian, Palestinian, and Lebanese), English, Jewish, French, German,
and other entrepreneurs and managers formed the principal artery of
industrialization, dominated commerce, and contributed considerably
to almost all sectors and enterprises. The immigrant distinguished
himself from the foreigner by permanently settling in Chile. Most
immigrants began as entrepreneurs, borrowed funds from banks, old
families, and even abroad, established their concerns, and subsequently
financed expansion by reinvesting profits. The extraordinary success
of such groups as the Arabs—who owned more than half the profits,
capital, and reserves in textile production during 1960–63—demonstrates unique entrepreneurial talents and high reinvestment propensity
from profit.[34] Direct foreign investment was, at $552 million in 1948,
70 percent of total foreign investment and, at $678 million in 1953,
66 percent, with more than 80 percent of that being foreign investment
from the United States.[35]

Direct foreign capitalists, especially from the United States, West
Germany, and other European countries, who had been almost always
present through agencies, subsidiaries, and so forth, became increasingly important and in the 1960s almost completely dominated some
industrial subsectors. This class of capitalists contributed to savings
through capital inflows and reinvestment of profits. It also caused
major resource leakages through repatriated profits, payments for
licenses, royalties, and other channels. Direct foreign investment
inflows during 1962–70 amounted to $1.546 billion, 44.6 percent of

34. See the excellent thesis by Andrés Sanfuentes Vergara, "La Influencia de los
Arabes en el Desarrollo Económico de Chile" (Santiago: Universidad de Chile, 1964,
typewritten).
35. Banco Central de Chile, *Inversiónes Extranjeras en Chile* (Santiago: Banco Central, 1955), table 17, p. 59. This study replaced an earlier one by the same institution
entitled *Inversiónes Extranjeras en Chile en 1948* and published in 1950. Hereafter the
1955 study will be cited as *Inversiónes Extranjeras*.

which was in large-scale copper.[36] Although these new investments have entered all sectors, those in mining and industry made up almost equiproportionately more than 95 percent of the total during 1965–70.[37] However, some expansion or even initiation projects were financed to a large extent by national resources.[38]

Although the great majority of these capital inflows constituted investment in the broad sense, they were not necessarily converted into fixed capital formation. The direct foreign private credits between 1964 and 1968, which amounted to $208 million, are an example. Of them only 15.5 percent were utilized for investment in machinery and equipment, 8.1 percent in construction, and 66.8 percent in other "real" operations. Direct foreign private contributions amounted to $99 million during the same period, with 22.6 percent used for investment in producers' durables, 7.2 percent for construction, 39.7 percent for other real operations, 11 percent for the purchase of stocks, and 16.1 percent for miscellaneous financial operations.[39]

The Giant Copper Capitalists

Among the direct foreign capitalists the corporate giants involved in copper extraction form a uniquely separate breed. Their contribution goes beyond investment to their capacity to earn foreign exchange and generate resource surpluses available for immediate satisfaction of needs through consumption or for future well-being through investment. The giant foreign copper corporations were a mosaic assortment of supermen. Mixed together were pioneers in technology; rough, sometimes ascetic managers; American engineers and hardened, excellent Chilean workers living in unhospitable desert or mountainous terrains; mammoth capitalists; and relentless risk-takers. They created vast riches and appropriated as much of them as Chile would allow. Everything connected with them was excessive: risks, efforts, capital invested, profits, losses. Their appearance on the Chilean scene about 1910 was as pyrotechnic as their expulsion in 1971 under President Allende was abrupt. They were no ordinary men of fortune but a class

---

36. CORFO, *Inversiónes Extranjeras en Chile* (Santiago: CORFO, May 1971), p. 2.
37. Ibid., p. 27. More than 50 percent of foreign investment in industry were in paper and paper products (ibid., p. 28).
38. CORFO, *Comportamiento de las Principales Empresas Industriales Extranjeras Acogidas al D.F.L. 258* (Santiago: CORFO, May 1970), p. 26.
39. ODEPLAN, *El Capital Privado Extranjero en Chile en el Período 1964–1968 a Nivel Global y Sectorial* (Santiago: ODEPLAN, 1970), table 7, p. 37; p. 39.

that creates gold out of deserts and impregnable mountains against the most unfavorable odds. The challenge of unearthing Chile's riches between 1970 and 1973 rested almost exclusively with the state, which claimed a capacity equal to or greater than the foreign capitalists. The Allende era was too short-lived to show whether enough progress had taken place in the last fifty years for the challenge to be met by Chileans without dependence on a new breed of "socialist men of fortune." Neither the Russians nor any other socialist experts did replace the Americans between 1970 and 1973. Under Chilean state ownership, production in large-scale copper mining increased from 571,000 metric tons in 1971 to 593,000 in 1972. The output increase in the El Teniente mine more than offset the output reduction in Chuquicamata and Exótica.[40] Serious production losses occurred, however, during the crippling two-and-a-half-month strike in El Teniente during April–July 1973.[41] The military junta started negotiations with Kennecott and Anaconda in October 1973 on the issue of compensation for their expropriated assets and their possible, partial return to Chile's copper mines to restore their resource surplus.

In the multifaceted relationship between Chile's copper sector and the saving–investment process, several dimensions are of paramount importance. They include the size of the large-scale copper-generated resource surplus, the sector's own profit reinvestment propensity, its ability to act as a quasi-capital goods sector, and finally its indirect capital inflow contribution. At this point we shall examine only the first and fourth points, which relate to saving. The other two will be discussed in the second half of this chapter.

The resource surplus can be defined either as the sum of taxes and profits or as value added in copper less subsistence consumption allowances for labor and capital. If the first definition is used, the copper resource surplus rose from $38.5 million annually during the 1930–39 period—always in 1961 constant prices—to $78.9 million during 1940–54 and to $140.2 million during the third, 1955–64 period.[42] The data required to estimate the resource surplus according to the second

40. See Salvador Allende G., *Mensaje Presidente Allende ante Congreso Pleno, 21 Mayo '73* (Santiago: Presidencia de la República, 1973), p. 349. Hereafter cited as *Mensaje 1973*.

41. See *El Mercurio*, internacional ed., July 2–8, 1973, p. 2.

42. See table 120, col. 3 and 6, in M. Mamalakis, "Contribution of Copper to Chilean Economic Development, 1920–67: Profile of a Foreign-Owned Export Sector," in Raymond Mikesell and Associates, *Foreign Investment in Minerals and Petroleum* (Baltimore, Md.: Johns Hopkins Press, 1971). This article will be cited as "Copper Contribution."

definition are available only for 1950–60. The resource surplus amounted to an average of $123 million a year, at least $8,200 per copper worker.[43]

Although massive, the size of the copper-generated resource surplus never matched the one generated by nitrate, which fluctuated between 10 and 15 percent of GDP during 1880–1930. The copper resource surplus during 1930–70 fluctuated between 0 and 5 percent of GDP but was normally less than 2.5 percent. Thus it was hardly enough to cover the amortization needs of global investment, let alone support a big push.[44] The effects of sectoral clashes, discrimination against mining, and unfavorable international market conditions are measured as much by the rising trend of the absolute size of the surplus as by its small share in GDP. The copper resource surplus fell to negligible amounts between 1970 and 1973.

The regional element, which was so important before 1930, also affected capital accumulation during 1930–73. The mining sector, predominantly located in the North, remained the major source of foreign exchange and to a lesser extent of a resource surplus. Although the North contributed only 9.2 percent of GDP in 1963,[45] 49.1 percent of the country's exports originated there.[46] In 1960 the net resource transfer to both the developed nations and Chile's Center was 117.1 million escudos, approximately half of which went to general government.

Even if we add all investments in the North to the net transfers to the national government, the total is only about 10 percent of gross capital formation in 1960.[47] Furthermore, throughout 1950–59 copper taxes from the Gran Minería contributed 25 percent of government revenues

43. This estimate was made by deducting $33 million from value added each year as subsistence labor and capital consumption and by using as employment the conservative figure of 15,000. All data were obtained from my "Copper Contribution," table 118, p. 412.

44. The resource surplus of the foreign-owned copper sector fluctuated generally between 1 and 2 percent of GDP before 1960 and might have at best reached a value of 3.5 percent. Even if we assume that the resource surplus equaled 50 percent of the mining sector's value added, which is given in table 3.6 of chap. 3, and use the adjusted income figures of the 1960–66 period, it could not have exceeded 5 percent of GDP.

45. Thelma Gálvez Pérez et al., *El Norte De Chile: Problemas y Perspectivas,* 3 vols. (Santiago: Universidad de Chile, Facultad de Ciencias Económicas, 1964). All statistics in this section concerning the North were derived from this study and the unnumbered "Resumen."

46. Although the North contributed 49.1 percent to exports, it accounted for only 17.3 percent of total imports in 1960.

47. See M. Mamalakis, "National Accounts," in "Historical Statistics," vol. 1, table IE1, p. A-126.

only once. Usually they amounted to 15 percent.[48] These figures clearly illustrate the lesser significance of the extractive export sector as a source of resource surpluses, potential savings, and government revenues from 1930 to 1973 compared to the 1880–1930 period.

The Indirect Foreign Capitalists

As Allende was shocked to discover after his celebrated nationalization of the American-owned copper mines, the foreign-owned export sector makes an important indirect contribution to capital inflow. The nature of ownership shapes the nature of the inflows. Private foreign ownership creates the business climate conducive to capital flows from the West. State ownership, established after expropriation, destroys what might be called a conducive "private business climate" and sharply reduces private capital flows. But it either generates or fosters a "state business climate" that attracts capital from the socialist or communist nations. At least in the case of Chile the 1971 copper nationalization profoundly damaged the private business climate. The foreign private capital attrition was so severe between 1970 and 1973 that the socialist countries were unable to alleviate it. To understand the external dimension of Chile's economic physiognomy, it is crucial to identify and measure the significance of these foreign, indirect capitalists, who held Chilean debt rather than equity. Their penetration power was a function of their unlimited ability to satisfy promptly almost any need through import or other credits, of the willingness of the domestic system to depend on them, and of the decumulation of institutional capital in banking.

The anonymous bureaucratic capitalists seated behind the desks of central banks, international credit agencies, private banks, and communist or socialist trade, banking, or aid agencies form the backbone of this group, which included in its portfolio Chilean private or public debts. Those debts were direct, whether or not they were guaranteed by the government. These private or state international capitalists as a group have almost always been by any standard the least known, conspicuous, or understood segment of the foreign capitalist class. Indirectly, as holders of Chile's governmental debt, they partly "owned" Chile and determined or assisted in its growth. Between

48. Mario Vera Valenzuela, *La Política Económica del Cobre en Chile* (Santiago: Editorial Universitaria, 1961), p. 121–22.

1970 and 1973 a rising segment of this class was composed of the Chinese, Russian, and Rumanian states.[49]

From 1970 to 1973 Chile had as an integral part of its spectrum of capitalists the Chinese, Russian, Japanese, Rumanian, Polish, Australian, Korean, and East German lenders who substituted for or became complementary to the fading pre-1970 American and European lenders. The abrupt termination of diplomatic and economic relations between Chile and most other socialist countries after September 1973 led to the disappearance of the socialist indirect capitalists and the return of those from the United States, Great Britain, and other Western nations. Some foreign lenders sought to stimulate to the maximum physical and human investment in Chile. Others extended credits to support government-budget or balance-of-payments deficits. Overall, their capacity as capitalistic lenders did not automatically convert them into investors or give them power over investment decisions. Their financial resources were used by Chile to satisfy any of its needs, and too frequently only current consumption needs were attended to rather than those in the future.

Thus, all foreign capitalists extending the compensatory credits knew in advance that they were used by the Central Bank to cover the balance-of-payments deficit. These indirect capitalists who owned Chile's nonamortized or new foreign debt during 1930–73 included the international credit institutions (World Bank, International Monetary Fund, International Financial Corporation, Inter-American Development Bank, International Development Association), the foreign governments already mentioned, including the Treasury of the United States, some private North American Banks, and even individuals.[50] Total economic and military aid to Chile from the United States was $906.7 million between 1946 and 1965. Of this only $147.7 million was in economic and $102.8 million in military grants.[51]

This amorphous, ever-changing class of indirect owners of Chile's

49. See Statement by Pedro Vuskovic, minister of economy, at the 1972 Washington CIAP meeting (*El Siglo*, Apr. 27, 1972, p. 13).
50. ODEPLAN, *Utilización de Créditos Externos*, pp. 7–8. See also Banco Central de Chile and Oficina de Planificación Nacional, *Estudio de Fuentes y Usos de Fondos Chile 1960–1964* (Santiago: Editorial del Pacífico, 1967), p. 49.
51. See U.S. Senate Committee on Government Operations, *United States Foreign Aid in Action: A Case Study*, submitted by Senator Ernest Gruening to the Subcommittee on Foreign Aid Expenditures (Washington D.C.: U.S. Government Printing Office, 1966), table 1, pp. 13–14.

production system lent to and received resources from Chile far in excess of those involved in the case of the foreign copper companies. They have exercised and would continue to exercise—especially if Chile had continued to transfer to, or had increased indirect foreign ownership through, Soviet bloc credits—an indirect influence of unparalleled proportions while contributing far less than the owners of the extractive industries. As Chile's case demonstrates, the conversion of a country's foreign ownership from direct to indirect can be very onerous. It may simply shift but not eliminate dependence.

Indirect foreign capitalism assumed increased strength not only because it was associated with direct foreign investment but also because the internal, inflation-induced credit asphyxy made Chile, in satisfying its operating and investment needs, increasingly dependent on foreign credit.[52]

There is no accepted definition of foreign saving. According to ODEPLAN, external credits from international organizations, banks, suppliers, and Western states financed between 15 and 30 percent of all private investments during 1965–68, with an increasing share of these credits guaranteed by the public sector.[53] Yet within the national accounts foreign saving is defined as the deficit of the nation on current account. Foreign saving could be also defined as saving generated by foreigners operating within and outside Chile, as the amount of resources made available to Chile from abroad, or in other ways. There exist gross, net, direct, indirect foreign saving.

In table 11.3 and figure 11.1 foreign saving is measured first by the domestic trade gap—that is, the difference between domestic exports and imports—and second by the national trade gap—that is, the difference between national exports and imports. National exports are defined as domestic exports less factor, amortization, and other nonreturned payments to and by foreign concerns.[54] If the domestic trade

52. Fuenzalida and Undurraga, Distribución del Crédito, p. 32.

53. See ODEPLAN, El Crédito Externo Como Fuente de Financiamiento del Sector Privado (Santiago: ODEPLAN, March 1970), pp. 3, 5–10.

54. It was statistically impossible to estimate a narrower variant of national exports defined as domestic exports minus all payments abroad by the foreign-owned export concerns. Although there exists information on interest and profit payments to most foreign-owned export concerns under item 2, table IIE2a3, p. A-584, "Historical Statistics," amortization payments were not separately available. In the final definition adopted here, payments to foreign capital include private and public interest payments, depreciation and reserves, stock exchanges in Chile, all expenditures made abroad, and movements of capital by mining concerns.

Fig. 11.1. Exports, imports, and trade gaps, Chile, 1920–64 (in millions of U.S. dollars, 1961 prices).

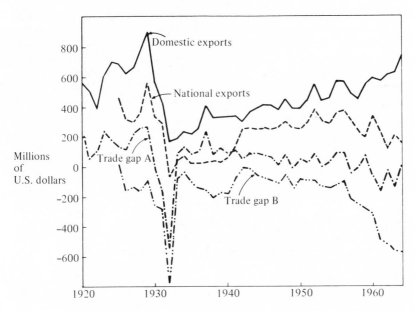

Source: Table 11.3.

gap, which comes closest to the Chenery–Strout definition of an export–import gap, is used as a measure of foreign saving, Chile exported resources throughout 1933–56, except for 1949. Foreign saving to Chile emerges primarily after 1957. However, the national trade gap was negative throughout 1925–64, with the exception of 1925. Thus, whereas the domestic trade gap shows a favorable trade balance and a flow of national savings abroad until 1957, the national trade gap shows trade deficits that become staggering after 1952 and huge foreign savings that permitted Chile to meet its trade and balance-of-payments commitments. The negative values of the national trade gap—eloquent proof that Chile's deep consternation with its balance-of-payments problem was well founded in spite of the domestic trade gap surpluses—show that foreign saving and external financing are. inevitably linked with dollar-servicing requirements of foreign debt and equity.

Much of the controversy concerning foreign saving arose from con-fusion between gross and net figures. It was believed that foreign saving

Table 11.3. Exports, Imports, and Trade Gaps, Chile, 1920–72
(In millions of U.S. dollars in 1961 prices)

	Domestic exports X	National exports X_n	Total imports	Domestic trade gap G_A (1–3)	National trade gap G_B (2–3)	Short-term foreign resource transfer F_s	Investable trade surplus X_i
	(1)	(2)	(3)	(4)	(5)	(6)	(7)
1920	572.7	—	334.3	238.4	—	—	303.0
1921	504.7	—	442.7	62.0	—	—	147.4
1922	389.4	—	278.0	111.4	—	—	165.1
1923	612.5	—	370.6	241.9	—	—	313.5
1924	702.5	—	420.4	282.1	—	—	363.2
1925	687.4	470.7	446.9	240.5	23.8	126.2	110.0
1926	625.2	328.0	488.0	137.2	−160.0	275.6	−65.7
1927	669.1	300.1	424.1	245.0	−124.0	98.0	−42.0
1928	767.6	355.0	506.9	260.7	−151.9	222.9	−71.9
1929	911.7	554.0	642.6	269.1	−88.6	131.9	37.2
1930	581.4	347.9	612.8	−31.4	−264.9	−97.5	−127.7
1931	428.1	293.9	576.0	−147.9	−282.1	−72.1	17.1
1932	168.8	−66.2	698.9	−530.1	−765.1	−107.6	−176.7
1933	197.0	42.6	104.0	93.0	−61.4	−27.5	−57.0
1934	237.3	84.2	107.8	129.5	−23.6	42.3	−9.1
1935	223.5	29.8	138.9	84.6	−109.1	−59.1	−85.2
1936	263.5	22.5	162.2	101.3	−139.7	−100.5	−107.3
1937	415.6	34.4	188.1	227.5	−153.7	−101.7	−101.1
1938	328.9	39.0	239.8	89.1	−200.8	−98.4	−141.8
1939	329.4	33.5	200.8	128.6	−167.3	−111.0	−131.4
1940	335.4	63.4	242.4	93.0	−179.0	−94.9	−136.9
1941	338.5	138.1	226.1	112.4	−88.0	−1.9	−50.6
1942	297.7	243.1	134.5	47.9	−6.7	0.2	23.4
1943	357.7	258.8	153.2	85.8	−13.1	−1.6	18.5
1944	390.4	254.6	174.5	82.9	−52.9	−35.3	−15.1
1945	406.1	258.0	186.8	82.5	−65.6	−45.0	−27.3
1946	403.8	253.9	224.0	63.9	−86.0	−67.4	−33.9
1947	382.9	264.1	300.8	11.4	−107.4	−89.1	−35.1
1948	445.7	298.5	305.9	96.7	−50.5	−4.5	20.0
1949	383.8	262.1	334.2	−17.7	−139.4	−48.6	−31.4
1950	386.3	252.9	285.7	56.2	−77.2	−28.3	0.8
1951	442.0	323.0	397.1	30.1	−88.9	−33.8	−0.1
1952	546.8	369.8	429.6	88.4	−88.6	−10.0	25.2
1953	440.4	308.0	398.0	9.8	−122.6	−62.8	−11.2
1954	454.5	289.3	394.5	28.6	−136.6	−82.8	−32.5
1955	576.3	355.3	445.3	97.1	−123.9	−45.7	4.8
1956	568.0	370.1	451.1	97.7	−100.2	−38.0	45.3

Table 11.3 (contd.)

	Domestic exports X (1)	National exports X_n (2)	Total imports (3)	Domestic trade gap G_A (1–3) (4)	National trade gap G_B (2–3) (5)	Short-term foreign resource transfer F_s (6)	Investable trade surplus X_i (7)
1957	483.2	311.1	521.8	−45.5	−217.6	−125.7	−24.3
1958	456.2	238.1	468.7	−12.0	−280.1	−117.0	−68.6
1959	545.7	193.3	474.2	72.9	−279.5	−166.3	−141.1
1960	586.2	341.2	659.2	−70.4	−315.4	−186.2	−114.1
1961	567.4	250.5	729.6	−162.2	−479.1	−262.9	−227.3
1962	609.4	119.6	641.8	−30.5	−520.3	−264.3	−308.6
1963	637.8	216.6	773.0	−135.2	−556.4	−306.2	−323.1
1964	743.2	158.1	724.1	20.6	−564.5	−275.5	−329.6
1964	675.4	—	711.3	−35.9	—	—	—
1965	759.5	—	701.0	58.5	—	—	—
1966	925.8	—	841.1	84.7	—	—	—
1967	931.7	—	859.2	72.5	—	—	—
1968	951.7	—	884.4	67.3	—	—	—
1969	1,159.1	—	964.3	194.8	—	—	—
1970	1,090.0	—	1,034.8	55.2	—	—	—
1971	799.9	—	963.3	−163.5	—	—	—
1972	663.3	—	1,123.5	−460.2	—	—	—

Sources: Original data are found in "Mining, International Transactions, Money and Banking, and Government and the Public Sector," in Mamalakis, "Historical Statistics," table IIE2a3, pp. A-580–A-592. For 1965–70 figures in current prices see ODEPLAN, *Antecedentes sobre el Desarrollo Chileno, 1960–70* (Santiago: ODEPLAN, 1971), table 303, p. 413. For 1971 and 1972 the data in current prices, which were subsequently converted into 1971 prices, were obtained from *El Mercurio*, internacional ed., July 30–Aug. 5, 1973, p. 2.

Notes: Domestic exports are total export revenues for the years given. National exports are domestic exports (col. 1) less all payments to foreign capital, private interest and profits, official payments to private capital, other nonreturned payments of foreign investments, amortization payments, and other payments to abroad. Domestic trade gap (G_A) is the difference between domestic exports and total imports. National trade gap (G_B) is the difference between national exports and total imports. F_S stands for trade gap B less long term capital inflows. X_i stands for national exports less imports of intermediate and consumer goods.

was beneficial as long as its net magnitude was positive or even rising. Positive and net foreign saving has as a corollary increased foreign investment and ownership in Chile and an increased foreign debt. This is exactly what happened in the 1960s. Total guaranteed public and private debt in foreign currency amounted to $1.5 billion at the end of 1968 and to $3.0 billion in December 1970.[55]

The composition of domestic saving in terms of foreign versus national origin underwent a massive transformation. With internal interest rates low, zero, or negative, national saving was discouraged; with interest rates on foreign debt positive, foreign saving increased secularly, especially in gross terms. The revolutionary reaction of Allende to the invited onslaught of foreign credits was of the same magnitude as the mounting challenge.

Even though the statistical evidence suggests a strong correlation between the fortunes of the export sector and the magnitude of gross capital inflows, it is difficult to provide an accurate measure of the size of the indirect inflows that have been generated by either nitrate or copper mining. According to Raúl Saez, the joint ownership copper projects of Eduardo Frei would have attracted $200–300 million annually, making possible a Chilean "economic miracle" of 6.5 percent income growth.[56] Between 1930 and 1957 these capital inflows were small, selective, heavily oriented toward CORFO-sponsored projects, and unable to offset the leakage caused by capital and profit repatriation. They blossomed, however, between 1957 and 1968 as unprecedented amounts of foreign aid and short-term credits were bestowed upon Chile. The copper sector itself and the government attitudes toward it supplied all or a major part of the collateral needed by foreign creditors or donors. The nationalization of all foreign extractive concerns by Salvador Allende during his first two years in office on the one hand removed this collateral and froze capitalistic inflows of resources and on the other hand closed the loophole of profit repatriation, which was the most irritating thorn in Chile's side. The net short-term benefits to Chile have been negative or negligible, but if the U.S. government could have continued its Chilean foreign aid by giving it to the expropriated Kennecott and Anaconda, little or nothing would have changed. As of 1973, therefore, no radical transformation in Chile's copper-related saving process has occurred. Such change will take place only when the mining sector in toto has assumed its inherited role of providing an investable surplus of 10–15 percent of GDP.

The economic independence of Chile, the "only guarantee of real

55. See CORFO, *Financiamiento Externo 1968* (Santiago: CORFO, 1969), p. 68, and unpublished information by CORFO, Departamento de Créditos Externos, "Deuda Externa de Chile," p. 188.

56. *Chile y el Cobre* (Santiago: Departamento de Cobre, 1965), p. 64.

political independence," and liberation from the alleged capitalist imperium could be achieved, according to Allende, only by nationalizing all large and strategic foreign firms as well as all the large and national private firms that, through their symbiosis with the foreign ones, had surrendered the country to capitalist imperialism, and by directly seizing the resource surpluses that had previously escaped abroad.[57] This argument failed to either recognize or sufficiently emphasize the absolute necessity of domestic effort, sacrifices, and, above all, saving in achieving independence. In his attempt to deliver the fruits of the dawning socialist nirvana to the masses immediately, Allende not only drew down the foreign exchange reserves and inventories accumulated by the Christian Democrats, but also had to renegotiate Chile's foreign debt through the Paris Club and seek aid from socialist nations.

The negative effects were profound. Total saving and investment fell in 1971 and 1972, to recover partially in 1973.[58] Public saving became negligible or negative. Reserves declined. Foreign saving, which Allende had promised to erase, climbed to 3.3 percent of national product in 1971 and to 6.0 percent in 1972 (as can be seen in table 11.1). A confidence crisis of staggering proportions gripped the nation in 1973. And Allende was politely but openly lectured by Chinese premier Chou En-lai, who argued that "it is very dangerous to depend excessively on foreign aid, in particular on the credits of the great powers, instead of basing the economy on the country's own efforts."[59] Chou En-lai's message was, rather ironically, adopted by the military junta that overthrew Allende. The domestic austerity and reconstruction programs introduced since September 1973 are as unprecedented in Chilean history as they are necessary for the nation's survival. Their success will depend on the ability to raise internal and national savings, whether public, business, or household.

INVESTMENT

Investment affects growth in many ways: by its size, its nature (whether in construction or machinery and equipment) its origin (national or

57. See Allende, *Segundo Mensaje 1972*, pp. 15–16.
58. See Pedro Jeftanovic P., "Ahorro e inversión," in *Comentarios sobre la Situación Económica Ier Semestre 1973* (Santiago: Universidad de Chile, 1973), pp. 161–63.
59. See letter to President Allende from Chou En-lai, released to the press and published in *El Mercurio*, international ed., July 23–29, 1973, p. 2.

imported), its labor intensity, its division among various sectors, and so forth. The division of investment by growth functions provides the analytical framework within which all other dimensions will be examined here.

Investment in the Food-Producing Sectors

Chile's agricultural capital stock consisted of rural land, including improvements in it, livestock, and machinery and equipment. Rising per capita income, demographic growth, secular urbanization, and improvement of dietary standards exerted increasing pressures upon all capitalists to increase all three forms of agricultural capital required to satisfy the society's individual and collective food needs. The social burden and responsibility for such multiple capital accumulation heaped upon the owners, operators, or toilers of land were not matched by equal amounts of individual pecuniary incentives and penalties, public social overhead investment, publicly financed technical progress, or incentives to the rural sector and to agricultural labor.

The agricultural capitalists included the large-scale latifundistas and estancieros, the medium-sized farmers, the minifundistas, the state in its role of satisfying collective needs, and agricultural workers, who held the key to converting much of free labor time into more and better land, machinery, livestock, and labor. None of these groups lived up to either the country's needs or expectations. The collective performance of the food-producing function emerged as the greatest failure of Chile's modern economic history.

A most prominent obstacle was the lack of incentives for agricultural labor. In 1940 almost two-thirds of agricultural labor consisted of transitory and permanent blue-collar workers who were paid the lowest wages in the country, primarily for peak-season harvesting. Since the colonial period this habitually floating population contributed little to the accumulation of agricultural capital stock. The tenant farmers— the other third of the agricultural labor force—enjoyed better incentives and performed more effectively than the afuerinos. Yet even they lacked the crucial incentive—ownership of land. Land reform, which would split up the large estates into smaller farms totally under private ownership, has always been the best incentive solution, but it was never introduced. Finally, even the incentives to the latifundistas were limited, negative, or contradictory. The terms of trade between agriculture and industry were unfavorable, competitive agricultural imports were subsidized, input prices were high, taxation was negligible and did not penalize inefficiency, and so on. However—as I have shown elsewhere and subsequent studies have confirmed—farmers were highly and readily responsive to price signals and the market mechanism.[60]

Government attention to agriculture in terms of investment during 1950–60 was dismal; less than 3.7 percent of public investment was allocated to it.[61] Approximately 15 percent of gross capital formation during 1962–66 went to agriculture, and of this more than 80 percent was private investment in construction and other works.[62] Public investment directed toward agriculture was very small throughout 1960–70. Direct public investment represented only 2.4 percent of total investment in that sector during 1962–66 and an average of only 6.2 percent of total direct public investment during 1961–70.[63] Indirect public investment in agriculture, the bulk of which was absorbed by the corporation for agrarian reform (CORA), CORFO–agriculture, and the Institute for Agricultural Development (INDAP), accounted for an average of 25 percent of total indirect public investment during 1961–70.[64] The third category of public investment—purchase of debt, equity, or other IOUs—remained insignificant. A unified, comprehensive, pragmatic governmental policy of agricultural modernization was never drafted and therefore could not be implemented even though all governments professed a desire to do so. Furthermore, in spite of a definite labor abundance, if not a surplus, emphasis was placed on imported, mechanized, capital-intensive techniques.

Moreover, the landowner class was dependent on CORFO credits to obtain foreign tractors and other agricultural equipment throughout 1939–73. Domestic industry failed to become a significant producer of agricultural machinery. The great majority of those landowners, though

60. See M. Mamalakis, "Public Policy and Sectoral Development: A Case Study of Chile, 1940–1958," in M. Mamalakis and C. W. Reynolds, *Essays on the Chilean Economy* (Homewood, Ill.: Richard D. Irwin, 1965), pp. 141–43. Hereafter cited as "Public Policy."

61. Wally Meza San Martín, "La Participación del Sector Público en la Economía Nacional," Memoria de Prueba (Santiago: Universidad de Chile, 1962, typewritten), p. 40. Hereafter cited as "Sector Público."

62. ODEPLAN, *La Inversión Geográfica Bruta en Capital Fijo por Sectores de Destino* (Santiago: ODEPLAN, Nov. 1967), pp. 1–33; ODEPLAN, *Inversión Geográfica Bruta en Capital Fijo por Sectores de Destino, Período 1962–1966* (Santiago: ODEPLAN, 1968), table 2, p. 4. Hereafter cited as *Inversión por Sectores de Destino, 26/3/68.*

63. ODEPLAN, *Antecedentes, 1960–70*, pp. 9, 380.

64. Ibid., p. 382, and ODEPLAN, *La Inversión Pública en el Período 1961–1970* (Santiago: ODEPLAN, 1971), tables 21, 22.

spared by President Frei's land reform program, had been reduced to small-scale farmers or replaced by state latifundism, farmers' cooperatives, minifarmers, and a whole host of combinations of these devices by July 1973. However, their disappearance did not improve the capital accumulation pattern. The imports of up to 10,000 tractors from Russia in 1972[65] and the continuation of CORFO's earlier ex cathedra efforts toward agricultural mechanization reflect the will of the state but not necessarily its agricultural needs.

Efforts toward agricultural mechanization may in fact hinder rather than stimulate the desperately needed investments in better education of labor, irrigation works, vineyards, land improvement, livestock care, and road and assorted building construction that only local labor can provide. All these areas have a high national component. Food production continues to be the Achilles' heel of state-controlled land use.

Transformation in agriculture's ownership pattern and employer–capitalist class did not bring about better investment incentives, new rules for the game, and higher production. This is demonstrated best, at least in terms of the government's 1971–76 plans, by the fact that agricultural investment of any kind continues to be neglected, perhaps grossly.[66]

In short, as the food crisis in Chile assumed alarming proportions, the government responded by promoting land reform and by leaving the desperately low private investment almost totally unaided. As the investment figures suggest, promotion of Chile's internal capacity to satisfy its food needs was deemphasized, underestimated, and granted a low priority even as government originally moved cautiously to reduce the number, and then abruptly eliminated the power, of the latifundista capitalists. The agricultural capital accumulation leakages were multiple and increasing rather than decreasing. Unused, free labor time convertible into land improvement or livestock raising was wasted. Foreign exchange, price, and import policies made horse-for-meat production lucrative until 1972 but forced beef production into bankruptcy. The government released more than $300 million for food imports in both 1971 and 1972 but spent less than $60 million for direct public agricultural investment.

Above all, the agricultural resource surplus was too small between 1930 and 1973 because of the low income share of, and low absolute

65. See *El Mercurio*, May 2, 1972, p. 27.
66. See ODEPLAN, *Resúmen del Plan de la Economía Nacional 1971–1976* (Santiago: ODEPLAN, 1971), p. 39. Hereafter cited as *Plan 1971–1976*.

and relative productivity in, agriculture and because of the inadequate incentives offered to the agricultural production agents. The Chilean experience illustrates that for the 1930–73 period a minimum agricultural surplus reinvested in agricultural food production was far more important than the transfer of an agricultural resource surplus to industry. The Frei–Allende land reform policies and the establishment of small-scale private ownership by the military junta may have created the institutional bases necessary for a comprehensive policy of agricultural modernization. And the rise of the agricultural income share during Allende's first year in power, even though it was short-lived, too small, and insufficient to solve the acute 1973 food crisis, may signal the beginning of an agricultural revival. This could be one of the more lasting contributions of his administration.

Investment in Industry and Energy

The industrial and energy sectors received major portions of the 1930 –73 capital formation, although the share received by public investment was not always high or stable. During the decade of the 1950s government attention increased markedly. Whereas energy and industry received only 12.5 percent of total public investment in 1950, they received 19.0 in 1960—and as much as 44.1 percent in 1959.[67]

Investments in industry ranged from 14 to 18 percent of gross fixed capital formation during 1962–66. The great majority consisted of imported machinery and equipment for the private sector that had a minimal capital goods production–employment effect. However, national producers' durables, which accounted for at least 20 percent of total investment, were the result of labor-intensive production techniques. During 1962–66 industrial investments rose continuously.[68]

In the only estimate of this nature available, the bulk of external credits to the private sector went to the combined industrial sector: a high of 66.4 percent in 1965 and a low of 41 percent in 1966. External credits financed 52.8 percent of industrial sector investment in 1965 and 31.2 percent in 1966.[69]

Because all governments before 1970 believed that the complex spectrum of industrial needs should be fulfilled by private investors, the direct role of government as an investor remained small. Between

67. Meza, "Sector Público," pp. 39–40.
68. ODEPLAN, *Inversión por Sectores de Destino*, 1962–1966, table 4, p. 6.
69. ODEPLAN, *El Crédito Externo Como Fuente de Financiamiento del Sector Privado* (Santiago: ODEPLAN, 1970), table 5, p. 11; 12–15.

1961 and 1970 only 7 percent of direct public investment went to industry, which accounted for only 5 percent of the sector's investment from 1962 to 1966.[70] Socialization of a major industrial segment under Allende must have led to a substantial increase in the public sector's investment share.[71] Indirect public investment in industry was larger, having a value of 13.6 percent during 1961–70 and growing to 20 percent of total direct public investment in 1970.[72]

No other policy of the Allende government aroused as much opposition, suspicion, and doubt within the country as the assignment to the state of the function of producing the industrial consumer or capital goods required by the masses of Chile. Probably no other policy could have so radically changed the ownership structure of production, destroyed the financial base of the opposition and traditional democracy, and affected so many national interests, entrepreneurs, capitalists, and workers.

Investment to Transform the Time, Quantity, and Location Dimensions

The share of gross capital formation allotted to investment that would bring the transformation of time, quantity, and location of goods and people ranged between 20 and 30 percent of the total during 1962–66. Investment in trade was minimal, and that in transport, storage, and communications was significantly greater than that in gas, water, electricity, and sanitary services. Real investment in transport and related areas declined rather sharply during 1962–66 as both imported and private investment shrank precipitously. Overall, there was a marked advance in the domestically produced component of investment in transport and communications. Of investment in gas, water, electricity, and sanitary services during 1962–66, more than 75 percent was internally produced.[73]

The capital/output ratio during 1963–66 for gas, water, and electricity ranged, depending on the method of estimate, between 9.5 and 21.5, while that for transport ranged between 5.5 and 10.6, and that for trade and commerce between −0.86 and 0.51. The marginal

70. ODEPLAN, *Antecedentes, 1960–70*, table 284, p. 380; table 10, p. 9.

71. Salvador Allende, *Primer Mensaje del Presidente Allende ante el Congreso Pleno, 21 de Mayo de 1971* (Santiago: Presidencia de la República, 1971), pp. 113–23.

72. ODEPLAN, *Antecedentes, 1960–70*, table 286, p. 382.

73. ODEPLAN, *Inversión por Sectores de Destino, 1962–1966* pp. 18, 23–24, 26.

capital/output ratios had very similar values.[74] This is an area in which the labor intensity of production could be increased.

The large differences between Chile's spatial distribution of natural and mineral resources on the one hand and the spatial distribution of its population, income, wealth, industries, and foreign markets on the other, created a high direct demand for land, water, and airport transport and a derived demand for resources investable in this sector. Most investment undertaken to permit the movement of goods and people was of the Schumpeterian autonomous rather than the induced kind. Much of it may have been unnecessarily imposed upon Chile.

As international transport technology advanced by leaps and bounds, such new inventions as the steamship, railroad, motorized vehicles, and the airplane were eagerly adopted, concurrently or consecutively. During 1930–73 most of these instruments for performance of the location-transformation function coexisted. Most foreign inventions were capital intensive and were often introduced before past transport investments had been amortized. In the case of railroads and air transport their deficits created a major drain on governmental resources.

Relative public investment expenditures may have fallen during one decade—in 1950–60, for example, those in transport and communications dropped sharply from 37.8 percent to 15.0 percent and those on ports and navigation from 2.4 percent in 1950 to 0.9 in 1960[75]— but they rose in the next. Transport, storage, and communications received an average of 26 percent of direct public investment during 1961–70, and water, gas, electricity, and basic services an average of 15 percent. Combined, the basic functions of moving people, goods, water, electricity, garbage, and so forth and of storing goods and informing people absorbed 41 percent of direct public investment.[76] Road building and railroad investment absorbed almost 60 percent of investment in transportation.[77] Indirect public investment in this area was trivial. More than half the investments to perform these functions were undertaken by the public sector.[78] Foreign credits financed 41

74. ODEPLAN, *Coeficientes Capital-Producto, Alternativas de Cálculo* (Santiago: ODEPLAN, 1968), tables 2–8. Hereafter cited as *Coeficientes Capital-Producto, 1968.*
75. Meza, "Sector Público," table 12, p. 40.
76. ODEPLAN, *Antecedentes, 1960–70*, table 284, p. 380.
77. ODEPLAN, *Inversión Pública, 1961–1970*, table 6.
78. *Antecedentes, 1960–70*, table 10, p. 9.

percent of public capital formation in transport, storage, and communication during 1965–68.[79]

The maldistribution of aggregate investment inherent in the oversized transport component was further accentuated by an internal maldistribution of this segment. There were selective overinvestment in railroads and social overhead, measures catering to private automobiles, and underinvestment in public mass transit and other urban transportation. Much of this was induced by often indiscriminate, duplicative adoption of foreign, highly advanced, and rapidly changing technology, pervasive price distortions, supply bottlenecks, and excessive protection. A lasting, universal Chilean transport revolution will have materialized when public mass transport needs have been satisfied and defense mechanisms have been established for selectively fending off costly and foreign transport inventions and innovations that have little social benefit.

Investment in Quality Maintenance and Improvement

The service sector that has as its function the maintenance or improvement of the quality of the stocks and flows of people and goods received a large and ever increasing share of investable resources. The treatment of the individual service subsectors—public administration, education, health, welfare, housing, and so forth—has been extremely uneven.

During 1950–60 public expenditures on social services declined sharply until 1954 but rose subsequently. Within social services, public educational expenditures remained stable, the share of social security expenditures increased abruptly, and that of the national health service fell from 13.3 percent of consolidated public sector expenditures in 1950 to only 5.6 percent in 1960. Within the public sector investment budget, construction and housing expenditures, which reflect the great deficits accumulated in the 1930s and 1940s and the pressures from the urban centers and middle classes, were the largest and most stable item: 42.4 percent in 1950 and 41.4 percent of gross public investment in 1960.[80]

Services that catered predominantly to urban needs, including ownership of dwellings, received at least 30 percent of gross investment during 1962–66.[81] All housing investment was financed equipropor-

79. ODEPLAN, *La Utilización de Créditos Externos por Parte del Sector Público* (Santiago: ODEPLAN, 1970) pp. 15–16.

80. Meza, "Sector Público," table 9, p. 33; p. 40.

81. ODEPLAN, *Inversión por Sectores de Destino, 26/3/68*, table 1-A, p. 18.

tionately by private and public savings. Most investment in services was public, and at least one-third of it consisted of imported machinery and equipment.[82] The capital/output ratios in ownership of dwellings ranged, depending on the estimate and year, between 11 and 61 (the marginal ratio ranged between 17 and 67) during 1964–66. Capital/output ratios in all services were between -2.2 and 9, with the marginal between 1.4 and 5.7.[83] Production of dwellings had a massive employment effect.

The growth contribution of dwellings construction cannot be measured correctly by capital/output ratios in housing, because value added is imputed in an erratic, inadequate fashion. It must be measured by the magnitude and quality of services offered. Furthermore, as Charles A. Frankenhoff correctly points out, the notion of a housing gap is misleading and inadequate since numerous partial housing markets with different degrees of development are defined by the type of services they offer. The problem is not to solve the housing problem, which will remain as long as humans exist, but to provide a flow of better, more, and equitably distributed human housing services.[84]

After 1960 government invested, directly and indirectly, most heavily in those sectors that maintained or improved the quality of inputs, output, and life. Housing and urbanization received 25 percent of direct public investment during 1961–70, public administration and defense 6.0 percent, education 5.2 percent, and health 2.7 percent.[85] Indirect investment in housing and urbanization absorbed 44.5 percent of total indirect public investment during 1961–70, reaching a peak of 59 percent in 1963 and declining secularly to only 19.3 percent in 1970.[86] Indirect public investment in public administration was small, and that in health and education trivial.

Although the quality-maintenance and -improvement functions thus received the government's paramount attention, the impact was highly uneven. Investments favored almost exclusively the rising urban population and its needs. Ultimately such treatment led to the establishment of private housing owners. Investments in health and education were too small to elevate their quality-improving ability to levels required by modern societies.

82. Ibid., table 8-A, p. 25; table 10A, p. 27.
83. ODEPLAN, *Coeficientes Capital-Producto 1968*, tables 2–8.
84. See Charles A. Frankenhoff, *Hacia una Política Habitacional: El Caso de Chile* (Santiago: Centro Interdisciplinario de Desarrollo Urbano Regional, 1969), pp. 21–18.
85. *Antecedentes, 1960–70*, table 284, p. 380. For services, 82 percent of the investment was public (ibid., table 10, p. 9).
86. Ibid., table 386, p. 382.

The critical role of investment in the latter area was demonstrated by Henry Bruton in a study of the productivity of education in the Greater Santiago area. Despite an increased flow of grammar, high school, and university graduates, the need for improved human capital was not properly satisfied, because of the low quality of the educational system. The major growth bottleneck was underinvestment not in education per se but in the educational system, especially at the primary and university levels, which had persistently underperformed. Inadequate or poor education, not relative abundance, caused the growing number of graduates to earn a rate of return on education that was below the likely 25 percent rate of return on conventional capital: 18 percent on resources in secondary education, something less than 16.5 percent in primary education, and about 14 percent for university education.[87] The Frei administration made a major attempt to improve the quality of this flow. Nevertheless, severe gaps persist throughout the educational system, and improvement is particularly needed in vocational training, schooling for the rural segment and urban poor, and university education. The political polarization and agitation within the educational establishment between 1970 and 1973 led to a deterioration in the quality of education services.

Throughout 1930–73 the omnipresent, powerful pressures of the urban elites, middle classes, and poorer masses forced government to allocate the overwhelming majority of its resources to satisfy their needs. Indirectly, more critical investment in agriculture, mining, industry, and even education, especially technical, suffered. Unlike Japan, where housing investment and urban development were neglected while export-catering industrialization was favored, Chile preferred the former investments. Even industry favored the domestic cities rather than become a link with world markets.

Investment in Multifunctional Mining

Investment in mining went through strong replacement cycles and had

87. Henry J. Bruton, "The Productivity of Education in Chile," Research Memorandum no. 12 (Williamstown, Mass: Center for Development of Economics, 1967), mimeo, pp. 16–17. Bruton's rate of return on capital greatly exceeds the Harberger–Selowsky estimate of 15 percent. Bruton also claims that the Harberger–Selowsky 218 percent average rate of return on educational investment is grossly overestimated. See Arnold C. Harberger and Marcelo Selowsky, "Key Factors in the Economic Growth of Chile: An Analysis of the Sources of Past Growth and of Prospects for 1965–1970," mimeo, pp. 22, 29. This paper was prepared for the conference "The Next Decade of Latin American Economic Development" held at Cornell University, Apr. 20–22, 1966.

a large import component. It was free of the foreign exchange constraint between 1930 and 1970 but subject to it between 1970 and 1973. It rose mildly each decade but always fell short of possible desirable levels. Although gross mining investment was substantial, its net magnitude was generally very small. Even though substantial investment occurred in petroleum, iron ore, coal, and small- and medium-sized copper mining, the lion's share of investment took place in large-scale copper production.

The resource surplus of pre-1971 foreign-owned large-scale copper mining was in part retained by Chile through reinvestment of profits and taxation. The share captured through reinvestment was small. In contrast the resource surplus acquired through taxation and kept in Chile was formidable. It grew from an annual average of $8.7 million during 1930–39 (in 1961 prices) to $37.0 million during 1940–54 to $92.9 million during 1955–64.[88] Alongside the foreign exchange contribution including investment, which increased from $42.8 million annually in constant prices during 1930–39 to $135.2 million during 1940–54 and to $214.2 million during 1955–64, it gained for Chile substantial investable resources.[89]

The leakage of copper resource surpluses due to foreign ownership was most severe during the 1930–40 laissez-faire period, when the surplus was at its minimum. The degree to which these leakages were offset through reinvestment varied. During the export collapse of 1930–31 the average propensity to reinvest out of copper profits was 30 percent; during 1936–40 it was only 5 percent.[90]

During the 1940–54 period of rampant discrimination and sectoral clashes, investment stayed conspicuously low except for a sudden spurt between 1948 and 1953. The average propensity to reinvest profits was about 6 percent between 1940 and 1947—if 1941, when it was 20.8 percent, is excluded.[91] The resource leakage was temporarily halted when, as a result of the building of a sulfuric plant at the Chuquicamata mine, the propensity to reinvest climbed rapidly and almost erratically from 13.5 percent in 1948 to 98.8 percent in 1951 and then to an impressive 207.6 percent in 1953, before collapsing to a dismal 1.4 percent of profits in 1954.

There was an improvement but no permanent correction in this

88. See my "Copper Contribution," table 121, pp. 418–19.
89. See ibid., table 120, pp. 418–19.
90. See my "Historical Statistics," pt. 5; "Mining," table IID, pp. A-499–A-500a.
91. See ibid., table IID, pp. A-499–A-500a.

resource exodus after 1955. As a consequence of the opening of the
El Salvador mine, needed to replace the defunct one in Potrerillos,
the propensity to reinvest out of foreign-company profits rose substantially. During 1957 and 1958 it was in excess of 100 percent.
Throughout the remaining years (excluding 1955), the propensity to
reinvest never fell below 33 percent. However, even this new investment was of the replacement type and did not produce a large increment
in the mining capital stock. Furthermore, the figures for the propensity
to reinvest during 1955–64 were slightly inflated because more liberal
depreciation allowances permitted American investors to repatriate
profits under the disguise of depreciation. The imperfection in capital
accumulation caused by this leakage prevailed until the nationalization programs of 1970–71.

Mining received less than 8 percent of fixed capital formation during
1962–66. The great majority of this investment consisted of machinery
and equipment imported by the private sector, whose share was relatively stable.[92] Free access to capital goods and foreign exchange
was greatly reduced after nationalization.

Finally, the state contributed only 5 percent of its direct investment
and 13.8 percent of its indirect investment to the jack-of-all-trades
mining sector during 1961–70.[93] Whereas direct public investment
in mining went almost exclusively for petroleum and medium- and
small-scale copper production in 1967–70 its indirect investment
became significant during this period, when government became a
partner in large-scale copper production through the Chileanization
of the foreign-owned companies.[94] After Frei's administration had
taken the long overdue decision to reinvest part of Chile's resources
in its fabulous copper mines, Allende abruptly confiscated the foreign
properties in his effort to recover Chilean natural resources. With
agriculture, transportation, and even some industrial sectors under-
performing in the pursuit of their respective functions, the copper
sector's fortunes assume an even greater significance in filling current
and future gaps between needs and expenditures on the one side and
internal production on the other.

Public Investment

The greater part of investment was either undertaken by government

92. ODEPLAN, *Inversión por Sectores de Destino, 26/3/68*, p. 5; table 3, p. 20.
93. *Antecedentes, 1960–70*, table 286, p. 382.
94. ODEPLAN, *Inversión Pública, 1961–1970*, p. 16, table 13; p. 23.

and its semiautonomous industries or was financed, guaranteed, and mediated by CORFO, the Housing Corporation, and other governmental entities. Government was propelled into investment projects in order to alleviate unemployment, as during 1932–38, in order to prevent foreign ownership, as in the case of petroleum, sugar, steel, and petrochemicals, because it sought housing, agricultural, and mining reforms. or because the state replaced private ownership. The inability of Chilean capital, entrepreneurship, and managerial capacity to pursue major investment projects and the advocacy of socialism after 1970 were largely responsible for government ownership and public investment since 1930.

Public investment rose sharply both in absolute and relative terms between 1950 and 1960. As the role of the public sector expanded, the share of investment in consolidated public expenditures doubled from 10.7 percent in 1950 to 20.0 in 1956, and with some fluctuations it remained close to that level until 1960.[95] Even so, this share was grossly inadequate for the country's needs.

The primordial role of public investment is demonstrated best through an examination of the 1961–1970 period, when total investment ranged between 17.4 percent of GDP in 1961 and 14.7 percent in 1967, reaching 15.0 percent in 1970.[96] Direct public investment in physical capital, which ranged from 6.8 to 8.6 percent of GDP, grew at an annual rate of 6.3 percent during 1961–69 and accounted for at least 50 percent of gross capital formation since 1950, even though value added by the public sector accounted for only 13 percent of GDP. If indirect public investment (i.e., public funds made available to private investors or used to purchase equity, for example) is added, the share of total public investment in gross domestic capital formation rises from 46.6 percent in 1961 to 74.8 percent in 1969.[97] As direct public investment increased, private investment declined in relative terms; it grew at an annual cummulative rate of only 3.2 percent between 1961 and 1969. Indirect public investment as a percentage of private physical investment rose from 12.5 percent in 1961 to 50.3 percent in 1969.[98] Only a portion of public indirect investment

95. Meza, "Sector Público," p. 38.

96. ODEPLAN, *Inversión Pública, 1961–1970*, table 3. See also the earlier study, ODEPLAN, *Inversión Pública Directa e Indirecta 1961–1967* (Santiago: ODEPLAN, 1968), pp. 1–32.

97. ODEPLAN, *Inversión Pública, 1961–1970*, pp. 4–10, 11, 15; tables 1, 3.

98. Ibid., p. 11 and table 5.

was ever used by private concerns for physical investment, whereas the majority led to transfers of assets because of land, copper, and other reform.

The nature, magnitude, and changes in the real and financial mechanisms that link saving with investment have been as important in determining the level and composition of capital formation as the direct determinants of saving and investment opportunities.

The Real Nexuses : The Supply of Domestic and Imported Capital Goods

The internal supply of raw materials, intermediate products, and other inputs needed for the production of dwellings, business buildings, and other private and public construction was sufficiently abundant to make the construction supply curve highly elastic between 1930 and 1973. As a consequence construction boomed and bottlenecks were limited whenever funds were plentiful, demand was rising, and financial intermediation efficient. There was no construction supply bottleneck of any serious nature between 1930 and 1973.[99]

In the area of producer durables the combination of an abundant, often artificially high, demand for machinery and equipment and an inelastic, limited supply forced the issues of interlocking mechanisms and of supply into the foreground. The supply of machinery and equipment was determined by the size of the domestic producers durables sector and the foreign exchange earnings available for machinery and equipment imports.[100]

99. For a more detailed examination of the market for dwellings see "Construction: The Neutral Sector," in my "Public Policy," chap. 2, pp. 83–116.

100. This point, which formed a central theme of my earlier study on Chile ("Public Policy," chap. 4) had been recognized by the Chileans at least as early as, if not earlier than, the 1940s. See, e.g., Ewald Hasche Sánchez, "El Proceso de Capitalización en Chile, 1938–1950," Memoria en Economía (Santiago: Universidad de Chile, 1950), mimeo, esp. pp. 10–11. For a formalized extension of the Harrod–Domar model to include the role of exports as a quasi-capital goods sector, see my "The Export Sector, Stages of Economic Development, and the Saving-Investment Process in Latin America," *Economia Internazionale* 23 (Nov. 1970): 283–307. My extension of the Harrod–Domar model was first published in Spanish in a slightly different version, "El Sector Exportador, Etapas de Desarrollo Económico y el Proceso Ahorro-Inversión en América Latina," *El Trimestre Económico* (México) 34 (Apr.–June 1967): 319–41. A similar point is made in the well-known work by H. B. Chenery and A. Strout, "Foreign Assistance and Economic Development," *American Economic Review* 56 (Sept. 1966): 679–733.

Domestic demand for primary capital goods (those used to produce capital goods) and secondary capital goods (those needed to produce consumer goods) gave rise to a domestic supply of about 10 percent of the total in 1940 and as much as 30 percent during 1966–72. The very limited total supply of domestically produced machinery and equipment compelled Chile to depend on imports for 70–90 percent of its producer durables needs.[101] The 1970–73 governmental efforts to diversify the state-owned metallurgical industries complex might increase significantly between 1974 and 1980.

Chile had to rely on export revenues, external credits, and foreign aid to fill the gap between internal demand and supply of producer durables. Although it was imperative that the export sector act as a quasi-capital goods sector between 1930 and 1973, the actual response left much to be desired. Before 1971 the export sector acted first as a quasi-financial sector with its revenues used to meet the servicing and amortization payments to all direct and indirect foreign capitalists. Almost simultaneously, these revenues were used to meet its own fuel, raw material, consumer, and capital goods import needs. Once the country's financial obligations and the export sector's immediate foreign exchange needs were met, the export sector was called upon— along with borrowing—to act as a quasi-agricultural sector, filling the rising gap between domestic demand for and internal supply of meat, sugar, dairy products, wheat, tea, bananas, and other foods.[102] Preference was given to the hardship provinces of the extreme South and North and their free ports of Arica and Punta Arenas. The external sector regularly functioned as Chile's leading parallel welfare and transfer institution—not a quasi but a real one—because it explicitly or implicitly financed enormous subsidies on all imports. The subsidy function associated with foreign exchange overvaluation reached its zenith under Salvador Allende in 1972–73. When domestic agriculture, which had already been neglected, was further penalized

101. For an excellent quantitative analysis of the role of the external sector see Alejandro Foxley, "Opciónes de desarrollo bajo condiciónes de reducción en la dependencia externa. Un análisis cuantitativo," in *Proceso a la Industrialización Chilena*, ed. Oscar Muñoz (Santiago: Universidad Católica de Chile, ODEPLAN, 1972), pp. 176–219.

102. Imports of consumer goods were particularly favored during periods of anti-inflationary policies, especially if they weighed heavily in the cost-of-living index. For some priorities established in the 1930s, see "Decreto-Ley Nº 295, Santiago, July 26, 1932. Decree with power of law Article 1," in *Disposiciónes Vigentes* (Santiago: Imprenta Molina Lackington y Cia., 1938), p. 21; "Decree Nº 1086, Santiago, October 3, 1933, Article 9," in ibid., p. 41, and also the documents on pp. 53–54.

by heavily subsized imports, the nation's food deficits became self-perpetuating in an upward direction. The disequilibria that prevailed during 1973 had been surpassed only by those of the Great Depression.

Once the export sector and foreign borrowing had performed as quasi-financial and-agricultural sectors, they were called upon to act as quasi-raw materials and -industrial sectors by facilitating imports of cotton, fertilizers, chemicals, heavy oil, automotive and appliances parts, and so on. Only then, and only ahead of luxury imports, were exports-cum-borrowing able to perform as a quasi-capital goods sector and partly fill the internal producer durables demand–supply gap. In some instances, for example between 1940 and 1945, export restrictions by supplier nations caused bottlenecks that interfered with the development efforts of Presidents Pedro Aguirre Cerda and Juan Antonio Ríos.

With some principal but short-lived exceptions, governmental policy used export-cum-borrowing revenues primarily to close the current internal consumption gap, regardless of the sacrifices in short- or long-term investment and production. Linking ex-ante saving with investment had less priority. However, copper tax revenues were earmarked for development projects to augment human or techno-logical capital, for the financing of local investment, and for the covering of public sector deficits, in particular of railroads. Because it was impossible to satisfy the investment plans of all firms, preference was given to CORFO-sponsored industries, such as steel, petroleum, electricity, sugar, and cellulose, before 1970 and to state-owned enter-prises since then. Export industries with comparative advantage within the Latin American Free Trade Area were also favored.

The limited, low, erratic supply of imported producer durables and spare parts frequently led to excessively high inventories of com-ponents and raw materials and/or to duplicate investments and/or to spotty excess capacity and/or to idle capital equipment. Also, actual depreciation of the capital stock fell far below that in developed countries because excellent maintenance and careful use had prolonged the life of machinery and consumer durables.

It is conceptually very difficult, even somewhat arbitrary, to mea-sure the export revenues available for producer durables imports. In order to measure it I shall rely on the concept of the investable trade surplus, which is defined as domestic exports minus consumer and intermediate product imports and subsistence financial payments abroad. As can be seen in table 11.3, the investable trade surplus was negligibly positive during 1929, 1931, 1942–43, 1948, 1950, 1952, and 1955–56 and negative during the remaining years. This indicates that the export sector was unable to provide a substantial and continuous surplus flow of foreign exchange convertible into imported capital goods. As a consequence foreign borrowing, whose magnitude is measured by the negative values of the investable trade surplus presented in table 11.3, was massively relied upon to finance imports of producer durables during 1930, 1932, the 1936–40 recovery period, and 1958–64 but also to a lesser degree during the remaining years. Even though copper and other exports and external borrowing were the quasi-capital goods sectors par excellence, they were unable to generate an equilibrium between demand and supply and turn Chile into a quasi-complete system, because they were called upon with even greater urgency to act on the external trade side as quasi-financial, -service, -agricultural and -industrial sectors.

According to the minerals subtheory of economic growth that emerged from the Chilean experience, the benefits derived from the foreign-owned export sector were admittedly greater than in Peru's guano case, where the producing country's share in export proceeds was dissipated in luxury imports by a backward plutocracy,[103] but contrasted disadvantageously with the benefits derived from exports in staples economies. In a minerals economy the export contribution to growth comes primarily from the export-induced effects of, and transformation in, income distribution and capital formation and (unlike staples economies) only to a limited degree from production linkages and spread effects. But even these forces were weak and fragmented in Chile. The lack of integration between the export-induced distribution and capital formation effects and the weakness of production were caused by the semiperpetual suppression of the export sector and the use of export-generated resource surpluses for consumption rather than investment.

A series of econometric tests based on the investment feasibility accounts prepared in my "Historical Statistics of Chile" aimed at determining the nature of a relationship between key balance-of-payments variables and imports of machinery and equipment.[104] The most valuable finding was that imports of capital goods display

103. Jonathan V. Levin, *The Export Economies: Their Pattern of Development in Historical Perspective* (Cambridge, Mass.: Harvard University Press, 1960), chap. 1, pp. 1–24; chap. 4, pp. 165–202.
104. See table IIE2a3, pp. A-584–A-591.

an unusually strong, positive, and significant degree of association only with current domestic export revenues, mostly after a one-year lag.

In the first test, least-square estimates using stepwise multiple regressions were made for 1920–64. Imports of capital goods were the dependent variable, and domestic exports, national exports, and the investable trade surplus with, respectively, a two-year lag, a one-year lag, and no lag were the independent variables. The highest explanatory value was possessed by domestic export revenues without or with a one-year lag (as shown in col. 1 of table 11.4), which demonstrates results typical of all tests. In the final step, four independent variables had been retained at the $F = 10$ percent level of significance, as presented in column 2 of table 11.4. According to both equations the association between imports of capital goods and domestic and national export revenues is strong and positive, while the association between capital goods imports and the investable trade surplus is negative.[105]

The second test covered only the 1942–1964 period. These more reliable data were also expressed in millions of U.S. dollars, and the independent variables were increased from 9 to 12 by adding the total foreign resource transfer, F_t, with a two-year, a one-year, and no lag. The multiple regression yielding the best results is presented in column 3 of table 11.4.

The relationship between capital goods imports and domestic export revenues with a one-year lag remains positive and highly significant. The variable with the highest explanatory value was again X_{t-1}, and only F_t, X_{t-1}, and Xn_{t-1} passed the $F_{.10}$ test. The relationship between I_m and X_n, which during 1920–1964 is positive, becomes negative during 1942–1964. There is a negative association between imports of capital goods and the total foreign resource transfer. This is not especially puzzling, since negative values in the basic series for F_t reflect a transfer of resources to Chile while positive values reflect a transfer of resources from Chile to abroad. Thus, the present equation suggests a positive association between capital goods imports and the total resource transfer to Chile and a negative association between capital goods imports and a total resource transfer out of Chile. Both tests suggest that domestic export revenues influence greatly the economy's imports of capital goods.

105. The national trade investable surplus with a one-year lag had the least explanatory value even though it was statistically significant. For further information concerning these variables see the footnotes of table 11.3.

Table 11.4. Imports of Machinery and Equipment and Key
Balance-of-Payments Variables

Variables	(1) I_m Coefficient (s.e.)	(2) I_m Coefficient (s.e.)	(3) I_m Coefficient (s.e.)
Constant	-49.40	-40.76	-29.605
X_{t-1}	$+0.377 (0.024)$	$+0.138 (0.060)$	$+0.384 (0.064)$
$X_{i, t-1}$	$-0.237 (0.052)$	$-0.107 (0.069)$	
X_n		$+0.316 (0.077)$	
X_i		$-0.378 (0.101)$	
F_t			$-0.257 (0.059)$
$X_{n, t-1}$			$-0.126 (0.064)$
R^2	0.87	0.92	0.96

Note: I_m = imports of machinery and equipment in millions of current U.S. dollars

X = domestic export revenues in millions of current U.S. dollars

X_i = investable trade surplus in millions of current U.S. dollars

$t-1$ = with one-year lag

X_n = national export revenues in millions of current U.S. dollars

F_t = total foreign resource transfer

The Financial Nexuses

The variety and depth of financial institutions operating in Chile between 1930 and 1970 were ample. Formal credit, money, and capital markets included the Central Bank, approximately thirty private commercial banks, a state bank, two stock exchanges, a series of insurance companies, at least one state institution for housing, two mortgage banks, various savings and loan associations, the Chilean Development Corporation (whose activities are discussed in chap. 12), and two or three mutual funds.[106] Their growth and extent of operations were inadequate for a variety of reasons. The actual flow of savings was small and a large portion of savings was generated by a few large firms or institutions. With persistently strong demand for capital there arose a great tendency to reinvest profits directly rather than rely on financial intermediaries. Inflation reduced the real interest rate on most fixed-price assets to zero or negative levels. Finally, inflation-proof deposits and other financial titles appeared only in the 1960s and were not widespread.

Chilean capital markets were deficient in some vital areas through-

106. See the excellent study of the Chilean capital markets by the World Bank, Banco Internacional de Reconstrucción y Fomento (BIRF), *El Mercado de Capitales Chileno* (Santiago: INSORA, Instituto de Administración, 1967), annex II, pp. 1–2.

out 1930–73. A market for government liabilities was absent as was a money market. Furthermore, a shortage of medium-term credits was coupled with an inability of firms to obtain funds by issuing stock or bonds to the public.

Money and capital markets did not generally stimulate saving and provided only weak links between saving and investment. Capital markets, in particular that for mortgages, were early victims of the government's industrialization policies of the 1940s, which engendered suppression of mining and neglect of agriculture. Excessive reliance of government on Central Bank credit proved counterproductive because it destroyed, through inflation, numerous financial instruments (time and saving deposits literally evaporated), reduced savings, and increased rather than decreased dependence on inflationary credit.[107] The massive distortions of the financial system during most of the 1940–73 period—many but not all were corrected between 1960 and 1970—were an unintended consequence of often inefficient and contradictory governmental production, distribution, and capital formation policies. The obvious inability of the financial system to capture available savings and transfer them to investors reflected what I believe can be best described as "financial attrition." There is no evidence that it was caused by a planned or intentional "financial repression."[108]

The pervasive nature and magnitude of the deterioration in financial intermediation were fully recognized only after Javier Fuenzalida and Sergio Undurraga published their classic 1968 study *El Crédito y su Distribución en Chile*. This articulated and tested the hypothesis that Chile's economic growth was being choked by a "credit asphyxy," defined as the inability of firms and economic sectors to obtain the amount of credit they consider necessary under the prevailing economic conditions and at the current interest rates. This asphyxy reached its peak when serious difficulties were generated within the financial system about the payment of debt and the financing of current operations by business.[109] This hypothesis was further elaborated by Pedro Jeftanovic, who demonstrated that financial intermediation suffered heavily because usury laws prevented money rates of interest from

---

107. Reduction in savings and a sharp deterioration in financial intermediation were singled out as major negative effects of government policies between 1940 and 1958 (see my "Public Policy," pp. 22–28).

108. The theme that "financial repression" is *the* bottleneck to development is found in Ronald I. McKinnon's *Money and Capital in Economic Development* (Washington: The Brookings Institution, 1973), pp. 68–88.

109. See Fuenzalida and Undurraga, *Distribución del Crédito*, pp. 2–3.

rising sufficiently to discount the fluctuating and secularly rising inflation risk. The deterioration in the institutional capital stock of the financial sector is measured by and mirrored in the share of deposits and titles in Chilean currency held by the principal financial institutions, which declined from 36.2 percent of gross national product in 1940 to 13.2 percent in 1959 and 22.6 percent in 1968. However, there was an uneven degree of discrimination against the money and capital markets institutions.[110] The real stock of money fell sharply between 1930 and 1955, and the income velocity of money climbed to high levels between 1940 and 1973.[111]

Within an environment characterized by cyclically rising inflation, legal inertia, and inefficient governmental policies, the interest rate became obsolete. Wide and unpredictable differences between the money and real interest rates deprived them of their capacity to act as a price signal and caused the obsolescence of many financial intermediation instruments. Credit rationing became the primary instrument of monetary policy. The institutional recovery of the late 1950s and 1960s, when the readjustable deposits, which were immune to inflation in the saving and loan associations, the Central Bank, and other institutions, were introduced, was only partial.[112]

The effects were profound. The links between suppliers and users of savings and credits were weakened. The credit shortage impeded the modernization of factories. By compelling almost total reinvestment of profits and extremely low dividend payments, it sapped the ability of stocks to act as instruments that would attract saving. An excessive proportion of executive energy—14 to 18 percent of their time—was devoted to financial matters, and financial operations grew inordinately, at the cost of production operations. All these forces combined reduced investment and production and had a negative employment effect.[113]

110. See Pedro Jeftanovic P., *Estudio sobre el Mercado de Capitales Chileno* (Santiago: Centro de Estudios Socio-Económicos, 1969), pp. 203–08.
111. See Instituto de Economía, Universidad de Chile (IEUCH), *Formación de Capital en las Empresas Industriales* (Santiago: IEUCH, 1961), pp. 76–77; John V. Deaver, "The Chilean Inflation and the Demand for Money," in *Varieties of Monetary Experience*, ed. David Meiselman (Chicago, Ill.: University of Chicago Press, 1970), pp. 28–35.
112. See ODEPLAN, *Mecanismos de Ahorro en Chile* (Santiago: ODEPLAN, 1970), pp. 1–2, and tables.
113. Instituto de Organización y Administración (INSORA), *El Financiamiento de la Industria en Chile, Encuesta a los Ejecutivos* (Santiago: INSORA, 1962), pp. 24–28; Instituto de Economía, Universidad de Chile (IEUCH), *Formación de Capital*, pp. xi–xxvi.

Direct investment in land, dwellings, automobiles, U.S. dollars, television sets, and paintings flourished. However, despite the reduced availability of internal credit, production and development continued to be financed, thanks to the reinvestment of profits, the rise in unorganized money and capital markets, increased foreign credits, the diminution of consumer credit, establishment of policies of deferred payments for raw materials, and in some cases sale of stock and debentures to the public.[114] A domestic institutional change occurred as a growing number of firms became informal financial institutions by extending credits out of secularly rising undistributed profits. This fragmented and costly parallel financial system became indispensable to the survival of the large-scale private enterprises, which, according to Fuenzalida and Undurraga, received a disproportionately small share of direct credits.[115] Although the use of undistributed profits for credit purposes helped short-run production, it hindered long-term growth by reducing the magnitude of reinvested profits. At the other extreme the needs of some rural families were satisfied by relying on the informal market, where credit was supplied by "friends, neighbors, relatives, patrons, village stores, itinerant traders, and money lenders." However, imperfect competition among creditors led to excessively high real interest rates.[116] Even more unnecessary and detrimental was Chile's growing dependence on foreign credit to fill the widening domestic gap between demand and supply for money and credit. The rising power of indirect foreign capitalists and the economy's continued dependence on external credits for operating and investment needs imposed unnecessary balance-of-payments burdens and delayed the introduction of governmental policies required for the revival of the financial, mineral, and agricultural sectors.

It is widely agreed that savings can be neither increased nor linked with investment unless capital markets are significantly improved and expanded. For this to occur, it is necessary in turn to have positive real interest rates, escalator clauses in all financial instruments, and specialized financial institutions, such as rural banks, saving cooperatives, and savings and loan associations.

---

114. See Fuenzalida and Undurraga, *Distribución del Crédito*, p. 34.
115. Ibid., pp. 148–49.
116. See Charles Nisbet, "Interest Rates and Imperfect Competition in the Informal Credit Market of Rural Chile," *Economic Development and Cultural Change* 16, no. 1 (Oct. 1967): 73–84.

Above all, however, it will be essential to define the role and objectives of monetary policy and their place within the broad spectrum of public policies. As long as monetary policy is held responsible for carrying out or supporting an industrialization and/or redistribution policy and as long as financial intermediation is subordinated to these supergoals, decumulation of financial institutional capital will be an expected, though undesirable, consequence. Calls for the restoration of monetary policy's time-honored goals of optimum liquidity, financial intermediation, and so forth are but one step. It will be necessary to introduce those tax, income, tariff, foreign investment, price, exchange, and other policies and reforms that should in the first place have carried out the goals directly or indirectly assigned to monetary policy. Only then will it be unnecessary for monetary policy to continue its inefficient pursuit of such alien objectives as promoting chosen sectors or redistributing incomes. Monetary policy and the financial intermediation goal are neither superior nor precede other policies and goals. Nor are they inferior. They are parallel to and just as important as other policies and goals. As such, solid foundations for optimum production, distribution, and capital formation, as well as maximum growth, may not be constructed without independent and effective monetary and financial policies.

The principal bottlenecks to development were found in capital formation. Positive stimuli to the heterogeneous sources and agents of saving were generally rare and often absent. The saving climate was dismal during 1940–58 and 1970–73 but definitely positive between 1958 and 1970. Households and government saved little, if any. Mining and agricultural resource surpluses generated between 1930 and 1973 were not only far below their levels between 1840 and 1930 but were even often deliberately reduced or destroyed by government. With saving choices limited because of the absence of profitable, inflation- and government-proof financial instruments, ex-ante household savings were dissipated into consumption. The size and contribution of net foreign savings were limited.

There were several major imperfections on the investment side. Public physical investment tended to replace rather than be added to private investment. Public investment funds transferred to private firms were not always used for investment purposes, as they were supposed to be. On the whole, total private and public investment remained grossly inadequate. It was unable to raise output in critical sectors to the level required to perform their respective functions.

It was lopsidedly directed to meet the immediate basic and growing needs of the urban centers and thus it neglected agriculture, the rural sector, and, in part, mining, industry, and advanced and technical education. With minor exceptions the supply of producer durables—especially those imported—fell short of the levels that were demanded and could have been absorbed by the system. The accumulation of human, physical, and institutional capital was too low, distorted, or even negative. What Chile has always needed most—a revolution in capital formation—did not occur and was not attempted between 1930 and 1973.

PART 3   TWO ASPECTS OF CAPITAL FORMATION

12

The Promethean Financial and Investment Endeavors of the Chilean Development Corporation

As the principal agent of the Chilean government's development efforts since 1939, the Chilean Development Corporation[1] has acted as a financier, entrepreneur, investor, innovator and researcher, and frontiersman. Through these roles the Corporation has dominated economic life. It controlled the lion's share of aggregate investment in machinery and equipment (more than 30 percent in ten of the years between 1939 and 1954), more than one-fourth of public investment, and as much as 18 percent (1954) of gross domestic investment.[2] Never before had Chile witnessed the presence and intervention of such a powerful, multifaceted government organization.

The Chilean Development Corporation was established in 1939 after a devastating earthquake and one year after the Popular Front had come to power under the aegis of Pedro Aguirre Cerda. Although the earthquake provided the excuse, CORFO was established as a powerful, autonomous fiscal organization to implement the Popular Front's development program.

CORFO was given the promethean task of bringing to Chile the secret fire that the industrial demigods of the developed nations had so successfully guarded in achieving self-propelled growth. If successful, the agency, seen as an expression of the power of the people united by the state, would herald that elusive goal of self-sustained growth, prosperity, and balance-of-payments equilibrium. Without ignoring Chile's traditional strength in nitrate, copper, and iron, CORFO aimed

1. The Chilean Development Corporation will be also referred to as the Corporation or the Development Corporation.
2. Calculated from information found in CORFO, *Cuentas Nacionales de Chile, 1940–1954* (Santiago: Editorial del Pacífico, S.A., 1957), table 54.

primarily to unravel the mysteries and harness the hidden power of modern industrial frontiers and to inject new life into the economic fabric by financing new, internally controlled, technology-oriented industrial enterprises. To achieve this goal it planned to add to the country's crude saving and investment framework the missing components needed to guarantee a large, smooth flow of savings, a high return to investment, and an ample supply of capital goods.

A major part of CORFO's constitution reflected the belief that low savings was a key growth bottleneck. It hoped to erect an impregnable defense against overpowering foreign interests and to become the benevolent shield under which new and nascent national industrial enterprises could emerge into a rapidly and efficiently growing giant. Thus, motivated as much by Friedrich List's proindustry nationalist ideologies as by Marx's pro-statist principles, CORFO forged the rings that chained the sponsoring government into a lasting coalition with its favorite, dominant industry. Deliberately or by default, it severed the government's weakening links with large-scale mining and agriculture.

Since 1964 the air has again been filled with the commercial and economic philosophy that swept over the country so irresistibly in the early 1940s. Starting in the Frei administration there has been a visible return to the Popular Front's philosophy that injections of public investment and extensive government intervention in capital accumulation and production are a sine qua non for accelerated economic growth. In the new setting of 1964–73 the agency's finance and investment roles were both renewed and expanded.

A review and evaluation of CORFO's major activities will unravel the mechanisms by which government has attempted to affect capital accumulation and production. Their effectiveness in an underdeveloped country can be evaluated and certain lessons derived for future policies both in Chile and elsewhere. A study of CORFO becomes particularly important in view of the unprecedented new responsibilities that were bestowed upon the agency by the government of the Unidad Popular and President Salvador Allende in 1970–73. This chapter will concentrate on CORFO's finance and investment activities, which are qualitatively and quantitatively of central significance, and will cover primarily but not exclusively the pre-1964 period.

In retrospect, the most interesting theoretical implications of the present chapter lie in the differences uncovered between the original goals of the Corporation and the reality formed by its actions, between the planned financial activities and those observed ex post, and finally between the explicit or intended investment criteria envisaged by the founders and the actual ones pursued by the CORFO decision makers.[3] We turn now to a discussion of the Corporation's financial activities.

FINANCING ECONOMIC DEVELOPMENT

Ever since the establishment of the Chilean state, government control of credit has seemed desirable. Camilo Henríquez recommended the establishment of a national bank in 1823 to no avail,[4] and according to Jobet and Cange the aristocrats overthrew President Balmaceda because of his attempts at the nationalization of credit in 1891.[5] But it was not until the Great Depression that the public sector assumed major responsibility in the financial domain.[6] Specifically, CORFO has extended credit both for working and investment capital, has guaranteed foreign loans to domestic enterprises, has participated in the equity of both public and private enterprises, and has established artificially low interest rates, favorable amortization, and other positive measures.

As a financial institution, CORFO can be best described as a sui generis investment bank. Although it is unquestionably *the* institution specializing in the financing of long-term investment, it operates as a nonprofit organization and dispenses its vast resources without applying the traditional rules of profit-motivated investment banks. Furthermore, it has been receiving yearly capital contributions from govern-

3. For a more detailed analysis of the Chilean Development Corporation see Markos Mamalakis, "Veinticinco Años de la Corporación de Fomento de la Producción," in Instituto de Economía, *Ensayos Sobre Planificación* (Santiago: Universidad de Chile, 1967), pp. 411–58. This essay includes a description of the other activities of CORFO, e.g., those in research, national accounts and planning, and the involvement of the CORFO subsidiaries in electricity, iron and steel, oil and sugar (pp. 451–58). See also my more recent and occasionally more detailed article, "An Analysis of the Financial and Investment Activities of the Chilean Development Corporation, 1939–1964," *The Journal of Development Studies* 5, no. 2 (Jan. 1969): 118–37. A very good cost-benefit study of the CORFO-sponsored sugar beet industry is found in Ernesto R. Fontaine, "La Industria de la Azúcar de Remolacha en Chile. Un Análisis de Costos y Beneficios," *Cuadernos de Economía* no. 8 (Jan.–Apr. 1966): 5–81.

4. See the unpublished Ph.D. thesis of Robert Milton Will, "Some Aspects of the Development of Economic Thought in Chile (c. 1778–1878)" (Duke University, 1957), pp. 98–100. José Joaquín de Mora advocated similar ideas (ibid., pp. 100–07).

5. Julio César Jobet, *Ensayo Crítico del Desarrollo Económico-Social de Chile* (Santiago: Editorial Universitaria, S.A., 1951), pp. 60–66.

6. See Fernando Lorca and Pablo León, *Financiamiento Externo* (Santiago: CORFO, Departmento de Créditos Externos, 1968).

Table 12.1. Investment Funds of the
Chilean Development Corporation by Type of Source
(In thousands of escudos)

	State contributions	External credits	Income from own sources	Other sources	Total investments
1939	8,515.8	—[a]	—	—	6,083.3
1940	12,661.9	3,093.5	—	13,956.8	29,712.2
1941	14,928.2	6,308.6	—	9,181.8	30,418.5
1942	7,807.1	5,818.0	—	12,580.8	26,205.9
1943	6,330.2	9,195.9	—	6,159.1	21,685.2
1944	6,199.8	6,199,8	—	3,635.7	16,035.2
1945	6,999.6	2,462.2	105.5	6,296.2	13,471.7
1946	3,248.3	5,312.7	91.1	8,409.2	13,691.6
1947	10,588.5	2,885.7	159.1	—	12,769.8
1948	13,672.3	12,979.0	635.5	539.2	27,825.1
1949	11,772.3	21,063.7	1,362.1	745.9	34,944.1
1950	11,927.9	10,871.7	2,379.9	605.5	25,785.1
1951	14,190.3	5,885.7	5,862.7	1,877.4	27,816.2
1952	17,392.5	10,708.9	7,909.1	—	32,899.7
1953	17,766.1	10,560.4	9,642.7	—	36,096.3
1954	13,886.5	8,462.9	8,751.1	3,838.4	34,938.9
1955	14,561.7	10,715.6	13,193.3	413.8	38,884.3
1956	22,627.1	8,571.1	22,171.6	—	40,900.7
1957	12,329.9	9,405.5	24,835.0	5,542.8	52,113.2
1958	14,643.0	13,655.0	32,738.0	8,516.0	69,562.0
1959	23,898.3	4,856.4	29,247.8	—	57,929.3
1960	27,750.5	4,373.6	13,972.9	—	46,097.0
1961	34,159.7	[b]			
1962	36,002.1				
1963	31,906.1				

Notes: The majority of the tables included in the present paper were originally expressed in pesos, the currency that was replaced in 1959 by the escudo on a 1,000 : 1 basis. The figures in 1958 prices were obtained by adjusting the figures in current prices with cost-of-living index.
Source: Department of Finance, CORFO.
[a]Dash indicates provisional figure.
[b]Blank indicates figure not available.

ment, has been borrowing from foreign institutions and individuals, and has also used the income it derived from its own financial, investment, and other economic activities. However, it has not floated its own liabilities, created species, or accepted deposits. The role of each of the various sources of funds, which are summarized in table 12.1, will be discussed separately.

State Contributions

As the government's instrument in industrializing Chile, CORFO has received a generous share of the public funds each year, both in national currency and in dollars. Normally, the first are destined for domestic expenditures, while the second serve to facilitate amortization of liabilities in dollars and the purchase of imported capital goods. The level of dollar payments has depended on the taxes paid by the large-scale copper mines, which have been explicitly earmarked for CORFO, on the nonearmarked dollar tax proceeds of the general government, and on the dollar needs of CORFO compared to those of other government agencies.

The government contributions fall into three major categories. Certain funds originate from taxes levied specifically to finance CORFO's activities. They are supplemented by general contributions from other tax receipts and by credits extended to government by the Central Bank of Chile.

Taxes assigned specifically to finance the activities of CORFO have been imposed almost exclusively on the foreign-owned, large-scale copper mining sector. One type accrues to the general budget of CORFO and can be used as the agency sees fit.[7] Such taxes contribute to a transfer of a resource surplus to industry from the highly productive mining sector, in particular from the mining North and O'Higgins Province to the Center of Chile, where most of the urban population and industry and services are located. These copper funds have been used predominantly for investment. Unfortunately, they have represented only a small fraction of taxes paid by the large American-owned copper concerns to the Chilean government. The other resources transferred to the Center through taxation have been used mainly to cover current expenditures, and thus for consumption.[8] Other tax contribu-

7. The 15 percent tax on the normal profits of the large-scale copper mines is an example of this class of contributions. It was imposed in 1942 on the difference between an assumed cost of production (which included a fair rate of return) and the actual cost of production; this tax was allocated to CORFO. The proceeds from this tax diminished rapidly from 167 million pesos in 1942 to 34 million in 1947 as the actual cost of production approached the legally fixed assumed cost. For details see Kalman H. Silvert, "The Chilean Development Corporation" (Ph.D. thesis, University of Pennsylvania, 1948), pp. 86–91.

8. See Clark Reynolds, "Development Problems of an Export Economy: The Case of Chile and Copper," in Markos Mamalakis and Clark W. Reynolds, *Essays on the Chilean Economy* (Homewood, Ill.: Richard D. Irwin, 1965), pp. 201–350.

tions to CORFO are restricted as to their use. For example, the so-
called copper law funds formed an integral part of the "New Deal"
legislation enacted in 1955.[9]

Although it is not possible to obtain a quantitative measure of the
credit received by the government from the Central Bank, some conjectures are possible. Despite the success of CORFO's activities in
raising public investment to an average of 45 percent of total investment,[10] there is no evidence of any increase in the share of investment
in national product. Gross investment during 1940–65 averaged only
11 percent of GNP and during many years hardly covered depreciation.
Only in the 1960s, after the advent of U.S. foreign aid, did the investment coefficient rise above 15 percent of GDP.

The original intention was to use all such borrowing for investment.
In reality, however, it was extensively—in some years exclusively—
used to amortize CORFO's foreign debt. Over the years dollar contributions became increasingly determined by the size of CORFO's current debt payments abroad. The need for greater dollar contributions
was used as an excuse to levy higher taxes on copper mining, and the
need for increased peso funds provided the excuse for increased dependence of the state on Central Bank credit and indirect taxes. The
outcome was a strengthening of sectoral clashes and an accelerating
inflation with virtually no investment increase except after 1960.

Foreign Credits

Until 1969 CORFO had received almost $969 million, used $662
million, and amortized $328 million of foreign credits. Thus, according
to almost any standard, foreign credits have been a major source of the
financing of the country's economic development. Such credits have
been applied to the financing of steel, electricity, cellulose, coal, gas and
oil, and sugar production, to the building of roads and irrigation pro-

9. The lawmakers were convinced that copper mining was subject to highly discriminatory treatment, to which its stagnation was being attributed, and also that the
unbalanced preoccupation of government with industry at the expense of mining was
matched by an inequitable participation of the Center in the fiscal revenues to the detri-
ment of the North and the O'Higgins Province. Thus it was prescribed that starting in
1952, a fraction of copper proceeds would have to be spent in the major copper-producing
provinces of Tarapacá, Antofagasta, and O'Higgins. The more equitable treatment of
copper was therefore accompanied by a balanced geographical allocation of tax
revenues.

10. Statistics on this issue are available only for the 1940–54 period. Thus, the share
of the public sector in gross domestic investment was 54.4 percent in 1940, as high as 71.5
percent in 1954, and as low as 22.9 percent in 1946. During six years it exceeded 50
percent.

Table 12.2. Distribution of Foreign Credits Received by CORFO according to Source, 1939–69
(In thousands of U.S. dollars)

Lending institutions	Amount of credits	Utilization to 12/31/69	Unutilized balance at 12/31/69	Amortization to 12/31/69	Balance to be amortized to 12/31/69	Amounts canceled without utilization
World Bank	196,026.5	146,199.1	49,692.0	53,974.1	141,917.0	135.4
Interamerican Bank	115,783.9	55,377.6	60,403.8	11,179.3	104,602.1	2.5
Eximbank	139,619.5	138,734.0	589.1	111,737.5	27,585.6	296.4
German Development Bank	52,814.2	41,239.1	11,575.1	819.7	51,994.5	—
France	67,454.5	10,586.4	56,868.2	775.6	66,678.9	—
England	11,400.0	1,978.7	9,421.3		11,400.0	—
Spain	17,402.9	5,899.1	11,503.8	276.9	17,125.9	—
USSR	54,000.0	—	54,000.0		54,000.0	—
Czechoslovakia	5,000.0		5,000.0		5,000.0	—
AID	43,300.0	42,670.4	590.8		43,261.2	38.8
Argentina	6,500.0		6,500.0		6,500.0	—
Private banks and financial institutions	57,307.9	44,929.1	12,378.8	11,272.7	—	—
Various suppliers	201,081.9	193,738.2	7,343.8	137,939.1	63,148.4	—
Debentures	1,100.0	1,100.0	—	110.0	990.0	—
E°	1,470.0	1,470.0	—	217.8	1,252.2	—
Total U.S. dollars	968,791.4	682,451.6	285,866.7	328,084.9	640,233.4	473.1
E°	1,470.0	1,470.0	—	217.8	1,252.2	—

Source: CORFO, Departamento de Créditos Externos, Financiamiento Externo, Estado de los Créditos Contratados por CORFO al 31 de Diciembre de 1969 (Santiago: CORFO, 1970), p. 7. This publication provides a detailed breakdown of foreign credits received by CORFO by year, use, interest rate, term, and so forth.

jects, to improvement of agriculture, fishing, and mining, and to transportation of materials for railways and public transport. This list mentions only the most important areas.

Table 12.2 provides a summary picture of the primary sources of foreign credits. The majority was subscribed with the Export and Import Bank (Eximbank), the International Bank for Reconstruction and Development (IBRD), the Interamerican Bank (BID), the Italian Emigration Institute (ICLE), the Agency for International Development (AID), the German Development Bank, and the French government.

A striking aspect of CORFO's external financial activities has been the radical change in the normally accepted procedures of investment financing. Although in theory, and also legally, it was supposed to act as an intermediary between foreign financial institutions and national enterprises, in reality it assumed new functions. Implicitly but unmistakably it converted the hard foreign currency loans to enterprises or agencies into domestic soft loans. This policy was mainly the consequence of the rampant inflation and the fact that CORFO was lending without a dollar or other escalator clauses. As a result only a fraction of the real value of these loans has ever been repaid by the recipient enterprises.[11]

Over the years a double standard was introduced. One set of rules applied to the international aspect and another to the domestic aspect of the same financial transaction. The first set, which was valid de jure, made the recipient enterprise directly and the Corporation indirectly liable for a loan. It was stipulated that the loan was both to be made and repaid in hard currency. The foreign agency was the creditor, the Chilean enterprise the debtor, and CORFO the financial intermediary. The credit was obtained with at least a vague understanding that the debt would be amortized by the enterprise on whose behalf CORFO was acting.

The second set of rules, developed de facto by CORFO and circumstances to cover directly the domestic aspect of its financial transactions, both contradicted and violated the original regulations. The recipient enterprise was not required to repay the international loan in *dollars* or in dollar-equivalent funds. While the foreign agency was still the creditor, the national enterprise the beneficiary, and CORFO

11. But even when a dollar clause was introduced, as in many cases after 1960, repayments were highly irregular and rarely, if ever, insisted upon by the Corporation. So, even though price stability might have reduced many problems, there is no proof that it would have prevented CORFO from turning hard loans into soft ones.

the intermediary, the state was the actual debtor, because it assumed the amortization payments. Furthermore, the recipient enterprise was not required to repay the loan, even in local currency, in part or in toto, and nonpayment never entailed bankruptcy or any similar punishment. Since CORFO had no obligation to repay such debts by drawing on its own resources, payment had little or no connection with the solvency, profitability, or success of the debtor enterprise. It was related strictly to the government's ability to acquire directly (through copper taxation) or indirectly (through the Central Bank and international borrowing) sufficient foreign exchange to service its debts.

In view of the fact that payments were made, it can be said that CORFO had complied with the first set of rules. However, these same rules were violated by the fact that a third party, namely government, rather than the recipients made the payments.[12] In reality, therefore, CORFO assumed the function of coordinating two separate actions of government. The first obtained hard currency loans from foreign creditors, and the second used the hard currency income to service and repay these debts. The net inflow of capital goods or foreign resources as a result of these operations was positive but by no means exceptional.

Two successive transformations were performed by means of CORFO's financial intermediation. According to the first a *loan to an enterprise* that was hard both because of the repayment requirement and in view of its dollar nature was transformed into a soft loan to an enterprise without these two requirements. The second, reverse transformation, which was at least as fascinating as the first, reconverted the soft loan into a hard one by turning it into a *dollar liability of the country*.[13]

12. As an example, credits authorized by Eximbank to landowners to purchase agricultural machinery and to ENDESA (National Electricity Company) to import electrical machinery constituted legally an obligation for CORFO, ENDESA, and the landlords, but in reality the credits were converted into a government liability because they were paid by the government and only on rare occasions constituted a direct and real liability of the actual beneficiary.

13. This anomaly, by means of which the burden of a firm was converted into a burden of the whole economy, existed regardless of the nature of CORFO's investment being in debt or in equity as long as the resources used by CORFO to repay these dollar liabilities originated from sources other than the individual enterprises concerned. It is certain that CORFO incurred an immediate loss only in those instances where investments were made in debt liabilities of enterprises vulnerable to inflation. Lack of a dollar clause implied a subsidy to the debtor equal to the difference between the dollar value of the investment plus the cost of servicing and the real burden of the debt to the individual, as determined by the rate of price increase and the money rate of interest. But even when equity investment was involved, the protection may have been a spurious one because the profitability of the enterprise in relation to the capital market conditions did not permit CORFO to recover its investment by means of sale of the equity.

This dual transformation process was carried, by both CORFO and the Central Bank, to the point where these artificially created dollar liabilities of the government and the country could no longer be serviced through either dollar tax revenues or current dollar earnings delivered to the Central Bank. Chile reached a period of crisis during 1960–62, and only the timely arrival of American aid prevented an external financial catastrophe. The increase in copper prices from 1966 to 1970, induced by the war in Vietnam, also boosted the economy.

The implications of the mechanism that emerged have been pervasive. The individual investments sponsored by CORFO have been consistently judged financially sound by the foreign financial circles involved—officially because their approval followed careful scrutiny and analysis of the individual plans submitted, in reality because government had guaranteed and, as experience revealed, paid for these liabilities through the Corporation. To the extent that government contributions were absorbed by amortization payments rather than new investment, the impact on investment and growth was clearly negative.[14]

As already mentioned, once it possessed funds, CORFO administered a credit-with-subsidy program that had a highly unequal impact upon sectors and enterprises. Subsidies were largest in the case of loans in national currency and smallest when CORFO controlled the equity. Whenever the debtor was an enterprise owned by CORFO, the gain from the subsidy accrued ex ante to all factors of production employed by the public sector. However, most frequently those who gained most were labor and, in particular, white-collar workers. This view is supported by the zero profit margins and negligible reinvestment levels by ENDESA[15] and most other government-owned enterprises. In such instances the subsidy program led to real wages and salaries in the public enterprises that exceeded productivity levels.[16] These subsidies

14. The Corporation was established to increase the domestic availability of commodities and in particular to raise the "feasibility" of investment by augmenting the imports of producer durables. This goal was only partially achieved because net foreign credits by CORFO have not been very large. Instances have been recorded when CORFO had started making amortization payments before having made use of the credit at all. Net foreign credits were negligible or zero during the first ten years, increased slowly during the middle of the 1950s, and were substantial in the early 1960s.

15. This picture has changed somewhat in recent years. ENDESA (the electricity company) profit rates became positive during the 1960–65 period.

16. Real wages and salaries exceeding productivity levels, a phenomenon quite prevalent in CORFO-financed enterprises, had an inflationary impact also through the cost-push mechanisms. These artifically high wages exerted a pull on wages in the rest

became evident in later years, when the real value of the effective repayments to CORFO fell short of what it would have been without inflation.

This de facto subsidy program had two effects, one of which was strongly inflationary. By reducing the real value of CORFO's outstanding credits, the amount of the subsidy impoverished the Corporation; it diminished the relative significance of CORFO's own funds of "recuperations" (as they were called by CORFO) as a source of future investment funds and increased its direct dependence on government for financial support and its indirect dependence on the Central Bank. Whenever foreign credits were involved, it was necessary to burden either the mining sector or the economy as a whole with additional taxes destined for the amortization of the dollar debt by the magnitude of the subsidy. This move was unavoidable even when CORFO controlled the equity.[17]

The presence of foreign credits, however, enabled CORFO to establish *an investment priority system*. Industries, whether private or public, that received CORFO-guaranteed foreign credits were able to break the foreign exchange bottleneck, bypass the Central Bank, and proceed with their investment plans. Moreover, the Central Bank was eventually forced to give these same industries scarce foreign exchange resources that were needed to service, maintain, and expand their investments.

Foreign credits permitted CORFO and the recipient enterprises to obtain the country's scarce dollars through the back door. First, without using export-earned dollars they were able to import capital goods; subsequently they obtained hard export-earned dollars simply by presenting to the Chilean government or Central Bank the bills for interest and amortization. Since the maintenance of a new industry required continuous future imports of capital goods, its establishment reduced the present and future dollar reserves available for other sectors. The dollar funds that remained after these operations were rationed among public and private investors. CORFO gave preferential treatment to the enterprises it patronized but diminished the

---

of the industry or in other sectors: the CORFO enterprise acted as a "wage leader." The induced demand for higher wages and salaries by the employees of the non-CORFO industries led to a greater demand for credit, in order to cover increased costs, and to increased prices in order to absorb increasing costs (cost push).

17. In more recent years, repayments of foreign debts were also made by obtaining additional credits abroad.

investment feasibility for those at the margin of the favored group, to which normally belonged the small national private enterprises and small investors.

Within such a financial framework it is almost impossible to measure the success of foreign credits. The claim of CORFO that its own success can be measured by its excellent repayment record is unfounded, because it actually has borne no relation to the success of the recipient enterprises. On the contrary the poor financial record of the recipients, as witnessed by their own limited repayments, suggests that a misallocation of resources is likely to have occurred. Foreign creditors contributed to the establishment of the new rules, which ultimately could lessen the ability of the economy to repay individual debts by showing no interest in *who* paid, as long as debts were paid.

Nevertheless, CORFO contributed to Chilean growth by means of additional, less spectacular financial and related activities. In negotiating foreign credits it adopted a sound policy of purchasing capital goods. Furthermore, CORFO established a favorable climate for foreign credits and foreign investments, especially in the field of manufacturing. In this respect its New York office has been particularly efficient.

Other contributions of CORFO included the contracting of low-cost foreign credits and preparation of both the Chilean national accounts and the first comprehensive development plan. It also carried out studies of a large variety of technological, economic, and environmental problems.

Revenues Originating from Own Sources

Internal funds—including moneys received from commissions, interest on and amortization of loans, sales of stocks, dividends on equity investment, sales of machinery, and so forth—became an important source of revenue in 1941 and maintained their importance in later years. In 1951 internal funds amounted to 20 percent of investment funds, and in 1959 their percentage contribution had increased to 40 percent.[18]

Dividends have constituted the single most valuable source of these internal funds. CORFO has forfeited its right to dividends payable

18. The major components were dividends, interest, and profits of companies and sale of securities.

whenever the debtor enterprise is engaged in an investment program that is so large that it requires, in addition to its internal funds, major contributions by CORFO itself. The National Electricity Company (ENDESA), for example, has not transferred dividends to CORFO even though it pays on its privately owned shares.

Interest payments have also been significant, especially because in the first years CORFO provided assistance primarily in the form of loans. They have provided significant revenue despite low interest rates and inflation, and the payments would have been far larger had the credit program of CORFO not been to a great extent a subsidy program. Finally, receipts from sales of stocks have fluctuated erratically because CORFO decided to sell securities.

CORFO, as well as the majority of its subsidiary enterprises, lacks the information for an objective estimate of the real value of profits. Their complicated finances and inflation make such an attempt a herculean task. The Development Corporation has been a financier only in the narrow sense of providing funds for investment projects, not in the more general sense of supporting the most (or more) profitable projects, of seeking a normal or minimum rate of return on its capital, or even of aiming to recover capital lent out. Such a behavior pattern did not violate any of its principles but formulated them. CORFO has attempted without success to use objective and rational criteria in its financial dealings with private and public corporations. However, the pressures in support of the use of objective criteria, either from inside the Corporation or from outside, have not been as yet strong enough, if they have existed at all. Any objective financial criteria used by the Corporation before 1970 were abandoned during the Allende years.

INVESTMENT AND INVESTMENT CRITERIA

No other institution has ever directly controlled or indirectly affected so large a percentage of the country's investment in producer durables as CORFO.[19] The investment criteria adopted by CORFO can be divided into explicit, implicit, and actual and subdivided as follows:

19. During ten of the years from 1940 to 1954 this percentage exceeded 30 percent, and in five of the years it was larger than 40 percent of total investment in machinery and equipment.

Explicit	*Implicit*	*Actual*
Standard of living criterion	Social rate of return criterion	Import substitution criterion
Balance-of-payments criterion	Foreign exchange criterion	Import substitution in power, raw materials, intermediate goods
		Capital intensity

Explicit criteria are defined as those stated in the legal documents that concern CORFO. Implicit criteria are those that, for an economist, underlie the explicit ones. Finally, actual criteria are those that have been used by CORFO in choosing among alternative investment opportunities. Despite the correspondence between the explicit and implicit criteria, there is no reason why the actual criteria should be identified with either type. Explicit and implicit criteria describe the intentions of CORFO, whereas the actual category refers to its actions and is revealed by the investment decisions.[20]

The explicit criteria used in establishing CORFO appeared for the first time in the organic law, which stated that CORFO's objectives were "to elevate the standard of living of the population and to improve the situation of the balance of international payments."[21]

The terms are vague, especially for the first criterion. It could be said that the social rate of return and foreign exchange criteria are their underlying components. Since virtually any investment raises the standard of living, the problem was to determine which investment contributed most to the income increase. To answer this question, a new criterion, import substitution, was developed.[22] Products were ranked

20. There exists a correspondence, albeit a vague one, between investment criteria and CORFO's principal policy objectives that can be also characterized as explicit, implicit, and actual. The explicit objectives, defined as goals contemplated in the organic law, included a higher standard of living and a balance-of-payments equilibrium; the implicit ones, which are defined as those the legislator would have spelled out had he been an economist using today's jargon, included greater capital formation, especially in infrastructure, increased productivity, and promotion of autarky and self-sufficiency. Finally, the actual objectives of CORFO have been those observed ex post. In a broad sense the most important actual objective has been industrialization and, in a narrower one, the substitution of industrial imports, excluding production of producer durables. The latter also involved the establishment of an infrastructure permitting future industrial expansion, including the development of energy sources.

21. Law 6440, Article 250, letter a.

22. The roots of the import substitution criterion are found as part of the vague description of the additional objectives of CORFO, namely "to aid the manufacturing

according to the absolute value of their respective imports. A commodity appearing at the top of the list was automatically a candidate for import substitution, and its rank determined the priority given in producing it locally.

The projects approved on the basis of this criterion fit three major categories. For those that contributed to import substitution in the final stages of the value-adding process, such as consumer goods manufacturing, the respective investments shifted the import needs of the country from final consumer goods to the intermediate, raw material, fuel, and capital goods categories and increased foreign exchange requirements for these groups. Into the second category fall projects leading to domestic production of fuels and raw materials, including steel, oil, and electricity. These projects increased the demand for capital goods imports but saved foreign exchange by reducing the country's need for raw materials, fuel, and intermediate products. Finally, the third category of projects includes production of capital goods, in particular producer durables, and has normally constituted the ultimate step of an import substitution that results in complete vertical integration and incorporation of industries into the domestic economy. Such projects usually saved foreign exchange by reducing demand for capital goods imports, especially if they produced machinery to be used to produce more machinery.

Indirectly, the organic law of CORFO had excluded an import substitution effort only insofar as it referred to production of capital goods.[23] By declaring explicitly and specifically that CORFO will aid "the importation of machines and other elements of production," it indirectly placed the effort of import substitution on consumer goods and intermediate products. Since neither the level of income nor the degree of industrialization provided a large enough market for the production of producer durables and since the technical know-how for such ventures was domestically missing, the decision was rational. Even today the producer durables sector is very small.

---

industry within the country" and "to propose and aid the adoption of means destined to augment the consumption of national products or to obtain a greater participation of Chilean interests in industrial and commercial activities" (ibid., Article 25, d and e). Even so, in 1939 there was little evidence that import substitution would be converted into the most powerful instrument in the government's development policy for more than two decades and that it would control investment process and resource allocation as well.

23. Capital goods are understood here to mean machinery and equipment and not construction.

In the other two categories import substitution was firmly advocated and selectively implemented. Although it was a pre-1940 phenomenon for the manufacturing sector as a whole, it remained significant to the growth of the industrial, electricity, and agricultural subsectors directly promoted by CORFO. Domestic-oriented industry became the most important growth sector after regular and substantial assistance. Its performance, better than that of any other sector, was desired and expected.

The quantity and variety of final consumer goods being produced today compare very favorably with those of 1939. Expansion of this sector was achieved without substantial direct public investment. Import substitution was invited by such indirect stimuli as import quotas, tariffs, tax exemptions, easy credit, and capital goods import licensing. With few exceptions the need for direct governmental participation did not arise, because in these ventures risk in expanding old or creating new enterprises was relatively low, capital requirements were within the reach of the private sector, and private enterprise had already been successful. The actual response vindicates the view that the stimuli offered would be adequate. Nonetheless, government investment has not been negligible and has entered riskier or more complicated ventures, including, for example, the sugar beet industry, milk processing, paper manufacturing, and construction of hotels for tourism.

The investments of CORFO and the government have been more extensive and direct in electric energy, raw materials, and intermediate products. The three projects that stand out in terms of investment outlays in this category are hydroelectric power, steel, and oil. Both the oil and steel industries were new ventures explicitly established to compete with imports. The hydroelectric plants and distribution facilities reflected an independent expansion of the existing network and indirectly reduced the country's fuel needs.[24]

Government policy promoted domestic vertical integration by adding to the existing consumer goods sector a wide range of intermediate and raw material industries. Given the capital requirements, which were often extremely high, and the desire to prevent foreign control of these industries, government investment became the natural choice.

Investments were divided by CORFO into two principal categories: contributions and loans, and direct (equity) investments. For invest-

24. Other investments in the line of raw materials and intermediate products included construction materials, copper refining, the rayon industry, cement, refrigeration plants, textile fibers, and so forth.

(In millions of U.S. dollars)

Accounting period	Savings generated by steel industry (CAP)[a]	Accounting period	Savings generated by oil industry (ENAP)[b]	Accounting period	Savings generated by sugar beet industry (IANSA)[c]	Accounting period	Savings generated by the electric power industry (ENDESA)[d]
1953	12.5	1953	−5.8	1954	0.4		
1954	18.8	1954	−1.3	1955	0.6		
1955	18.6	1955	7.2	1956	1.1		
1956–57	26.0	1956 1st sem.	7.3	1957	3.3		
1957–58	24.7	1956–57	8.1	1958	3.0		
1958–59	31.0	1957–58	9.4	1959	4.0	1959	16.8
1959–60	23.5	1958–59	8.9	1960	5.6	1960	15.0
1960–61	28.0	1959–60	14.4	1961	2.7	1961	20.0
1961–62	43.1	1960–61	14.0	1962	5.3	1962	20.0
1962–63	56.8	1961–62	23.5	1963	19.4		
1963–64	68.5	1962–63	32.4				
		1963 2nd sem.	25.4				
Total saving since CAP's establishment . . . 389.6		Total saving since ENAP's establishment 121.8		Total saving since IANSA's establishment 45.2			

[a]CAP stands for Compañia de Acero del Pacífico S.A. The information on dollar savings has been obtained from the company's yearbooks. Total saving was calculated by the company itself and is not the sum of the figures presented in the table, because some years are missing.

[b]ENAP stands for Empresa Nacional del Petróleo S.A. Dollar-saving figures throughout the table have been rounded off. Savings in this column have been calculated by taking the difference between the dollar equivalent of ENAP's total sales and its actual dollar expenditures, which include all international payments. Expenditures for the establishment of the oil industry started as early as 1942. Sales of output began in 1950, and by 1955 the dollar value of output exceeded the international dollar payments. Remarkable as this performance may be, it conceals the fact that crude petroleum imports to Chile, which started in 1955, did not decline but rather increased in absolute value, even though they have declined dramatically to 20 percent of total consumption. The negative values for 1953 and 1954 indicate that international dollar payments for ENAP's operations exceeded its sales income.

[c]IANSA stands for Industria Azucarera Nacional S.A. Calculation of dollar savings is not completely correct, since it does not take account of the cost of servicing foreign credits as a component of dollar expenditures. Nevertheless, the resulting error is minor because the total value of these credits has been small. The information required to correct this error has not been available.

[d]ENDESA stands for Empresa Nacional de Electricidad S.A. Savings have been crudely calculated as the difference between the dollar value of its sales and ENDESA's current dollar expenditures.

ments of the first category repayment is normally expected. If at a later date CORFO receives shares in repayment of the debt instead of cash, the original contributions or loans are reclassified as direct investments.

The dollar savings generated by the four major industries supported by CORFO are presented in table 12.3. Since the terminology employed in the discussion of import substitution in Chilean literature is rather vague, some clarifications are made here. An enterprise established on the basis of the import-substitution criterion creates dollar saving if the sum of the value of its exports and production for the domestic market exceeds the sum of its current dollar expenditures and the servicing costs of long-term foreign debt. An industry earns dollars or generates dollar earnings if the value of its exports exceeds its current dollar expenditures plus the cost of servicing its long-run dollar debt.[25]

The notion of saving dollars is a somewhat dubious one because every domestic industry "saves" dollars by producing goods that as a consequence do not need to be imported and therefore to be paid for in dollars. The savings based on such a conditional event are very indefinite. By the same token it can be said that an industry "spends" dollars if, as a result of its lack of growth, the economy spends dollars to import commodities that this industry could have produced. Thus, while investment in the steel industry permits the economy to save about $60 million, this and other similar investments, at the same time, could force the economy to spend $100 million to import agricultural products that could have been saved had investment taken place in agricultural instead of in steel production. Thus, unless such savings can be measured per unit of investment for different sectors and industries, the net or overall saving of foreign exchange for the economy, as a result of an investment, cannot be calculated. Net saving will occur only if the decline per unit of investment in imports is greater than the increase of imports incurred as a result of omitting to invest a unit in another sector.

The notion of dollar earnings per unit of investment has a higher operational value. If an industry contributes more per unit of investment to dollar revenue earnings than to dollar expenditures, it has such earnings. As far as the balance of payments is concerned, an industry makes a clearly positive contribution only if its dollar (export) revenues exceed its dollar expenditures (direct and indirect). An economy runs

25. Although the concept of dollar savings has been readily used by Chilean planners, that of dollar earnings is introduced by the present essay.

into trouble, as in the case of Chile, if practically all investments lead to dollar savings but none or very few lead to earning of dollars. Obviously, it is possible that more investment will be directed toward industries that create dollar savings than toward industries that create dollar earnings. In that case both revenues and expenditures of dollars will decline either in absolute value or as a percentage of total income, but the former more rapidly than the latter. As to Chile it is doubtful whether investments over time have led to an overall import substitution, which would be evidenced by a decline of imports as a percentage of gross national product,[26] let alone have led to dollar earnings.[27]

CORFO's second objective, equilibrium in the balance of payments, has never been attained. From the beginning the means for achieving it were insufficient. Equilibrium could be attained by raising exports or decreasing imports. The de facto chosen alternative was the second, and the policy was not successful. The world oil crisis led in 1974–75 to Chile's worst balance-of-payments situation since the Great Depression.

In the very narrow sense of producing domestically previously imported commodities, CORFO can claim substantial credit. Chile now produces a variety of commodities, which represents a radical change in the composition of the industrial sector, and fares well in comparison to some other less developed nations. However, the policy ignored or neglected two elements fundamental to any trade policy.[28] Indirectly, traditional exports were put at a disadvantage either because of discriminatory taxation and foreign exchange and other policies, as in the case of the copper industry, or because of inflation, neglect, and administrative inertia, as in the case of agriculture, forestry, and tourism. Some exports declined, and in extreme instances commodities

26. A primary aim of Chile's import substitution policy was to reduce the share of domestic resources used to import commodities.

27. Although the import substitution policy of CORFO was successful as far as final and intermediate industrial products and fuels are concerned, it was a failure of omission as far as agricultural exports or imports are concerned. Net agricultural imports have thus increased from $7.6 million in 1942 to $83 million in 1962 as a result of a narrow interpretation of the import-substitution criterion both with respect to time as well as to sectors affected. The time horizon rarely exceeded the present, and normally interest was confined to the industrial sector and electric power.

28. In determining the foreign exchange saving component of alternative investment options, the potential constellation of future consumer goods imports as a product of present investment policies was not taken into account. Even today, with heavy agricultural imports, the import-substitution criterion has not been applied in favor of agriculture.

normally exported were now heavily imported.[29] The concept of import substitution should probably be refined to include both commodity imports and other financial payments abroad.

According to Chenery [30] import substitution is measured by the difference between the potential total supply (domestic output plus imports if the ratio of imports to total supply remained unchanged) and actual supply. The absolute figure yielded by this measure is normalized by the difference between actual output and its potential had output grown proportionately with national income. Thus, import substitution, γ, can be written as

$$\gamma = \frac{(U_o - U_1)Z_1}{X_1 - \lambda X_o},$$

where U is the import proportion in total supply (or the commodity import coefficient), Z is total supply (equal to the value of gross domestic output, X, plus the value of imports, M), λ is Y_1/Y_0, $<o>$ indicates initial values, and $<1>$ indicates terminal values.

This notion of import substitution is narrow in the sense that it measures only the relative decline (or increase) in the country's dependence on commodity imports. However, if investments leading to import substitution are financed from abroad, the decline in foreign exchange needs resulting from a relative reduction in commodity imports will be offset at least partially by an increase in amortization and factor payments abroad. Therefore, a more accurate measure of an industry's success in substituting payments abroad is the relative decline in its *overall dependence* on foreign exchange rather than on foreign exchange to be used exclusively for imports of final goods. To obtain this measure the equation is revised to include also *other* foreign

29. This is true, as we have seen, with various agricultural products. Most of the new products are not export oriented and place a strain on foreign exchange reserves by requiring capital goods and raw material imports, as well as frequently servicing of capital imports. In 1965 the country found itself in an even more serious balance-of-payments disequilibrium than in 1940 and with a matching desire to eliminate it. The balance-of-payments problem was worse in 1975 than it ever was in the past.

30. The traditional definition of import substitution and its various ramifications are presented, discussed, and elaborated in the writings of Hollis Chenery, Carlos Díaz-Alejandro, and Steuer and Voivodas. In particular see Hollis B. Chenery, "Patterns of Industrial Growth," *American Economic Review* 50 (Sept. 1960): 624–54; Carlos Díaz-Alejandro, "On the Import Intensity of Import Substitution," *Kyklos* 18 (July–Sept. 1965): 495–511; M. D. Steuer and C. Voivodas, "Import Substitution and Chenery's Pattern of Industrial Growth—A Further Study," *Economia Internazionale* 18 (Feb. 1965): 47–82.

exchange needs measured by the production foreign exchange coefficient, f. The new definition of foreign exchange (import) substitution then becomes

$$\mu = \frac{[(U_o + f_o) - (U_1 + f_1)]Z_1}{X_1 - \lambda X_o},$$

where f is the ratio of foreign exchange required to maintain the current level of gross domestic output, X, to total supply, Z.

The implications of the new formula are clear. The greater the decline in the ratio of overall foreign exchange requirements $(U + f)$ to total supply of a commodity, the greater the coefficient of foreign exchange substitution. However, the greater the rise in the production foreign exchange coefficient, f, generated by a reduction in the import coefficient, U, the smaller the foreign exchange substitution coefficient.

This new definition of foreign exchange substitution has distinct advantages over the narrower one. It provides a complete picture of the balance-of-payments debits leading to and generated by import substitution. Moreover, it demonstrates that a mere shift of debits from the trade account (decline in imports) to the factor payments account (rise in repatriated profits) or a simple shift of debits from the current to the capital account—instead of commodity imports capital payments abroad—does not always involve a solution of the balance-of-payments problem and does not always satisfy the foreign exchange investment criterion.

The accepted definition of import substitution deals with imports needed to satisfy final demand that can be used for consumption as well as investment. If import-substitution coefficients are calculated for all industries in the economy, the traditional definition will provide an accurate overall insight into the process of import substitution because it will include industries in the intermediate products and raw materials lines. However, it will never take into account a change in the country's or industry's dependence on foreign exchange caused by factors other than imports.

It should be evident that the import substitution investment criterion is not the same as the foreign exchange substitution investment criterion. Chile's difficulties in solving its balance-of-payments problems have largely resulted from the adoption of the former rather than the latter. Besides, as mentioned earlier the negative import-substitution policies adopted with respect to agriculture offset the positive effects of the same policy in industrial subsectors.

The country possesses steel, oil, and sugar beet industries, a publicly owned electricity network, and numerous other medium or minor enterprises in the area of industrial raw materials and intermediate and final products, all as a result of the efforts of CORFO. Import substitution and industrialization have only partly included the crucial producer durables sector, which is still very small. Its presence would have made Chile a complete economic system capable of entering a path of self-sustained growth with the assistance of its own capital goods sector and without dependence on imports of machinery and equipment. But this alternative was hardly open to Chile. At best it can enter a few lines of machinery and equipment production.

Even though the dependence on industrial consumer goods, intermediate products, fuel (this has been reversed since 1973), and some imports of raw materials from other nations has been reduced since 1939, the lopsided development pattern of the country has promoted an increased dependence on agricultural consumer goods and producer durables imports. The balance-of-payments disequilibria in 1965, in 1970, and worst of all in 1974–75 show a deterioration over that of 1939, and leave unfulfilled the second principal objective of the Chilean government. Dependence on the outside world has changed in type by shifting toward food and machinery imports, interest and amortization payments, and in 1974–75 to fuel. But efforts toward greater economic independence have not succeeded. Actually, dependence has increased. Since the possibility of obtaining a domestic producer durables sector has been and still is remote, the future of the country lies in its efforts to augment its exports in general and to import less food and less fuel. It remains to be seen whether both the economy and CORFO can overcome a traditional aversion to trade. Necessity may provide the crucial impetus.

By the end of 1974 CORFO's resources had been eaten away by internal inflation, sectoral clashes, and payments to its foreign creditors. There had been some replenishment through copper taxes, foreign aid, and new credits, but the mending of capital accumulation and some industry failed to supply the growth power enjoyed by the developed nations. Instead, it appeared as if such a secret fire could be acquired only by relying on and harnessing Chile's internal strength, which is bountifully dispersed among its mountains, seas, and sectors.

13

Negative Personal Saving in the Chilean National Accounts: Artifact or Reality?

Few items have puzzled the users of the Chilean national accounts as much as its negative personal saving of approximately -5.0 percent of family income during 1940–65.[1] Since this represents an integral part of the saving and investment accounts, the reliability of all those figures has been strongly questioned. Furthermore, an independent estimate of personal saving for the city of Santiago suggests that personal saving has been positive and possibly about 5.0 percent of family income.[2]

The views of the critics are summed up in the following quote from the Report on Chile by the Committee of Nine:

> The Committee believes that the estimates of saving and investment included in the national accounts are significantly inferior to the real ones....
>
> It must be noted that the level of saving and investment presented in these estimates is markedly inferior to those needed to be consistent with other indicators of economic activity. In support of this point the following can be cited:
>
> a) Net national saving of the private sector has been negative, according to these estimates, in all years falling between 1940 and 1962, with the exception of 1944, 1945, 1946, 1948 and 1953. This does not appear to be compatible with the development experi-

---

1. Personal saving in most other countries of the world for which information is available has ranged between 5.0 and 18.0 percent of family income.
2. See Pedro Jeftanovic P., "Estudio sobre el Ahorro Familiar en el Gran Santiago" (Santiago: Centro de Estudios Socio-Económicos, Oct. 1970), mimeo, pp. 1–89. A summary of the study by Pedro Jeftanovic was published in *El Mercurio* Feb. 20, 1971, p. 3. The methodology of this study is different from the one used in the national accounts but its main finding is largely valid in spite of its numerous methodological limitations.

enced by the Chilean economy in general and the private sector in particular, during those twenty five years.

b) Imported machinery and equipment constitutes, according to the national accounts of Chile, 50.1 percent of gross fixed capital formation as an average of the years 1940–1963. This is an exorbitantly high percentage, if compared with the other countries of Latin America. For example, this average for the years 1950–59 has been in Colombia, 26.3 percent, and in Venezuela 23 percent, according to the national accounts and imports statistics of these two republics.

c) Net investment in fixed capital realized by Chile in the last 23 years amounts, in total, to only E^0 609,1 millions, in 1961 prices, which results in a net capital–output ratio for these years of 0.20.[3]

I believe that much of the data underlying the saving and investment accounts are reliable. To provide an explanation for the idiosyncratic presence of negative personal saving, I shall first present the background information and theoretical framework used in preparing the accounts. A detailed analysis of the problems and issues related to specific items in the accounts will then be developed, along with suggestions and recommendations about possible improvements in the estimates and methodology.

The dissaving that has occurred in every year since 1954 reached in 1960 a stunning − 523.2 million escudos, 10.52 percent of gross domestic product. Even during 1940–1953 personal saving was positive only during five years (1944–46, 1950, and 1953).

The factors that are jointly responsible for and can explain household dissaving fall into the three broad categories: methodological and statistical, behavioral, and real and structural. Most of my analysis

3. "Las Cuentas Nacionales de Chile Durante los Ultimos Años," *Economia*, 2nd and 3rd trimesters, 1964, pp. 93, 95. The note published in *Economía* on pp. 93–115 is an excerpt from the unpublished report, Comité de los Nueve (Report of the Committee of Nine), *Informe sobre la Ejecución del Programa de Desarrollo Económico y Social de Chile*, Dec. 1963, pp. 79–83, and 114–18.

The allegations included in the Report of the Committee of Nine were disputed and repudiated by the research group of the Chilean Development Corporation in charge of the national accounts in the short document: CORFO, Dirección de Planificación, Departamento de Investigaciónes Económicas, *Comentarios Acerca de las Referencias a las Cuentas Nacionales en los Informes sobre el Programa Nacional de Desarrollo Económico y Social Presentados al Gobierno por el Comité de los Nueve de la Alianza para el Progreso* (Santiago: CORFO, Feb. 1964), pp. 1–8. Translation of quotes or documents from Spanish into English has been made by the author.

will concern the methodological and statistical factors, although some attention will also be devoted to the other categories.[4]

SAVING AND INVESTMENT ACCOUNT:
ESTIMATION AND METHODOLOGY

Chile, like many other underdeveloped countries, has found it impossible to make estimates for all items suggested by the United Nations. The components of the investment and saving accounts for which estimates have been consistently made throughout 1940–65 are presented in three sets of definitional equations.[5]

4. After reading the present chapter in 1969, the ODEPLAN office informed me, among other points, of the following. First, personal saving is calculated as a residual in many countries in addition to Chile; second, an independent estimate of personal saving is extremely difficult not only because of the natural statistical difficulties but also because the concept of saving used in national accounts differs considerably from the concept as generally understood and used outside the national accounts; and, third, if other items are calculated correctly there should be absolutely no fear in calculating family saving as a residual. A major aim of this chapter is to show the weaknesses of the national accounts methodology as applied in estimating personal saving in Chile, and only to a far lesser extent to question the reliability of specific estimates. I am questioning definitions, notions, and methodological procedures primarily as they were inherited in Chile from elsewhere.

5. There are three sets of basic documents that deal with the saving investment accounts. The first set covers the 1940–54 period and gives detailed estimates made according to the U.S. Department of Commerce methodology. These estimates are presented in CORFO, Departamento de Planificación y Estudios, Sección Investigaciónes Económicas, *Cuentas Nacionales de Chile, 1940–1954* (Santiago: Editorial del Pacífico, S.A., 1957), text and Appendix tables. This book, which is an invaluable source of information, contains the most detailed methodology of the national accounts. Very useful background information on saving and investment for the years 1938–50 is also found in the thesis by Ewald Hasche Sánchez, "El Proceso de Capitalización en Chile, 1938–1950," Memoria en Economía (Santiago: Universidad de Chile, 1950), mimeo.

The second set, covering the period 1940–65, presents in three mimeographed documents estimates made according to the United Nations methodology. The three documents are the following: CORFO, Dirección de Planificación, Departamento de Investigaciónes Económicas, "Cuentas Nacionales de Chile, 1940–1962" (provisional revised figures) (Santiago: CORFO, June 1963), mimeo; CORFO, Dirección de Planificación, Departamento de Investigaciónes Económicas, "Cuentas Nacionales de Chile, 1958–1963" (provisional revised figures) (Santiago: CORFO, June 1964), mimeo; Presidencia de la República, Oficina de Planificación Nacional, "Cuentas Nacionales de Chile, 1964–1965" (estimated figures) (Santiago: ODEPLAN, July 1966), mimeo. The first document, which will hereafter be cited as "Cuentas Nacionales, 1940–1962," contains final estimates for the years 1940–57. The second document, to be cited hereafter as "Cuentas Nacionales, 1958–1963," embodies the revised national accounts estimates for 1958–63. The third document, which will hereafter be cited as "Cuentas Nacionales, 1964–1965," presents the latest estimates for 1964–65. The final revised estimates of all national accounts are also found in the author's "Historical Statistics of Chile, 1840–

According to the first, which is the standard Keynesian formulation, gross domestic capital formation equals gross domestic saving:

$$I = S. \tag{13.1}$$

The second equation defines the subcomponents of the investment account as follows:

$$I = I_o + I_i, \tag{13.2}$$

where I_o is the change in inventories and I_i gross domestic fixed capital formation. This is broken down into

$$I_i = I_c + I_m \tag{13.2a}$$
$$I_c = I_{cb} + I_{cg} + I_{ce} \tag{13.2b}$$
$$\text{and } I_m = I_{mn} + I_{mf}, \tag{13.2c}$$

where I again is investment and the subscript c represents construction, m machinery and equipment, cb construction in buildings, cg construction in public works, ce other construction, mn nationally produced machinery and equipment, and mf imported machinery and equipment.

The components of the savings account are presented in the third equation:

$$S = S_f + S_n, \tag{13.3}$$

according to which gross domestic saving equals the sum of foreign saving (S_f) and national saving (S_n). Foreign saving is defined as the surplus or deficit of nation on external account. That is,

$$S_f = (M - X), \tag{13.3a}$$

where M is current payments to abroad and X current receipts from abroad.

Furthermore, since national saving has three components—government saving (S_{ng}), saving by firms (S_{nb}), and personal saving (S_{np})—we obtain

$$S_n = S_{ng} + S_{nb} + S_{np}. \tag{13.3b}$$

1965." All tables in the present chapter have this document as their source.

The third set of primary documents includes the revised national accounts estimates by ODEPLAN for the 1960–71 period. The latest publication in this series is ODEPLAN, *Cuentas Nacionales de Chile. 1960–1971* (Santiago: ODEPLAN, 1972). These ODEPLAN estimates are possibly more accurate than the previous ones but also follow the methodology described in this chapter. Although used elsewhere in this monograph, they are omitted here in order to avoid repetition.

The last equation referring to the savings account states that business saving (S_{nb}) is composed of capital consumption allowances (S_{na}) and retained earnings of corporations (S_{nz}). Equation (13.3c) can therefore be written as

$$S_{nb} = S_{na} + S_{nz}. \tag{13.3c}$$

The items of the investment and saving account that are included in the aforementioned equations are presented for selected years in table 13.1.

Personal saving has been used as an accounting device to bring into balance household revenues and expenditures on the one hand and on the other hand, gross saving and gross investment. Personal saving has been calculated as a residual both in the 1940–1954 period, when it was calculated first and primarily as the difference between household receipts and expenditures and secondarily as the difference between gross domestic investment on the one side and the sum of foreign, business and government saving on the other side.[6] Personal saving was also calculated during 1955–65, first and primarily as the difference between gross domestic investment on the one side and the sum of foreign, business, and government saving on the other side, and secondarily as the difference between household receipts and expenditures. Certain estimation biases for both procedures were present throughout the 1940–65 period even though their degree of importance changed depending on the particular procedure emphasized. This calculation as a residual produced estimates that indicated dissaving.[7]

In the 1940–1954 national accounts, independent estimates of consumer revenues and expenditures were made and the difference was (dis)saving. But no definite attempt was ever made to obtain an independent estimate of personal saving. This residual estimate of the household account was subsequently entered in the saving account, and any discrepancies were resolved by entering a statistical error item.[8]

6. Saving by persons and nonprofit institutions appears both in the household account (*Cuentas Nacionales, 1940–1954*, p. 78, account III) and in the gross saving and investment account (ibid., p. 83, account VI). Interestingly enough, in the national accounts estimates, according to the Department of Commerce methodology for 1940–54, personal saving is positive only in 1946 and 1953.

7. It has been impossible to apply the 1940–54 method of estimating personal saving to 1955–65, and to apply the 1955–65 method to 1940–54, mainly because the basic worksheets needed for such an exercise were not available.

8. This statistical error item is not included in the earlier definitional equations.

Table 13.1. Gross Domestic Capital Formation Account, Selected Years, 1940–65
(In millions of escudos, current prices)

Gross domestic capital formation	1940	1945	1950	1952	1955	1960	1962	1965
A. Gross fixed capital formation	2.4	4.7	14.3	24.5	86.8	513.0	812.0	2,599.0
1. Construction and other works	1.3	3.4	7.6	12.9	53.5	205.0	411.0	1,158.0
a. Buildings	1.1	2.6	5.9	8.6	37.7	110.4	242.0	575.0
b. Public works	0.2	0.5	1.4	3.2	11.0	77.0	135.0	467.0
c. Other construction	0.0	0.3	0.3	1.1	4.8	17.6	34.0	116.0
2. Machinery and equipment	1.1	1.3	6.7	11.6	33.3	308.0	401.0	1,441.0
a. Imported	1.0	1.1	5.9	10.2	28.8	276.0	362.0	1,297.0
b. National	0.1	0.2	0.8	1.4	4.5	32.0	39.0	144.0
B. Change in stocks	0.1	1.3	3.3	-2.0	-2.0	22.0	21.0	51.0
C. Gross domestic capital formation	2.5	6.0	17.6	22.5	84.8	535.0	833.0	2,650.0
Gross domestic saving								
D. Income retained by producers	3.1	5.9	17.1	43.0	148.4	816.1	663.0	2,144.0
1. Capital-consumption allowances	2.5	5.1	14.6	25.9	88.5	675.7	469.0	1,721.0
2. Retained earnings of corporations	0.6	0.8	2.5	17.1	59.9	140.4	194.0	423.0
E. Personal saving	-1.4	0.9	1.0	-17.6	-76.9	-523.2	-178.0	-475.0
F. Government surplus on current account	1.1	1.3	3.0	3.5	13.1	125.7	90.0	817.0
G. Less surplus of nation on current account	0.1	-0.6	0.2	-1.2	-2.4	148.4	163.0	164.0
Statistical discrepancy	-0.4	-1.5	-3.7	-5.2	2.6	-32.3	95.0	—
H. Gross domestic saving	2.5	6.0	17.6	22.5	84.8	535.0	833.0	2,650.0

This procedure concealed biases that have strongly contributed to underestimates of personal saving.

The biases, which also led to overestimates of consumer expenditures and underestimates of consumer revenues,[9] developed for a number of reasons. First, some expenditure estimates, such as those for medical, other personal, and lodging, were made by multiplying the number of persons[10] in a profession by an estimated volume of gross revenues.[11] However, not all these gross revenues were traced to various income groups to ensure appropriate adjustments on the income side. Instead, and this is the second reason, income estimates were based on official, mostly published information and have thus generally tended to be on the conservative side. A downward bias in income estimates was also introduced because of tax evasion on high incomes and understatement of the wage bill to evade the very high Chilean social and welfare taxes on wages. The resulting underestimate of income has very probably ranged between 10 and 20 percent. In the same way, expenditures were imputed without corresponding imputations on the income side.

Both expenditure and revenue estimates have possessed a degree of arbitrariness that makes any claim about accurate personal saving estimates void of any meaning. The degree of arbitrariness is indicated by the fact that consumer expenditures in 1952 were 191 million pesos according to one estimate,[12] 179 million pesos according to a revised one,[13] 205 million pesos according to the final estimates using the U.S. Department of Commerce methodology,[14] and 211.6 million pesos according to the final estimate using the United Nations methodology.[15] To suggest the arbitrary role of personal saving as an adjustment factor, one need only note that the sign has been changed

9. It is possible that both receipts and expenditures have been overestimated in Chile but that the expenditure overestimate has exceeded the one affecting receipts.

10. Or the number of hotels, restaurants, and so forth.

11. For a detailed overall evaluation of the Chilean national accounts and a detailed examination of income and expenditures, see my "Historical Statistics," pt. 1, "The Chilean National Accounts: An Evaluation."

12. Instituto de Economía de la Universidad de Chile, *Cuentas Nacionales de Chile, 1950–1951–1952* (Santiago: Editorial Universitaria, 1953), p. 29. In contrast to all other national accounts documents, the present one has a positive estimate for personal saving in 1951 (ibid., p. 17). Much of the basic information used in the national accounts is not publicly available and checks cannot therefore be made.

13. Universidad de Chile, Instituto de Economía, *Cuentas Nacionales, Informe al Ministro de Hacienda* (Santiago: Editorial Universitaria, 1954), p. 18.

14. See "Cuentas Nacionales, 1940–1962."

15. *Cuentas Nacionales, 1940–1954*, table III, p. 145.

Fig. 13.1. Gross domestic capital formation and saving account for Chile, 1952.
(The figures are percentages of gross domestic capital formation.)

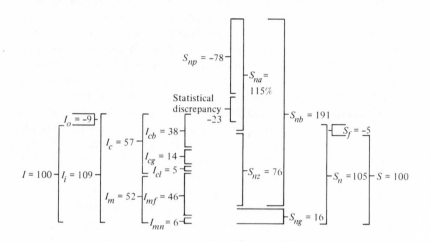

from positive (implying saving) to negative (implying dissaving) from one estimate to another.[16]

These methodological biases become even more explicit in the estimates of saving covering the 1955–1965 period. Since personal saving was defined as $I - (S_f + S_{ng} + S_{nb})$, and since I, S_f, S_{ng}, and S_{nb} were estimated independently, the estimate of personal saving followed as a residual in the saving–investment account. But underestimates of I and overestimates of S_{ng} and S_{nb} have led to an underestimate of the actual value of personal saving.[17] The residual nature of personal saving makes it just another statistical discrepancy item and therefore reduces its usefulness for planning purposes.

Figures 13.1 and 13.2 link and contrast the investment account statistics with the saving account statistics. The first, which covers 1952,

16. The 1950 estimate for personal saving was positive first (Instituto de Economía de la Universidad de Chile, *Cuentas Nacionales de Chile, 1950–1951–1952*, p. 17), negative in the second Instituto estimate (Universidad de Chile, Instituto de Economía, *Cuentas Nacionales, Informe al Ministro de Hacienda*, p. 19), then negative in the early CORFO estimates but positive in the final CORFO estimates. (See *Cuentas Nacionales, 1940–1954*, table III, p. 148, for the dissaving figure for 1950, and "Cuentas Nacionales, 1940–1962," household account, for the positive figure.) A similar pattern from saving to dissaving estimates, for the same year, can be also found in the aforementioned publications for the years 1951 and 1952.

17. On the other side, as it will be seen below, foreign saving may have been underestimated and thus have resulted in an overestimate of personal saving.

expresses the components as percentages of gross domestic capital formation. The second, which covers 1960, presents the components in their absolute values and as percentages of gross domestic product.

Both figures give the investment components in the left half and the saving components in the right half. Figure 13.1 uses the symbols presented in equations (13.1)–(13.3c), whereas figure 13.2 provides a complete identification of the various items included in it. These data will be used in describing and evaluating the method of estimation of each item.

Gross Domestic Investment and Its Components

Gross domestic investment is estimated independently of other national accounts items and can be regarded as being, *mutatis mutandis*, comparatively accurate. Gross domestic investment is calculated by using both direct, relatively complete, information (e.g., in the case of public works and imported capital goods) and indirect, less accurate information (as in the case of construction and nationally produced capital goods).[18]

Gross domestic investment in machinery and equipment, which was the largest component of gross fixed capital formation during the 1940–1960 period, is estimated from the supply or production side as the sum of imported and nationally produced producer durables. As shown in figure 13.1, I_m accounted for 52 percent of total investment; in 1960, as shown in figure 13.2, it accounted for 6.2 percent of gross domestic product and almost 60 percent of I. Furthermore, throughout the period under discussion imported capital goods have accounted for almost 90 percent of the machinery and equipment component of investment. This is true also for 1952 and 1960 and can be seen at the lower left side of figures 13.1 and 13.2.

The data on which the estimates for the imported investment component are based are highly reliable and are obtained from publications of the Central Bank, especially the annual *Balanza de Pagos*. The imported component of investment is estimated by converting the dollar figures appearing in the *Balanza de Pagos* into escudos and adding local expenditures related to marketing, transportation, and installment of machinery. The underlying quantitative information is accurate, and the estimate of this item is one of the most reliable in the

18. United Nations, Economic Commission for Latin America, *Seminario de las Naciones Unidas sobre Cuentas Nacionales para América Latina* (Rio de Janeiro, Brazil. II June 26, 1959) (ST/TAO/SER.C/44), pp. 164–65. Hereafter cited as UNECLA, *Seminario*.

Table 13.2. External Transactions Accounts, Selected Years, 1940–65
(In millions of escudos, current prices)

	1940	1945	1950	1952	1955	1960	1962	1965
Receipts from abroad								
Exports of goods and services	3.7	7.0	17.0	33.8	96.8	562.0	671.0	2,578.0
Factor income from abroad	—	—	—	—	0.4	—	—	—
Transfer payments to individuals	—	—	—	—	—	38.9	15.0	60.0
Transfer payments to government	—	—	—	—	—	—	—	—
Current receipts from abroad	3.7	7.0	17.0	33.8	97.2	621.2	686.0	2,638.0
Payments to abroad								
Imports of goods and services	2.7	5.6	14.5	28.3	80.1	690.9	745.0	2,412.0
Factor income paid abroad	1.1	0.8	2.7	4.3	14.6	79.0	104.0	390.0
Transfer payments from individuals	—	—	—	—	0.1	—	—	—
Transfer payments from government	3.8	6.4	17.2	32.6	94.8	769.9	849.0	2,802.0
Current payments								
Surplus of nation on external account	−0.1	0.6	−0.2	1.2	2.4	−148.7	−163.0	−164.0
Current payments to abroad and surplus	3.7	7.0	17.0	33.8	97.2	621.2	686.0	2,638.0

national accounts. Although smuggling in machinery and equipment has been periodically uncovered, it is hardly so important in Chile as elsewhere in Latin America. The import statistics have been adjusted for smuggling, and there is little reason to consider its impact on the estimate of I_{mf} as significant. Gross construction investment is in part estimated from the expenditure side, as in the case of public works and explorations, and in part through a sui generis income–product approach for housing construction, in which a housing index and a cost-of-production-per-square-meter-of-construction index are combined to obtain an estimate of construction investment.

Despite the high degree of accuracy of some components of investment, the global gross domestic investment estimates are imperfect for a number of reasons. First, *nonmonetary capital formation*[19] is underestimated. Little or no official information is available concerning capital goods produced by and within such sectors as agriculture, small- and medium-scale mining, and some services. However, it appears, mainly from firsthand observation, that such capital formation as the building of rural unregistered homes and of mining equipment, and the opening of roads and canals, which is not adequately covered in the accounts, is important. When workers are paid in agriculture to make physical improvements that are rural investment, their income may be accurately reflected in the national accounts, but their output —rural investment—is ignored or underestimated.

The second, and possibly gravest omission is *maintenance, repair, and improvement expenditures*. Their exclusion from the national accounts[20] produces a substantial underestimate of investment. Certain maintenance and repair expenditures are necessary for the performance of a capital good during the normal life expectancy assigned to it in the country that produces it.[21] I do not believe that such expenditures should be included in the national accounts as investment. But another type of repair and improvement expenditure multiplies the normal life expectancy of a capital good and therefore has a distinct function. Since for all practical purposes, new capital goods are created as a result of such expenditures, their exclusion from capital formation leads to omission of a significant part of national capital goods production. Both the annual gross capital formation and the capital stock are underestimated. It can be said that in Chile there exists a repair

19. Capital formation is nonmonetary in the sense that the respective capital goods do not pass through a market.
20. UNECLA, *Seminario*, p. 165.
21. This country would normally be a developed one.

quasi capital goods sector that uses secondhand capital goods as inputs for the production of new ones. The very scarcity of imported machinery and equipment provides the inducement for such operations, and the extremely high prices paid for secondhand and old capital goods proves that repairs have indeed been prolonging their useful life. In Chile it is not difficult to find moderately priced, efficient machines and other capital goods from the nineteenth century.

Furthermore, investment figures are likely to have been underestimated because of the use of inadequate methods for converting dollar values into escudo values as well as because of inadequate deflation indexes. The variety of regulations covering imports of capital goods, the presence of free ports in Arica and Punta Arenas, the continuous but uneven inflation, and the diversified origin of capital goods cast doubt on CORFO's (and since 1965 ODEPLAN'S) procedure of using one exchange rate for all conversions of dollar values into escudo values. Although this is regarded by many as the only operational procedure, it has tended to underestimate the relative escudo value of capital goods imports because of the overvaluation of the peso in general and because of the even higher degree of overvaluation with respect to many capital goods imports.

The annual undervaluation of gross investment arising from these major biases is estimated to be in the neighborhood of 20–40 percent although it could be larger or smaller in some years. In order to measure the impact of this underestimate on personal saving, two revised sets of the investment account were prepared. In the first set, gross investment was adjusted upward by 20 percent; in the second set a 40 percent adjustment was made. A corresponding adjustment was made only in the construction component of investment even though at least part of this adjustment should be attributed to the machinery and equipment component. A more exact estimate would require access to ODEPLAN's information.

Gross Domestic Saving and Its Components

Gross domestic saving has not been estimated independently but has been assumed to be equal to gross capital formation. Hence the global figures of investment and saving, which appear in the extreme left and right sides of figures 13.1 and 13.2, are always identical.

Because personal saving has been estimated residually, its magnitude depends on the value of investment on the one side and on the values of the various saving components deducted from investment to reach personal saving on the other. Given the three biases in the investment, estimate, it is clear that personal saving has been underestimated by as much as investment has been underestimated. The next step is to examine and evaluate the various saving components that are being deducted from gross saving to obtain personal saving.

The *surplus or deficit of the nation on external account*, which we have also called foreign saving,[22] is calculated in the external transactions account. This item, which is presented in table 13.2 for selected years, is subsequently entered in the saving account. If the external transactions account shows a deficit, foreign saving in the saving account is positive, and vice versa. Foreign saving is entered in the lower right side of figures 13.1 and 13.2.

The external transactions account shows that Chile had a deficit in 1940, a surplus during 1941–1946, 1948, 1952, and 1954, and deficits in the remaining years until 1965. A continuous deficit of the nation on external account started after 1956. During seven years between 1940 and 1950 the nation had a surplus on external account, but only during three of these years were savings of persons and nonprofit institutions positive. It does not therefore follow that a surplus on external account is causally linked with positive personal saving. Moreover, both in 1950 and 1953 personal savings were positive even though the nation was incurring a deficit on external account. An examination of the foreign trade statistics also shows that between 1940 and 1956 imports exceeded exports only in 1949 and even then only by a small margin. Again, it does not follow that negative personal savings are exclusively caused by a deficit on external account. Such a deficit can be a major, but by no means the only, cause for negative personal saving.

It is important to analyze three major definitions of foreign saving. The first and narrowest treats it simply as the excess of imports over exports:

$$S_f^1 = M' - X', \qquad (13.4)$$

where M' stands for imports and X' for exports. The unique characteristic of this definition is that it excludes factor payments on both sides.

A second, broader definition has been used in the Chilean national

22. If Chile has an excess of current account receipts over payments, Chile "invests" abroad. If Chile has an excess of current account payments over receipts, foreign countries are "investing" in Chile. Neither of these items, however, appears on the investment side of the investment–saving account but rather on the saving side. This is why the terms positive or negative foreign saving seem more accurate and consistent than positive or negative foreign "investment" and are used in this essay.

Fig. 13.2. Gross domestic capital formation and saving account for Chile, 1960 (absolute figures and as a percentage of GDP; in millions of escudos, current prices).

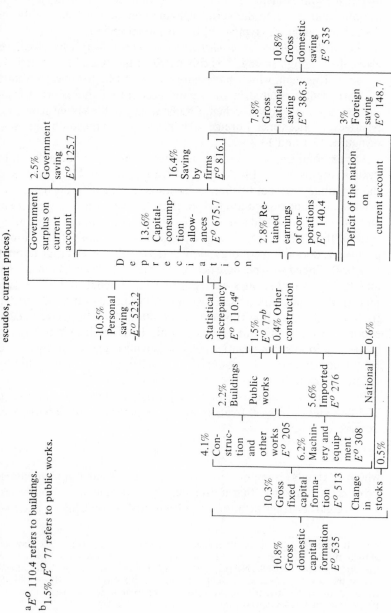

^aE^o 110.4 refers to buildings.
^b1.5%, E^o 77 refers to public works.

accounts and was presented earlier. It states that foreign saving is equal to the surplus or deficit of the nation on external account:

$$S_f^2 = M - X. \qquad (13.5)$$

According to this definition foreign saving is the sum of the trade gap, as defined in equation (13.4), and net repatriated income of foreign factors of production (Y_f). That is,

$$S_f^2 = M' - X' + Y_f. \qquad (13.5a)$$

Thus, if factor payments are excluded from both the export and the import side, the first definition is obtained; if they are included, the second is obtained. In either case foreign saving is determined by an accounting procedure and has little or nothing to do with the actual stock of foreign investment or saving in the country or with the total financial flows with abroad.

The size of S_f^2 determines the net foreign borrowing that the economy has to undertake in order to maintain its actual level of imports and foreign factor payments. Since the term $(M' - X')$ represents payments for the use of foreign-produced commodities and Y_f reflects the actual price the economy has to pay over a one-year period for the services provided by foreign capital and labor, I can see no reason why one type of payment for the use of foreign resources is included in the first definition of foreign saving [viz., $(M' - X')$] while another type of payment (i.e., Y_f) is excluded.

However, even the second definition provides an inadequate picture of what an economy is receiving from or giving abroad. To cure this deficiency, which will be further explained below, a third concept of foreign saving is presented. This includes also the volume of external resources the economy needs to meet its actual depreciation and amortization (A) payments on its external debt. Thus

$$S_f^3 = (M' - X') + Y_f + A. \qquad (13.6)$$

The rationale behind this definition is simple. In order for an economy to maintain the observed levels of investment and consumption, it is forced to borrow from abroad sufficient funds to meet its current contractual amortization payments, its current income payments to foreign factors of production, and also whatever payments are due for the excess of imports over exports.

The value of S_f^3 describes the gross foreign resource requirements of an economy. These needs can be usefully contrasted with the net foreign resource requirements arising from a simple excess of imports over exports. Models of the import or foreign exchange gap normally deal with the net rather than the gross gap and corresponding resource (aid) needs. Presumably, it is the real resource influx that matters, and this is adequately measured by the magnitude of $M' - X'$.[23] But this rather simplistic approach assumes first that the refinancing of foreign debt is an easy matter, second that the magnitude of $M - X$[24] that an economy can maintain or aim for has no relationship to the size of the economy's foreign debt, and third that insofar as planning of external financing is concerned, the use of net magnitudes is superior to the use of gross magnitudes.

Both for consistency and practical reasons it may be essential to redefine foreign saving as broader than the surplus of the nation on external account. The consistency factor is the most compelling one. Currently, the savings account includes an internal saving flow and a foreign saving flow. The former is a gross figure, with a replacement and a net saving component, whereas the foreign saving flow is a net amount that excludes the component of the foreign saving flow needed to replace the foreign debt component that is amortized. The present formulation of the foreign saving component is also inadequate in the sense that it does not provide an accurate measure of the total or gross contribution of foreign countries to the domestic development effort and also underestimates the future needs for external financial resources.

Table 13.3 presents S_f^2 and S_f^3 as percentages of gross domestic product, investment, and imported machinery and equipment. Note that S_f^3 has been consistently and substantially higher than S_f^2. Furthermore, during many years, especially between 1942 and 1952, when the economy was lending resources abroad according to the S_f^2 definition of foreign saving, it was actually borrowing heavily from abroad according to the more general S_f^3 definition of foreign saving. Most significantly, S_f^2 and S_f^3 have not always moved in the same direction. It is in fact possible for them to develop completely different patterns because foreign dollar expenditures of Chile can be classified as belonging to either the current or the capital account, depending on a number of factors. As an example repatriated profits of foreign investors consistently appear in the capital account because of special legal dispositions. Also, foreign enterprises are influenced in classifying their repatriated funds as profits or amortization by changing laws. Note

23. Most of the so-called two-gap models deal with foreign saving as determined by $(M'-X')$.
24. Or $M'-X'$.

Table 13.3. Foreign Saving and its Relation to Investment in Chile, 1942–1964

	S_f^2 as % of GDP (1)	S_f^3 as % of GDP (2)	S_f^3 as % of I (3)	I_{mf} as % of GDP (4)	Col. (2) as % of col. (4) (5)	Col. (1) as % of col. (4) (6)
1942	−1.9	0.31	3.53	2.4	13.0	−79.2
1943	−2.8	0.55	5.84	2.2	25.0	−127.3
1944	−0.9	1.89	15.86	1.9	99.5	−47.4
1945	−1.2	2.27	20.29	2.1	108.1	−57.1
1946	−0.3	2.51	15.43	2.8	89.6	−10.7
1947	1.9	3.48	55.60	4.4	79.1	43.2
1948	−0.7	1.47	12.06	3.6	40.8	−19.4
1949	2.0	3.41	29.81	4.5	75.8	44.4
1950	0.1	2.16	19.44	3.7	58.4	27.0
1951	1.0	2.43	23.85	4.3	56.5	23.3
1952	−0.5	2.07	24.18	3.9	53.1	−12.8
1953	0.7	2.46	19.66	3.2	76.9	21.9
1954	0.3	2.24	34.95	2.2	101.8	13.6
1955	−0.2	2.00	24.54	2.7	74.1	−7.4
1956	0.1	2.02	20.20	4.3	47.0	2.3
1957	3.1	5.81	58.16	7.5	77.5	41.3
1958	2.1	5.49	54.68	7.5	73.2	28.0
1959	0.7	4.76	47.22	5.3	89.8	13.2
1960	3.0	6.94	64.58	5.6	123.9	53.6
1961	4.7	9.54	71.09	6.7	142.4	70.1
1962	2.5	8.97	72.16	5.4	166.1	46.3
1963	2.2	9.94	77.90	6.7	148.4	32.8
1964	2.5	8.34	62.24			

Notes: Column (1) presents the surplus of the nation on external account as a percentage of gross domestic product. All statistical information necessary to make this calculation was extracted from official CORFO and ODEPLAN documents. A negative sign in front of the figures means that the country had a surplus, while a positive sign implies the presence of a deficit of the nation on external account.

Column (2) presents the foreign exchange deficit of Chile as a percentage of its gross domestic product. This deficit was measured by contrasting all current earnings of Chile, i.e., exports of goods and services, plus transfers, plus various miscellaneous earnings listed in the current account of the *Balanza de Pagos*, with all current expenditures, including amortization and other nonreturned revenues of foreign investors. This deficit was identical to the sum of long- and short-term capital inflows.

also that the rising share of S_f^3 in total saving, which is shown in column (4), leads to a secular reduction in the share of national saving and, *ceteris paribus*, also to a reduction of personal saving. Thus, the possibility of obtaining a residual estimate of personal saving with a negative sign increases if S_f^3 is adopted for the national accounts instead of S_f^2. Finally, column (6) shows that foreign saving defined by S_f^3 has frequently exceeded the total value of capital goods imports. This explicitly indicates that such saving has been used for consumer goods imports. Not only are the limitations of the existing methodology readily apparent, but the different definitions of foreign saving have pronounced if indirect impact on the magnitude of personal saving.

The second item in the saving account, which is estimated independently, is the *government surplus on current account*. This item is introduced from the general government current expenditure account, which is presented in table 13.4. Although government has shown a surplus on current account throughout the 1940–64 period, there are strong reasons to suspect the accuracy of this estimate. First, the government may run a continuous deficit but present a nominally balanced budget at the end of the calendar of fiscal year. Because of continuous and rapid inflation, the revenues collected at the end of the year (when, until 1965, it had been customary in Chile for most of the taxes to be paid) have the same nominal value but a substantially lower real value than the same expenditures incurred during the course of the year. It has been estimated that during 1929 and 1957, owing to the administrative lags between the date of the accrual of a tax liability and the date of tax payment, the real value of some (primarily direct) taxes was reduced 1 percent for each 1 percent increase in the price level.[25] The procedure of lumping together receipts and expenditures as if the timing of the respective transactions were of no material consequence may be acceptable in an economy with no significant inflation, but in an inflationary economy a deficit or surplus can be measured accurately only if revenues and expenditures are deflated properly and expressed in real terms. Only monthly (or even daily if inflation is rampant) revenue and expenditure statistics, deflated by an appropriate price index, can provide an accurate comparison. One year's inflation in Chile has been as much as forty years' in the United States, and it would be patently absurd to call the government's budget balanced if expenditures of thirty or forty years ago were covered by the depreciated currency of today. For the same reason the receipts that come at the end of the year must be discounted for inflation if they are to be comparable to earlier expenditures. Without the use of an appropriate discount factor the receipt and expenditure items are not strictly comparable.

The government surplus on current account has also been inflated by shifting current expenditures into the capital account for window

25. See Kenneth G. Ruffing, "The Effects of Inflation on the Yield and the Structure of the Fiscal System of Chile" (Ph.D. diss., Columbia University, 1971), p. 125.

Table 13.4. General Government Current Revenue and Expenditure Account, Selected Years, 1940–65

(In millions of escudos, current prices)

	1940	1945	1950	1952	1955	1960	1962	1965
Current Revenues								
Payments by producers								
1. Corporate profit taxes	0.5	1.3	3.5	9.2	31.0	152.1	193.0	728.0
2. Property income paid to government	0.3	0.4	1.9	2.5	10.4	60.8	53.0	167.0
Payments by individuals								
1. Social security contributions	0.7	2.0	6.6	11.6	51.6	364.3	480.0	1,621.0
a. By wage and salary earners	0.3	0.9	2.1	4.5	16.6	98.6	130.0	423.0
b. By employers	0.4	1.1	4.5	7.1	35.0	265.7	350.0	1,198.0
2. Taxes on personal income	0.2	0.8	2.0	2.9	9.1	49.9	72.0	390.0
Transfer payments from abroad	—	—	—	—	—	25.6	10.0	9.0
Total receipts	3.1	7.9	25.0	44.1	182.4	1,141.9	1,488.0	4,989.0
Current expenditures								
Government current expenditures	1.6	5.0	13.7	24.4	106.8	510.7	761.0	2,143.0
Subsidies	0.1	0.3	2.0	4.7	14.4	136.4	156.0	515.0
Transfer payments to individuals	0.3	1.3	6.3	11.5	48.0	369.1	481.0	1,514.0
Transfer payments to abroad	—	—	—	—	0.1	—	—	—
Surplus on current account	1.1	1.3	3.0	3.5	13.1	125.7	90.0	817.0
Total current expenditures and surplus	3.1	7.9	25.0	44.1	182.4	1,141.9	1,488.0	4,989.0

dressing purposes. Basically, the Chilean capital account includes expenditures, such as administrative wages and salaries, that are not included on the investment side of the investment–saving account. To be specific, general administrative expenditures of the Land Reform Corporation and other agricultural corporations appear under agricultural investment in the capital account.[26]

It is possible, even though it cannot be proved here, that government has run a deficit in its current account for many years.[27] The presence of such a deficit automatically raises personal saving above the figure currently reported in the national accounts.

Saving by firms is composed of undistributed profits, adjustments in the valuation of stocks, reserves for depreciation, indemnification for accidental damage of fixed assets, and the statistical discrepancy.[28] Undistributed profits are estimated residually by deducting from total profits direct taxes and distributed profits. "The figures have an error inherent in all estimates of profits, in addition to the one present in the estimates of distributed profits."[29]

The adjustments in the valuation of stocks are based on the inventories of industry and trade, on data concerning the assets of industry published in the continuous official statistics, and on information about the assets of the commercial joint-stock corporations. Since such information is reputed to indicate stocks inferior to the real ones, it is almost certainly true that the estimates of adjustments in the valuation of stocks contain errors. However, it has been impossible to correct them because no background information about the size of the underestimate is available.[30]

Finally, according to the official CORFO document, "Capital consumption allowances are an estimate of depreciation at replacement value based on data concerning the age of equipment and the assets of

26. For the figures concerning agriculture see tables 25 and 28 in República de Chile, *Balance Consolidado del Sector Público de Chile, Año 1964* (Santiago: Talleres Gráficos "La Nación," 1965). The same is true for other sectors also though to a lesser degree (see ibid., tables 22–23, esp. summary tables 23, 27, and 28).

27. According to published, official information the general government incurred a deficit in its total (current plus capital) account between 1950 and 1957 although the national accounts have reported a surplus in its current account.

28. UNECLA, *Seminario*, p. 164. In the final revised estimates of saving both by CORFO and the Planning Office, saving by firms is merged into undistributed profits and capital consumption allowances.

29. Ibid.

30. Ibid.

enterprises or the valuation of fixed capital goods. The use of this statistic, which suffers from sizeable and fluctuating underestimates, creates complex problems which have not yet been totally resolved even though this is in the process of being done."[31] Among the various components of business saving, it is the estimate of depreciation allowances that is most questionable. The margin of error in the other items is relatively small.

Changes in depreciation allowances have no effect on gross domestic product, on gross investment in the investment account, or on retained corporate profits in the saving account, because these variables are estimated independently of depreciation. For example, retained earnings of corporations are estimated independently and rather accurately. Then, an economy-wide independent but incorrect, excessively large estimate of capital consumption is prepared. Subsequently, saving by firms is expressed as the sum of retained earnings and depreciation. Through this procedure the overestimate of depreciation is passed on and becomes an overestimate of saving by firms.

Most students of Chilean national accounts have been confused because they start at the end, that is, with the false assumption that saving by firms is calculated first, independently and accurately. Then, accepting my argument that depreciation is overestimated, they conclude that retained profits are estimated residually and must be by necessity underestimated by an amount equal to the overestimate of depreciation. But as it was already pointed out, retained profits were not estimated residually.

However, changes in depreciation allowances affect the residually estimated personal saving, net investment, domestic income, and the difference between domestic income and gross domestic product. Thus, although it is true that if depreciation allowances are overstated, net investment is understated, it is not also true that retained profits are understated. If that were the case, a reduction of depreciation allowances would be compensated by an increase in retained earnings, leaving household saving unaffected. In fact, overstatement of depreciation allowances has reduced the value of personal saving in the saving account. Furthermore, in order to make the saving account consistent with the household account, the national accountants have,

---

31. Ibid. The estimates of the indemnification for the accidental damage of fixed assets are based on information originating from insurance companies. They constitute complete and reliable information (p. 165).

deliberately or unknowingly, underestimated household expenditures.

For depreciation purposes, capital goods have been divided into four major categories: (1) rolling material, with a useful life of six years; (2) furniture, tools, and fixtures, with a useful life of ten years; (3) machinery and equipment, with a useful life of twenty years; and (4) buildings and installations, with a useful life of fifty years. Until 1949, depreciation allowances were calculated on a global level. Since that time, however, and increasingly in recent years, attempts have been made to estimate capital consumption allowances on a sectoral level and on the basis of more detailed estimates of the life expectancy of a variety of capital goods.[32] The four categories were first developed by the Internal Revenue Office and subsequently introduced in the national accounts.

Capital consumption allowances, which have exceeded investment in

32. A serious effort to obtain more realistic estimates for the useful lifetime of capital goods was started by the Planning Office in 1966. Presented below is a list of the useful life (vida útil) assigned to capital goods by the Planning Office, which is currently in charge of the preparation of national accounts. In agriculture, irrigation works, drainage and constructions are assigned a useful life of 50 years; installations, closures, and fruit plantations, 10–50 years; vineyards, 30 years; forest plantations, 8–20 years; artificial meadows with more than one year's duration, 2–6 years; pastures with more than one years' duration, 2–4 years; livestock, up to 10 years; machinery, 10–30 years; and tools and fixtures, 10 years.

For construction, estimates were prepared until 1967 on a global basis, and thus even today there exist no estimates of the useful life of capital goods. No capital consumption allowances are estimated for government. The useful life assigned to capital goods in industry has been the following: buildings, 50 years; machinery, 20 years; furniture, tools, and fixtures, 10 years; and transport material, 6 years.

The estimates for useful life of capital goods in mining were made in 1958 and are currently being revised. They have been used to calculate depreciation since 1949. Before 1949 depreciation was calculated on a global level and an attempt was later made toward sectoral estimates. The following useful lives have been assigned to capital goods in mining: constructions and buildings, 50 years; rolling material including railroads, 15 years; plants and installations, 25 years; tools and fixtures, 10 years; furniture and utensils, 10 years; machinery and equipment, 20 years.

The useful life assigned to capital goods in services has been buildings and installations, 60 years; machinery and equipment, 20 years; furniture, utensils, and fixtures, 10 years; rolling material, 6 years.

Finally, the useful lifetime of capital goods in transport, storage, and communications was estimated to be as follows: vehicles, 6 years; fleets and vessels, 20 years; furniture and utensils, 10 years; buildings and installations, 50 years; machinery and tools, 20 years; floating material, 30 years; telephone plants, 25 years; railroad buildings, 40 years; railroad routes and works, 30 years; railroad tools and instruments, 15 years; railroad machinery, 25 years; rolling material and railroad traction engines, 30 years; motorized equipment, 15 years; trolley buses, 20 years; and buses, 12 years.

The aforementioned statistics were made available by ODEPLAN.

eight years[33] and have ranged between 50 and 100 percent of investment during the remaining years of the 1940–65 period, appear to be
strongly overestimated. The life expectancy assigned to them is not only
below that used in developed nations for such items as buildings but
also substantially below the real period of useful life they seem to enjoy
in Chile. Although only the recent research efforts by the Planning
Office can provide the evidence necessary to revise the tables applied to
capital goods, I suggest that, on the average and for the majority, actual
useful lives are at least twice as high as the figures used. Because it is
believed that depreciation allowances were overstated during 1940–60
by at least 50 percent, figures showing a 50 percent downward adjustment were presented by the author in an earlier and more extensive
version of this chapter.[34] Although these revisions are essentially
suggested recommendations, I believe they come very close to reality.
The two new estimates of personal saving, along with the original,
official one, are presented in figure 13.3. It is worth noting that the
second revised estimate, which results from a 50 percent reduction in
depreciation allowances and a 40 percent increase in investment, leaves
personal saving negative only in 1954.

Further indirect evidence supports the view that depreciation allowances are too liberal and useful life estimates too conservative. All types
of automobiles and vehicles enjoy extremely high market values; the
1940 models are as expensive as new cars in the United States. This is
also true of virtually all machinery and equipment. It appears that in
Chile the only reason a capital good will not operate is the lack of
imported spare parts. The high resale value of old, secondhand producer durables and their lengthy utilization are also important factors.

Chile is forced to import almost all necessary producer durables and
has operated since 1930 under a severe balance-of-payments constraint

33. In 1952, as shown on the right side of fig. 13.1, capital and consumption allowances
exceeded gross investment by 15 percent. As fig. 13.2 shows, capital consumption allowances have exceeded gross investment in 1960 by more than 50 percent. Even during
earthquake years such depreciation levels are excessively high.

34. See Markos Mamalakis, "Negative Personal Saving in The Chilean National
Accounts: An Artifact or Reality?" Center discussion paper no. 36, August 1967, Economic Growth Center, Yale University, tables 5, 6. These two tables include current
price figures of the gross domestic capital formation account with upward corrections
of 20 and 40 percent, respectively. Gross fixed capital formation figures were increased
by 20 or 40 percent, and analogous changes were introduced in the items of construction
and other works. The figures for capital consumption allowances were reduced by 50
percent. Finally, the figures for gross capital formation, personal saving, and gross
domestic saving were adjusted accordingly.

Fig. 13.3. Personal saving as a percentage of gross domestic product.
——first revised figures, —second revised figures, · · · · original figures.

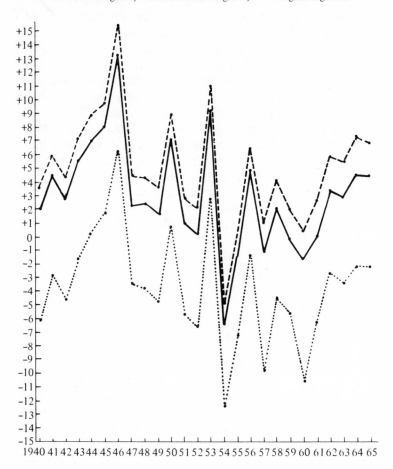

that has repeatedly led to heavy rationing of capital goods imports. Machinery and equipment are not easily replaceable, and the economy has relied on large-scale spare parts imports and repair and maintenance expenses to prolong the lifetime of such goods. Because of the relative abundance and low cost of labor, the capital/labor ratio is being reduced below the figure originally incorporated in the capital good. Labor is constantly applied to prolong the capital good's useful life. Heavy maintenance and repair expenditures and a prolonged lifetime are actually a method by which imported capital-intensive technology is adapted to the local resource endowment and transformed into a labor-intensive one.

The second major factor leading to an overestimate is related to the method developed to estimate depreciation in replacement values. Hernán Kappes, who was assigned in the middle 1950s the task of eliminating the distorting impact of inflation from the depreciation estimates, developed a method of expressing investment, depreciation, and capital stock figures in "replacement values."[35]

This depreciation formula has the serious shortcoming that, if applied partially, it can distort the relation between gross and net investment. In the Chilean national accounts an error arises because gross domestic investment is estimated by one method (viz., the mixed product–expenditure procedure described earlier), which does not take complete account of the inflationary price rises, and because depreciation is calculated at replacement values, which are linked not to the cost of foreign exchange but to the domestic cost-of-living index. Thus depreciation figures estimated by the Kappes method are inflated upward, if compared to gross investment, by the difference in the rate of increase of the cost-of-living index and the index of the dollar's escudo price. Some of the inflation-induced distortions in the components of the saving account would have been eliminated if they were expressed in constant prices. Unfortunately, such a task had not been undertaken as late as 1972.

Finally, it seems that the coverage of depreciation estimates has been more extensive than that of investment. As a consequence, items were being depreciated that had not been previously included in the investment estimates. This appears to have been the case with respect to construction and related works in agriculture, mining, and services.

35. For a detailed description of this method see Hernán Kappes Barrientos, "Cálculo de Depreciación para Uso en Cuentas Sociales. Un Método General Aplicado a la Industria," Memoria en Economía (Santiago: Universidad de Chile, 1959), mimeo.

BEHAVIORAL FACTORS AFFECTING
PERSONAL SAVING

Whatever the biases or errors in the statistical methodology might be, they do not provide a complete explanation for the low level of personal saving. The vast transfer payments from government to households, which are an effect and symptom of the welfare state, have had a downward impact on personal saving. These transfers have either exceeded or been very close to the total employer and employee contributions to the social security system during 1950–65. Family allowances are the most significant of these transfers, and households have apparently treated them as gifts and have adjusted their consumption patterns upward.

In a welfare state it is possible that the behavior of government rather than that of households causes low overall household savings. If the poor, who presumably consume all they are given, receive an amount of resources exceeding the savings of the upper-income households, total personal savings can be lowered and possibly turned negative.

Furthermore, to the extent that government converts part of the income of the business sector that could be invested into subsidies to the poor by means of high employer's social security contributions and high transfers, as is the case in Chile, it introduces an unsettling and negative element in the growth process. The funds that if invested would provide future employment and higher income for all, including the poor, are spent on current household subsidies and consumption. This process has a transitory short-run palliative effect but substantial negative long-run growth consequences.[36]

Under such circumstances the phenomenon of overall negative savings of the household sector reveals little about the average and marginal propensity to save of the upper- or middle-income groups.[37]

36. An extensive discussion of nonstatistical factors influencing directly the level of investment and indirectly personal saving is found in Markos Mamalakis, "Public Policy and Sectoral Development. A Case Study of Chile 1940–1958," in Mamalakis and C. W. Reynolds, *Essays on the Chilean Economy* (Homewood, Ill.: Richard D. Irwin, 1965), pp. 54–82, 149–68. This earlier study does not contain an evaluation of the national accounts or any specific item of the accounts.

37. Juan Crocco presents figures on saving provided by persons and on saving received by persons for 1950–62. These figures indicate that some persons saved vast amounts, while these same or other persons proceeded to borrow even vaster amounts. See Juan Crocco Ferrari, "El Ahorro y la Inversión," *Geografía Económica de Chile*, rev. ed., CORFO (Santiago: Editorial Universitaria, 1965), tables 1 and 2, pp. 858–59.

For example, household savings from income, excluding transfers, could run a healthy 3–4 percent of domestic product, with all saving done by the rich, but net government transfers to the household sector of 5 percent of domestic product would wipe out all personal saving by subsidizing the nonsaving lower-income groups.

A legal ceiling might be set on such transfers. One ceiling recommends that not more than 80 percent of the household sector's nontax contribution to government could be returned in the form of transfers.

REAL AND STRUCTURAL FACTORS AFFECTING PERSONAL SAVING

It is not sufficient to point out that government prefers to consume rather than invest. After all, the government's investment and development program has shown that it can be a massive, if not always efficient, investor. Moreover, it is also not sufficient to argue that households will consume rather than save their disposable income. During some years they have displayed positive savings, and it is also known that in earlier decades this dissaving process did not take place. Other factors must explain the process that has permitted households to dissave at all. Did they increase their liabilities to government and business firms? Did they continually liquidate previously accumulated net assets? Or did government, business, and foreign transfers fill the gap between current earnings and other receipts and consumer and other expenditures?

In fact, households were able to borrow whenever they wished even as the real value of their outstanding debt fell. Households borrowed from firms, firms from banks, and banks from the Central Bank. Inflation eliminated most of the household sector's debts as well as those of firms and banks that lacked escalator clauses.

Several real, structural, or institutional factors seem to have facilitated household spending or reduced household saving. Until 1965 the almost unlimited possibility of borrowing without an escalator clause attached to debts[38] was coupled with the expectation that inflation would lessen the real burden of debt. Escalator clauses have been strongly and effectively objected to by households, which relied on inflation to reduce the real value of their debts. Furthermore, there was a lack of symmetry between real foreign debt and real domestic debt.

38. According to Juan Crocco, who until 1965 was in charge of the preparation of national accounts, personal dissaving was made possible by the credit extended to the household sector by enterprises.

Chile's foreign indebtedness rose from $800 million in 1955 to almost $2 billion in 1964 without any traceable increase in internal indebtedness of government, firms, or households. Households were able to consume far more than they produced without increasing, thanks to inflation, their liabilities. With no built-in constraint on excessive consumption in terms of either reduced or more expensive borrowing, burdenless dissaving increased. Finally, and this is by no means a complete list, saving was made difficult by the lack or small number of inflation-proof assets until the late 1960s.

It would be inaccurate to claim that households were able to annually increase their indebtedness by an amount equal to the size of their annual negative personal saving.[39] That households were able to increase their indebtedness to some degree during certain time periods is certainly true, particularly with respect to social security institutions. The latter frequently took their member contributions and lent them out on low-interest mortgages to senior and politically privileged members. Since such institutions belong to the government sector in the Chilean accounts, part of the mortgages amounted to transfer payments to the household sector and should be so counted.

Without question one of the principal reasons why savings were not higher during the years of inflation was the lack of adequate savings channels.[40] Savings deposits in banks[41] were not readjusted until the 1960s, and because the interest rate authorized was repeatedly extremely negative, these deposits in effect were eliminated. A 1965 law introduced a cost-of-living index clause to saving deposits, but it has not yet resulted in any substantial increase in saving, mainly because the State Bank has a monopoly in accepting saving deposits.[42] Further-

39. For a discussion of the relationship between inflation and negative personal saving, see ODEPLAN, *Cuentas Nacionales de Chile, 1960–1969* (Santiago: ODEPLAN, 1970), pp. 6–12. In these pages, ODEPLAN attempts to place the burden of explanation of negative saving of households on inflation and rising indebtedness and answers some criticisms raised in this chapter.

40. Instituto de Economía, unpublished study on saving and investment.

41. The lack of adequate money and capital markets in Chile and its negative impact upon personal saving are described in detail in International Bank for Reconstruction and Development, International Development Association, *Development of a Capital Market in Chile, The Report*, (Washington, D.C., and Chile: IBRD, Jan. 19, 1965), pp. 1–13 and appendexes.

42. Banks cannot receive deposits in dollars, and although stockbrokers received dollar deposits in the late 1950s, to be re-lent in large part for import deposits, a number of brokers went bankrupt at great loss to the depositors so that this channel was not considered reliable. Even if the brokers had not gone bankrupt, this channel would not have been open for the great mass of small investors.

more, insurance has been used exclusively for protection and not for investment.[43] Also, although the social security institutions had a considerably greater income than their current payments and although a significant a part of this surplus was invested in housing construction, another important component was dissipated in fixed value loans to favored members of the pension plans.[44]

The Chilean stock market also proved to be an unsatisfactory investment opportunity because many shares failed to increase enough in value to compensate for inflation.[45] Besides, the anti-inflationary policy introduced at the end of 1964 and lack of confidence have caused an unprecedented decline in stock prices.

One of the best investment opportunities during inflation has been agricultural land. A study by the Institute of Economic Research showed that in the period 1940–1958 such property increased in value much more rapidly than the dollar on the free market and increased in real terms whether deflated by the cost of living, wholesale prices, or agricultural prices.[46]

43. A discussion of the effects of inflation on the insurance companies is found in Jorge Bande, *La Política del Seguro Privado* (Santiago: Editorial Universitaria, 1953), pp. 112–20.

44. A discussion of this problem can be found in the report of the Klein–Saks mission, *El Sistema de Previsión Social Chileno*.

45. The results of three studies of the return on stock investments are in Luis Escobar Cerda, *El Mercado de Valores* (Santiago: Editorial del Pacífico, 1959), 274 pp., which contains a general description of how the Chilean stock market operates.

46. Instituto de Economía, Universidad de Chile, *La Tributación Agrícola en Chile, 1940–1958* (Santiago: Instituto de Economía, 1960). Some of the first measures of the Alessandri government were intended to improve savings and investment opportunities. Banks were permitted to receive deposits and the government itself sold dollar bonds, thus providing the investor with a partial hedge against inflation.

Another significant innovation was the establishment of personal savings accounts by the Corporación de la Vivienda (CORVI), a government institution charged with the construction of low-cost housing in Chile both for its own account and for the account of the social security institutions. At present, private individuals can open an account and sign a contract with CORVI in which they promise to deposit a certain sum monthly in their account. When they have accumulated a minimum sum under the terms of the contract, they are entitled to a housing loan from CORVI. Both the savings deposit and the construction loan are readjustable in line with general wage increases. In 1964 a 1 percent payroll tax was established, the proceeds of which go to CORVI. For the worker the tax is, in effect, forced savings because part of it will be credited to his savings account in CORVI if he has one.

Another innovation, the establishment of private savings and loan associations, was made possible by government decree in the late 1950s. Long urged by the Cámara de Construcción and supported by Point IV, the associations would receive readjustable deposits and make readjustable construction loans. Two studies published in 1965 in Santiago by the Instituto Chileno del Acero describe the proposal and demonstrate how

In conclusion, the introduction of escalator clauses in most consumer and other types of credit and assets can be a most efficient means of raising personal saving. Such clauses could reduce, or even wipe out, the massive net borrowing of the debtor part of the household sector and possibly stimulate further saving by the creditor segment of the household sector.

Nevertheless, it is clear that the presence of negative personal saving in Chilean national accounts has to a large extent been a methodological artifact. The accurate estimates of personal saving needed for planning will not be obtained so long as this item is calculated residually. The nature of Chile as a medium-sized underdeveloped country relying heavily on imported producers' durables and suffering from acute secular inflation is largely responsible for the methodological problems faced by those making the estimates. However, any attempt to raise personal savings in the future, once accurate estimates have been obtained, will have to include policies that can deal with the money and capital markets, taxation, the social security program, the balance of payments, and inflation.

---

it could work out in practice: *Antecedentes para el establecimiento de un sistema de ahorro y préstamo para la vivienda*, and *Asociaciónes de Ahorro y Préstamo para la vivienda, análisis de su funcionamiento*. Since 1965 the Christian Democratic government has introduced saving accounts protected from inflation.

14

Summary of Findings and Conclusion

Progress and change in Chile between 1840 and 1973 have been remarkable. Yet a general economic theory relevant to it and other less developed countries does not yet exist. As Hla Myint has argued, there is no need to eliminate major segments of present economic theory; instead, the orthodox economic theory must be greatly expanded before it can adequately cover the present-day developing nations.[1] My analysis has not only recommended the theoretical framework within which I believe such extension must occur but has also applied it to Chile.

I have suggested, first of all, that growth in general (as well as for Chile in particular) should be analyzed in terms of changes in production, distribution, and capital formation. Furthermore, in order to understand the structure of the economy it is necessary to identify the morphology of each of these three processes as well as the interactions among them. I have defined economic development as the integrated, continuous, and substantial transformation in production, distribution, and capital formation. Per capita income increase is the major result of such development.[2] The transformation in Chile's production, distribution, and capital accumulation can, I believe, be described in

1. "Economic Theory and Development Policy," *Economica* 34, no. 134 (May 1967): 119–21, 123–27.
2. Existing approaches to economic development are inadequate because they cover or emphasize only one of these three processes. Thus, the dualistic agriculture-industry and export-versus domestic-derived growth frameworks concentrate on production and pay scant or no attention at all to distribution and capital formation. The Marxist approach concentrates on distribution. More recent work views everything from the angle of capital formation. See Harry G. Johnson, "Towards a Generalized Capital Accumulation Approach to Economic Development," in OECD Study Group in the Economics of Education, *The Residual Factor and Economic Growth* (Paris 1964), pp. 219–25, reprinted in Gerald M. Meier, *Leading Issues in Economic Development, Studies in International Poverty* (New York: Oxford University Press, 1970), pp. 628–33.

a manner that records and summarizes the progress achieved, focuses on the major forces that determined growth, and isolates the critical bottlenecks that prevented an even better performance.

PRODUCTION: PROBLEMATIC PROGRESS

The race between output and population increase was as important to Chile as to most LDCs. Population grew mildly until the late 1920s, when sharply falling death rates and a relatively stable birth rate led to a significant rise in population growth. Income growth resulted from the simultaneous interaction of internal and international demand and supply forces. Internal demand was strongly affected by the level and distribution of income, population growth, and urbanization. Supply was determined by the rate of absorption of land, including mineral and other resources, and the increase in the quantity and quality of labor, capital, and technological progress. Unfortunately, the data are not yet sufficiently accurate to permit a valid estimate of the relative contributions of capital and technological progress to growth. During most of the 1840–1973 period output growth was unsatisfactory because of low formation of physical, human, and institutional capital and inadequate technical progress and resource discovery.

A dominant feature of the changes in production was entrenchment of pluralism, whether defined in terms of labor income or sectoral productivity. Within an extraordinarily broad range the lowest labor income and productivity were found in agriculture, the highest in mining, gas, water, and electricity. Construction, personal services, transport, industry, trade and banking, and government evenly filled the gap between the two extremes. There is no evidence supporting the presence of production dualism.

Agriculture and Food

The greatest contrast found in comparing 1840 and 1973 is in agriculture. In a classic retrogression Chile changed from a self-sufficient food-exporting nation into a cripple that was dependent on food imports worth $700 million in 1974.[3] Agriculture, the only sector that directly carries out the primary critical function of food production, underperformed. Thus, in order to correct the rising imbalance between demand and internal production, the export sector was forced to in-

3. See *El Mercurio*, internacional ed., Dec 3–9, 1973, p. 1.

directly perform this function. It acted as quasi-agriculture by making food domestically available in exchange for present or future exports.

The Chilean agricultural paradox emerges from its production changes, which are associated and coincide with its retrogression, being similar or identical in form to those experienced by nations that have undergone an agricultural revolution. Relative agricultural employment declined secularly, falling below 23.9 percent of the total in 1971. The share of income generated in agriculture not only dropped secularly to less than 10 percent in 1972 but has also been markedly lower than—indeed, normally only half as high as—the share of employment in agriculture. Consequently, relative agricultural productivity was low both during the pre-1930 and land-abundant and the later land-scarce periods of development.

Before 1930 a substantial but stable surplus of consumer goods was generated jointly in a semiclosed environment by land and a mass of illiterate peasants. This small surplus was increasingly diverted away from export toward the urban centers, where it supported the aristocratic urban–rural elite, government, and other embryonic services. Agricultural productivity grew substantially before 1930, when government and agriculture were at least in harmony, if not in partnership. In short, before 1930 agriculture was prosperous and performed adequately although the spread effect on the quality of agricultural labor was minimal. It was between 1930 and 1973 that agriculture's long-term inability to perform its food-supplying function led to the conversion of the small pre-1930 food surplus into the staggering food deficit.

Agriculture was never a major source of resource surpluses. It made a small foreign exchange contribution between 1840 and 1940 but none afterward, and it caused an increasing drain on foreign exchange between 1940 and 1973. It offered only a weak market for industrial consumer goods and failed to generate autochthonus technical progress. An agricultural revolution, in the sense of the acquisition of the capacity for self-modernization and -transformation, did not materialize. In spite of the ever worsening food crisis between 1940 and 1973, no government organized a comprehensive plan for complete and effective modernization—or, had one been available—had the political and financial power to implement it. Agricultural research was neither organized nor systematically pursued although substantial resources were devoted to the many land reform plans. Neither a latifundio nor a minifundio technology was prepared. Resources—labor, surpluses, capital—were not released; they simply fled agriculture, a sign of retrogression rather than progress.

Especially after 1930, agriculture was unable to perform some of the traditional growth functions because of negative incentives, such as price controls, deteriorating terms of trade, subsidized imports, inadequate extension work, and land reform. Each and all of these factors furthered its neglect and suppression. The ill-conceived attempt by the nonagricultural population to extract a surplus through these instruments became doubly counterproductive. Agricultural living standards fell in relative and sometimes even in absolute terms, and transferable surpluses shrank. Even though agricultural investment had a higher social rate of return, it was the less necessary and less socially profitable investment in industry that materialized.[4]

Perhaps the most damaging, if the least noticed, factor during 1930–73 was the "latifundio psychosis." Almost all Chile's real ills, and many imaginary ones as well, were attributed to the land tenure structure. Excessive preoccupation with the notion that Chile was a latifundio society, based on, oriented toward, and dominated by agriculture, diverted attention away from the requisite positive price and capital formation policies. Thus this allegedly rural–agricultural economy was led to the debacle in which it imports more than half its food requirements.

The full-scale tenure reform of 1962–73 induced a comprehensive subdivision and redistribution of land and eliminated the already weakened landed aristocracy. By ending the latifundio trauma, it may permit development of a rational agricultural policy. Once those who implement policy have learned all about argiculture's secondary functions of releasing labor and savings, making a market contribution, and such imaginary goals as providing control over the political apparatus, they may recognize and pursue agriculture's primary function of producing food.

Exports and Mining

Production frontiers expanded profoundly after 1840 as independence from Spain permitted export demand to become the primary growth

---

4. See on this issue Howard S. Ellis, "Accelerated Investment as a Force in Economic Development," *Quarterly Journal of Economics* 72 (Nov. 1958): 486, 491–95, reprinted in Meier, *Leading Issues,* p. 401.

determinant. Wheat, copper, nitrate, silver, wines, and the like found favorable markets abroad. Because exports had a definite mineral bias, mining provided the economy's heartbeat.

International demand did not absorb an unused surplus of the mining sector but rather created this sector because it created income. Natural resources were made valuable, and a totally new production apparatus was built. With a speed reminiscent of the Californian and Alaskan gold rushes, the empty, inhospitable nitrate deserts boomed from 1880 to 1930.[5] With mining profoundly and idiosyncratically shaping the country's destiny, what can be called a minerals production pattern or theory of economic growth emerged. The nature of the mineral product—an inorganic, durable, exhaustible, irreproducible material extracted from natural capital—formed the crux of the theory. The growth rate of mining income equaled the depletion rate of the stock of mineral capital. Technical progress not only made the nitrate stocks valuable in 1860–1880 but also made those not already depleted obsolete between 1920 and 1930 by discovering synthetic substitutes. Chile's production between 1880 and 1930 was centrally affected by the stock, depletion, and obsolescence of its natural mineral capital.

The composition of aggregate demand had a large export share. It was heavily oriented toward mineral exports, which constituted between 15 and 30 percent of GDP before 1930 (primarily nitrate) and between 5 and 12 percent during 1930–74 (primarily copper). Furthermore, minerals—mostly nitrate and copper—constituted 80 percent of total exports between 1880 and 1974. The level of aggregate demand was also determined by and linked with the international demand for minerals. Because of its concentration on a few products, countries, and markets, the highly volatile export segment imparted instability to the rest of the economy through truncated multiplier–accelerator effects.

Depletion of the fabulous mineral capital stocks increased the productivity of labor in mining far above the rest of the economy. After labor and physical capital had been compensated, significant surpluses or quasi-rents remained that amounted to as much as 20 percent of GDP between 1880 and 1930.

Production and surpluses, especially between 1880 and 1955, were part of the developed, international production system—even though

5. See Hla Myint, "The 'Classical Theory' of International Trade and the Underdeveloped Countries," in *Readings in International Economics*, ed. R. E. Caves and Y. G. Johnson (Homewood, Ill.: Richard D. Irwin, 1968), pp. 318–38.

geographically located in Chile. The unequal intrusion of the international market system into Chile's sectoral production structure led
to the lopsided creation of income and investable funds by export
mining before 1930.

Because production imperfections in mining and the rest of the
economy were deep and many, trade had less impact on Chile's destiny
in terms of immediate and lasting effects than in preindustrial and
takeoff Japan, Germany, and England. In Chile the forces shaping the
expansion of demand *and* supply—with the exception of wheat and
early mining—originated from the foreign, mostly developed nations
that needed Chile's exports. The low level or absence of educational,
financial, technological, and other forms of man-made capital generated weak interaction mechanisms between mining (where natural
capital decumulated) and the rest of Chile but strong ones with the
developed West. Although this was neither negative nor detrimental
per se, it illustrated the primary challenge that had to be met within
a changing economic physiognomy. The production imperfections
caused by insufficient past accumulation of man-made forms of capital
were perceived early and corrective policies were recommended. Between 1840 and 1930 a significant but not sufficient effort was made
to implement the policies that would have converted the mineral capital
being depleted into other far scarcer forms of capital (educational,
technological, institutional) that would strengthen the interaction
mechanisms.

Even though the sectoral growth pattern caused by mineral exports
was patently unbalanced, it did not foster dualism but production
pluralism. Within mining, which on the whole was more modern,
capital intensive, and productive than the rest of the economy, highly
advanced large-scale production (copper, iron, and even nitrate before
1930) coexisted with medium-scale mines, which were less capital
intensive and productive, as well as with erratic small-scale mines.
Moreover, selected segments of the economy—some public utilities,
steel production, and so forth—were highly productive and efficient
before as well as after 1930.

The contribution of mining to Chile's development was mainly indirect in that it never possessed the ability to create massive employment.
In exchange for satisfying urgent raw material needs of the industrial
nations, Chile received labor inputs, consumer goods, machinery and
equipment, and financial capital. Expansion of industrial, service, and
construction employment was in part determined by the extent to

which the mineral capital exported was converted into employment-increasing, scarce capital forms. Between 1880 and 1974 the mining export sector did perform as a quasi-financial, -educational, -technological, -consumer and -capital goods sector, thus greatly increasing economic welfare. However, by concentrating on consumer goods (agricultural since 1950), it was associated with only a limited conversion into scarce capital forms and indirect employment increases. The danger of treating mineral depletions as permanent rather than transitory income was exposed when technical progress made natural nitrate stocks obsolete about 1930. Nitrate's previously unlimited substitutability into other forms of consumer goods or capital fell to zero and anciliary capital was also wasted.

Fortunately, and unlike Cuba, Chile was not totally beset by a "minerals mentality"—emphasizing nitrate before 1930 and copper after that date—in the sense that it excessively linked its economic future to the fortunes of mineral exports.[6] But signs of a copper mentality did develop after 1935, when foreign ownership in large-scale copper and export dependency were singled out as growth constraints.

Industry

Industry played a key role in the transformation of production between 1840 and 1974. Industrial income rose to 26.1 and employment to 19.2 percent of their respective totals in 1971. Much of the growth before 1940 resulted from import substitution, which has continued on a narrowly selective basis until the present. However, because import-substituting industrial investment did not satisfy the more general investment criterion of foreign exchange substitution, the balance-of-payments crisis of the 1930s was only aggravated. Although industry has developed to a point where it supplies Chile with an impressive variety of consumer and intermediate products, overprotection and preferential treatment by government have contributed to excessive diversification. Even its dominance between 1938 and 1973 has failed to turn industry into either the most productive or the most dynamic sector.

During the process of forced-draft industrialization its interaction mechanisms with agriculture were deliberately severed. The weak expansion of neglected and suppressed agriculture dragged down overall

6. Henry C. Wallich has coined the expression "sugar mentality" See *Monetary Problems of an Export Economy* (Cambridge, Mass.: Harvard University Press, 1960), p. 12.

growth. The interaction mechanisms between industry and mining were also distorted by incorrect policies in extracting mining quasi-rents. However, the forward and backward linkages within industry and between industry and construction blossomed, establishing an interconnected development pattern. In short, although industry was the backbone of the booming construction sector, it failed to become a significant source of technical or other progress for either mining or agriculture. Also, besides not performing the quality-improvement function, it was largely responsible for the negative price policies toward mining and agriculture. Despite the impressive quantitative industrial growth (much of the relative manufacturing expansion be-tween 1915 and 1960 was offset by the decline in artisans), the nation's self-transformation and modernization ability remained limited in adjusting to shifts in demand level and composition.

Chile was persistently plagued between 1840 and 1974 by imbalances between production of consumer and capital goods as well as within capital goods production. Its overall capacity to produce capital goods directly remained small. Its indirect capacity, through exports, has been discouraging since 1930. And within the capital-goods-producing sector, the favored segment was construction, primarily in the form of housing, which immediately and directly augmented the production of services.

Size and Functions of Services

Services boomed between 1840 and 1974. Their share of employment climbed to more than 40 percent of the labor force with their relatively stable income share being in excess of 50 percent of GDP between 1915 and 1972. Relative productivity has been above average but declined since 1940.

My framework of analysis not only challenges the Fisher–Clark theme of primary, secondary, and tertiary sectors but also offers what I believe is a far more meaningful categorization according to the functions performed. Services complementing commodity production perform the time-, quantity-, and location-transformation functions. Since no production, exchange, or final use can occur without them, they are as primary and necessary as any other sector. Although wholesale and retail trade adequately fulfilled the time- and quantity-transformation functions to a certain extent, they failed to provide equitable income to some producers (agricultural) and to generate export outlets for production surpluses. Furthermore, even though transportation was a major recipient of investment, it performed the location-changing function only partially and at a high cost; intra-urban mass transport was neglected. Health, education, housing, welfare, and government performed adequately the quality-maintenance but not the quality-improvement function. Dietary, health, educational, sanitation, and housing deficiencies declined sharply between 1840 and 1972, especially in the cities and among middle and upper classes. For many of the rural and urban poor, however, the deficiencies were as great in 1970 as in 1840, and the improvement under Allende between 1970 and 1973 was largely transitory. Chile's central challenge was to increase its stock of human, physical, and institutional capital in education, government, health, and personal services as well as in the commodity sectors that could improve quality throughout the economy and thus strengthen the weak inter- and intrasectoral interaction mechanisms.

Last, in a third category, the money function was performed well by the financial sector between 1840 and 1930 but suffered during 1940–55 and 1970–73 because of excessive reliance on inflationary Central Bank credit. The performance of communications and publishing was unparalleled in Latin America until 1973, when it became a victim of the disguised but relentless 1970–73 civil war. Finally, some personal services provided the cultural and religious enrichment so desperately needed to balance and enrich the human soul and spirit.

DISTRIBUTION: ENIGMATIC PROGRESS

The class, international, sectoral, and regional dimensions of income distribution between 1840 and 1970, which were dominated by significant inequalities and a high concentration of income and wealth, reflected as well as shaped the changing pattern of production and capital formation in Chile. The inequalities arising from this distribution were important but less so than the available statistics suggest.

The profound and largely irreversible changes in income distribution and ownership of means of production between 1970 and 1973 were inspired by the Left's belief that the historical distribution pattern within Chile's political democracy prevented economic democracy. As the primary goal and accomplishment of Salvador Allende's Popular Unity, these changes were the pyrotechnic culmination of trends at least forty years old. But they were also responsible for the chaotic economic, social, and political atmosphere of 1973, the demise of Allende's presidency, and the destruction of the truly unique democratic tradition that had permitted a Marxist takeover by the ballot.

According to crude aggregate national accounts statistics, labor generally earned less than 50 percent of income—but its share was growing—and capital more than 50 percent before 1970. This unequal pattern was first mildly modified under President Eduardo Frei and then revamped under President Salvador Allende; the labor share rose to 66 percent of income in 1971.

But the picture provided by the national accounts is somewhat inaccurate because it is based on data before rather than after taxes, subsidies, and transfers and thus underestimates the labor share. Also, the traditional distinction between capitalists (those who receive income generated by physical and financial capital) and workers (who receive income generated by human capital) is strongly blurred. As much as 20 percent of income before 1930, and at least 5 percent since then, represented mining quasi-rents that developed from the decumulation of natural capital. This income belonged to but was not equally distributed among all Chileans. Furthermore, much of capitalist income—at least 25 percent of income during most years—was a return to labor in unincorporated enterprises.

Chile has been marked by subtle but substantial income gradations among and within the marginals, the poor, the middle classes, the rich and the superrich. The extremes of the spectrum are, however, so far apart that the contrasts in living standards and productivity have been enormous. The inequalities in the interclass distribution of income were part of this elongated, pluralistic distribution and shaped it.

The employer–capitalist class was heterogeneous and pluralistic in its control over capital as well as in its orientation. It included the foreign capitalists in mining, industry, and services (whose power was determined by their direct control over physical, financial, and technological capital and indirectly over natural capital), the assorted land owners (whose uneven incomes were derived primarily from land), the wide spectrum of private Chilean capitalists (who controlled all forms of capital), and the Chilean state (which after 1880 and before 1930 derived most of its income from the decumulation of natural resources). There is no evidence of generally high incomes or of a binding capitalist ethos among the diverse private capitalists, who ranged from kite vendors to the Guggenheim colossus.

Inequalities in income distribution and lack of homogeneity were also obvious within labor and still exist. Between 1880 and 1970 white-collar workers in all sectors, though heavily urban based, slowly gained a privileged economic and social status that set them apart from most menial workers and often close to or even above some employer–capitalists. Among the blue-collar group were the well-off, militant copper, steel, and sheep-raising union members, the servants of upper- and middle-income salaried workers, the industrial workers, the poor tenant farmers, and other employees in service or commodity production. In addition, there was a quasi-lumpenproletariat, part of which floated within and between the urban *callampas* (slums), the fringes of the latifundios, and even nations. The variations in the quality of human capital represented by the various workers were so great that labor was not and could not be treated as a homogeneous entity. Even under Salvador Allende the sectoral consciousness of many workers greatly transcended their class awareness, as the copper workers, truckers, and others demonstrated. However, income differentials within labor often exceeded any obvious quality differences, and these gaps contributed to social tension and unrest. Furthermore, the changes in labor income were repeatedly too erratic to be explained away in terms of unequal productivity.

At least in part, the interclass as well as the intralabor income inequalities can be explained by the pattern of income distribution among sectors. Actual welfare was determined by each sector's production plus (or minus) the resource influx (or outflow) from other sectors. The pre-1930 intersectoral distribution of income was characterized by a massive and unequal transfer of mining income to services, industry, and agriculture, which coalesced with government to extract these quasi-rents, as well as to the capitalists of the industrial nations. Because the surplus-receiving sectors, especially services and industry, enjoyed expenditures above their own production, the returns to their inputs were inflated. Labor costs in some sectors rose to levels far above Chile's long-term capacity to pay them. The quantitative and qualitative influence of the quasi-rents created a minerals income distribution pattern before 1930. Distribution was shaped not only by the classical relationship between man and man-made capital and by the primitive relationship between man and land, but also by the relationship between man and decumulating mineral capital. A new, powerful man-to-man relationship emerged as the unequally distributed mining quasi-rents were converted into higher quality, income-generating human capital.

The crash came between 1930 and 1933, when technical progress made Chile's natural nitrate capital stocks obsolete and the resource transfer of quasi-rents to other sectors became minuscule. Living standards in all sectors retreated to levels that could be sustained without nitrate aid. The adjustments were extremely painful because each sector attempted to maintain its pre-1930 living standard. As industry and urban services entered a new coalition with government, they attempted to maintain or improve their status by extracting (through inflation, protection, subsidies, and other means) quasi-rents from the recovering, high-productivity copper sector but also from perenially weak and poor agriculture. This misguided distortion of intersectoral distribution of income—and of production incentives— caused a less than desirable decumulation of the stocks of raw copper, a reduced income transfer from copper mining to other sectors, a decreased rate of return for all inputs and thus a decline of income growth in agriculture, and less economic welfare. Government inter- vention in favor of some sectors and against others begins to explain the lack of harmonious interaction among production, distribution, and capital formation in the economy as well as within specific sectors.

The sectoral distribution of income was interwoven in a regional pattern. The mining and agricultural hinterland transferred resources to the urban sectors concentrated in Central Chile. If sustained develop- ment is to be achieved, the incentives offered to and the income share received by the rural hinterland must rise appreciably.

The class, sectoral, and regional dimensions had a direct impact on the international distribution of income. Although international distri- bution was favorable to Chile during the import surplus periods of 1844–1850, 1930–32, 1957–64, and 1971–73, the welfare of the nation during most years between 1860 and 1957 was below that suggested by domestic production. It would appear that because of a net export surplus or resource exodus, Chile is a donor rather than a resource recipient.

The dual, mutually offsetting impact of foreign ownership caused only a fraction of the net outflow. Direct foreign ownership created a resource leakage through income and capital repatriation and an inflow through investment. On balance, the flow was negative. Indirect foreign ownership led to resource inflow through the acquisition of direct or indirect government liabilities, aid, and credits and to outflows through servicing and amortization of foreign-owned Chilean financial capital.

On balance, the flow was positive and normally exceeded the direct investment leakage. However, a third force was operating, especially after 1880: monetary, price, fiscal, and foreign exchange instability caused a massive flight of resources out of Chile between 1880 and 1930 and a lesser one since 1930. During the presidencies of Jorge Alessandri and Salvador Allende all statistical evidence shows an international distribution of income favorable to Chile—in both instances at a high social cost. Allende's nationalization of direct foreign investments in copper, nitrate, iron, and numerous other sectors proved only a partial solution to the international distribution problems; it was associated with increased flight of national capital and was offset by a rise in indirect foreign ownership.

The distribution of income to various functions played a critical role in shaping growth. The time-, location-, and quantity-transformation functions received extremely favorable income to their factors of production. The rates of return to their human and physical capital were kept high either by transferring mining quasi-rents to them, as in the deficit-ridden railroad transportation, or by permitting them to enjoy monopoly or monosony profits through quotas, tariffs, licenses, and so on, as in wholesale and retail trade. As income was redistributed in favor of its inputs, industry became excessively diversified in its production of intermediate and consumer goods. The sectors performing the quality-maintenance function, such as housing, education and welfare, were given indirect preferential treatment.

An unfavorable distribution of income reduced rates of return for inputs performing the food production, quality improvement, and money functions. The worst treatment was bestowed upon desperately needed agriculture, whose rates of return to all inputs were artificially reduced and which recorded a dismal performance. The financial sector was plagued by negative rates of return, partly because government attempted to bypass a major segment of it by relying on Central Bank credit and inflation. Decumulation of financial capital and the resulting credit asphyxy, which were as detrimental as the agricultural deficit, were caused by the distorted incentives and distribution of the 1930–73 government–industry coalition. Relative stagnation in mining, the sector capable of performing all functions, was in part brought about by the inability of government to extract only, but no more than, the quasi-rents from natural resource depletion. Whenever government overshot the mark, output stagnated; whenever it undershot, foreign capital and local labor enjoyed incomes they did not deserve. Finally, inadequate returns were given to inputs performing the quality-improvement function, whether through capital goods or service production. Thus, human and technical capital was always in short supply.

These inequalities, which are largely attributable to the unequal distribution of mining quasi-rents, have been carefully examined, thoroughly if not excessively publicized, and often greatly exaggerated, if not misinterpreted, within a free and democratic press. Furthermore, because Chile's inequalities were not matched by high investment but were, rather, consumption promoting, they were never considered so redeeming as the investment-promoting inequalities of the industrial revolution. However, as Allende's experiment in income redistribution and ownership transformation demonstrated (it was thus valuable but still too costly), some inequalities were production promoting. Even partial elimination of them had a significant adverse effect on production.

The challenge is to strike a balance between the extremely great, often distorted, socially untenable, and economically too costly inequalities and the utopian complete equality, which is consumption promoting but incentive stifling and investment depressing. Chile's growth, which was hampered because its distribution either was too close to one extreme or the other or moved from one to the other, will hopefully follow the middle of the road in the future. For this to be achieved, the mineral quasi-rents must be distributed in a fashion that favors the critical bottleneck functions: food production, quality improvement, and money. Such a policy may demonstrate that some crucial missing pieces of the distribution jigsaw puzzle were discovered during Chile's development experiment.

CAPITAL FORMATION: PROGRESS AND RETROGRESSION

If revolutions are won or lost in the economic battlefield, it can be safely said that Chile's weakest fronts have been in capital formation. Capital endowment was inadequate in 1840 and, in spite of continuous growth, remained so in 1974, although the shortage was not the same in all categories of capital. Natural mining capital, proved abundant by repeated discoveries, decumulated through intensive exploitation and technological substitution. Human capital was accumulated rapidly but unevenly; severe shortages in technical skills and rural education and a brain flight plagued the nation in 1973. Accumulation of physical capital between 1840 and 1973 was cyclical and significant but overly concentrated in housing and social overhead. Decumulation of natural capital was offset by a sharp accumulation in industry. Political capital, the pride of Chile, was transformed and adjusted under pressure from successive shocks; it suffered a full-scale collapse during the battle between the Popular Unity of the Left and the rest of the nation between 1970 and 1973. Monetary institutional capital increased between 1840 and 1930 but after 1930 declined cyclically and sharply until 1973.

Saving

Each form of capital generated investable resource surpluses. Especially between 1880 and 1930 economic expansion was shaped by the size and use of sectoral surpluses. Resource surpluses were rarely low in Chile. Saving was determined by the size of the aggregate resource surplus and the system's ability to appropriate and use it for investment purposes. The aggregate resource surplus consisted of the surplus generated in Chile (whether foreign- or Chilean-owned) and the inflow of private or public foreign capital. Ex-post saving, in terms of disposable income put aside for investment purposes, was generally low.

The Chilean case may be unique, particularly before 1930, in that resource surpluses consisted primarily of quasi-rents in mining. Thus there was a much smaller capitalist surplus from profits and rents than in the classical and Lewis models.[7] Mining quasi-rents, defined as income generated by nonreproducible natural capital, generated a share of resource surpluses that was high and dominant between 1880 and 1930. Surpluses created by human and physical capital increased secularly and became dominant between 1930 and 1973.

By exploiting natural capital and benefiting from the assistance of foreign, human, financial, and physical capital, nitrate and copper mining generated a resource surplus that ranged between 12 and 20 percent of GDP from 1880 to 1930. During the same period the Chilean government appropriated from these surpluses amounts ranging from 6 to 8 percent of GDP. The remaining surpluses, including significant mining quasi-rents, leaked abroad—primarily to Europe—as repatriated profits and capital flight induced by monetary and fiscal

7. See W. Arthur Lewis, "Economic Development with Unlimited Supplies of Labour," *The Manchester School of Economic and Social Studies* 22 (May 1954): 156–58.

instability. As much as half the mining resource surpluses, which may have never exceeded 5 percent of GDP between 1930 and 1973, leaked abroad as returns to foreign capital.

The export-dependent mining resource surplus created in the aftermath of Europe's and North America's industrial revolutions was tangible and durable. It could be converted into modern physical and human capital through investment in machinery, equipment, and education and it was transferable to any country and sector. It was volatile and unstable because of its links to international demand but replaceable and substitutable as a consequence of rising modern technical obsolescence.

In terms of resource surplus creation Chile had at least three distinct sectors. Agriculture, which was poor, created a small surplus, released labor, and required significant modernization to become a positive element in growth. Export mining, which was rich, often overmechanized, highly capitalistic and productive, possessed limited capacity to absorb labor but generated as well as released massive resource surpluses. And the urban service–industrial complex, even though it always received mining resource surpluses, generated an increasing share of the nation's savings. It also absorbed most of the labor force increments resulting from population increase and the labor released from low-productivity agriculture. Thus the mining surplus led, through multiplier effects, to service–industrial savings.

In national accounting terminology, business profits in mining and agriculture were the main saving sources before 1930. The preponderance of savings between 1940 and 1973 consisted of depreciation and retained profits by business—with industrial profits becoming dominant between 1950 and 1970. The role of the state as a saver was ambivalent. Foreign saving was significant. Periodical pre-1930 foreign capital inflows fluctuated between 2 and 4 percent of GDP, bringing the total export-generated resource surplus to 8–12 percent of GDP. Foreign capital inflows from 1939 to 1959 amounted to 1.5 percent of GDP, thus partially offsetting the 2.5 percent leakage of mineral profits. American foreign aid between 1959 and 1970, private capital inflows, and massive socialist credit and aid between 1970 and 1973 greatly exceeded the resource leakages caused by servicing and amortization of direct and indirect foreign debt. Household savings were marginal; if intersectoral resource transfers could be properly accounted for, savings of most of the households between 1880 and 1973 were negative or nil. Ex-ante savings or resource surpluses ranged from 15 to 30 percent of GDP, with at least one-third diverted to consumption or abroad. Actual investment almost always fell short of potential savings.

Investment

Gross investment tended to be 10–20 percent of GDP between 1840 and 1973. It occasionally surpassed the upper value before 1930 and repeatedly fell below the lower value after 1930. Investment varied significantly among the various forms of capital.

The highest rate of accumulation occurred in human capital. Although the quality of the stock of human capital in 1974 is among the highest in Latin America, the formation of such capital for the rural labor force, the urban poor, and specific vocational, technical, and university skills has been inadequate because of limited access to and availability of educational services. The pre-1940 selective immigration of human capital has been replaced by a selective emigration since 1955. The quality of labor producing consumer goods and services improved, but investment in labor that could augment instrumental capital goods production and determine the economy's transformation and modernization ability was limited.

Accumulation of physical capital in consumer production was significant and continuous. Such investment occurred primarily in transportation services. It was also significant, but less important, in industrial consumer goods production. Physical investment in agriculture was minimal.

Investment in capital goods production was almost totally confined to construction. Increased output directly augmented Chile's stock of physical overhead capital (dwellings, roads, airports, government buildings, and so forth) and the flow of housing services. Investment in the production of quality-improving instrumental capital goods, whether primary or secondary, stayed small.

Investment in mining had two interrelated components. The flow of mining income was equal to the depletion of natural mineral capital. This rate of disinvestment in mineral capital was determined by the rate of physical investment needed to extract the mineral and by technical progress. Investment in mineral capital is by definition impossible because this capital only decumulates. Investment in ancillary physical capital remained too small throughout Chile's modern history. Even though the amount of natural mineral capital decumulated between 1840 and 1973 vastly exceeded the investment amounts that could be absorbed in ancillary mining-physical capital, the actual reinvestment in mining was far below the optimum required to achieve higher mining income through decumulation of natural capital.

As the Chilean experience shows, investment in any form of capital cannot be indiscriminate. Human resources, in addition to minimum skills, require specialized training to perform the quality-improvement function. And physical investment that can reduce sectoral productivity differentials and accelerate each sector's self-transformation ability should supersede in importance such investments as employment-creating public works.

The Nexus between Saving and Investment

Even though Chile possessed an abundant flow of sectoral resource surpluses, potential savings, and investment opportunities over long periods of time, the profit or surplus reinvestment ratio remained perenially low and a sustained investment boom failed to materialize.

Significant efforts were made to improve the intermediation between savers and surplus sectors on the one side and investors on the other, but the stock and accumulation of intermediation capital remained grossly inadequate. The money and financial functions were constantly underperformed by the financial nexus: the organized and unorganized money and capital markets provided by government, foreigners, national private business, and households.

Before 1930 government played a crucial role in converting a major part of mineral quasi-rents into human capital through education, although this element received low priority in bottleneck areas. Through CORFO, the government's sui generis investment bank, an additional effort was made to convert depleted mineral capital into industrial and overhead capital. Despite these two major intermediation efforts, government acted even more powerfully as a force diverting ex-ante savings away from capital formation into consumption through welfare transfers, wage and salary payments to public employees, and direct and indirect subsidies to domestic and imported consumer goods. The most important change necessary for economic development is the conversion of CORFO into a full-scale investment bank. Endowed with capital gained from mining quasi-rents as well as saving deposits, it should extend credits and buy private and government bonds and stocks on fully commercial terms. An efficient government financial nexus is essential for an efficient and equitable conversion of depletable natural resources into other forms of capital. Each Chilean should own an equal nontransferable amount of CORFO shares that earn an annual dividend.

Domestic private financial intermediation has been persistently inadequate. The private financial system was one of the best in Latin America from 1900 to 1930. Nevertheless, fiscal, price, monetary, and foreign exchange instability discouraged domestic reinvestment of part of the national resource surplus and encouraged its emigration. Organized money and capital markets deteriorated substantially between 1940 and 1955, and the country was plagued by a severe credit asphyxy and financial attrition. Large and erratic differences between monetary and real values deprived interest rates of both their incentive power and their credit-rationing function. The 1958–70 institutional recovery, which was substantial but not complete, contributed to the investment boom of the 1960s but suffered a relapse between 1970 and 1973. A parallel financial system emerged between 1950 and 1970 as major corporations used retained profits to extend credit.

The recurrent lack of financial capital between 1940 and 1973, which was caused by a severe decumulation in the real financial capital of the banking system, forced Chile to rely on external credit for its operating and investment credit needs. Thus, a large portion of Chile's income, which was appropriated by foreigners through factor payments, was returned in the form of credits from the developed nations' banking system and financial intermediaries—Central Banks, World Bank, Export–Import Bank, AID, and others. External financial intermediation was not only unnecessary—it provided only operating capital and was based on mistaken domestic monetary policy—but very costly since it created a further leakage by raising the nation's foreign debt. Chile had to pay for foreign financial services with its most valuable resource, natural capital. To regenerate national loanable funds and discourage credit-subsidized consumption, real interest rates on all financial instruments should be raised to 10–20 percent.

Chile remained throughout 1840–1973 an ex-ante incomplete system in need of imported machinery and equipment. The export sector, which acted as a quasi-capital goods sector, provided the real physical capital links between savers and investors. The ability to convert financial into physical was determined by the depletion rate of the internationally marketable natural capital. With such capital converted abundantly into producer durables, Chile was a quasi-complete system free of bottlenecks in capital goods or other imports between 1840 and 1930. But the nitrate collapse of the 1930s and copper's subsequent lackluster growth left the economy partially incomplete between 1930 and 1973. Because of internal and external supply constraints, Chile has faced a shortage of producer durables since 1930. To accelerate growth, the Concepción–Talcahuano instrumental goods complex should be offered incentives to produce a selection of the machinery and equipment needed by agriculture, mining, and industry.

The domestic construction capital goods sector experienced increased production capacity and was capable of providing the real links between savers and investors, between social overhead and housing capital: railroads, ports, educational and health facilities, public buildings, housing. It remained the fastest growing form of physical capital between 1840 and 1973.

Chile was plagued by capital formation gaps between actual and potential (primarily mineral) resource surpluses, between actual and needed supplies of producer durables, between actual and desired financial intermediation, and between actual and desirable surplus/reinvestment ratios. These gaps can be in part explained by the lack of flexibility and limited conversion of one form of capital, whether mineral or housing, into another, such as machinery and equipment. Problems were presented by a spectrum of returns to capital shaped by unequal and unstable mining, inflation, and protection quasi-rents, the destruction of potential and actual resource surpluses, and leakages to consumption and abroad, which reduced the conversion ability of potential into actual savings.

With the wisdom of hindsight, one can argue that all sectoral surpluses should have been invested. Some surplus has to be used for consumption to demonstrate progress, some for investment to augment both consumer and capital goods output, some to reduce income inequalities for the benefit of the poorest, and some in the most backward sectors to reduce intersectoral productivity differentials. Capital formation and income distribution did not reach the desirable patterns, not only because within Chile's democracy surpluses were used primarily for consumption but also because they were wasted in the form of import subsidies and other supports.

It would be sterile and may even be impossible to list the constraints inhibiting Chile's growth. One reason for this is that there are so many of them: technical progress, physical capital, skills, financial intermediation, technical education, agriculture, and on and on. Also, as the result of chain reactions, constraints appear and disappear simultaneously almost everywhere.

More government intervention or stimuli are needed to remove institutional bottlenecks and promote investment. There should be less interference with market incentives, and discriminatory government intervention should be eliminated when it leads to growth-inhibiting relationships among production, distribution, and capital formation. Equitable income distribution rules should provide stable, consistent, and only mildly differentiated incentives for the rapid accumulation and cooperation of inputs in all functions, with emphasis on those performed inadequately. Only then can the growth rate of production be permanently accelerated, income differentials reduced, and the elusive goal of economic independence reached.

Index

Accelerator effect, 349
Accumulation of capital, 350. *See also* Capital formation
Aconcagua, 125
Administrative council, 170
Afuerinos. See Migrant labor
Agency for International Development (AID), 299, 300
Agrarian reform, 94
Agrarian Reform Corporation. *See* CORA
Agricultural bank, 247
Agricultural Colonization Bank. *See* Caja de Colonización Agrícola
Agricultural country: Chile as, 11, 120; notion questioned, 120
Agricultural lumpenproletariat, 219
Agricultural research, 347
Agricultural revolution, 347
Agricultural surplus, 246, 270, 360
Agriculture: long cycle, 10; labor force, 10, 132; output, 12; markets for, 34; and income distribution, 47; and exports, 81; saving by, 81, 246; golden era, 120; roles and functions, 120, 123, 347, 348; Chilean and Argentine compared, 121; food surplus, 121; and nitrate, 122, 123; capital inputs, 123; frontier defined, 123, 124; production of, 124; social structure, 125; aristocratic, 126; heterogeneous population, 127; size of, 129; production indices, 130; perverse model, 132; ownership in, 135, 237; supply elasticities, 136; technical progress in, 136; mechanization, 141, 270; and military junta, 142; artisan shops in, 145; and industry, 148, 153; labor productivity, 167; maltreated workers, 218; salary/ wage ratio, 219; salaries in, 220;

production functions, 246; profits in, 248; capitalists described, 268; capital stock, 268; and modernization, 269, 347; as market for industry, 347; relative productivity, 347; flight of resources, 348
—capital formation: investable surplus, 132; by government, 269; leakages, 270; surplus reinvestment, 271; nonmonetary, 325. *See also* Quasi-agriculture
—employment: underestimated, 11; relative, 11, 15, 129, 347; growth of, 167
—and government: discrimination against, 105, 247; policy, 138; neglect of, 142; penalty against, 142; suppression of, 351
—incentives: diminution, 95; restored, 96; product, 136; production, 137; general, 268
—income: relative, 15, 129, 347; generated by, 121; "fair" share, 141, 238; growth of, 167; share, 236
—performance: as failure, 37; as success, 37; crisis in, 91; eclipse of, 122; lessons from failure, 142; retrogression, 346
—unemployment: 9, 133; disguised, 134; open, 134; quasi-Keynesian, 135
Agriculture Marketing Corporation (ECA), 240
Agrorural, 123
Aguirre Cerda, Pedro: policies, 93; monetary policy, 103; and agricultural mechanization, 141; and industrialization, 163; and Allende, 198; development efforts, 282; and CORFO, 293
Ahumada, Jorge, 89

Economic Growth Center Book Publications

Werner Baer, *Industrialization and Economic Development in Brazil* (1965).

Werner Baer and Isaac Kerstenetzky, eds., *Inflation and Growth in Latin America* (1964).

Bela A. Balassa, *Trade Prospects for Developing Countries* (1964). Out of print.

Albert Berry and Miguel Urrutia, *Income Distribution in Columbia* (1976).

Thomas B. Birnberg and Stephen A. Resnick, *Colonial Development: An Econometric Study* (1975).

Benjamin I. Cohen, *Multinational Firms and Asian Exports* (1975).

Carlos F. Díaz Alejandro, *Essays on the Economic History of the Argentine Republic* (1970).

Robert Evenson and Yoav Kislev, *Agricultural Research and Productivity* (1975).

John C. H. Fei and Gustav Ranis, *Development of Labor Surplus Economy: Theory and Policy* (1964).

Gerald K. Helleiner, *Peasant Agriculture, Government, and Economic Growth in Nigeria* (1966).

Lawrence R. Klein and Kazushi Ohkawa, eds., *Economic Growth: The Japanese Experience since the Meiji Era* (1968).

A. Lamfalussy, *The United Kingdom and the Six* (1963). Out of print.

Markos J. Mamalakis, *The Growth and Structure of the Chilean Economy: From Independence to Allende* (1976).

Markos J. Mamalakis and Clark W. Reynolds, *Essays on the Chilean Economy* (1965).

Donald C. Mead, *Growth and Structural Change in the Egyptian Economy* (1967).

Richard Moorsteen and Raymond P. Powell, *The Soviet Capital Stock* (1966).

Douglas S. Paauw and John C. H. Fei, *The Transition in Open Dualistic Economies: Theory and Southeast Asian Experience* (1973).

Howard Pack, *Structural Change and Economic Policy in Israel* (1971).

Frederick L. Pryor, *Public Expenditures in Communist and Capitalist Nations* (1968).

Gustav Ranis, ed., *Government and Economic Development* (1971).

Clark W. Reynolds, *The Mexican Economy: Twentieth-Century Structure and Growth* (1970).

Lloyd G. Reynolds, ed., *Agriculture in Development Theory* (1975).

Lloyd G. Reynolds and Peter Gregory, *Wages, Productivity, and Industrialization in Puerto Rico* (1965).

Donald R. Snodgrass, *Ceylon: An Export Economy in Transition* (1966).